THE
DEVIL
IS IN IT

THE DEVIL IS IN IT

A History of the American Acoustic Guitar

JOHN STUBBINGS

UNIVERSITY OF TEXAS PRESS
AUSTIN

Printed in the United States of America
First edition, 2025
Illustrations by Drew Christie, Kalakala Co. Animation, LLC

♾ The paper used in this book meets the minimum requirements of ANSI/NISO Z39.48-1992 (R1997) (Permanence of Paper).

Library of Congress Cataloging-in-Publication Data

Names: Stubbings, John, author.
Title: The devil is in it : a history of the American acoustic guitar / John Stubbings.
Description: New edition. | Austin : University of Texas Press, [2025] | New edition of The devil is in it—Gratitude and acknowledgments. | Includes bibliographical references and index.
Identifiers: LCCN 2024060635 (print) | LCCN 2024060636 (ebook)
ISBN 978-1-4773-3258-0 (hardcover)
ISBN 978-1-4773-3259-7 (pdf)
ISBN 978-1-4773-3260-3 (epub)
Subjects: LCSH: Guitar—United States—History. | Guitar music—United States—History and criticism. | Guitar makers—United States. | Guitarists—United States. | Folk music—United States—History and criticism. | Blues (Music)—History and criticism. | Country music—History and criticism. | Rock music—United States—History and criticism.
Classification: LCC ML1015.G9 S84 2025 (print) | LCC ML1015.G9 (ebook) | DDC 787.87/1973—dcundefined
LC record available at https://lccn.loc.gov/2024060635
LC ebook record available at https://lccn.loc.gov/2024060636

doi:10.7560/332580

THE UNIVERSITY OF TEXAS PRESS GRATEFULLY ACKNOWLEDGES THE BRAD AND MICHELE MOORE ROOTS MUSIC ENDOWMENT FOR ITS SUPPORT OF THIS PUBLICATION.

For Mo and Ray

Contents

Preface

Waiting for the delivery of two new handcrafted guitars, at the time my fourteenth and fifteenth, I could not disguise my excitement. But, as pleased as I was, I knew the pair were evidence that I had contracted an extreme and unreasonable enthusiasm for guitar acquisition. Before I inevitably acquired more, I needed to understand how this had happened. How had the eighteenth-century European classical or Spanish guitar been transformed by the twentieth century into the modern American steel-string flat-top that had taken such a hold of me? I needed to better comprehend the allure, power, and influence of this once little-respected instrument that reshaped twentieth-century music. How had it become the defining instrument of our age, democratizing music making over a dozen decades and influencing not just music but social politics and popular culture?

Like many guitar enthusiasts and "accidental collectors," I knew some of the history of the guitar. But I wanted to connect the dots, see what links the European classical guitars that arrived in America in the nineteenth century to today's ubiquitous American flat-top dreadnought that every teenager uses to play their versions of Taylor Swift's "Tim McGraw" or Ed Sheeran's "The A Team."

How, and why, did the physical shape, design, and size of the guitar evolve? What influences caused the small-bodied parlor guitar of the mid-nineteenth century to morph into the single, double, and triple 0s, via the OM, into the relatively gargantuan dreadnought and jumbo and ultimately into the modern modified dreadnought?

In search of more answers, I read extensively around the topic: books about guitars and their history; academic papers; and interviews with guitar players, makers, collectors, and dealers. I also disappeared down the various rabbit holes of the World Wide Web. As I dug deeper and ever wider, a friend suggested I should follow the flat-top guitar's own journey from Europe to America.

That journey and the people I met along the way helped me better understand the history behind the defining instrument of our age. As I travelled from New York to Pennsylvania, through the Carolinas into Tennessee and Mississippi, south to Texas and on to the Mexican border, and then looped up through Northern California, I began to appreciate how the guitar had superseded the banjo, violin, mandolin, and ukulele, all of which had been much more popular at one time.

I also learned why so much of the music we love today was inspired and facilitated by the acoustic guitar—and how so much of the music we listen to today not only came from the poorest sections of America's Black and white communities but also was inspired and facilitated by the steel-string flat-top acoustic guitar. The people's instrument.

THE
DEVIL
IS IN IT

Introduction

I was driving south on Highway 61, a route that originally started at the Canada-US border and ran for 1,714 miles south to New Orleans. In Minnesota it runs through Duluth, where Bob Dylan was born. In Mississippi it passes by the birth- and workplaces of Muddy Waters, Charley Patton, Son House, and Elvis Presley. Bessie Smith, the "Empress of the Blues," died in 1937 on Highway 61 just outside Clarksdale, Mississippi, where her speeding car sideswiped a truck. The doctor who attended her as she lay dying in the middle of the two-lane blacktop reckoned she had lost a lot of blood. She died beside a road that had been built mostly by the labor of Black chain gangs that were leased to highway departments by state prisons.

Highway 61 is steeped in the blood, sweat, and tears of the blues.

As a teenager living in England, over five thousand miles from Highway 61, I had no reason to know of its existence or much about it. Yet I did.

When I was in my mid-teens, the English folk singer Shirley Collins visited our high school art class. Our teacher, Mike Clifton, had sung on and created the cover art for her then-most-recent album, *Anthems in Eden* (1969). We sat and listened to a few tracks, and afterward she talked about how a decade earlier, in 1959, when she was only a little older than us, she had visited Mississippi with the American song collector Alan Lomax. She told us how she first saw the Black blues singer Mississippi Fred McDowell. I'm sure none of us at the time had any idea who he was or why Mississippi was of any significance, but she was an entertaining storyteller. Many years later, on a BBC Radio interview, she told the same story she had told us in 1970. What she had seen more than sixty years earlier had clearly moved her and remained lodged in her memory.

> He appeared through the trees wearing his work overalls and carrying his guitar. . . . He'd been picking cotton all day and came into the clearing where the shacks were . . . [,] sat down, and "61 Highway Blues" was the first thing that he played. And it was the most wonderful sound. That shimmering metallic sound of the guitar, his wonderful voice, and the wonderful blues itself. It was so extraordinary, and Alan and I were just looking at each other and shaking our heads in wonder. Alan wrote one word in his notebook, which he'd never written before. "Perfect."

Lord that 61 Highway. It the longest road I know.

Four weeks into my American road trip, I arrived at the crossroads where Highway 61 meets old Highway 49—not just any old road junction but the one where Robert Johnson made his Faustian pact with the Devil when he traded his soul for mastery of the guitar.

I had finally reached Clarksdale, home of the blues. W. C. Handy had lived there in 1903 and regularly played with his band, not just in the town's swanky uptown restaurants but in the less salubrious saloons and boogie-woogie joints of the area.

After many weeks and hundreds of miles of solitary travelling, I had begun to better understand the guitar's strange energy to induce addiction and obsession among guitarists and guitar-builders alike. I also realized that in America the acoustic guitar was much more than a musical instrument. It doesn't just provide a musical accompaniment to the social and political history of the United States; it is at its heart.

• • • • • •

The guitar that came to America in the hands of white European migrants in the early 1800s was still largely an instrument of classical rather than popular purpose. Around this same time, the banjo appeared in the hands of enslaved people, the instrument an iteration of the simple folk instruments they knew from Africa. But what followed and has influenced modern popular music for over a hundred years is much more complex and more collaborative (albeit accidentally) than the familiar trope that "white kids' rock 'n' roll just stole the Black blues." What actually happened was a series of baton exchanges between Euro-American and Black musicians.

In the mid- to late nineteenth century, early domestic guitar makers like

C. F. Martin & Co. perpetuated the guitar's classical heritage, initially producing bespoke, highly ornate instruments destined for white players in the concert halls, salons, and prosperous homes of East Coast America.

Around the same time, the banjo was taken up by white performers appearing in blackface minstrel shows. From 1820 onward, minstrel-show music was by far the most popular music performed in America. Minstrelsy led to an eighty-year-long miseducation among its majority audience (young white males), imprinting upon them its crude, caricatured portrayals of Black men and women as lazy, stupid, deceitful, and dishonest.

During America's industrial revolution and through the Civil War and the social tumult that followed, the guitar was democratized. Its journey south from prosperous East Coast cities to an impoverished Appalachia created a white blues—what became known as hillbilly and old-time music. Farther south, Black players started picking up cheap, factory-made, mail-order guitars, and the six-string flat-top widely replaced the banjo. Joining the Great Migration of African Americans that had started around 1910, many players moved north to earn their living in Chicago and New York.

The music Southern Blacks played in the Northern cities was a blend of jazz, gospel, white hillbilly ballads, dance tunes, and ragtime. By the 1950s, and now as older players, they found themselves in need of a new audience, and Black blues musicians travelled across the Atlantic in search of one. They found it in England. By the early 1960s, white British beat groups that had "borrowed" Black blues and rhythm and blues reimported it back to the United States. The "British Invasion," with the guitar leading the charge, reinvented and reignited American interest in rock 'n' roll and changed the face of popular music forever.

Although the British Invasion was largely electric, it was the acoustic guitar that became the weapon of the '60s protest singer and the constant companion of the '70s singer-songwriter. It was almost killed off by disco in the 1980s, only to be rediscovered by '90s baby boomers as electric rock 'n' roll "unplugged." By the end of the century, a new generation of players was reinvigorating the acoustic guitar's musical journey in genres like Americana, alt-country, and new folk.

In each of those decades, the guitar enabled musicians—regardless of sex, creed, class, or color—to make their names and put their own stamp on the shape of popular music.

This is the story of the instruments they played, the music they made, and the influence it has had on us all.

Fernando Sor playing an 1828 Louis Panormo Spanish guitar.

The Origins of the Acoustic Guitar

We live in a world dominated by music made and reproduced by machines. Music is everywhere: in every room of our houses; in our cars, stores, elevators, shopping malls, and garage forecourts; overflowing from cars on the street or even from the earbuds of the person sitting next to us on the train and the plane. The irony is that despite this ubiquity and the apparent importance of music in our lives, few of us today can create it ourselves, even for our own amusement. There are no definitive figures, but a reasonable consensus of various sources suggests that less than 10 percent of adults in developed, industrial societies can play a musical instrument to a level where people don't throw shoes at them.

I'm just about old enough to remember a time when most ordinary homes had an upright piano in the front room or parlor. Most families had someone who could play that piano or at least an aged aunt or uncle who could do a musical turn. Not that long ago, our connection with music was as active participants, whereas now we are, in the main, only listeners. In fact, since the early 2000s, we can now listen to everything without even going to the record store and paying for it.

Does it matter that while we might have access to all the music on the planet, we are missing out on the practical, often casual, amateur involvement that created the varied musical world we live in?

Music making is largely in the hands of a minority rather than the majority. And that's important because musical invention is a numbers game. When thousands of players from different walks of life and musical persuasions are borrowing, sharing, and exploring, magic happens. Where they overlap is usually where the truly inventive and original occurs. When a fiddle player from Appalachia meets a hillbilly singer from Texas; when a guitarist from Glasgow emulates a prison singer from Mississippi; or when two very different middle-class schoolboys start trading skiffle songs after a church fete in Liverpool.

American band leader John Philip Sousa, the composer of "The Stars and Stripes Forever" and known as the "March King," expressed his fears for continuing musical creativity in a prescient essay titled "The Menace of Mechanical Music" (1906). While celebrating the fact that in 1906 the United States was awash with pianos, violins, guitars, mandolins, and banjos, Sousa's big concern was that machine-made mechanical music would soon dominate listening. He worried that live music would be made only by the "professional executant" and that "children wouldn't bother to learn the technique of playing an instrument; that mothers would no longer sing lullabies but put their child to sleep with a recording and that the natural pause when a dance band takes a break would no longer allow a period when people could be afforded the opportunity for general sociability."

Sousa's concerns went beyond our musical health. He recognized that music making promotes human well-being through interpersonal contact. It sparks our imaginations and has the power to give life additional meaning and value. Poor Sousa even feared for the very existence of mankind, the notion that "boy" would no longer "meet girl" at a dance, talk to her in the band's interval, and eventually "make whoopee." Sousa feared that "now a tireless mechanism can keep everlasting at it, and much of what made the dance a wholesome recreation is eliminated."

So apart from writing one of the world's abidingly popular marches, co-inventing the sousaphone (a doubtful accolade, I would accept), and leading a band that over forty years played over fifteen thousand concerts, Sousa foresaw the age of disco, the DJ, and the MP3 file that allowed the uninterrupted playing of 120 beats per minute (bpm) music through the night. He feared not only that mechanical music might affect the earning potential of the dozens of Sousa bands that toured the world but also that without amateur music making, we might turn into a bunch of well-listened but musically inept numbskulls.

Given the decline of amateur music making over the last one hundred years, I believe that while Sousa would be disappointed to find that his predictions were largely correct, there is some good news for him. Amateur music making may be much-diminished compared to his day, but he would be surprised to find that the humble guitar, a little-respected instrument in Sousa's time, has done more to keep amateur music making alive than the piano, violin, mandolin, and banjo combined.

• • • • • •

The guitar, itself part of a family of instruments, belongs to an even larger group, chordophones, or instruments that make sound via vibrating strings. But the rise in popularity of the guitar during the eighteenth and nineteenth centuries was driven by a number of factors: the relative speed and ease of learning its basics compared to the piano; its modest purchase price; its portability; and its social acceptability and general association with the home and polite society rather than the music hall or minstrel show where the equally popular banjo was usually found.

Its uptake by amateurs and casual players lay in the factors above, but an additional, unique aspect cemented its popularity. Not only is it an instrument that can be played while the musician is singing, but it sits extremely well with the human voice in terms of pitch, volume, and tonality. You can sing while playing most instruments in the violin family, but the guitar's fretted fingerboard makes it easier for the player to sing and play accurately at the same time. Frets make it easier to navigate. They are signposts and waypoints, mapping out where to put your fingers, helping the amateur player get pitch-perfect notes every time while making both simple and complex chords. Singing along to chords led to the acoustic guitar becoming a folk music instrument rather than an orchestral or band instrument.

Folk music (i.e., music made, played, or sung by ordinary folks) was often considered culturally inferior, but many modern classical composers, from

Bartók to Ralph Vaughan Williams, Dvorák to Copeland, have incorporated or adapted folk songs into their compositions. Louis Armstrong, asked in the 1960s his view of the folk music coming out of Greenwich Village during the American folk revival, responded with what is now the folk music axiom: "Well all music is folk music. I ain't never heard no horse sing a song," adding, "There ain't but two kinds of music, good and bad. If it sounds good, you don't care what it is, you're just gonna enjoy it. So anything you can tap your foot to is good music, and that's the kind I play."

Thus the legitimacy and popularity of folk music situated the guitar, with its easy-playing versatility and adaptability, at the center of the American home. The banjo and the mandolin, both also fretted folk instruments, had their brief moments in the sun, but the steel-string flat-top guitar has done more to democratize music making than any other instrument.

To understand how and why this came about we need to step back to a time when musical entertainment was still necessarily self-made, whether by court musicians or members of the family.

• • • • • •

As early as the sixteenth century, and encouraged by Elizabeth I, herself an accomplished lute player with an active interest in all things musical, families thought it more important for an Elizabethan woman of status to learn a musical instrument than to read or write. While music was an everyday part of life at the Elizabethan court and in the great houses of nobility, it was also becoming commonplace in the homes of the gentry and a growing upper class of increasingly wealthy merchants. Domestic servants were often expected to be able to play an instrument as part of their household duties, and all towns had waits, official musicians who provided music for general festivities and religious holidays. While music making was more commonplace for the upper classes, listening was becoming part of everyday life.

The seventeenth century saw the advent of cheap printing, and broadside ballads—covering topics as diverse as politics, natural disasters, and notable murders and subsequent executions—were being sold on the streets of Britain by the hundreds of thousands. Old, traditional ballads had previously been passed on orally from generation to generation, and "serious" music was commissioned and reproduced through patronage by the upper classes, but these new "stories in song" were sung in alehouses and workshops and on the streets by anyone who could read and then were passed along by rote. They led to an explosion in popular music and amateur music making. Printed crudely on single-sided sheets and sold for a penny by ballad-mongers, who usually performed the song as well, they marked the beginnings of commercial music publishing.

While there was music on the streets for the masses, anyone familiar with Jane Austen's *Pride and Prejudice* and *Emma* knows that by the eighteenth century, cultured young ladies in hope of a good marriage needed to be accomplished at the keyboard. If a young lady was not totally accomplished, then she should at least be able to rattle out a pretty minuet on the pianoforte or harpsichord in the brief interlude between meeting Mr. Right and bearing him a brood of children. Social commentary of the time reinforced the view that "any young woman unable to take her proper place in a vocal or instrumental ensemble became the laughing-stock of society."

Throughout the eighteenth century, the expectation by the middle and upper classes was for children of both sexes to learn an instrument to entertain both their families and visitors to the household. The pianoforte was the musical instrument of choice for those with the space and the funds to buy one. (In Jane Austen's time a plain, basic piano cost around £100, the annual income of a professional engineer.) But by the first quarter of the nineteenth century, it was the Spanish guitar, costing from £2 to £10, that was more often seen in the parlors of the upper classes of Europe. Such was the guitar's popularity that virtuosos filled European salons and concert halls. Nicollò Paganini, remembered today for his furiously paced violin playing, was a celebrated guitarist first, describing his guitar as his lifelong "constant companion." Because of its fashionability in high society, hundreds of guitar pieces were written during this period.

But what were the origins of this melodic, sympathetic, and easily played instrument? Where had it come from and how long had it been around?

• • • • • •

The guitar we know today has multiple roots, but the earliest and strongest originate from Central Asia three thousand years ago. Many stringed folk instruments have names that end with *tar*, the Sanskrit word for string, and an instrument with four (*char*) strings is called a *chartar*. By the eighth century CE, the Arabic word for four, *guit*, had been affixed to the now broadly used word for strings. Travelers, traders, and merchant seamen brought the Arabic lute (or *ud*), the *guit-tar*, and the four-string, narrow-waisted Persian *chartar* to

Europe—specifically to the merchant trading centers of Italy and Spain. From the ninth to twelfth centuries, the Iberian Peninsula was an Islamic caliphate and a culturally rich melting pot in which eleventh-century Indian, Greek, Arabic, and Persian art forms, especially music, influenced the many bardic troubadours now accompanying their poems of courtly love with *el luto*.

During the fifteenth century, the fretless Arabic *oud*, or *ud*, morphed into the fretted European lute, its name in English a mispronunciation of *al'ud* ("al" meaning "the"). The instrument quickly developed a reputation outside of innocent, courtly romance, and by the late sixteenth century, its rich, delicate tones were closely associated with both sensuality and unbridled lust.

> *He capers nimbly in a lady's chamber*
> *To the lascivious pleasing of a lute.*
> *RICHARD III*, ACT 1, SCENE 1

While the lute—and an English, flat-backed derivation, the orpharion—was immensely popular at the Elizabethan court, the wyre, the stringed gittern, or cittern, an English version of the pear-shaped Spanish *chittara*, was popular with the middle and lower classes. A regular habitué of the tavern, these loud instruments featured eight wire strings that were played with a plectrum and were said to be hanging on the wall of every barbershop in London for the use of waiting customers:

> *Is she a whore?,*
> *A Barber's cittern for every man to play on?*
> THOMAS DEKKER, "THE HONEST WHORE," 1604

By the 1600s, in mainland Europe the *vihuela*, with five pairs of unison-tuned gut strings, had developed into an instrument beginning to look and sound like the modern Spanish guitar. Gut frets, which had to be tied onto the neck and required some skill to place accurately, gradually started to disappear, replaced by metal or ivory frets permanently mounted on the neck and upper body of the guitar.

For the next hundred years, many variations in shape, the number of strings, and tunings appeared. But by the 1770s, Romantic-era guitars that featured six single gut strings and flat-backed bodies were popular in Spain, France, Italy, Germany, and Austria.

However, in Britain in the mid-1750s, an instrument with a similar name, but quite different in design and construction from the European guitar, had arrived in polite London society. The English wire-stringed guittar took its body shape, fretted neck, and nine to twelve wire strings from the cittern and its predecessor, the gittern. Recognized as an instrument that was relatively cheap, elegant sounding, and easy to learn, it was characterized as "an amusement, but not a study." A gentrified variant of the Elizabethan barbershop cittern, the flat-backed, wire-string English guittar quickly gained popularity as an instrument played predominantly by women in fashionable society. It was introduced into Britain by immigrant German craftsmen who based the design on their native Moravian cittern, an instrument used as part of their religious worship and typically played by female members of the congregation. In many ways these instruments were a closer antecedent of the steel-string guitar of the modern era than the gut-string Spanish guitar. Existing examples, including a pear-shaped guittar made by the celebrated London maker John Simpson in the late 1770s, have a loud, complex but predominantly trebly sound. An eighteenth-century Italian composer and music theorist wrote in *The Art of Playing the Guittar or Cittra* that "the sweetness and brilliancy of sound peculiar to the Guittar, together with its convenient shape and size, and the easyness of performing on it, has already render'd it exstreamly fashionable in the polite world."

That the guittar was intended as an instrument to accompany the voice is supported by the existence of holes drilled in between the first few frets of the neck to accept a *capodastro*, an accessory designed to adjust the pitch to match the singing voice.

While the English guittar was the most popular plucked stringed instrument in Britain from the middle of the eighteenth century to the start of the nineteenth, in Europe the small-bodied, hourglass-shaped European guitar was being further developed by Joséf Pagés, a leading member of the prolific Cadiz school of guitar makers. Pagés's improvements, particularly fan strutting (bracing) and a slightly domed top, were praised by composer-players like Dionisio Aguado and were further refined by a small group of makers producing instruments for the urban upper classes and landed gentry in fashionable European musical centers. Johann Georg Stauffer in Vienna introduced a number of modifications to his guitars, most notably further raising the fingerboard above the level of the soundboard (the flat top of the guitar) and fitting hard-wearing alloy frets. In France, Pierre-René Lacôte's guitars featured a defined, narrow waist, a shape still echoed in instruments today. He also improved tuning machine mechanics, enabling instruments to be tuned more accurately and to stay in tune longer.

In London's fashionable West End, the Paris-born maker Louis Panormo popularized the use of tuning machines over violin-style pegs but moved away from the French style of instrument then popular in London. Panormo favored the Spanish guitars played by the influential player and teacher Fernando Sor. Panormo improved the tone of his instruments by using lightweight construction and Pagés's method of fan bracing. In addition to Sor, Panormo courted the attentions of the growing community of London-based Spanish guitar superstars of the day, including Madame de Goñi (of whom more later) and the notorious womanizer Antonio Huerta, to whom Panormo married off his fourteen-year-old daughter, Angelina. Keen to promote his specialization in making Spanish guitars, and possibly encouraged by this newly acquired and famous son-in-law, in 1828 Panormo pasted the legend "The only Maker of Guitars in the Spanish style" above his Bloomsbury workshop.

Panormo was keen to differentiate himself from the domestic makers of the English guittar and the still-popular cittern. Despite their continued popularity, these instruments—with their bright, steely tone that sounded like a spinet or harpsichord—now lacked both the sonorous aural finesse and the social standing of the gut-string Spanish guitar.

Burnished by the romantic allure of its Spanish heritage and now established as an instrument popular in the fashionable salons of Europe, the guitar had come of age. Its popularity brought about *la guitaromanie*, a term coined by the French composer and guitarist Charles de Marescot in his book of the same name. Richly and wittily illustrated, it not only contained guitar pieces suited to both the novice and the experienced guitarist but also described and fueled the guitar mania that gripped European society in the early 1800s. Guitar virtuosos like Sor travelled from London to Vienna to Paris to St. Petersburg, inspiring men and women of style and substance to listen to and learn the instrument. Polite society was, for the first time, gripped by guitar fever.

• • • • • •

As the European colonization of the Atlantic Seaboard continued through the 1700s and early 1800s, it wasn't surprising that immigrants of all nationalities and classes brought the portable, and now highly fashionable, guitar on board the ships taking them to America. Aside from reduced shipping costs and added convenience, leaving their large, expensive pianofortes at home was understandable when many didn't know where they might finally settle in their new homeland.

The first Continental Europeans from Spain and Italy had brought their Spanish guitars, while the early English settlers brought and stayed loyal to the cittern and the "English guittar." Tuned to an open C major chord, the latter were easily accessible instruments for the farmers and "middling sort of English colonist." Their popularity with these largely Protestant English settlers also stemmed from a continuing suspicion of anything Spanish as being at best Papist and at worst having the ability to "engender licentiousness."

Between 1820 and the outbreak of World War I, over eight million Germans emigrated to America, forming one of the largest immigrant diasporas in the country. Alongside the millions of German builders, bakers, farmers, and furniture makers escaping religious intolerance or seeking their fortunes in America during the nineteenth century, there were a few instrument makers. One, a builder of Viennese and German-style guitars, was Christian Friedrich Martin, a thirty-seven-year-old immigrant fresh from Saxony. As a teenager he trained in Vienna and initially returned home to Germany to build guitars, but he was foiled by the restrictions that the German craft guilds were imposing on independent guitar makers. Seeking to freely ply his trade in America, Martin became the father of the modern acoustic guitar, starting a business in 1833 that still thrives today as the premier maker of acoustic guitars.

C. F. Martin Sr.

The Birth of Martin Guitars

In 1832, Christian Friedrich Martin was working in Markneukirchen, a town near the Czech border that was at the center of German musical instrument making in Saxony. In the early 1800s, a large proportion of the world's violins, violas, cellos, and basses were made in or near this one town.

As with all artisans, Martin depended on his local craft guild for his license to operate. Since the early medieval period, skilled craftsmen in major European towns and cities had been strictly controlled by their individual guilds. These legally recognized associations were formed to maintain craft standards and skills through a strict accreditation and apprenticeship system. Local laws supporting the craft guilds enabled them to effectively operate a monopoly against whoever their members saw as outsiders or a threat to their business livelihood.

The makers of string and fretted instruments were members of the Geigenmacher-Innung, the Guild of Violin Makers. They saw themselves as the most skilled of all instrument makers, able to precisely and painstakingly carve the arched backs and tops of violins from solid blocks of maple and spruce and craft a finished instrument. Violin makers occasionally turned their hand to making guitars (even the master violin maker of Cremona, Stradivarius, made a few baroque guitars in the late 1600s), but guitars were not as popular or as lucrative as violins, and builders generally saw constructing the box-like instrument as beneath them.

Although the two instruments share some similarities, the guitar—with many more parts to fashion and requiring some degree of engineering skill to construct—has a fundamentally different and arguably more complex construction than the violin. The best cabinetmakers showed they were capable of much more than just making the wooden carrying and shipping cases for violins. Made under contract to the violin makers, many cases were often highly ornate themselves, and their makers soon had a nice sideline going in building the increasingly popular guitar.

By the early nineteenth century, the six-string guitar had increased in popularity, and as demand grew, some members of the cabinetmakers guild now concentrated solely on making guitars. This put the noses of the closed-shop violin makers seriously out of joint. In 1826, the violin makers of Markneukirchen filed a legal petition in hope of seeing off the encroaching cabinetmakers and seizing the business for themselves. The petition specifically named C. F. Martin and his friend and fellow guitar maker Heinrich Schatz. It stated that compared to violin makers, "whose work not only showed finesse but gave evidence of a certain understanding . . . and cultured taste," cabinetmakers were "nothing more than mechanics . . . (whose) product consisted of all kinds of articles known as furniture."

Martin was far more than a "mechanic" or simple artisan: he was a highly accomplished guitar maker, a skilled repairman, and an experienced instrument shop foreman. He had been trained initially by his father and apprenticed at fifteen to "the celebrated Johann Georg Stauffer," whose workshop was in Vienna, the epicenter of classical music and home to Mozart, Haydn, Beethoven, and Schubert. He worked under this master instrument maker for fourteen years before marrying the daughter of his next employer, a harp maker, and returning to Saxony to build guitars for the wholesale dealers in the town. After further petitions by the violin makers, Martin believed it would be only a matter of time before the authorities were persuaded to curtail his livelihood as a guitar maker. At the age of thirty-seven, and following the death of his father, he chose to seek his future and his fortune in America.

Arriving in New York in 1833 with his family and his eighteen-year-old apprentice Louis Schmidt, Martin immediately launched his business. Working initially out of rented rooms in a boardinghouse, he soon set up a combined family home, workshop, and retail store on Hudson Street, an arrangement not dissimilar to that of Louis Panormo in London around the same time. Besides repairing guitars, Martin imported instruments of all types, including cheap guitars from wholesalers back in Germany, still recognized as the source of some of the best-quality musical instruments. But as early as the summer of 1834, he was making guitars in-house and found a ready market selling mainly to the various quality retailers or music houses in New York City. He also sold a few instruments directly to amateur players and to students of guitar teachers who received a small commission on each sale.

Martin traded in various other instruments and subcontracted specialized repairs from among the skilled craftsmen, or journeymen, of Kleindeutschland, the large German immigrant community living in the Lower East Side area of New York. He focused on crafting high-quality guitars made in the German and Viennese styles, the latter using the long, curved asymmetric Stauffer headstock with the buttons, or Viennese "tuning machines," running along just one side. (This style of tuning machine and headstock was adapted in the 1950s by electric guitar pioneers Paul Bigsby and Leo Fender. It remains the trademark headstock shape found on today's electric Fender Telecasters and Stratocasters.)

In the mid-1830s, Martin was the sole domestic maker of guitars listed in the New York trade directory. The instruments coming out of Christian Frederick Martin's workshop (the founder's name now anglicized) were not only characterized by their quality but also by their shape and size. During his first years in New York, Martin made guitars mainly in the Germanic, Stauffer style: most featured narrow waists, with the upper and lower bouts (the curves in the body) of almost equal width, reminiscent of an hourglass.

Although in 1836 he made a guitar with a Moravian cittern–shaped body, by the late 1830s Martin had adopted a body pattern and other design features heavily influenced by Spanish guitars, where the lower bout was proportionately wider than the upper—a look we are familiar with today. Martin was aware that Spanish guitars were capable of greater volume and a fuller bass, and these changes in style made his instruments achieve a sound superior to German-made instruments. In addition, whereas many European guitars made during these decades were ornate and featured filigreed decoration on the body, Martin established an austere, pared-back aesthetic. These features, together with other Germanic stylistic cues, were ultimately adopted by his rivals as *the* look of a contemporary American guitar.

Another feature Martin retained from the European standard was the size of the instrument. Most of the guitars he was producing would today be considered very small, almost child-size. Until the end of the nineteenth century, his best-selling guitars had body widths under twelve inches, a third narrower than today's popular acoustic guitars. A relatively large number of these early instruments still survive in playable condition, and, despite their small size and the limitations of gut strings, sound surprisingly loud—quite capable of filling a small auditorium. Although Martin prided himself on building guitars with a balanced tone, their main sonic difference, compared to larger modern guitars, is a less full sound with a weaker bass. However nearly two hundred years on, they certainly don't sound like a diminutive relic from another age.

The music being played by amateur players on these early guitars would have included a mix of favorite hymns and arrangements of classical pieces, often transcriptions of popular opera arias. Fernando Sor's *Method for the Spanish Guitar* was translated into English in the early 1830s and was an immensely popular source of pieces designed for the dedicated amateur player and arranged for the clean-cut timbre of guitars of the period. Popular ballads like "My Pretty Jane," published in 1832, would have been sung to a guitar accompaniment.

Strumming or "framming" the guitar with the bare fingers or a plectrum had been popular since the earliest days of the instrument, but in 1825 the Neopolitan player and prolific composer Ferdinando Carulli published the first treatise to explore the use of chords and arpeggios (often called broken chords). This style was perfect in allowing the guitar to accompany and complement the voice, laying the foundations for modern pattern or fingerpicking.

The buyers and players of Martin's instruments at this time were white and middle-class, and they were often women who played in the intimate setting of a front parlor. Just as the guitar had conquered the drawing rooms of London, Paris, and Vienna, so it now gained fashion as the instrument used to entertain family and friends in the homes of New York, Boston, and Philadelphia.

Responding to the demands of these clients, Martin made his guitars with expensive but nonetheless restrained ornamentation. Ivory was used to fashion bridges, and rich Brazilian rosewood, with exquisite figuring, was shaped to make bodies. Martin quickly built a reputation for producing the best-made, best-looking, and best-sounding instruments.

However, in mid-1839 the Martin business was still a small family enterprise when it moved out of New York City and relocated eighty-three miles west to the small, deeply devout German Moravian enclave of Nazareth in upstate Pennsylvania. In addition to C. F. Martin and his son, Christian Frederick Jr., the only other full-time employee was C. F. Hartman, Martin's nephew. Martin almost certainly outsourced some of the time-consuming inlay work on his guitars to German-speaking journeymen living in New York. Only much later did he recruit the best one or two of these craftsmen, trained within the strict German guild system, to join his small guitar manufactory. Somewhat paradoxically, while Christian Frederick had learned his own craft outside of the guild system, he was well aware of the system's benefits. Apprentice luthiers, having completed their training under a guild master, were expected to complete their *Wanderschaft*, when they were to gain experience as journeymen. The term derives from their instructions to journey beyond their guild master's workshop for at least three years, working in a variety of workshops as a paid employee. Only after gaining experience under various masters, during which time he may have made hundreds of complete guitars, would an experienced journeyman be invited to present their *Meisterstück*, their "masterpiece," to the guild. This marked him eligible for elevation to guild master and qualified to establish his own workshop.

Martin's small workforce operated slightly differently from the traditional guild system workshop where individual craftsmen built whole guitars. It was likely that the small team divided the construction processes between them, each worker making a number of necks or backs and sides. Martin guitars were still handmade by skilled craftsmen, but each individual guitar might be the creation of many pairs of different hands. Records from the period show that this small team could fulfill a bespoke order for a high-quality guitar in as few as eight weeks, sometimes even more quickly.

Importantly, during this period Martin experimented with the way he braced his instruments—the system of internal reinforcement that keeps the guitar from collapsing under the tension of the strings and also helps shape the sound of individual guitars. Before 1840, almost none of his two models were braced in the same way. His exploration into the best method of internal bracing was driven by his desire to create instruments that were both loud and sweet-sounding. By 1843, when X-bracing first appeared, his experimentation had diminished, and by 1850, he was bracing most smaller, more basic guitars with Spanish-style fan braces and his higher-grade guitars with more complex X-bracing. Producing guitars while maintaining consistently high standards of materials, build quality, finish, and sound enabled Martin to command a premium price in the US market. While a basic factory-made guitar from the industrial dynamos of New York, Philadelphia, and Chicago might start at $5 and retail as high as $45, Martin guitars started at the latter price. A specially ordered Martin with elaborate appointments might be as expensive as $100 or more.

The guitar's continued growth in popularity created a scramble for market share in the 1850s, something music historian Philip Gura terms "the New York guitar wars." The upsurge in sales during this period led to some of Martin's employees branching out on their own. His original apprentice, Louis Schmidt, partnered with a Martin subcontractor, George Maul, and became one of the small-volume makers competing with his old master. But the real competition was from larger-scale East Coast guitar manufactories. One of these was started by English engineer James Ashborn, who used distributors to take his product to market and to bankroll the rapid expansion of his business.

The four dominant New York music houses, which combined wholesale facilities with lavish retail emporiums, all offered either to sell guitars on consignment or buy them outright from makers; the house would then handle distribution and sales to other retailers. The upside to this arrangement was that makers could concentrate on manufacture. The downside required makers to brand their guitars with the name of the retailer. James Ashborn initially manufactured guitars of reasonable quality in the style of Louis Panormo, the celebrated London maker, but he sold them through the Broadway retailer Hall & Son. Virtually all of Ashborn's guitars were marketed as "Hall's Guitars," and Hall & Son made sure they worded advertisements in a way that more than intimated that both design and manufacture were handled in-house.

Ashborn was, in today's terms, being treated as an anonymous own-label supplier, something that all major brands from Kellogg's to Colgate studiously avoid doing. Despite the short-term gain—manufacturing product without having to worry about marketing or sales—it always brings long-term misery as your trade customer starts to become your competitor, and you fail to build consumer loyalty to your own branded business. Martin had the foresight to decline the wider overtures of the New York music houses, but he did supply some unbranded guitars to retailers, keeping the arrangement at arm's length. Martin's focus was always on building his brand reputation, and it's undoubtedly one of the major reasons why both Martin's antebellum guitars and reputation survive to this day. Ashborn made good, quality instruments, but none sounded as good as Martin's, and few had the build quality that would enable them to last to this day. Ashborn's guitars were designed and standardized for mass production. They were all the same size and shape and were made of cheaper spruce and maple that was then veneered with mahogany or rosewood. The all-important neck joint was a much-simplified affair from that used by Martin. While the guitars made by Schmidt & Maul and Henry Schatz (Martin's fellow countryman who had first encouraged him to travel to America in 1833) rivalled Martin's, those luthiers were, like him, producing instruments in very small numbers. Unlike Martin, neither the Schatz nor Schmidt & Maul businesses continued after their founders' deaths; thus, alongside Ashborn, they are consigned to be footnotes in the history of the guitar. To be fair, it is unlikely that contemporary players would be either as interested in or reverent of early Martins were it not for the continued and continuing success of the Martin brand into the twenty-first century.

But Martin's general unwillingness to supply the music houses with own-brand guitars initially put him at a disadvantage to makers who had strong ties to the powerful New York retailers. With no physical retail presence in New York, and realizing that retailers and wholesalers would push their own-brand guitars before his, he needed players to ask for or demand a Martin guitar by name. European makers like Louis Panormo in London and Josef Pagés in Spain had both used the endorsement of, or at least the recommendation of, celebrity player Fernando Sor to introduce their instruments to new players. Martin was to employ a similar strategy to introduce his guitars to players.

• • • • • •

America's enthusiasm for the guitar was helped by its break from Georgian England after the War for Independence. The United States, once free from the English Protestant antipathy to anything Catholic, quickly developed a love affair with all things Latin. This included the Spanish guitar, still at the center of a European guitar mania that had crossed the Atlantic. The guitar had become indelibly associated with the racy imagery of an exotic Latin society and the allure of the darkened cantina and lovers and temptresses dancing in the street by moonlight. "El Fandango," a dance played on the guitar, was said by its executants to transform "even the most frigid of souls." Attracted by the promise of a warm welcome in the new nation-state, professional musicians from southern Europe arrived in America in the early part of the nineteenth century to perform and give guitar lessons (and perhaps more) to moneyed, middle-class students. (The numerous stories of European music masters seducing the daughters and wives of their employers were perhaps just stories, but the tales no doubt added to the exotic image of the Spanish guitar.)

Martin was recognized as the leading manufacturer of concert-grade instruments and soon became the professionals' choice. The company made special models for these artists to recommend to their students, which they did in return for a sizeable commission. The most notable of these performer-tutors was a woman as exotically mysterious as she was exquisitely beautiful. Her name, as equally colorful as her reputation, was Madame Delores Nevares de Goñi.

Señora de Goñi arrived in America with her husband Jean, also a guitarist, from Liverpool in November 1840. The American press acclaimed the Spaniards' first concerts, and by 1842 she was regularly performing (both on and off the stage) with George Knoop, a celebrated cellist, giving recitals at East Coast theaters and in wealthy private homes. After attending a Knoop concert in Boston, the American schoolroom poet Henry Wadsworth Longfellow, of *The Song of Hiawatha* and "Paul Revere's Ride" fame, wrote a letter to a friend about her. "With [Knoop] there is a sweet Spanish Lady, playing the guitar; La Señora de Gony—delicious. . . . La Señora de Gony, whose guitar delights me more, perhaps because it awakens sweet remembrances of early youth and Spain; perhaps because a woman plays it, and the devil is in it." The combination that so entranced Longfellow served to enhance her image and garnered much press coverage for the guitar superstar of her age.

When, in 1843, Señora de Goñi performed at a female academy in Bethlehem, she stayed at the Martin family home in Cherry Hill, near Nazareth, for a few days. As so often happens when guitar builders meet great players, Martin asked what features the artist most sought in a "perfect instrument." Señora de Goñi wanted not only an instrument with balanced tone that fitted her frame, but most importantly she longed for greater volume. (Before amplification, the louder the instrument, the bigger the auditorium, and the more tickets sold.) Martin must have listened closely and examined the Spanish-made fan-braced guitar she was playing. When she next played at his home, she was presented with a new design of Martin guitar.

The De Goñi guitar had revolutionary internal top-bracing in an X configuration, as opposed to the Spanish fan pattern or ladder of parallel braces used on most domestic guitars to date. It delivered exactly what de Goñi needed: increased volume without sacrificing a well-balanced tone. The instrument was instantly adopted by de Goñi, who requested that Martin build her a second guitar to the same design. Martin made a big play of this, and although he stopped short of claiming that she was endorsing Martin guitars, he did make public, in the *Albany Evening Journal*, the letter de Goñi wrote to him and John Coupa, Martin's main New York dealer. It is possible, however, given the carefully crafted language and inclusivity of her praise, that Martin or Coupa may have had a hand in its drafting.

> Messrs Martin & Coupa,
> Gentlemen,
>
> Before leaving New York, I feel compelled to express my satisfaction and admiration of the two guitars manufactured for me. I unhesitatingly pronounce them superior to any instrument of the kind I have ever seen in this country or EUROPE, for tone, workmanship and facility of execution. These remarks are not intended to apply peculiarly to those you have made for me. Those which I have examined in your room are not less deserving of my praise and I confidently recommend them to the public.
> DELORES N. DE GOÑI, NEW YORK, NOVEMBER 8, 1843

The instruments are accepted by historians as the missing link or bridge between the traditional "Spanish" classical guitars that Martin and others were making in the early part of the century and the modern X-braced guitars the company continued to make for the next 150 years. But as this small revolution in guitar design was taking place in the quiet rural backwater of Nazareth, a tension was building across the country that had an unimaginable effect on American society, commerce, and music.

Martin had left New York in 1839 following a series of violent antiabolitionist riots that took place only a few blocks from the Martin home and workshop on Hudson Street. He was leaving a turbulent and at times dangerous city. The Great Fire of 1835 and an economic crisis had exacerbated both the squalor and tensions in slums like the Five Points, where the once predominantly Black community was now living cheek by jowl with a massive influx of Irish Catholic immigrants escaping famine in Ireland. Slavery had been formally abolished in Pennsylvania as early as 1780, largely due to pressure from German religious communities like the one in Nazareth. New York and other Northern states were emancipated in the 1830s, but slavery proliferated in the South and its prosperous slaveholding economies. In Nazareth, Martin and his family may have felt protected from the tumult that was brewing, but in just a few years one of the biggest battles of the Civil War would be fought barely a hundred miles from their home.

Francesca Dibblee playing an 1868 Martin 2½ Style 17.

Popular Music in the Civil War and Beyond

The first shot of the American Civil War was fired at Fort Sumter, South Carolina, at 4:30 a.m. on April 12, 1861. The war, and its many long-lasting repercussions, changed America forever—socially, economically, and politically. Four years of war also hugely influenced the shape of American music, which was a critical driver at the inception, heart, and aftermath of the conflict.

• • • • • •

One of America's most popular forms of professionally performed entertainment in the nineteenth century was blackface minstrelsy. Long before that first shot was fired, minstrelsy played a key role as a provocateur in the politics of slavery and abolitionism that divided the Northern from the Southern economies.

Blackface minstrelsy was popular in America from the mid-1820s. White performers had been blacking-up their faces to create lurid, distorted stereotypes of enslaved people (or of their urban, emancipated or freeborn counterparts) since the late eighteenth century. Even Black performers applied the red lips and white eye circles—perpetuating a theatrical convention originally imported from Britain, where white actors performing impersonations of "Negros" had been popular since the mid-1700s. Whatever the intentions of British performers, in the United States, North and South, blackface minstrelsy took on a uniquely sinister hue. It played a much more provocative role in racial politics, shaping society's view of Black people across the country. It also spoke to a very different audience. In Britain, blackface was cross-class and cross-gender. In America, minstrelsy's role in the social and political tensions leading up to the Civil War came from its influence on young, white, working-class males, who made up much of its popular following.

Because most white Americans rarely saw, let alone regularly interacted with, Black people, much of their perception of Black folks came from the exaggerated portrayals of the minstrel show. By the 1830s, this racial burlesque had formalized into the big red lips, outsize clumsy feet, and large, bulging eyes regularly adopted by most performers. Frighteningly, there is plenty of evidence that many in the audience believed they were watching actual Black performers. Even those who realized that the minstrels were white people playing blackface often remarked on the accuracy of the minstrels' look, speech, singing, and dancing.

However faithful audiences felt the representations to be, minstrelsy for many Southerners was primarily about mocking the lazy, inarticulate "plantation darky" and showing open hostility toward any threat of abolition. In the so-called enlightened North, where many states had long abolished slavery, there was still a widely held view that Black people, who were often held to be intellectually inferior, might be better off under the care of "compassionate" masters who gave them shelter and food in exchange for labor. Yet the idea that denying any person their freedom was wrong was becoming more accepted, which led, in part, to many Northern minstrel songs being less viciously mocking. Some songs were ultimately reappropriated for an abolitionist agenda. Recruitment songs, patriotic anthems, and battle hymns became a daily part of the bitter conflict.

• • • • • •

Music has always been part of the machine of war. Fifes and drums had long beat out the speed of the march and spurred soldiers into the fight. Animal horns and their descendant, the bugle, carried military commands across battlefields as well as marking mealtimes and the closing of the day. But the military ferocity of the American Civil War far surpassed the steady, gentlemanly advance of red-coated soldiers bearing swords and muskets. The conflict marked the first time ordinary citizens of a modern, rapidly industrializing nation were pitted against each other in battle. Music's role was evolving. It became a recruiting tool—tuneful propaganda to justify the war to the citizens and soldiers on either side. It also offered solace to families missing their sons and to soldiers far from home. As music became more influential to more people in more places, the means of producing it would also evolve.

The industrialized musical instrument factories of Connecticut supplied ever-cheaper instruments to the fife-and-drum bands that formed a key part of the military machine. Regiments' wealthy sponsors and private benefactors recruited and paid the wages of professional brass bands to augment their fife-and-drum field musicians in parades and to inspire their troops in battle. At the Battle of Fredericksburg in 1862, bands from each side played their adopted anthems to taunt the enemy.

The North had sequestered "The Star-Spangled Banner" as well as the newly penned "Battle Cry of Freedom," which made the case for Northern victory. The South had new songs, such as "The Bonnie Blue Flag," as well as its de facto anthem "Dixie" (a.k.a. "I Wish I Was in Dixie"), which had originated as an 1850s blackface minstrel song.

Oh, I wish I was in the land of cotton,
Old times there are not forgotten.
Look away, look away, look away, Dixie Land!

In Dixie Land, where I was born in,
early on one frosty mornin'.
Look away, look away, look away, Dixie Land!

I wish I was in Dixie. Hooray! Hooray!
In Dixie's Land I'll take my stand,
to lib and die in Dixie.

Away, away, away down south in Dixie!
Away, away, away down south in Dixie!

There's buckwheat cakes and Injun batter,
Makes you fat or a little fatter.
Look away! Look away! Look away, Dixie Land!

Then hoe it down and scratch your gravel,
To Dixie's Land I'm bound to travel.
Look away! Look away! Look away, Dixie Land!

"Dixie," the most famous song associated with the Civil War, continues to cause controversy. Is it a fond remembrance of the culture and hospitality of the Old South? Or is "Dixie" an unpleasant reminder of a slave-reliant economy and an apologist's view of the benefits of racial separation?

"Dixie" was written in New York in 1859, before the outbreak of war, by musician and minstrel show performer Daniel Emmett. It was a so-called walkabout song-and-dance routine for Bryant's Minstrels, a blackface troupe regularly playing the Mechanics' Hall in New York. Its lyrics reflected the theme of many Northern minstrel songs of the time, that of a free person of color living in the North but pining for his life on the old plantation. Written in mocking, "comic" Black dialect, the "Look away!" refrain is probably a poor transcription of the Southern dialect "looky way," as in "look aways down there" or "let's away to the South." The song's original lyrics (there are myriad adaptations and variations) were intended as a satire on the Southern secessionists' argument that enslaved African Americans were happier in bondage. The song was a favorite of Abraham Lincoln's and was used as his 1860 presidential campaign song. Yet by the middle of that same year, it had spread to New Orleans and the South, where it was quickly adopted by the secessionists, who focused on the first verse and the rallying couplet, "In Dixie's Land I'll take my stand, to live and die in Dixie."

That it was written by a Northerner was quickly passed over, and various lyrical adaptations over the years of the Civil War removed any inconvenient lyrics. But the song's totemic power, and its ability to raise the blood of Southern and Northern audiences even now, was recognized just one day after the surrender of Robert E. Lee that ended the war.

• • • • • •

After the South surrendered at Appomattox on April 9, 1865, President Lincoln made numerous conciliatory comments and gestures to placate what was a defeated South. But on April 10, speaking to an audience on the White House lawn, Lincoln stated:

> I propose now closing up by requesting you play a certain piece of music or a tune. I thought "Dixie" one of the best tunes I ever heard. . . . I had heard that our adversaries over the way had attempted to appropriate it. I insisted yesterday that we had fairly captured it. . . . I presented the question to the Attorney-General, and he gave his opinion that it is our lawful prize. . . . I ask the Band to give us a good turn upon it.

Reclaiming a proslavery song that had become such a totem for the South may have seemed less than placatory. Only four days after this speech, Lincoln was assassinated by John Wilkes Booth, a Confederate sympathizer and white supremacist.

Given music's consistent role on and off the battlefield, it's no surprise that the Civil War was called by some the "Singing War." Battle hymns, sentimental ballads, minstrel ditties, recruitment songs, and patriotic anthems made up most of the ten thousand songs published and copyrighted during the years between 1861 and 1865. Over 9,500 of these songs were published in the North.

Sentimental songs like "The Vacant Chair" were popular with the soldiers of both armies and the families back home.

> *We shall meet but we shall miss him,*
> *There will be one vacant chair.*
> *We shall linger to caress him,*
> *When we breathe our evening prayer*

That and songs with similar themes continued in popularity in the United States into World War I and became part of a movement popularizing simple ballads sung to the accompaniment of the guitar.

The tradition of marching brass bands continued in the US Army after the Civil War and led to the inclusion of trumpets and cornets in early New Orleans jazz. While the numerous fife-and-drum bands gradually disbanded, the concept of a melody instrument played alongside a drum prospered in New Orleans's Congo Square and in small Black communities in Mississippi, Georgia, and Tennessee—and this current ran deep in American popular music.

Performing at weekend picnics and on public holidays into the 1940s, the simple cane fife took the melody while separate snare and bass drums played either a shuffling marching rhythm, matching the syllables of what was often a single repeated vocal line, or an infectiously danceable "second-line" backbeat. Most of these drummers could also play distinctly African syncopated polyrhythms, as recorded by the music collector Alan Lomax in the South in the 1940s and again in the '50s. (The second-line rhythms of fife-and-drum bands from the Civil War link directly to country, electric blues, and generations of pop music. The rhythm reappears as the highly influential Bo Diddley beat in the singer's eponymous 1955 debut single and from there in everything from the Rolling Stones' cover of "Not Fade Away" to "Faith" by George Michael.)

Music from the Civil War period went on to impact the civil rights movement long after the war was over, and one song in particular gave name to the statutory inequality that continued to divide America after the failure of Reconstruction and the rise of Jim Crow.

The war, fought to maintain the Union and to outlaw slavery, had a lasting and long-term effect on the future of the whole nation, especially when Lincoln successfully overturned the constitutional right to own human beings across the whole of the country. Some may have hoped that this settled the issue of slavery forever, but the many and various "Black Codes" introduced in 1865 and 1866 under Southern state laws and local ordinances restricted the very freedom of emancipated African Americans. The codes included everything from the so-called walking tax, whereby out-of-town Black visitors had to register with the police and pay for a permit that allowed them to walk the streets, to the "Separate Car Law," the practice of forcing Black passengers to use separate and usually inferior railroad cars, trollies, and buses. African Americans and civil rights activists still describe the unfair, segregationist practices introduced in the mid-1870s after the defeat of Radical Reconstruction as "Jimcrowing," itself a term with roots in the same minstrel music that had contributed to the war.

Come listen to me, galls and boys
I's just from Tuckahoe
I'm going to sing a little song,
My name's Jim Crow
Weel about and turn about and do jis so,
Eb'ry time I weel about I jump Jim Crow
THOMAS DARTMOUTH RICE, "JUMP JIM CROW," 1828

Jim Crow, a dim-witted, degrading Black stereotype, was the creation of one of the first white performers to wear blackface makeup, Thomas Dartmouth "Daddy" Rice—the "Daddy" acknowledging him as "the Father of Minstrelsy."

Rice, who became successful and wealthy as a performer in both Northern and Southern states, had borrowed the song, character, and name Jim Crow, after watching a gammy-legged Black coach driver entertain a small crowd in the street. The Jim Crow character originated from a West African folk tale popular with enslaved people. "Jim" was a trickster crow, prototype for the Br'er Rabbit character, who acted foolish and got what he wanted through guile. Rice dropped the guile and played up the stupidity and laziness by blacking-up into a character that remained popular throughout the 1830s and '40s. The character later gave name to the "separate but equal" laws that legally perpetuated segregation and discrimination for another hundred years.

Rice was more than a vaudeville entertainer, and his performance was more than a piece of harmless fun. When he took his Jim Crow act to Great Britain in the autumn of 1836, he likely had a political agenda. On November 9, 1837, following his return to the US, the *Baltimore Sun* reported that after a well-received performance he had delivered a speech. "Ladies and Gentlemen: Before I went to England, the British people were excessively ignorant regarding 'our free institutions.' They were under the impression that negroes were naturally equal to the whites, and their degraded condition was consequent entirely upon our 'institutions.' I effectively proved that negroes are essentially an inferior species of the human family and they ought to remain slaves."

• • • • • •

The musical legacies of the Civil War were many, but the most important was the evolution of a non-European, truly American style of music. Soldiers from small towns and hamlets, alongside many from isolated southern Appalachian valleys or hollows ("hollers," in Appalachian dialect), had been pulled together to form fighting units, many meeting men from places and states they hadn't known existed. They brought with them tunes with distinctly different musical styles, imported Irish jigs, Scottish reels, English hornpipes, and Protestant hymns among them. These were cross-fertilized, mixed with local folk songs, and for the first time influenced by the fiddle and banjo music of the many different races living in the region.

Black people were living in Appalachia as early as 1780, part of the estimated 14 percent of African Americans who were designated free before the Civil War theoretically freed all enslaved peoples. Alongside these Black Appalachians were some twenty thousand free people of color, a group of multiracial people variously called "mulatto," "creole," or "Melungeon." The group, whose communities were spread across the region, were of Black African, white European, and Native American descent.

Whatever their origins or skin color, they were rarely recognized as Americans by those writing at the time. But the complex multiracial, intercultural influence of their music gave much more than the "tinge of character" suggested by many modern narratives describing the role of Black and mixed-race people in the development of Appalachian music. Far from being rare or token participants, since the 1650s Black fiddle players and Black string bands were playing reels, hoedowns, and frolics in both New Amsterdam (New York) and Virginia. Dancing was the major form of rural community entertainment before 1900, and according to American dance historian Phil Jamison, "Every town and village had its ballroom, and its musician [was] almost always a negro fiddler."

Alongside the fiddle—whether a homemade, single-string native gourd or a cheap, factory-made, four-string European classical violin—was the gut-string banjo. At this time, the banjo was a fretless, low-tuned instrument played primarily by Black musicians in a style that linked back to its West African roots. "Stroke-style" playing (known now as frailing or clawhammer) involved striking down on the strings with the back of the fingernail and thumb and combining melody and rhythm in a way that encouraged people to dance. The popularity of minstrelsy and the exposure to this playing style during the Civil War led to a rise in the national popularity of the banjo. The instrument, first introduced by enslaved people in the 1600s, is believed by historian and archivist Jim Bolman to be an amalgam of the African gourd lute and the *vihuela*, a Spanish guitar–like instrument also prevalent in the cultures of early enslaved peoples. It's unlikely that any slave traders would have allowed any of their victims to bring a spiked lute or gourd banjo with them: Enslaved people arrived in America without possessions but no doubt carried the concept of instruments, many still played in Africa today, in their heads and hearts. These early primitive banjos, more suitable for rhythmic than melodic playing, gradually became more sophisticated, and what was initially a popular, portable folk instrument ultimately became by the late 1800s "America's Instrument," played in concert halls by primarily white players dressed in tuxedos.

Fiddle and banjo tunes popular during the war, like "The Boatman" and accompanied ballads like "I'll Twine 'Mid the Ringlets," became part of American folk music.

I'll twine 'mid the ringlets of my raven black hair
The lilies so pale and the roses so fair
The myrtle so bright with an emerald hue
And the pale aronatus with eyes of bright blue.

The latter's melody and words, reimagined and popularized by the Carter Family as "Wildwood Flower" in 1928, remain at the heart of American country music today.

Popular campfire ballads like "Aura Lee," a favorite for both armies, remained obscure, incubating for almost a century; this tune in particular popped up in 1956 as Elvis's first hit ballad, "Love Me Tender." Elvis's manager, "Colonel" Tom Parker, had noticed that "Aura Lee" was then out of copyright, so the estate of the original composer could not benefit from the royalties. Despite contributing neither tune nor lyrics, Elvis and Parker most certainly did profit. The song's legitimate author, George R. Poulton, from rural England, arrived in America with his parents in 1835 as a seven-year-old. Growing up in New York, Poulton can rightly be regarded as part of the first generation of American songwriters. But many traditional pre–Civil War American songs were often simple adaptations of the songs brought over by the first British immigrants.

A quintessential American jazz and blues standard like "St. James Infirmary" started out in the 1780s as the English folk song "The Unfortunate Rake."

As I was a-walking down by St James Hospital
I was walking down by there one day
What should I spy but one of my comrades
All wrapped up in flannel though warm was the day

Popular in the Appalachian Mountains well before the Civil War, it morphed into many other versions, including a Texas traditional song called "The Sad Death of My Sweetheart" or "The Cowboy's Lament." The song continued to live a colorful existence all the way through to 1927, when it appeared in Atlanta, Georgia, reworked by bluesman Blind Willie McTell as "The Dyin' Crapshooter's Blues."

Eight crapshooters to be my pallbearers,
Sixteen bootleggers to sing a song . . .

Just twelve months later it had reached New Orleans, and Louis Armstrong made the first jazz recording of the tune with yet another modified lyric. A further twelve months later, a tune that had managed quite well for over one hundred years with "Traditional" listed as the writing credit had miraculously gained a composer. Irving Mills slightly modified the tune that went on to become the basis of the 1960s Marty Robbins hit "Streets of Laredo," albeit with much detail of the cautionary tale removed (such as catching syphilis from so-called city girls and its painful treatment by the application of mercury salts).

• • • • • •

While the guitar continued to grow in popularity both before and during the Civil War, the popularity of the gut-string banjo was driven after the Civil War by the many blackface minstrel shows that toured the country and filled the playbills of the vaudeville theatres and music halls in towns and big cities.

With many professional musicians and vaudeville players favoring the banjo, the guitar remained something of a minority interest, played by professional touring classical players or enthusiastic amateurs. Although playing primarily for their own enjoyment or entertaining friends and family, many of these amateur guitarists were nonetheless serious students of the instrument, playing classical pieces but also arrangements of the popular songs of the day like "Polly Wolly Doodle" and "Turkey in the Straw." Some players, though, were ordinary workers who took a guitar with them to provide entertainment at sea, out on the range, while panning for gold, or on lonely farmsteads. The instruments they played were sometimes homemade, but usually they were basic factory-made models costing just a few dollars.

But in the second half of the 1800s, during a time when a month's salary for a skilled worker was $34 and still only bought a relatively basic Martin guitar, who were the amateur musicians buying guitars from Martin & Co.?

It was the wealthy, of course, for whom the Martin guitar had the cachet of quality, excellent sound, and durability. In 1868, one such customer of a Martin 2½-17 student model was a prosperous, forty-five-year-old Californian landowner. Thomas Bloodgood Dibblee was on honeymoon in New York with his bride, nineteen-year-old Francesca, the granddaughter of a Spanish-born California grandee.

The Dibblees' honeymoon took them from Santa Barbara, California, to New York, where Thomas Dibblee had been born, and involved uncomfortable passages by ship, stagecoach, and train. Francesca followed the tradition of the daughters of high-born Spanish Californian families in being able to sing a large repertoire of traditional Spanish folk songs, and Thomas commemorated their visit to New York by buying his new bride a Martin guitar. Given their considerable joint wealth, it's perhaps surprising that the guitar purchased was one of Martin's less expensive models. But it was a highly practical choice considering the rigors this wooden-cased instrument endured on the homeward journey. Regardless of its monetary value, Francesca long relished playing the instrument, as a visitor to the Dibblee home in 1890 reported:

> The Dibblee House . . . is built of stone to represent an old castle. . . . We spent an evening there. . . . After a time we went around to a veranda at the back and sat about a table and ate figs. . . . After we had eaten the figs Mrs. Dibble [*sic*] took a guitar and began to sing. A mantilla was on her head; she sang with the dash and style and coquetry of her Spanish blood. Not one atom of it has gone from her, or of the grace which only a Spanish woman possesses.

The exotic appeal of a Spanish lady playing the guitar was still working its magic, even in the hands of forty-one-year-old Francesca Dibblee.

Francesca's Martin guitar served her well for over fifty-seven years. During the devastating Santa Barbara earthquake of 1925, the *Santa Barbara Daily Star* reported that when family and servants were fleeing out of the grand Punta del Castillo, known locally as Dibblee's Castle, Mrs. Dibblee, now seventy-six years old and long widowed, was still thinking of her treasured honeymoon gift; she called out, "Save the guitar, save the guitar!"

It obviously survived. Today, the same guitar, still playable and in excellent condition, sits in the Santa Barbara Historical Museum alongside her black dress and lace mantilla. Chris Jensen, the local guitar store owner who was called in to assess and repair the guitar after it was discovered in the late 1990s, reported that the instrument was fitted with steel strings.

> Their condition strongly suggested that these were the original strings from when Mrs Dibblee played it. Many players of that period used steel strings,

they were louder, lasted much longer and therefore, in the long run, were significantly cheaper than gut strings. A set of new gut strings would almost certainly be imported from Spain or Germany and could cost the same price as a decent guitar of the time. Therefore, it was quite usual to find that when the original gut strings wore out, they were replaced with steel. A second Martin guitar from the same period was found a few years ago in another ranch house owned by the de la Guerra family. It had been hidden behind a piano for years and also had steel strings. It's evidence that Martins, braced for gut but capable of carrying steel strings, were being made as early as the 1860s. That both instruments lasted so long and were in playable condition was a testament to their build quality.

Consistency of product quality had always been the pillar of Martin's business, and anyone looking for a serious guitar during this period knew Martin was the brand to buy. Although the most expensive guitar in their printed catalog was $90, Martin still had customers specifying guitars with ivory and gold appointments that cost as much as $275. Yet despite its relative fame, Martin & Co. was still a small, fragile enterprise. Its capability to produce guitars of the highest standard year after year was undoubtedly an enormous asset, and Martin concentrated solely on producing quality instruments and became more introspective as a business. It didn't seem too interested in expanding, failing to capitalize on the full power of marketing, especially in reaching out to the emerging Western states and cities. Its more bullish competitors embraced the new age of selling to the whole nation enabled by mass advertising and catalogue selling.

By 1888, and under the leadership of a new head-of-family, twenty-two-year-old Frank Henry Martin, grandson of the company's founder, the business faced a difficult time. The East Coast in particular entered a period of economic depression following a panic in 1893, and sales of luxury goods, and unsurprisingly, the more expensive Martin guitars, came to a virtual standstill. Business was so slow that for a month or more Martin stopped production. Their main distributor, and key New York wholesaler and retailer, was carrying so much inventory it announced it would not be ordering any new guitars for at least six months. While retailers did carry stock of popular models, Martin rarely made instruments on spec (that is, done on a speculative basis); everything was usually built against a firm retail order, so firing skilled workers looked inevitable.

Despite the century-long passion for blackface minstrelsy finally fading and banjo sales starting to fall, the guitar market was, at best, static. Surprisingly, a growing musical craze in the 1890s for the mandolin not only stopped the Martin business from foundering but influenced acoustic guitar design for at least the next one hundred years.

Charley Patton playing an early Stella six-string.

Minstrelsy and the Blues

The growth and dominance of the guitar as the democratic musical instrument of the twentieth century has always been reliant on new players—regardless of creed, class, or sex—being not just attracted to the sound of the guitar but also convinced that learning to play was relatively quick and easy.

Although being able to play a simple tune on the guitar *is* relatively easy for a novice, as with any instrument, reaching a level of pleasing proficiency takes time, dedication, and usually a little instruction. For this reason, music teachers have been highly influential in building the guitar's popularity, although the style and way that tuition was delivered have varied over the years.

How we learn today was heavily influenced by two regulars of New York's 1960s Washington Square music scene. In the late '60s, the guitarist Happy

Traum pioneered long-distance teaching using the tablature notation system in books like his immensely popular *Finger-Picking Styles for Guitar* (1966). By the early '80s, when VCR recorders and VHS home tapes had become affordable domestic standards, Traum started Homespun Tapes. Alongside the videos produced by Stefan Grossman's Guitar Workshop and Vestapol archive films, home video tuition was widely available. With the adoption of split-screen video came the guitar teacher who never tired and never slept! He could demonstrate to the slowest learners, over and over, how to perfect the style of Bert Jansch or show them exactly how the long-dead Elizabeth Cotten or Rev. Gary Davis actually played. Today, online downloads and largely free videos through YouTube dominate, teaching everything from simple chord accompaniment to note-by-note breakdowns of the finger-busting pyrotechnics of bluegrass player Tony Rice or the English finger-style player John Renbourn.

For generations of British teenagers in the mid-twentieth century, one man was synonymous with learning to play the guitar—Bert Weedon. A dapper, jobbing dance-band guitarist, Weedon almost single-handedly facilitated the highly influential British guitar boom of the late 1950s through his hugely popular *Play in a Day: Guide to Modern Guitar Playing* tutorial. He helped and inspired a whole generation of young amateur guitarists, including teenagers Eric Clapton, Paul McCartney, Mark Knopfler, and Pete Townshend. He even influenced Hank Marvin, having been the first to record "Apache," the song that Marvin and the Shadows turned into their first hit. Prior to Weedon's arrival on the scene, the typical young amateur guitarist in Britain was, almost by default, learning to play classical guitar under the instruction of a serious-minded professional teacher. With a background in jazz and dance-band music, Bert Weedon's home-taught method focused on the melody and rhythm of playing of popular tunes rather than a stuffy classical repertoire. Weedon billed himself as "the man who taught the world to play guitar." Obviously an exaggeration, yet in the 1950s and '60s, it convinced a generation of young people that after only a few days' practice in the privacy of their bedrooms they could be entertaining their friends and family and, perhaps more importantly, potential romantic partners.

Learning to "play in a day" may have been unrealistic, but over a hundred years earlier, *Elements of Guitar-Playing*, a printed guitar "method" from American music professor James Ballard, reassured potential students that "persons who had a taste for music . . . and [wished] to play a few pleasing pieces . . . could do so without any serious encroachment upon the time devoted to every-day life."

Ballard's method book, originally published in 1838 and still in print sixty years later, along with earlier works from European masters Fernando Sor and Matteo Carcassi, was intended to be used alongside the services of a professional teacher. Early mass production of guitars made the actual instrument financially more accessible in America, but only the wealthy and well positioned could afford the services of a qualified music professor or a leading professional player-tutor like Madame de Goñi, the early guitar superstar for whom Martin built guitars.

For the less prosperous middle classes, help came in the shape of Henry Worrall, a Liverpudlian guitarist who arrived in New York in 1835, just two years after C. F. Martin. Neither of these Old World immigrants could have imagined their enormous influence on the guitar, and guitar music, in the New World.

In the 1860s, Worrall and his instruction books helped a generation of young East Coast ladies and gentlemen learn to play guitar. Having left England an enthusiastic amateur guitarist, in America he developed into an accomplished musician, teacher, and composer. By 1856, he had published *The Eclectic Guitar Instructor*, a proto–*Play in a Day* for the American market. His book was written for the student without access to a professional teacher. Rather than tutor someone who wished to perform professionally, its aim was to teach "the instrument so as to be played for pleasure." The idea of the guitar as an instrument that was both quick and easy to learn had been established.

As a teaching professor, Worrall knew the attraction for new, inexperienced players to guitar pieces written for open tuning (which allows the player to play a chord with no strings fretted) rather than the more complex classical tuning (E, A, D, G, B, E) used by professional players like Sor and Carcassi. In 1860, he arranged and copyrighted two simple instrumentals for guitar, "Spanish Fandango," a jaunty dance tune in 3/4 time, and "Sebastapol," a military march piece celebrating the Siege of Sebastapol in the recently ended Crimean War. Both were easy to play ("Fandango" required the guitar to be tuned to an open G chord), and they soon became staples for the Victorian parlor guitarists' repertoires.

Both tunes might have remained obscure, long-forgotten in the ever-increasing mountain of old sheet music, were it not for the curiosity of the 1960s British finger-style guitarist John Renbourn. He realized that these two songs had almost certainly influenced the style and repertoire of countless Black Delta blues musicians in the 1920s and '30s.

Renbourn, a longtime fan of American parlor music of the early twentieth

Worrall's "Fandango," from Frances Weiland's Instructions for the Spanish Guitar, *published in Philadelphia in 1855. (Library of Congress, call number M1.A12 I)*

century, noticed that Worrall's "Spanish Fandango," when played in a more common 4/4 time, had a "bluesy feel" to its dance-like rhythm. (The word "fandango" has long been used in English to describe a style of Spanish or Spanish-American dancing.) Renbourn also worked out that "Sebastopol," in a different open tuning from "Fandango," used chord shapes and musical intervals that felt much like those being used by the Black blues players sixty years after its publication. He realized that the melody of "Sebastopol," with just a slight change of position of one left-hand finger on the fretboard, easily slipped into the phrasing and "blue notes" used by Delta blues players. By the 1920s, that change of time signature from 3/4 to the simpler 4/4 and a little added pace transformed a pseudoclassical piece from the Victorian parlor of a New England home into a staple for Southern country blues players like John Dilleshaw and the String Marvels, Furry Lewis, and Mississippi John Hurt. The tune was also remembered by the veteran blues player, now much-celebrated in folk circles, Elizabeth Cotten, who knew it as "Spanish Flang Dang." Cotten gave numerous interviews in the 1980s, when she was in her nineties, in which she recalled playing it in the 1920s as a young girl. (It is ironic that the family responsible for her rediscovery in the 1960s, the leftist Seeger family, at the time employed the sixty-year-old as a domestic servant.)

Further evidence of how these two instrumental compositions reached across the decades and down to the Delta is in the names that blues guitarists used for the open tuning they deployed on slide guitar tunes. In the 1920s, as they do today, blues guitarists refer to open G tuning as "Spanish tuning" and open D as "Vestapol."

Cheap mail-order guitars, shipped in the 1920s in simple pressed cardboard cases by companies like Montgomery Ward, came with a basic tutorial booklet, often written by Septimus Winner, which invariably included versions of Worral's two most popular songs. So popular, and easy to play, were "Fandango" and "Sebastopol" that most other booklets contained versions of these songs, often slightly altered to avoid infringing Worrall's copyright. With minor modifications and accidental variations, the classical chord harmonies of Worrall's two instrumentals provided the basis of the "blues scale." Combined with the simple, percussive, repetitive work songs and "field hollers" of Southern field hands and sharecroppers, the roots of the recorded blues of the Mississippi Delta are revealed. It is the music that influenced, or was unashamedly plagiarized by, bands like the Rolling Stones and Led Zeppelin.

• • • • • •

The acoustic guitar is today almost synonymous with the blues and most other roots music from the early 1900s. But in the 1890s, the guitar was still vying for popularity with the five-string banjo, an instrument that at the time had something of a multiple personality. The banjo figured at the heart of the still-popular blackface minstrel shows as well as being played as a rural folk instrument. But it had also entered the concert hall and the homes of the middle classes, where a guitar-like fingerpicking, or "classic" playing style, was being used by both amateurs and professional entertainers. Distinct from blackface minstrel playing, where the banjo was primarily an accompanying instrument, classic banjo music featured instrumentals in ragtime as well as popular ballads and even older classical compositions.

While the minstrel banjo was already popular in 1833 when C. F. Martin first arrived in New York, the primary folk instrument of America was the fiddle, brought over by, and popular with, virtually every European immigrant cohort. But the banjo continued growing in popularity, due in large part to the ubiquity of the touring shows featuring banjo-playing blackface minstrels. The American banjo's origins—the *banza*, which used multiple strings vibrating against a piece of animal skin stretched across a hollow gourd (like a tambourine)—traces back to the French and British Caribbean of the early 1600s. There it was originally made and played by enslaved Black Africans before being brought to America by those same enslaved people sold from Caribbean sugar plantations to American tobacco and cotton plantations.

By the 1830s, the Americanization of the banjo and its misappropriation from its African origins had begun. Joel Sweeney, a white Virginia farmer's son, was taught to play banjo by enslaved workers on his father's farm. Legend holds that it was he, in 1839, who was the first white man to perform solo on a New York stage playing a five-string banjo. The Sweeney narrative also credits him as the inventor of the modern banjo, responsible for replacing the gourd body with a circular wooden hoop (allegedly repurposed from a cheese-making mold used in the family dairy) and for adding a fifth drone string to the instrument. Although those claims are incorrect (scholars have catalogued these developments as happening long before Sweeney was born, let alone picked up an instrument), he was undoubtedly a talented player. He had also helped popularize the instrument in America and was one of the first performers to introduce the banjo to Britain when he toured extensively as a blackface minstrel in the 1840s. Sweeney and other American players who visited Britain laid the foundations for a British banjo craze that ran from the late 1860s into the next century. British banjo fans included Queen Victoria, for whom Sweeney gave a command performance, and her playboy son Edward VII, who was said to be a more-than-competent player following lessons from the Virginian. (The minstrels' arrival also encouraged domestic banjo makers, who eventually branched out into making guitars once the banjo craze diminished in the early twentieth century.)

Sweeney had a broad repertoire of minstrel songs, some borrowed and some that he allegedly composed himself, including "Jenny Get Your Hoecake Done" and "Old Tar River." But he was just one of any number of blackface minstrels who played Stephen Foster's "Oh! Susanna."

I came from Alabama,
Wid a banjo on my knee,
I'm gwyne to Louisiana,
My true love for to see.

The song became the unofficial anthem of the California gold rush, and many of the three hundred thousand gold-seekers, and all other kinds of chancers, took the simple, portable banjo to play on their knees in the gold fields from 1849 through the 1850s.

In the cities, blackface banjo-playing minstrels were still extremely popular at the turn of the century, by which time the intentionally derogatory material in their repertoires had become even more insulting. So-called coon songs (e.g., "Coon, Coon, Coon," "Every Race Has a Flag but the Coon," and "All Coons Look Alike to Me") were so well known in New York, and so knowingly offensive, that whistling the first few notes was an easy and sly racial street taunt. Even before the Civil War, many blackface minstrel lyrics were intentionally mocking or belittling Black people, but they were nothing as strong as the material being publicly sung for entertainment in the 1890s and early 1900s.

No matter the cause, it is easy to regard these songs, and minstrelsy in general, as something that happened a very long time ago, that now, thankfully, has been long forgotten—written off as a regrettable period in musical history. But blackface continued into the twentieth century: many Delta blues and country players spent periods of their career wearing the grotesque makeup. Even Jimmie Rodgers, the white hillbilly "Father of Country Music," was "blacking-up" early in his career in the 1920s when he was playing in bar bands and travelling medicine shows. Blackface minstrelsy continued in Hollywood into the 1940s. Shirley Temple appeared with blackface, blackarms, blackhands, and blacklegs hiding from Union soldiers in her 1935 vehicle *The Littlest Rebel*. The following year Fred Astaire danced blackface as Bill "Bojangles" Robinson in *Swing Time*, while Bing Crosby appeared bizarrely as a blackface Abe Lincoln in his 1942 hit *Holiday Inn*. Live minstrel shows continued across the country well into World War II. But perhaps more shockingly, as recently as the late 1970s *The Black and White Minstrel Show* (1958–1978) was a primetime TV variety program broadcast nationally by the BBC in the UK. It was perhaps a more innocent version of minstrelsy compared to the coarsely cruel pre-1900 American vaudeville style, but despite the Campaign for Racial Equality petitioning the BBC to remove it in the 1960s, it ran until 1978. The show featured clean-cut white males sporting blackface and curly black wigs, singing and waltzing with white, blonde-haired Southern belles—something that would have resulted in a lynching party in parts of the Southern states in the 1950s. Today it feels as bizarre as it is offensive, but at the time it clearly didn't seem odd or wrong to its regular Saturday evening family audience of twenty million. The program was defended as a continuation of the purportedly innocent British tradition of music-hall minstrelsy that had started in the 1750s. Its repertoire featured "good old Southern songs" like "Old Black Joe," "Oh! Susanna," "Camptown Races," and "Old Uncle Ned."

> *Den lay down de shuffle and de hoe-o-o*
> *And hang up de fiddle and de bow*
> *No more hard work for old Uncle Ned,*
> *He's gone where the good n——s go . . .*

The white writer of the songs mentioned above was Stephen Foster, once celebrated as "the Father of American Music" and author of popular sentimental ballads like "Beautiful Dreamer" and "Old Folks at Home."

His most popular song, "Camptown Races," written in 1850, is about one of the many camped or tented hobo towns. It features racetrack ladies singing "doo-dah," local slang for the services performed by women of accommodating morals, and feckless Black racegoers squandering what little money, or "tin," they have on gambling at the notorious Pennsylvania track. Its apparently innocent lyrics entertained many a British family gathered round the television on a Saturday evening:

> *De Camptown ladies sing dis song—Doo-dah! Doo-dah!*
> *De Camptown race-track five miles long—Oh! Doo-dah day!*
> *I come down dah wid my hat caved in—Doo-dah! Doo-dah!*
> *I go back home wid a pocket full of tin—Oh! Doo-dah day!*

Another Foster song, "Oh! Susanna," which sold over a hundred thousand copies in its first year of publication, is known now only in its edited and sanitized version. But even the opening nonsense verse has its sting.

It rain'd all night the day I left, the weather it was dry,
The sun so hot I froze to death; Susanna, don't you cry.

That verse and others in the song played to a popular minstrel trope: a dandified, urban free Black man (or "zip coon") who thought himself as smart as whites but whose ignorance is illustrated through his regular misuse of language. The song, written in traditional minstrel dialect, painted a picture of a stupid narrator who, in the original version, tells us

I jumped aboard the telegraph,
And trabbled down the riber,
De lectric fluid magnified,
And killed five hundred n——s.

The singer is portrayed as so unworldly (or perhaps stupid) that, with warped logic, he thinks he can travel down the newly invented telegraph line. Electricity, considered at the time to flow like a river and thought capable of expanding uncontrollably, nonchalantly killed five hundred other Black folks. Foster eventually moved away from writing minstrel songs in dialect, and his realization of the deliberate taunting and racism of the original sheet music cover art of his earlier material caused him to persuade publishers to change it. His change of heart is seen by many modern-day critics as a case of too little too late. Ironically, Foster appears to have hidden his own antislavery views due to his financial reliance on his conservative family: one of his sisters had married the brother of president-to-be James Buchanan (1857–1861). (As the fifteenth US president, Buchanan did little to avoid the impending Civil War.) Foster songs like "Old Folks at Home" (or "Swanee River") were criticized for romanticizing slavery, although "the old folks at home" are sometimes explained as the singer experiencing a longing for the people and traditions of Africa rather than life on the plantation. "My Old Kentucky Home, Good-Night!" is itself based on *Uncle Tom's Cabin*, with all its inherent contradictions and complexities.

Illustrations on the covers of the millions of copies of sheet music that sold Foster's songs invariably featured Black minstrels playing the banjo. These and other such drawings show how the simple, fretless, three-string gourd banjo originally introduced to America by enslaved African Americans steadily transformed into a more technically complex and often highly ornamented instrument. By the 1860s, the banjo had become associated with polite society and white male and female college glee clubs.

The transformation of the banjo from a primitive African folk instrument into an instrument played by middle-class ladies was not a simple one. Black players not only passed the banjo habit to the middle class and influenced white professional musicians; they also passed it to poor, white mountain farmers in the South. Moreover, it was Black players who developed the fifth drone string, not a white American, contrary to the Joel Sweeney tale that had been advanced for many years.

Commercial banjo makers continued working hard to disassociate the instrument from the crude minstrelsy circuit and promote both a classical, and a classic, repertoire. There was even a fruitless attempt to change the spelling to "banjeau," but the old banjo did come up in the world. Some fancy instruments with ornate inlay and decorative heel carvings sold for double the price of the best guitars in the Martin catalogue. Banjo makers like S. S. Stewart and Fairbanks produced many highly ornate instruments, and while Martin's customers continued ordering one-off deluxe guitars with the fanciest appointments, the average guitar was still quite plain.

Professional and amateur banjo orchestras became popular in the 1880s and 1890s in both America and Britain. But the banjo could be a temperamental instrument for an amateur to keep in tune. In humid weather, retightening the vellum head and coping with slipping friction tuning pegs and gut strings proved difficult for a solo player; keeping an orchestra of instruments in tune was often impossible. By the early 1900s, and with the meteoric rise in popularity of the mandolin, banjo orchestras and the five-string banjo itself had fallen out of fashion in America.

The demise of the five-string, gut-string banjo didn't mean that the banjo, per se, was dead. As the mandolin grew in popularity, it inspired the banjo-mandolin. As the name implies, this was an eight-string cross between a banjo and a mandolin. A subsequent development, the tango-banjo, with four single steel strings rather than gut strings, was louder than its five-string predecessor and again provided an easy switch for mandolin players wishing to transition to what became known as the tenor banjo. Popular as a rhythm instrument, it could cut through the sound of the brass section in the orchestra. Players who wanted a deeper, sweeter, more mellow sound and a way to play both rhythm and lead lines leaned toward the longer-necked plectrum banjo. Both instruments were popular with jazz orchestras and became essential parts of the 1920s jazz sound. But musical tastes and dance styles changed after the Great Depression. The metallic twang of the jazz banjo was superseded by the archtop or jazz guitar, which offered a smoother, more liquid sound better suited to the dances of a new era.

The five-string banjo's fall from fashion at the start of the twentieth century, its indelible association with blackface minstrelsy, and its cultural appropriation as a middle-class American instrument all served to confuse and obscure the banjo's authentic Black heritage. When the five-string banjo, with steel strings and an amplifying resonator like its tenor brother, fully reemerged in the 1940s, it was associated primarily with white, mountain hillbillies and bluegrass music.

• • • • • •

A few years after Stephen Foster's heyday, another musician who had played blackface in minstrel bands himself became a second American musical patriarch, this time heralded as "the Father of the Blues."

Born in 1873 in Alabama, as a teenager W. C. Handy was a keen guitarist, but his pastor father banned the instrument, branding it "one of the devil's playthings," so Handy took up the cornet. (Clearly Handy Sr. hadn't heard Charlie "Buddy" Bolden play "Funky Butt" on the cornet in the 1890s.) The cornet served Handy Jr. well, and he was soon leading his own band. As a touring musician he played all styles of music, but he also heard his fair share of what he termed "primitive" music, and in 1909 he wrote the song "Memphis Blues." It is often cited as the first blues song, but more correctly, it is the earliest vocal blues to be written down. In many ways it's a specious claim, given that much blues music has an oral tradition.

Handy acknowledged in his autobiography that he "got the blues" orally in 1903, while waiting for a train in Tutwiler, Mississippi, when "a lean, loose jointed Negro had commenced plunking a guitar beside me while I slept. . . . As he played, he pressed a knife on the strings of the guitar in a manner popularized by Hawaiian guitarists who used steel bars. The effect was unforgettable. His song too, struck me instantly—'Goin' where the Southern cross' the Dog.' The singer repeated the line three times, accompanying himself on the guitar with the weirdest music I had ever heard."

The reference was picked up a few years later by Handy in his "Yellow Dog Blues"; over a hundred years later, Bob Dylan cribbed the line in "Nettie

Moore": "Where the Southern crosses the Yellow Dog." ("Yellow Dog" was the nickname for the Yazoo Delta branch railroad, or "dog" [as in dogleg] line.)

Bluesologists are always looking to connect the dots, wanting to believe that the loose-jointed singer in Tutwiler singing about a railway branch line famous in the days of cotton was Charley Patton, a mixed-race man of African American and Cherokee ancestry who lived on the nearby Dockery Plantation. The dates and locations coincide, and it would make a beautiful, symmetrical confluence to link the Father of the Blues with one of its greatest and most influential guitar players.

W. C. Handy's official photograph pictures a white-haired-uncle figure in suit and tie who looks prosperous, smartly dressed, and benevolent. With a crisp white handkerchief peeking from his breast pocket, it's easy to write off Handy as a rather stiff professional composer with none of the coolness or street credibility of a typical blues legend like Charley Patton. But Handy knew the Delta and many musicians, like Charley Patton, whom we revere today.

Patton is credited with both teaching guitar and mentoring several of his fellow workers at Dockery. His informal students included formative blues players Son House, Willie Brown, and Tommy Johnson. He was, by all accounts, also an amazing showman, capable of playing the guitar behind his head or back, skills that ensured him regular paid engagements in juke joints and at dances held at other plantations. Dockery Plantation was connected by the old Peavine railroad branch to Moorhead, the main passenger and freight connection from Mississippi to the North and West—"where the Southern cross' the Dog."

Handy's "Memphis Blues" was by no means a pale or formalized imitation of a blues style. It had echoes of field music and songs Handy had often heard solo singers and rural three-piece string bands play. Not following the verse and chorus structure of popular songs of the time, the tune had begun life as "Mister Crump Blues," a specially commissioned political campaign song for "Boss" Crump, a dubious Memphis mayoral candidate. Having served its initial purpose for Mayor Crump, Handy published the song in 1912 as "Memphis Blues." It was subsequently covered in the 1950s by everyone from Louis Armstrong to Nat King Cole.

Although "Memphis Blues" was a blues song in structure and feel, at this point in the genre's popular evolution the blues was essentially dance music—played in cities by brass bands and small dance orchestras and in rural areas by local string bands. Handy, through a succession of songs, including "Memphis Blues," "Beale Street Blues," and "Saint Louis Blues," formalized the twelve-bar structure and introduced the term "blues" to a wider audience. But it was still a few decades before blues music became synonymous with the guitar and a major driver of the instrument's popularity.

• • • • • •

Meanwhile, a few hundred miles east of Memphis, a different sort of music was being created by a different sort of people. If the blues was initially born of poor Black musicians from the Delta, at about the same time a "white blues," what later became known as country music, was being born of poor white people in the mountains of West Virginia, Tennessee, Kentucky, and North Carolina.

The southern area of Appalachia, with its rolling hills and rocky, hardscrabble hollers, was first colonized in the seventeenth century by poor Scots-Irish immigrants who had originally immigrated to Pennsylvania as indentured servants. After working out their terms of servitude, as free people they often found land in the North too expensive or unavailable to settle, so whole families migrated south. In search of cheap, fertile land, a contingent headed to Virginia. But the migrants found the good flatlands between the hills and the sea either too expensive or already occupied by land companies. They had little choice but to migrate west into the valleys and hollers of the Appalachians, the mountain range that runs from Maine to Georgia. Once there, they occupied land largely unwanted due to its inaccessibility and poor soil. Life in these small, isolated communities was tough, and the religion and music from the settlers' homelands provided social cohesion and moral solace.

God—and music to worship him by—was especially important to the descendants of the fervent Protestant settlers from Scotland and Ulster. Many were outcasts or deported supporters of King William III of England (who ruled England, Scotland, and Ireland from 1689 to 1702). Supporters fondly called him "Prince Billy," and they were known colloquially as "Billy's Boys." Therefore, given their location, these Southern uplands immigrants became known as "hillbillies." The region also included descendants from early Scots Presbyterians who, as signatories to the National Covenant petition for a Presbyterian government in Scotland, had fled the subsequent British religious persecution. Another story, equally apocryphal, has it that many signed the petition in their own blood, and their descendants wore a red neckerchief as a badge of honor. Whether this, or days spent working in the fields in the hot sun, led to the term "redneck" is unclear. However, the largely erroneous belief that many indentured servants were transported criminals, the inevitable intermarriage of cousins and closer blood relatives in these isolated mountain communities, combined with limited educational opportunities and abject poverty, did lead to Appalachian outsiders using both "redneck" and "hillbilly" as highly pejorative, interchangeable terms. This group of poor people living in isolation, with precious little distraction outside of subsistence farming, provided the straw in the tinderbox for the creation of white American blues music. It just needed a spark to ignite it, and that spark came in the shape of religious revivalism.

Revivalist Protestantism was in the ascendant in America from the mid-1800s through the early 1900s. Manifested most publicly in church camp meetings led by roving preachers, it was an integral part of a period of religious activism known as the Third Great Awakening and provided important social glue in these God-fearing areas. Instrument playing and group singing at these camps reinforced the popularity of music and included revivalist songs, spirituals, and evangelical gospel, all much livelier than the dirge-like hymns that had preceded it. Religious music merged with the secular, much of it Anglo-Celtic in origin, and focused on fiddle-based dance tunes and British folk ballads. Largely sung without accompaniment by women, the usual guardians of familial heritage, the repertoire leaned toward story ballads that the women identified with. Often these ballads were cautionary tales of decent girls wronged by deceiving men, as in "Pretty Polly" and "Blackwaterside." Also popular were much darker tales of incest and femicide, songs like "The Ballad of Lizzy Wan."

"I have a cause to grieve" she said
"And a reason for to mourn;
For the babe that lies in the cradle asleep,
Dear brother it is your own."

He took her by the lily-white hand
And he led her to the woods;
What he did there I never can declare,
But he spilt fair Lizzy's blood

This tradition of sweetheart murder ballads reappeared in 1934 in Alberta Hunter's jauntily eerie reading of "Miss Otis Regrets." It emerged again in 1950s country music in songs like "Tom Dooley" and carried over into the 1970s with the dark country-gothic of Bobbie Gentry's "Ode to Billie Joe" and then Kate Bush's 1978 reworking of the Lizzie Wan story, "The Kick Inside." It's a rich vein and is still mined today by musicians like the Handsome Family in what has become known as gothic Americana or dark country.

The guitar was the critical influence in the development of secular music in this, the home of country music. Fiddles, brought by the settler-pioneers in the 1700s, together with banjos from the 1800s, formed the basis of early nineteenth-century string bands playing instrumental dance music. The guitar didn't start appearing widely until the early 1900s, when industrialization and mail order distribution made it more affordable and accessible to mountain folk who were still extremely poor and isolated. Initially "frammed" (what we now term "strumming"), the guitar played a percussive role in shaping the music. It allowed more ornate melody lines to be sung over the chorded, rhythmic bed it provided. Gradually, songs that had been sung for decades by a single, unaccompanied voice were now backed by a strummed guitar and took on a stricter rhythm that served to tidy up traditional songs into the regulated verse-and-chorus structure that we recognize today. Without the acoustic guitar, this reshaping of popular vocal music may never have happened.

• • • • • •

As the guitar steadily grew in popularity, new makers capitalized on the increased demand. In the more musically conservative Northern states of early twentieth-century America, neither hillbilly tunes nor guitar blues had made an impression, especially in the relatively genteel world of the parlor guitar. It was still being used by classical musicians and sophisticated urban players, many playing formal arrangements of popular songs or accompanying four-part harmony singing groups.

Martin & Co., recognized as the maker of the highest quality guitars of the time, catered to these professionals as well as to wealthy amateur players, but despite the company's growing reputation, it was still a low-volume producer. Lyon & Healy, the most prolific maker of the time, had a five-story musical instrument factory in Chicago making everything from guitars to harps and brass band instruments and, leaning heavily on hyperbole in its advertising, boasted of "producing 100,000 instruments annually." The business focused on supplying guitars, sold under various brand names, through the growing number of mail-order catalogs selling to working people, whose numbers were expanding as they spread out across America. Through the Sears and Montgomery Ward catalogs, the guitar began to reach the pioneers and homesteaders living "out West." Guitars were soon in the hands of miners, gold-panners, farmers, cowboys, and railroad workers, and the democratization of music in America had started.

Martin & Co. and Lyon & Healy weren't the only makers. There were single individuals and small enterprises producing guitars during this period—companies like Harwood, Waldo, and Stewart & Bauer, most now long forgotten. Even the mighty Lyon & Healy was wiped out by the Depression, so for most of the twentieth century, only one other quality instrument manufacturer from the period, Gibson, prospered alongside Martin as a maker.

• • • • • •

In 1896, Orville Gibson, a former shoe store assistant and restaurant clerk in the thriving Midwestern town of Kalamazoo, Michigan, formally pronounced himself "a maker of musical instruments." Gibson, a forty-year-old bachelor, was a keen mandolinist and a passionate instrument maker. He was also a perfectionist. His first instruments were carved-body mandolins and guitars, each produced with numerous unique features using innovative building techniques. While he had some early sales success, it's unclear if he made anything more than a basic living from his early backroom endeavors.

Gibson, ever a purist, never underestimated the difficulty of making quality instruments. A characteristic story surrounds his response to a request for business terms and a delivery date from a trade customer in New York who wanted five hundred mandolins. Gibson allegedly replied that he would require $100 per mandolin and that delivery would take five hundred years.

When he was approached in 1902 by five local entrepreneurs, he saw it as his big opportunity. He willingly sold them his designs and patents and became an employee of the company that still carries his name today.

The investors had seen the growing popularity of the mandolin, and Orville Gibson provided their way into the market. But in 1909 a critical, demanding, eccentric, and often petulant Orville Gibson was squeezed out of the company. He never returned to work and was eventually admitted into a sanatorium, suffering from nervous exhaustion. By this time the company was successfully producing instruments using mass-production processes but ironically utilizing few of the ideas and techniques it had acquired from Orville. And this is still the defining difference between the two outstanding companies of the modern guitar era. Martin was started by a master maker and has, since 1833, been a company run by a Martin family member focused on making quality instruments. Gibson, although founded by an inventor and innovator with a love of musical instruments, became a company run by businesspeople manufacturing musical instruments.

As an illustration, when Orville was still a salaried employee, the board of directors, now his employers, were regularly "shocked at the ridiculous price" of the "instrument-quality" wood he was ordering. The five businessmen, no doubt looking at under-forecast profits, asked "how instrument wood could be five times the price of ordinary lumber." Orville had sold his business to lawyers and accountants, and this was not the first or last time these and similar questions were asked by the company's board. The strained relationship between founder and owners leaves Orville's actual legacy a little uncertain. His innovative redesign of the traditional mandolin and the initial development of the archtop guitar are certainly important, but unlike C. F. Martin, who was a skilled luthier and designer, Gibson's early instruments are considered historically interesting but not great-sounding. Yet the mandolins and guitars that the Gibson company developed after Orville had left the business stand today as the archetypes for all modern mandolins and archtop guitars.

Now driven by the need to return a profit to investors, the Gibson company became professional and innovative marketeers. Its catalogs and advertisements, now featuring fetching photographs of flirtatious young ladies playing Gibson mandolins, were supplemented by a sales channel originally employed by Martin but abandoned in favor of distributors. Gibson developed a nationwide network of teacher-agents. The once humble and poorly paid local music teacher could become an agent and buy Gibson instruments at net price and sell them on to students at a handsome markup.

The logic was impeccable—teachers were trusted and quite able to up-sell students to a quality Gibson mandolin rather than a mail-order brand of unknown quality. The company also offered, via their teacher-agents, credit terms, ready access to specially arranged mandolin sheet music, and a network of Gibson-sponsored mandolin clubs and orchestras.

The labels in early Gibson instruments bear the legend "Gibson Mandolin-Guitar Mfg. Co. Ltd.," and although the company built guitars from the outset, based on recent analysis of their serial number lists, their focus was mandolins. The instrument was all the rage in America, which explains why the five entrepreneurs had leapt at the opportunity to acquire Orville Gibson's patent.

Italian immigration to the US had peaked in the 1880s, and many arrivals brought with them their native instrument, the Neopolitan, or bowl-back, mandolin. This small, high-tuned instrument was a member of the lute family;

it carried four pairs of strings that were plucked with a plectrum to provide a loud and captivating tone. Europe had experienced a mandolin craze in the late 1870s, when crowds of up to thirty thousand people attended outdoor concerts. Within a couple of years, individual virtuosos and mandolin troupes were touring the American vaudeville circuits, showcasing the Italian mandolin and fascinating audiences with its distinctive, penetrating sound. Ironically, it was the arrival in New York of a troupe of Spanish musicians playing something that looked like a mandolin but was actually a pear-shaped *bandurria* that really ignited the craze.

The Estudiantina Española Fígaro (Figaro Spanish Students) first appeared in New York in 1880 dressed in a pantomime version of the costumes of Renaissance strolling players. They took New York City musical halls and theatres by storm. Within weeks of their arrival, the Italian community started to regain its cultural hegemony over the mandolin with the appearance of rival Italian groups drawn from the ready supply of Italian professional violinists who were only too happy to don velvet breeches and swap violin for mandolin. (It also helped that the mandolin shares the same basic tuning as a violin, so the crossover was not that daunting for violinists.)

It's difficult to overstate just how big the mandolin craze was. A newspaper from Michigan reported that the mandolin was so popular in the "fashion-conscious Eastern cites of New York, Boston, Washington DC, and Philadelphia" that in order to give the false impression that they were society ladies, "shop-girls" carried around empty mandolin cases to keep their packed lunches in.

Meanwhile, back in Nazareth, Martin & Co., having noticed the rising popularity of mandolins, soon started producing its own version of the instrument. Between 1906 and 1909, Martin made more mandolins than guitars. The mandolin epidemic gripped America. Lyon & Healy, the Chicago mass producers, boasted, again with a now-natural leaning into hyperbole, "At any time you can find in our factory upwards of 10,000 mandolins in various stages of construction."

The big catalog retailers serving the Midwest and West Coast cities further drove the boom, offering a wide range of mandolins and printed mandolin tutorials. Other manufacturers were using their sales forces like Gibson did by establishing local mandolin orchestras and selling into smaller local retailers.

Before the advent of cinema and the broadcast age, working people still had limited spare time but wanted to use what time they did have gainfully. The ideals of the self-made individual and of social and creative self-improvement were popular concepts. Playing an instrument was not only self-improving but provided an opportunity to meet people—especially potential romantic partners. Many advertisements of the time showed a young swain enthralling his girl with a turn on the mandolin.

Mandolin clubs (and, to a lesser extent, banjo and guitar clubs) became popular among middle-class youths on college campuses and in towns and cities throughout the United States. The guitar was still being played solo in the parlor, but the instrument was also being used as an accompanying instrument in the growing number of mandolin ensembles, played alongside the steel-string—and therefore much louder—mandolin. Designed as a solo instrument for small rooms or auditoriums, with more expressive but quieter gut strings, the guitar was now being drowned out by the smaller, louder, and more affordable mandolin.

For the first time, but not the last, the development of the guitar was driven by the need for "louder."

Guitar bodies have bracing on the inside of the instrument's top, or soundboard, to do two things. First, it maintains the top's physical integrity, preventing it from distorting or, in the worst case, breaking up, from the upward pull of the strings. The second is to affect the way the top vibrates and amplifies the harmonic vibration of the strings, which creates the actual sound of the instrument. The balance between the amount of bracing and the relative thickness of the top has always been a key part of the alchemy required to get a guitar correctly voiced, or sounding at its best. A thicker top with robust bracing will last forever but sound dead, a bit like attaching strings to a heavy wooden box. Thin out the top and reduce the number of braces and their mass, and the guitar's sound will come alive—but the box could collapse after only a few months playing. A few guitar makers started producing accessories, promoted as "patented improvements," that allowed a guitar made for gut strings to carry the longer-lasting and louder steel strings that many players were using to compete with the mandolin and banjo. In many ways it was a backward step: the eighteenth-century English guittar and its ancestor the orpharion had both used brass or wire strings, but both instruments were superseded by the sweeter sounding, gut-string Spanish guitar.

C. F. Martin had started changing the way his gut-string guitars were braced in the 1830s. The X-brace pattern he had experimented with on Madame de Goñi's guitar enabled him to make the top (soundboard) thinner and lighter.

X-braced guitar top. (John Stubbings)

By allowing the top to vibrate more freely, the instrument had greater volume as well as a more balanced tone; essentially, each string when plucked with equal force delivered the same volume.

Surprisingly, Martin's X-bracing remained a uniquely American modification. European makers of gut-string Spanish or classical guitars continued to use, as they do today, fan bracing, satisfied that it provides the right amount of support for lightly built guitars specifically designed for lower-tension gut strings. The many rock 'n' roll teenagers in the 1960s who restrung their school-issued classical guitars with steel strings, only to be left with a pile of broken timber, could testify to how lightly built these guitars were.

Received wisdom has it that even as late as 1920 Martin was not interested in steel strings, ignoring a trend that its many competitors had long adopted. But while it's true the Martin company was committed to making instruments designed for classical playing, it was not blind to the demand for louder, steel-string instruments. The first catalog appearance of a steel-string *only* model was in 1922, but archival research by Greig Hutton shows that for at least a decade before, Martin was offering most of its guitars with the option to be set up or "regulated" for gut, steel, or Hawaiian playing. Regulation involved setting up the nut of the guitar to take either gut or steel strings. (The nut is the narrow string support and slotted spacer at the top of the neck, derived from the German word *nuten*, meaning groove.) Hawaiian guitars were all the rage by the 1910s, and Martin not only shipped guitars with extended nuts and steel strings for "Hawaiian steel" but also sold thousands of "Kamiki" nut extenders to allow customers to convert existing guitars.

In addition to this, Martin had been gradually thickening tops and adjusting bracing for a number of years, enabling the guitars to be fitted with steel strings with virtually no adaptation of the standard X-bracing. When it formally started shipping steel-only Martins in the 1920s, its instruments not only held their own in an ensemble but retained their sweet, balanced tone. Martin had in X-bracing solved the problem of "volume with tone" that guitar makers had been working on for decades. Its breakthrough, never actually patented by Martin and adopted by virtually all flat-top guitar makers to this day, would ultimately serve to save the still financially fragile company. Although not just yet.

Vahdah Olcott-Bickford playing a
1915 Martin Olcott-Bickford Artist Model.

5

Ukuleles and Hawaiian Guitars

Across the 1910s Martin, while producing mandolins in relatively large numbers, was still focused on making guitars for parlor and classical players, albeit very few of them every year. In 1911, they sold fewer guitars than they had fifty years earlier. At a time when many of their competitors were promoting louder, steel-string instruments, Martin looked seriously out of step with what the market wanted and was buying in large numbers. The company was now led by forty-four-year-old Frank Henry Martin, grandson of the company's founder and the last head of the company capable of building a complete guitar from scratch. Like his grandfather before him, Frank Henry believed in the sonic superiority of gut-string guitars for both the parlor and concert hall.

Leading the charge for serious recognition for the guitar in America for the first half of the twentieth century was a former child prodigy, Vahdah Olcott-Bickford (1885–1980). Alongside performing and publishing popular guitar method books, she founded the American Guitar Society in 1923 to "promote interest in the classical guitar." Frank Martin seemed enamored with both the cause for musical legitimacy for the guitar and the charismatic player. He broke his company's strict rules on "Martin brand first" and in 1913 produced a range of plain but nonetheless expensive instruments branded the Olcott-Bickford Artist Model. These Style 44 guitars were available to order alongside Martin's standard range in a variety of music stores in New York and Chicago and were sold to students and fans of Olcott-Bickford.

Collaborations with other influential concert performers followed, and Martin introduced several minor design developments in the years that followed. By the end of the 1910s, the company, along with makers like the Larson brothers, was producing steel-string instruments. Many of Martin's instruments were specifically aimed at the latest guitar craze spreading through California and beyond—Hawaiian slide guitar. This, alongside the popularity of vaudeville guitar star Nick Lucas, who played fast solos using a flat pick on steel strings, jump-started the shift from gut strings to the steel strings found on the modern acoustic guitar. The high-minded Olcott-Bickford was suitably horrified when she played a concert tour of California and discovered that the "real" guitar (i.e., the classical gut-string instrument) was fast fading in popularity. The guitar as a classical instrument would ultimately be reinvigorated in America by the Spanish maestro Andrés Segovia, who first toured the United States in 1928. But Segovia's popularity came at some cost to the American classical guitar tradition. From the outset, Segovia only played and promoted guitars made in the style of the Spanish maker Antonio Torres. He and his many US-based disciples were convinced that only this style of guitar—played the "Segovia way"—was authentic and correct. Segovia plucked the strings with fingernails rather than in the American manner, with bare fingertips, and very soon other classical players, and the American-made gut-string Martin guitars they played, were deemed "inauthentic." Fortunately, by the late 1920s, Martin had moved on to produce almost exclusively guitars with steel strings. Since that time, the company has rarely been associated or identified with classical guitars. As Martin moved away from small parlor and classical style instruments, by the end of the decade the company had built a prototype of what became the modern acoustic flat-top guitar.

• • • • • •

But we need to go back seventy years to fully understand how small parlor- and classical-size guitars metamorphosed into the large-bodied dreadnought.

We are largely able to travel back because Martin & Co. started keeping detailed business records from the mid-1830s, when it first opened for business at 196 Hudson Street, New York. The company subsequently archived the majority of their meticulous records, which detail everything from the acquisition of bulk timber to the purchase of a box of pencils. The company even filed away the most mundane letters received from customers, retailers, and business associates. Because the company remained family-owned when other makers were regularly bought and sold, most of these ordinary working documents were retained. While many records were not examined for decades, recent archival work means the history of Martin & Co. is now extremely well documented—especially the development of the dreadnought guitar.

However, the dreadnought—the signature look and sound of the majority of acoustic guitars made today—was not the pure invention of Martin.

As Martin was establishing his workshop in New York in the 1830s, Oliver Ditson opened his first store in Boston selling sheet music. By the late 1850s, Ditson was not only a retailer but America's major publisher of printed music. It was both a notable and highly profitable achievement and the key to the development of American popular music. Prior to the introduction of the gramophone record in the 1890s, sheet music, theatres, and vaudeville *were* the music business. But printed music continued to be hugely popular even after the advent of the gramophone record. In the 1910s, the sheet music for popular songs sold in the millions to home music-makers, including amateur guitarists. Sheet music sales vastly surpassed the sale of records of the same song, and the record was usually only released once sheet music sales had peaked, to prolong the life of a song that had neared the end of its mass popularity.

While music publishing remained the most important part of his business, Oliver Ditson & Company music stores in Boston, Philadelphia, and Chicago started to sell the means to play the music they published, including Martin guitars. Having previously resisted making guitars under any retailer's brand name, something must have changed for the Martin company to make Ditson-branded guitars for the retailer. Either the high volume of guitars Ditson was ordering persuaded the company to set aside its original misgivings, or, due to tough trading times, Martin was prepared to do whatever it had to do to generate sales.

Ironically, Ditson was both a major Martin retailer and a manufacturing competitor. Oliver Ditson had bought the inventory of a bankrupt musical instrument company in 1861 and, in collaboration with John C. Haynes, opened a new store in Boston to sell the stock. A few years later, having set up a subsidiary company manufacturing some basic guitars and banjos under various brand names, Haynes hired Pehr Anderberg, a talented Swedish guitar maker. Production of quality guitars, some featuring expensive woods and fine inlay, soon commenced under the Bay State banner. (The name saluted the Commonwealth of Massachusetts, the Bay State.)

Ditson, an entrepreneurial mentor, later encouraged the two managers of his Chicago store, George Washburn Lyon and Patrick J. Healy, to set up their own company, which initially just distributed but later manufactured instruments sold through the Ditson chain of stores. From the outset, Lyon & Healy was organized as an instrument factory rather than a single builder's workshop, making Washburn-branded guitars alongside accordions, harps, and various other band instruments. To stimulate demand and feed their production capability, they produced perfectly adequate factory-made guitars and sold them through the many mail-order catalogs in circulation.

Washburn guitars tried to compete at the quality end of the market with both Martin and their own sister brand, Bay State, producing some fancy guitars, many at the same price point as high-end Martins. However, both contemporary sales and current critical opinion show that Washburn never achieved the quality of sound, finish, and playability of a Martin, primarily because it had started out as and continued to be a volume manufacturer. Its guitars were often made from mahogany, and the early promotional material argued strongly for the "bright, sweet sound" that mahogany delivers and falsely maligned the "flat, muddled tone" of rosewood. Somewhat underhandedly, the company offered mahogany as a premium-priced option; the publicity material failed to mention that wholesale, mahogany was a third of the price of rosewood. It also failed to point out that the visually striking rosewood was significantly more difficult to craft than mahogany—a material better suited to their production-line workers than skilled craftspeople.

Regardless of quality, Washburn guitars sold extremely well. By 1913, Lyon & Healy promotional material was claiming it produced more guitars *annually* than Martin had made in its then-eighty-year history. The company was certainly covering all the bases, making everything from cheap student models to elaborate rosewood-bodied guitars with "abalone on every corner," instruments that no doubt appalled the conservative Martin company.

Alongside guitars, Lyon & Healy was producing thousands of mandolins, feeding the still-vibrant mandolin craze. However, the austerity that followed World War I ultimately put an end to both Bay State and the fancy Washburn guitars as well as slowing down their claimed one-hundred-thousand annual production runs.

The sheer number of instruments sold by Bay State and Lyon & Healy had a huge impact on home music making in the period before and after World War I. Compared to Ditson's guitar factories, Martin focused on high quality and low volume. Indeed, the company motto during this time was *Non Multa Sed Multum*, "not many but much." As steady and careful innovators with a conservative eye for design, Martin influenced the guitar industry for decades after its competitors had been consigned to the history books, but it was the factory brands that equipped the nation with an affordable means of making music in the home.

While brands like Bay State and Washburn are today footnotes to the history of the flat-top guitar, the Larson brothers, Carl and August, who could easily be dispatched as a footnote to the footnote, have special significance. Their importance lies in their position as one of the first makers to exclusively build quality flat-top guitars designed specifically to carry steel strings. Unlike Bay State, Lyon & Healy, and even the antebellum James Ashborn, from 1900 to the outbreak of World War II, the Larsons produced around 2,500 guitars out of what was effectively a two-man operation. Their obscurity was largely self-inflicted—the Larson name never appeared on any of the headstocks of their many different models. Maurer, Prairie State, Euphonon, Dyer, Stetson, and Stahl guitars were all made by the Larson brothers. Jimi Hendrix owned and played a Larson-made Stahl parlor guitar when he lived in London in the 1960s, although whether he knew its historical relevance is unknown. By the 1990s, all the Larsons' many guitar brands were collectible and still sought after as highly playable instruments. The multimillionaire serial collector Scott Chinery amassed a huge number and regularly tipped them as an investment opportunity, although today only the most ardent enthusiast is likely to have even heard of Carl and August Larson.

The immigrant cabinetmakers arrived in Chicago from Sweden in the 1880s and first started making guitars in the 1890s, under the Champion brand name. They were among any number of experimenters and innovators of the time exploring the design possibilities of the guitar. Their innovations included everything from harp guitars (which were a brief success) to metal fingerboards that created a resonator sound (which never caught on).

While contemporary makers like Bohmann and Wolfram were short-lived enterprises, the Larsons, who spent much of their working lives occupying a dirt-floor workshop housed in a rural barn, perhaps subsisted more than prospered, but they did continue innovating. Most of their ideas served the cause of louder instruments. As serial inventors, they introduced laminated top-braces, internal metal bracing rods, and guitars with slightly arched backs and tops "built under tension" to improve the volume and brightness of sound. They even produced a short run of banjo-guitars. As a two-man shop they could experiment with limited runs of guitars, and they did so to the point that it is difficult to define a typical Larson style. Decades before Taylor or indeed Fender employed bolted-on necks, the Larsons trialed them on a few guitars in search of both easy adjustment and greater strength. Equally, although most of the Larsons' guitars were standard-sized, nearly all other guitars of the time were dwarfed physically, although not sonically, by their Prairie State twenty-one-inch special model, measuring an enormous twenty-one inches wide by six inches deep. The guitar delivered an interesting and unique sound, but according to those who have owned or played one, the strings were inadequate to drive the huge top to make the guitar louder—the primary purpose of the larger build.

Clearly not everything the Larsons invented or adopted worked as intended or caught on, but they deserve a place in guitar history. They built many fine guitars, even though some surviving models show they could make guitars with awkward aesthetics and limited appeal. Unintentionally asymmetric instruments surface on occasion, built by a no-doubt-exhausted Carl Larson. Sadly, but perhaps inevitably given their production and business model, while the Larson name may have been well known in the Chicago area during their lifetimes, it faded quickly after their deaths in the mid-1940s.

Somewhat bizarrely, the Larsons also have their place in the development of the electric guitar. Sometime around 1934, a local radio station guitarist who performed under the stage name Rhubarb Red asked them to make a couple of guitars with a one-inch-thick solid maple top. The guitarist's real name was Lester Polsfuss, later shortened to the more stage-friendly Les Paul, one of the most famous names in the history of the guitar.

It's impossible to accurately measure the true importance and influence of the Larsons on other makers of the time. However, then as now, the world of guitar makers is a relatively small one, and makers were rarely shy to adopt a winning idea, as illustrated by the widespread adoption of Martin X-bracing by most US makers.

But in 1914 in rural Pennsylvania, Martin was still developing its mandolin business. The firm had started making Neapolitan-style mandolins in the mid-1890s but converted to building what today looks like an ill-conceived range of flat-backed versions to compete directly with those made by Gibson and Washburn. Flat-backs could be made more quickly (and therefore more cheaply) than the old-fashioned bowl-backs, and although Martin did produce top-end models, their basic $10 Style A outsold all others ten to one. Rarely for a Martin instrument, they sounded anemic compared to the more expensive Gibsons and were unsuited for country or old-time playing. Lacking power and not as comfortable to play as the Gibson, Martin mandolin sales did nonetheless help the company stay afloat when the sales of gut-string guitars flattened in the late 1910s.

Things were still on a knife-edge for a small company under increasing pressure from the ever-expanding competition. As Martin's sales stagnated, another musical craze came to the rescue and once again ensured the company's long-term future.

• • • • • •

The little Hawaiian ukulele seemed an unlikely instrument to grip America, and the folk songs and tribal dances of a small Polynesian nation an odd combination.

Pronounced "oo koo lay lay," the diminutive instrument was not actually native to Polynesia. Immigrant sugarcane workers from the Portuguese island of Madeira brought their small, four-string *braguinha* and five-string *machete de rajão* to the Hawaiian Islands in 1879. A few of these first Portuguese settlers used the readily available koa wood to make local variants of the instrument, and the native wood gave them their characteristic bright sound. "Ukulele" in the Hawaiian language translates roughly as "jumping flea" either a nod to the instrument's crisp, insect-like sound; to the speed that players' fingers moved over the fretboard; or, as one story has it, to the excited antics of the first arrivals to the island when they jumped off the boat after their four-month sea voyage. One of those early arrivées was Manuel Nunes, who had emigrated to Hawaii with his Madeiran *braguinha*. After a short period working in the cane fields, he subsequently set up shop making what were known locally as "taro-patch fiddles"—a derogatory term coined by the Anglo-American planter elite. In addition to working the cane fields, the Madeiran laborers were also employed in the taro fields (or "patches") harvesting the taro root, the staple starch in the native Hawaiian diet. The name "taro-patch fiddle" was eventually superseded by "ukulele," although Martin catalogues still listed a small range of eight-string, larger-bodied taro-patch fiddles into the early 1920s.

As the popularity of the instrument grew, Hawaii had its own ukulele craze when the island's ruler, King David Kalākaua, known as "the Merrie Monarch," started playing. King David, resisting Protestant missionary attempts to convert the islands to Christian worship and values, used the ukulele and his passion for native music and dancing to keep local culture alive. He is credited with combining ukulele and Hawaiian steel guitar bands with hula dancers at formal royal events. It was then down to a touring Hawaiian guitarist, July Paka, visiting San Francisco in 1899 with his small "native Island" band, to export and establish the steel guitar and ukulele as Hawaiian inventions. Paka married a part-Hawaiian actress, and together they created a show featuring guitar, ukulele, and a dancer gyrating in a grass skirt—clearly a winning formula. The guitar Paka played was a Hawaiian steel guitar, using a unique style of playing invented in the late 1880s by Joseph Kekuku and played on a converted steel-string Spanish-style guitar—an instrument first introduced to the islands in the early 1800s by Mexican gauchos brought in from California to manage the ever-expanding herds of wild cattle that roamed the main island. Utilizing a short, solid-steel bar to get Kekuku's trademark glissando effect (gliding over the pitch between the notes), Paka's guitar sounded like nothing the mainland had heard before. The growing number of passenger ships plying their trade between the US mainland and the islands of the new territory of Hawaii were soon staging exotic, island-style onboard entertainment. Musicians playing the Hawaiian steel guitar and the humble little uke accompanied girls dancing a modernized, alluring version of the ancient hula dances, and the combination soon became the signature look and musical sound of the islands. By the turn of the twentieth century, following the annexation of Hawaii by the United States, contemporary Hawaiian music fast became all the rage along the West Coast of America.

With the help of the recording industry, Hawaiian music, ukuleles, and steel guitars spread across America relatively quickly. "The Banjo King," Vess Ossman, recorded "Honolulu Cake Walk" in 1899 using his five-string banjo to imitate the sound of the Hawaiian steel guitar. Columbia released on wax cylinder the first recording of *authentic* Hawaiian music in 1901, the immensely popular "Aloha Oe" ("Farewell to Thee"), played on steel guitar. A few years later, the Victor recording company logged an astonishing fifty songs when they visited the islands with a recording machine.

W. C. Handy's recollection in 1903 of a guitarist who pressed a knife on the strings of the guitar in a manner "popularized by Hawaiian guitarists" shows just how fast the Hawaiian steel sound appeared in the blues guitar music of the Mississippi Delta. Blues players already performing "Spanish Fandango" had long been exploiting the guitar's ability to be tuned to an open chord, what Hawaiians refer to as "slack key tuning," making the adoption of a slide an easy step. Delta players preferred to use a bottleneck or, as was the case for Handy's player, a steel knife in place of the original polished steel railroad spike used by the Hawaiians.

In 1912, a Broadway show, *The Bird of Paradise*, focused on the exotic and *erotic* appeal of the islands as its subject. The show's somewhat thin and often ludicrous plotline was rescued by scantily clad women in grass skirts and an erupting volcano. But its authentic Hawaiian musicians, ukuleles, and hula dancing further educated mainland America to the delights of a commercialized version of Hawaii. Although only a modest hit on Broadway, the show toured to great acclaim in major cities and across small-town America for a number of years, even visiting Europe in 1919. Following the lavish Hawaiian music shows at the 1915 Pan-Pacific Exposition, held in San Francisco, the craze for the ukulele and all things Hawaiian reached fever pitch. Hawaiian groups were appearing everywhere, and by 1916, the Victor record company reportedly sold more Hawaiian records than any other style of music. Once again, in an age when entertainment was largely homemade, a boom in sales for the easy-to-play ukulele was up and running.

Frank Herbert Martin had first experimented with making ukuleles as early as 1907. They were made at the request of James Bergman, the Martin company's official dealer in Honolulu. Bergman, one assumes, sent a Hawaiian-built example to Nazareth for the company to copy, along with some boards of koa wood. Initially, Martin's guitar heritage led it to build robust, over-engineered versions, making what were effectively mini-guitars. Apart from sounding stolid, they were expensive to make and unlikely to have impressed players had they gone into full-time production. However, by the time the Hawaiian boom was in full swing, Martin had realized that a lightly built model—made out of cheaper, thinner mahogany and with minimal internal bracing—not only sounded good but was cheap and quick to manufacture. Martin launched its first production model in January 1916 and by using marginal pricing managed to build sales quickly—a first for a company that had only been known to focus on expensive luxury instruments. While they made little from each $10 retail sale, the sheer number of units sold certainly made sense. The popular ukuleles spread the Martin name, and the company gradually expanded its range to include more ornate, and therefore more profitable, versions.

Sales figures show how important the ukulele became for Martin. In 1915, before full-time ukulele production and on the back of the mandolin boom, Martin sold two mandolins for every guitar. However, by the end of 1920, when mandolins and guitars were each selling equally at about 1,500 per year, Martin sold over 3,000 ukuleles. Overall, from 1916 to 1930, ukuleles made up a massive 65 percent of all instruments the company sold. It was a remarkable performance from a standing start and enabled the company to expand their factory and put a little money in the bank. While the mandolin had itself been a partial savior of the company in the first fifteen years of the century, accounting for 56 percent of sales in that period, mandolins sank to just 9 percent of total sales from 1916 to 1930.

This ability to quickly switch production from the now-unfashionable mandolin to a full range of ukuleles allowed Martin to invest in bigger premises in Nazareth. The ukulele meant the company was also able to keep its skilled workforce of guitar makers gainfully employed and have the capital funds behind it to weather the approaching Great Depression.

The diminutive instrument once again became important to the company in the years immediately following World War II. The sales spike was due in part to American troops returning from their postings on Hawaii with ukuleles and in part to the popularity of a ukulele-playing TV show host, Arthur Godfrey. His eponymous TV talent show, paired with his TV and radio variety shows, had an estimated fan base of over 40 million, and the Hawaiian-shirted uke player rebooted the ukulele for another generation. In 1950 alone, Martin produced 12,000 ukuleles, almost matching an earlier sales peak in 1926, and, largely thanks to Godfrey, went on to sell another 42,000 across the rest of the 1950s. While Martin will always be seen as the premier guitar maker of the twentieth century, it's paradoxical to think that its continued existence is owed not just to the guitar but to both the mandolin and the humble ukulele.

There is, however, a more subtle but nonetheless fundamental influence of the ukulele boom and Hawaiian music on Martin's guitar business. Between 1916 and 1930, Martin was almost solely focused on keeping up with the extraordinary demand for ukuleles, including more ornate versions with improved margins. This meant that the guitar side of the business was often left to its own devices. But if Martin wasn't focused on introducing new guitar models, its retailers were. It was the Ditson company, instrument retailer and music publisher, who encouraged Martin & Co. to make a guitar that secured both its reputation and fortunes for another hundred years.

• • • • • •

Harry Hunt, the manager of the Ditson New York store (one of Martin's biggest commercial accounts), was already ordering Martin-manufactured but Ditson-branded bowl-back mandolins. In 1916 he asked Martin to make a series of Ditson-branded ukuleles, mandolins, and guitars, all with wide-waisted, flat-backed, baroque-style body shapes. They were set up for playing in the still immensely popular Hawaiian steel style. It was not a totally alien concept for the company. Martin had been supplying regular flat-top guitars to the Hawaiian market since the 1880s, and a variety of professional Hawaiian bands used their instruments in preference to locally made models.

In early 1916, Martin completed a unique jumbo-sized guitar for the celebrated Hawaiian steel player Major Kealakai, leader of the Royal Hawaiian Sextet. Bigger guitars were generally becoming popular, but there is evidence that the Kealakai jumbo, larger than anything the Martin company had made previously, acted as a prototype for what became the wider-waisted Ditson dreadnought.

On behalf of Ditson, Hunt specified six sizes, including standard, concert, and the biggest—borrowing from a paper body pattern of the Kealakai model—an extra-large. Almost certainly made in prototype by finishing shop foreman John Deichman, this guitar was designated Style III, and with a lower bout width of 15⅝-inches, larger than anything the company had made before. For Martin it was a no-risk piece of product development since Ditson guaranteed payment for anything they commissioned. Martin was so back-ordered on ukuleles that they were probably delighted when Ditson requested they use "Chicago style" bridges manufactured by their affiliated company Lyon & Healy.

Martin production specification sheets designated these guitars "Ditson Hawaiian Models," the name signifying that the instruments were designed with the Hawaiian lap-style slide player in mind. These early forerunners of the dreadnought were not a particularly popular model at the time. Ditson ordered only twenty in the period from 1916 to 1930, the point at which the Ditson company ceased trading due to the Depression.

A few months after Ditson wound up its business, Martin started building the same size of guitar under its own brand name. It formally designated it the

Dreadnought—borrowing the name from the huge capital battleships that dominated World War I naval battles.

These initial dreadnoughts aside, the near glacial evolution and relative conservatism of Martin guitar design have been, perversely, critical factors in the success of the company's instruments in the modern age. While Gibson was quick to introduce new designs or follow the influence of fleeting stylistic fads, Martin's conservatism had the unintended benefit of rendering their guitars almost timeless. Even to an expert eye, ten Martins from each of the decades of the twentieth century are difficult to date without close inspection and access to individual serial numbers. This enduring look has been part of the allure of its guitars for serious players and collectors alike. While instruments from the years before World War II command enormous premiums, those made in the 1970s, '80s, and '90s have the same classic look and appeal and give owners the confidence that they may possess a future classic.

George Beauchamp holding a prototype Ro-Pat-In Frying Pan Electric.

The Birth of Jazz and Country Music's Big Bang

The end of World War I brought with it a period of unprecedented change in Europe and America. Traditional values gave way to more permissive moral codes that, despite Prohibition in the United States, ushered in the Roaring Twenties. Across both America and Europe, men and women were going out more, dating more, drinking more, and dancing more. The Charleston, black-bottom, five-step, and foxtrot were no longer being danced to string-heavy orchestral music but to syncopated jazz. The combination convinced the *Ladies' Home Journal* of 1921 to pronounce that jazz was putting the "sin into syncopation."

While early jazz was largely guitar-free, it laid the foundations for blues and country music, where the guitar did dominate. And all musical styles were helped in the 1920s by the coming of age of the cinema, the gramophone record, and radio. Improved personal income and increased free time meant that ordinary working people gained an appetite for leisure, and entertainment wasn't just for the wealthy and the new middle classes. Records, radio, and cinema competed for a share of their audiences' attention and money, which not only had a massive influence on the overall popularity and styles of music people listened to countrywide but also created a new phenomenon: nationally recognized screen, recording, and radio stars.

In 1910, the still relatively young US recording industry sold an unprecedented thirty million records. But no one could have predicted how fast sales would grow. The first recordings were etched onto expensive and fragile wax cylinders; the medium later adopted cheaper and more readily available shellac discs. Output had initially been largely classical—orchestral, operettas, and solo voice—as well as ballads and patriotic war songs like "It's a Long Way to Tipperary." The Italian opera phenomenon Enrico Caruso was the recording industry's first star, and even John Sousa—despite his dislike of "mechanical music"—released numerous records.

But a new, younger generation, with more free time and money, had little interest in playing the classical music and sedate waltzes their parents enjoyed. They liked the idea of "jassing" things up, a term on the lips of most New Orleans working girls that was synonymous with the activities and music of the city's red-light district—as in "Do you want to jass it up with me, honey?" The first American "jass" record, "Livery Stable Blues," a lively foxtrot recorded by the all-white Original Dixieland Jass Band, was released in 1917. Selling over a million copies, it outsold both Caruso and Sousa and was an indicator of the shape of music to come. Sadly, for the guitar, banjo, and mandolin industries, this first jass band used no string instruments, just brass, woodwind, piano, and drums. However, they did kick off a style of music that soon showcased and popularized first the jazz banjo and later the jazz guitar.

"Jass," effectively just a sophisticated form of ragtime, was soon overtaken by music with roots more firmly in marching brass bands and New Orleans "second line" parades. Second lines, or jazz funerals without a body, described the collection of dancers, drummers, strutters, and assorted tagalongs who followed the "first line," the official brass bands that led a licensed parade. Emanating from the Sunday dancing on Congo Square, most second lines included drummers improvising complex polyrhythms off the brass bands' formulaic, four-beats-to-the-bar songs.

The music that soon became known as "jazz" grew in popularity and attracted a new, younger audience. Importantly, its combination of second-line rhythms, Black blues, and ragtime could be danced to and was pioneered and recorded by bands like King Oliver's Creole Jazz Band and Johnny Dunn's Original Jazz Hounds. Anyone listening to Dunn's "Hawaiian Blues" (a tune released in 1922 that borrowed only its name from the still-current craze for all things Hawaiian), with its flattened fifths, syncopation, and ad-libbed jazz trumpet solos, will recognize that the type of jazz we listen to today had arrived. Even with this new jazz, there was still no guitar in the mix, only the tenor, or jazz, banjo. Played with a plectrum, it was used primarily as a percussive rhythm instrument, replacing the double bass, whose low-frequency thump had caused the stylus on early acoustic recording equipment to jump out of the groove.

Records were key in growing the popularity of jazz. Across the coming decades, recordings played an equally pivotal role in popularizing the blues in its many forms—and with it the guitar and guitar-led music. By 1922, record sales in the United States reached a hundred million a year, with much of the increase coming from the popularity of jazz and the "music of the devil," blues. Feared by parents and polite society and vilified by the church for their corrupting influence, jazz and blues were therefore massively attractive to the young record-buying public. In a pattern to be repeated across subsequent decades, young people rebelled against the music their parents liked, and a more relaxed moral code created a place for this new, faster, infectiously danceable music. It was providing what Irving Berlin called "the rhythmic beat of our everyday lives," and that rhythm was nearly always syncopated, or "ragged" (as in lacking uniformity—literally "ragg-ed time," as opposed to strict, on-the-beat playing).

Ironically, many of the United States' earliest jazz, ragtime, and blues artists—Black players who were playing ragged time and syncopated rhythms—were first recorded in England and Germany rather than at home. The players travelled to Europe as early as 1900 and were recorded by the Gramophone Company in London and its sister organization, Deutsche Grammophon, in Hanover, Germany. These were the European operations of the US-based Berliner Gramophone Company, started in the late 1890s by a German-born American, Emile Berliner, the inventor of the mass-produced gramophone record that replaced Edison's earlier and inferior wax cylinders. In Europe, Black musicians were largely free from the state-sanctioned racial discrimination they experienced in the United States and were further drawn by the opportunity to perform for both lucrative and appreciative European audiences. Being paid to record discs was a bonus. The embryonic US recording industry at the time couldn't see white record buyers being interested in Black artists; thus, companies exclusively recorded white artists—Mamie Smith and Bert Williams were the first and only Black artists recorded by major US labels in the early years of the record industry. In the years before and during World War I, Europe, and London in particular (because of the common language of English), became home to many Black American musicians, including the mandolin virtuoso Seth Weeks and the banjo-based string band the Versatile Four. These artists played music familiar to urban Americans, but it was new, original, modishly frenetic, and exotic to European ears. These touring musicians provided live entertainment in many of the estimated 150 legal and illegal music and dance clubs in London's Soho district.

Only through the lifetime passion of an obsessive German collector of early gramophone records, Dr. Rainer Lotz, do we know how wild and revolutionary the music was. His collection contains some of the only copies of these pre-1920s Berliner discs, each one a testament to otherwise forgotten examples of early Black jazz and blues. They are what many regard as the missing link between Black American minstrelsy of the nineteenth century and the music of the jazz age.

The popularity of jazz and blues drove record sales in both Europe and the United States. It also helped turn the nascent record business into a major industry and along the way brought the concept of one person singing and accompanying themselves on guitar to the attention of new audiences. When Berliner merged his business with the US Victor company in 1901, he helped place Victor, later RCA Victor, in a dominant position. Victor and its main US rival, Columbia, held a virtual duopoly of both record production and the phonographs that played them, marketing their record players as Victrolas and Grafonolas, respectively. Such was their dominance that the US government stepped in to break up the arrangement. A more liberal market led to the birth of many smaller, inventive specialist disc producers who helped popularize many under-represented folk music forms, including blues-driven guitar music. Within a white industry targeting white, urban record buyers there emerged "race records," Black music made especially for Black record buyers.

Black Swan Records, set up in Harlem in 1921, was the first record label wholly owned and managed by Black businesspeople and musicians geared to sell records to a primarily Black audience. The soon-to-be "Empress of the Blues," the earthy and raw Bessie Smith, was one of their first signings. But it was the more sophisticated blues and jazz singer Ethel Waters, backed by house pianist and band leader Fletcher Henderson, who gave the label its first success.

Black Swan also pioneered the idea of touring their artists to generate record sales. In the winter of 1921–1922, a nine-month, twenty-one-state tour by the Black Swan Troubadours, featuring Waters and Henderson's Jazz Masters, was a huge success, establishing both the label and its artists from New York to New Orleans.

Black Swan's early success encouraged mainstream, white-owned and -managed record labels like Paramount, Columbia, and OKeh to develop separate and extensive race record catalogs. Finally recognizing the importance of Black record buyers, they actively promoted their catalogs of race records, taking, for the first time, advertisements in Black newspapers. Initial recordings concentrated on "city blues," a mixture of jazz and blues that usually featured established female singers from the touring tent-show circuit and urban vaudeville and often using artists lured from the Black Swan stable like Bessie Smith, Ethel Waters, and Alberta Hunter.

Further broadening its catalog, the label's attention soon turned from the sophisticated urban blues to rawer, rural "country blues." Locally popular in Southern towns and cities, country blues featured smaller, jug-band groups and individuals singing and playing guitar. The shift in emphasis helped break the blues guitar as a solo or accompanying instrument into the mainstream of Black music. Sylvester Weaver's "Guitar Blues" and "Guitar Rag," recorded in late 1923 with Weaver using a knife as a slide on a Stella guitar, were the first solo blues guitar recordings. (The knife had become the way most Black players created the whiny slide sound.) Papa Charlie Jackson's "Papa's Lawdy Lawdy Blues" and "Airy Man Blues," recorded a few months later in 1924 on Columbia Records, were big hits, and for the first time brought a solo blues singer accompanied by just a guitar to a bigger audience. Although Jackson did play both guitar and ukulele extremely well, on these first recordings he was using a Larson brothers Euphonon guitar-banjo, giving him sound close to that of a guitar but with the increased punch and volume offered by a banjo.

Their success encouraged Maya "Ink" Williams, the Black producer of Jackson's first hit records and A&R man at Columbia, to set up the now-legendary Black Patti record label. Releasing fifty-five discs in its brief seven-month history and recording songs from the rare but highly influential "Boar Hog Blues" to the much-copied "Stack O' Lee Blues," the label introduced recordings that are today highly sought-after by collectors. Williams was also responsible for further shifting the focus of blues recordings from popular female tent and cabaret singers like Bessie Smith, Ma Rainey, and Ethel Waters to male singer-players like Blind Lemon Jefferson, Tampa Red, and Blind Blake, proving the commercial viability and popularity of Black blues singers accompanied by a lone guitar.

These players made a living but were never rolling in cash, and the guitars they used were often low-cost mail-order Stellas. If a recording sold well and an artist had managed to score a deal that granted him or her a royalty of a few cents for every disc sold, rather than a flat fee for the session, they might have afforded a more expensive, metal-bodied, National resonator guitar. The choice of guitar might affect or enhance an artist's playing style. Blind Blake played a complex ragtime syncopation over his singing, rarely resorting to framming or playing accompanying chords; Tampa Red accompanied himself with glistening slide guitar; while Blind Lemon Jefferson used a loose improvisation of chords alongside a conversation between bass and treble runs.

While most successful vaudeville, cabaret, and tent-show singers were women, often accompanied by a pianist or a small orchestra, women accompanying themselves on guitar were in a minority. This was unsurprising, given that most solo blues players toured the rowdy barrelhouse and juke joint circuit where poor rural laborers could drink cheap liquor, gamble, and find female company. Often located on cotton plantations themselves or on the outskirts of towns, they were not places where respectable women would go. Many female players were initially tied to the home or small-holding and performed only locally and for friends. Those women who did play the rural blues circuit usually played with a male partner (often a relative) or another woman.

Geeshie Wiley, who released the bewitchingly haunting "Last Kind Word Blues" on Paramount in 1931, toured and sang duets with another woman player, Elvie "L.V." Thomas. Bottleneck player Flora Molton, who toured and recorded in the early blues period of the late '20s and early '30s, was a former Washington preacher who became a street musician to help support her family by playing gospel-style songs. Etta Baker, born in 1913, was an astonishing, delicate Piedmont guitarist who was taught guitar as a young child by her grandfather and father. Although she started playing when she was just six, she wasn't "discovered" until the 1950s, when she became known for playing songs like "One Dime Blues" and "Railroad Bill." After her rediscovery by folklorist Paul Clayton, she travelled and recorded a few sides with John Jackson and was still appearing with him in the 1990s.

These blues players were primarily singing to English-speaking audiences and working their way across the Southern states, but farther south, toward the Rio Grande, a group of musicians were entertaining poor, working-class communities of Spanish speakers living along the Texas-Mexico border.

La Familia Mendoza toured the rural border towns of southern Texas in the 1920s, playing street markets and migrant camps where seasonal agricultural workers lived. The family group, as poor as their audiences, hitched lifts from one community to another. The standout singer was twelve-year-old Lydia. Already a more than competent mandolin player, Lydia learned from her mother, after much pestering, how to play six-string guitar and from her father how to handle the more challenging twelve-string (as played by Huddie "Lead Belly" Ledbetter and Blind Willie McTell—tuned a fourth below standard tuning). He also taught Lydia how to play the *bajo sexto*, known as the Mexican guitar, but with the twelve strings tuned a full octave below standard.

The family eventually recorded some sides for the OKeh label in 1928 after answering a newspaper advertisement requesting local talent. While Lydia was the standout singer and guitarist in the group, she continued to perform with her family and as a trio with her two sisters.

In 1934, Lydia recorded "Mal Hombre," a song she had learned as a child, which would become her signature song and just one of the two hundred songs in her repertoire. While a talented singer and inventive guitarist, Mendoza was also a striking figure, as evidenced in the many iconic postcard photographs of her playing the twelve-string guitar made for her by San Antonio luthier Guadalupe Acosta.

Music historian Michael Corcoran calls Mendoza "the Mother of Tejano," a musical style that is now widely known as Tex-Mex and is part of the rich mix of American roots music that started developing in the 1920s. Tejano repertoires include Spanish and Mexican ballads as well as German and Czech polka melodies that were popular with immigrant workers living in border communities. As we have come to learn in this history, it is rare to see a woman, and a twelve-string guitarist at that, leaving such an indelible mark on a musical genre at the heart of Americana. Mendoza performed for six decades; toured extensively in the United States, Canada, and Latin America; and released over fifty albums. Although she was born in Houston and lived in Texas for most of her life, she rarely spoke a word of English.

Record labels like OKeh were eagerly searching for new artists and the next big thing. Having taken notice of the growing popularity of guitar-led country blues and Tejano, they also put spirituals and gospel music, popular across the Southern states, on record. They heard the proto-country music of artists like Emmett Miller, a blackface performer who, while working the minstrel and medicine-show circuit, pioneered a unique singing style. Miller would break into falsetto in the middle of a word, pioneering what became known as "blue yodeling." He used it on his recording of "Lovesick Blues" in 1924, the prototype for Hank Williams's 1949 hit version, but Miller also influenced everyone from Jimmie Rodgers to Rex Griffin and Bob Wills.

Emmett Miller recorded for OKeh, which along with Paramount, Columbia, and Victor released a huge amount of white folk or old-time hillbilly music from the rural counties around the Appalachian and Ozark Mountains of West Virginia and Alabama. The labels' search for content was driven not only by competition within the record industry but also by a fight for survival against a newer, cheaper, and more accessible rival—radio.

• • • • • •

The 1920s Jazz Age coincided with the beginning of the age of radio, which began with the launch of the first US commercial radio station in 1919. By 1922, five hundred radio stations broadcast across the United States, but with early radio sets retailing for over $200, they were airing in fewer than a million upper- and middle-class households that could afford sophisticated technology housed in an ornate and expensive piece of furniture. Improved and cheaper technology eventually brought down the cost, and volume production of radios started just a few years later. With many radios now costing less than $35, soon over a thousand mainly short-reach, local stations beamed into 10 million households.

These new stations were broadcasting using the latest electrical microphones to the latest radios with the latest in speaker technology. Radio now played music much clearer than scratchy, wind-up gramophones with a speaker horn; unsurprisingly, record sales started to decline. The record industry, terrified that radio would destroy their business, persuaded President Herbert Hoover's government to legislate that radio stations could broadcast music only if performed live, which suited both musicians and the powerful Musicians Union—if not the public.

Enhanced technology enabled local stations to increase their signal strength and, together with network syndication, by 1925 the national radio audience was approaching 40 million people. In between the many commercials that funded every station, the family audiences listening were mainly tuning in to the sophisticated, popular dance music played by small orchestras broadcasting live from big-city studios and hotel ballrooms. However, the boom in radio station listenership also gave increased exposure to local performers, so when radio reached the rural South, hillbilly fiddle and string-band players got their chance to perform for its huge audiences.

The early '20s also saw a revival in rural square dancing and with it the old-time fiddle and string-band music that accompanied it. The revival was sponsored by the unlikely figure of automobile magnate and industrialist Henry Ford. He apparently longed for "a lost youth of neighborly dancing" and a segregated, bucolic rural past. He publicly criticized dances like the tango and the Charleston and the Black jazz music that accompanied them. To Ford and his many supporters, jazz, and the salacious dancing it encouraged, was un-American and unsuited to the "Northern temperament." Ford funded and promoted, through his own newspaper and many car dealerships, a campaign "to nationalize a revival of the old dances." The net effect of Ford's campaign is not known, but ring and square dancing as well as fiddling contests became a brief nationwide craze ripe for exploitation on the radio. In 1925, the Tennessee radio station WSM launched its version of *Barn Dance*, a syndicated weekly Saturday night radio show, and it was soon one of many stations and shows featuring Southern rural music. Although the various radio barn dances were primarily playing white hillbilly music, not all the bands or artists were as "Northern" (i.e., white) as Henry Ford would have liked. Radio, a color-blind medium, regularly featured the music of Black artists, including one of *Barn Dance*'s most popular acts, DeFord Bailey, "the Harmonica Wizard." Black artists were intentionally unacknowledged; few were even credited by name on records or shows catering to white listeners. It was another forty years before the *Grand Ole Opry*, a show aimed at a white audience, first acknowledged a Black artist, Charley Pride.

The station broadcasting *Barn Dance*, WSM, was funded by the Nashville-based National Life & Accident Insurance Company, whose advertising slogan, "We Shield Millions," gave the call letters to the station. The successor show to *Barn Dance*, the *Grand Ole Opry*, came about one evening in 1927 when a new compere and presenter of the show, "Judge" George D. Hay, introduced *Barn Dance* in his thick Southern twang immediately after NBC's nationally syndicated classical grand opera program: "You've been up in the clouds with Grand Opera; now get down to earth with us in a shindig of Grand Ole Opry!"

Barn Dance was now officially the *Grand Ole Opry* and, having achieved steady success in building an audience for its prime sponsor, a more powerful fifty-thousand-watt transmitter using a unique parabolic antenna was installed at WSM. This was Tennessee's first "clear-channel" station, which allowed the nighttime signal to reach across the nation, weather and wind permitting. With its near-national coverage, WSM established Nashville as the center of old-time music performing and recording and made "country" the United States' national music for many decades.

The mighty 878-foot red-and-white transmitting mast of WSM, albeit slightly reduced these days for technical reasons, is still broadcasting, and the station celebrated its ninetieth anniversary in October 2015. The original early engineers and broadcasters gathered for the anniversary celebrations tell of an intriguing and, in parts, comical tussle for sheer power of voice. It was potentially a struggle to the death between WSM and XER (later XERA), the brainchild of a Kansas-based quack "doctor" broadcasting from a five-hundred-thousand-watt station just south of the US border in unregulated Mexico. Aided by a boosting antenna, XERA claimed that with an output of one million watts it was "the world's most powerful broadcasting station," capable of being regularly picked up two thousand miles away in New York.

A number of "border blaster" transmitters were set up across the southern US border in the early 1930s, all pointing directly north and transmitting English-language music and advertisements to the large American audience. XERA, located in the Mexican border town of Villa Acuña, was one of the first and most powerful; at the time WSM engineers feared for the health of anyone living directly under the antenna, explaining, "You didn't need a radio aerial, on most nights you could pick up the signal on a rusty fence-post—it was that powerful."

WSM's lucrative nighttime signal was overwhelmed by its border-blaster rival until the bogus medical advice of "Doctor" J. R. Brinkley, the station's owner and primary advertiser, began to cause rather than cure "male ailments." It appeared that his cure-all powders ($5 a dose by mail-order for a potion based on powdered goat testicles) and the purported surgical implantation of goat gonads into the testicles of brave patients with $750 to spare, were bogus. The US government passed new legislation banning any link between US-based businesses and "out-of-country radio stations." The action effectively stifled Brinkley's promotional activities and, uniquely for any piece of prior or subsequent legislation, saved American male lives and the testicles of several hundred goats.

Quack doctors aside, the radio industry continued to rapidly expand its listener base while the record industry struggled to find a way to compete with what was effectively free entertainment. XERA carried on broadcasting into the late 1930s, and artists from the Carter Family to Woody Guthrie spent periods living in Del Rio, Texas, just across the Rio Grande from the station from which they broadcast daily radio shows to the forty-eight states.

Record industry competition was also coming from radio stations in the recording centers of New York and Chicago, and many record labels sent producer-scouts into the Mississippi Delta to find and record popular but unsigned local artists for an audience that might not be able to afford even the cheapest radio set. Known as "the land where the blues began," the Delta provided rich pickings for record company scouts. Itinerant musicians had been drawn to the northwest of the state of Mississippi in the late 1890s—in particular to the area around the town of Clarksdale, Coahoma County—by the increased prosperity brought by the continued growth of the local cotton industry. A young W. C. Handy, then a widely travelled leader of a small band, boasted, "I made more money in Clarksdale than I had ever earned. . . . This was not strange, everybody prospered in that Green Eden."

His autobiography also describes how Clarksdale was a magnet for musicians and a melting pot for good blues music. He described how "blind singers and footloose bards . . . surrounded by crowds of country folks . . . would pour their hearts out in song . . . and rarely did their creations lack imagination."

For many local entertainers and blues legends in the making, playing music in the 1920s was more often than not a part-time job. Apart from providing an appreciative local audience, Clarksdale also provided a backstop of steady, paid employment in the cotton industry. The great blues singer and guitarist Son House regularly performed at night while in the day driving a tractor on Dockery Farm, a plantation in Tutweiler, near Clarksdale. Tommy Johnson, the first blues guitarist to claim he had sold his soul to the devil, moved to another plantation near Dockery in 1916 and based himself in the area playing alongside House and his longtime partner Willie Brown.

Muddy Waters grew up in nearby Stovall, playing when he could in one of the informal and often rowdy juke joints found on most plantations. Waters bought his first guitar, a Stella, for $2.50 when he was seventeen, and, like Robert Johnson, he was heavily influenced by Son House. Waters recalled how the player "was all through the Delta back then, and I used to love to hear him play guitar. He had that bottleneck thing, and he could make that guitar real whiny. That man was the King!"

Blues players in the Delta, and particularly around Clarksdale, were part of a close-knit community. Waters's longtime pianist, Willie "Pinetop" Perkins, also drove a tractor on the Hopson plantation just outside Clarksdale until the late 1950s. Hopson is now where the Shack Up Inn operates, a boho colony of shotgun shacks catering to the many blues fans passing through Clarksdale seeking Robert Johnson's "crossroads," these days officially located at the junction of Highways 49 and 61. Guitarists and blues singers Howlin' Wolf, B. B. King, and Bobby Rush all spent time playing in the town, as did John Lee Hooker and Ike

Turner, who were in fact born there. Like so many Delta blues players, they then travelled north with their own takes on the Clarksdale guitar sound.

But how had Clarksdale become such a fertile ground for blues musicians? And why is the Delta so important in shaping the music we call the blues, and particularly the guitar blues?

The Mississippi Delta should not be confused with the delta at the mouth of the Mississippi River south of New Orleans. The Delta isn't an expanse of water but solid land, a vast inland alluvial floodplain sitting along and between the Mississippi and Yazoo Rivers. Seventy miles across at its widest point, it stretches from Memphis in the north to Vicksburg, Mississippi, two hundred miles to the south. The land was often cheaply and sometimes brutally acquired by white settlers from Native American farmers in the early 1800s, aided in large part by the state-sponsored ethnic cleansing allowed by the 1830 Indian Removal Act. Having gained the land and removed its Indigenous peoples, the white planter elite then cleared it of its dense hardwood forest using enslaved Black labor. The rich, sedimental soil that was revealed ran so deep that there was no need to either fertilize or let any previously cultivated land lie fallow. Farmers just turned the soil and replanted season after season. It was rightly described by Tennessee Williams's Big Daddy in *Cat on a Hot Tin Roof* as "the richest land this side of the Valley Nile!" It was the ideal bed for the lucrative cash crop of cotton that formed the basis of Southern prosperity.

In the period leading up to the Civil War, cotton growers dubbed their crop "King Cotton" to remind the federal government of its ability not only to generate unimaginable wealth but also to provide prosperity for the region, albeit both were gained off the backs of enslaved people. The patriarchs of the South believed that the financial importance of King Cotton in American, British, and world commerce protected them from ever having to raise arms to preserve "their way of life" from the North.

Oh Dixie, the land of King Cotton
The home of the brave and the free
A nation by freedom begotten
The terror of despots to be
JOHN HILL HEWITT AND JOSEPH AUGUSTINE SIGNAIGO,
"DIXIE, THE LAND OF KING COTTON," C. 1863

But after the Civil War and emancipation, former enslaved people, who had been promised land ownership and the chance of limited prosperity via the much vaunted "forty acres and a mule," were thwarted economically, socially, and politically. The idea that a small parcel of land constituted reparation for what they suffered was never made law in the statute books, and after the war foreign investors and domestic speculators remade the Delta into an industrial, rather than a traditional, agricultural community. African Americans once more provided cheap labor, no longer as enslaved people but as tenant farmers tied to factory plantations. By the early 1900s, white landowners prospered while the prospects of their tenant farmers, who were predominantly Black folks, grew ever bleaker. No wonder the music that came out of the region was blue. The field hollers and work songs of their enslaved ancestors eventually developed into the mournful sound that we associate with the guitar and solo-voiced country-blues of the 1920s.

Clarksdale was just another town amid the widespread poverty of tenant farmers, sharecroppers, and general plantation workers. But when highways and railroads replaced steamboats and horse-drawn carts, it became the "Golden Buckle of the Cotton Belt." Sitting where the main highways crossed and intersected with the newly built Illinois Central Railroad, it became a hub for transporting cotton to the ports of New Orleans and Mobile, Alabama. Local workers spent what little free time and loose change they had in Clarksdale and helped make it into W. C. Handy's "Green Eden." Even if you had no money, you could still have a good time . . . of sorts.

Clarksdale the town laying heavy on my mind
Clarksdale is a town laying heavy on my mind
I can have a good time there and not have one lousy dime
Every day in the week, I go down to Midtown
Every day in the week, I go down to Midtown Drugs
Get me a bottle o' snuff, and a bottle o' Alcorub
SON HOUSE, "CLARKSDALE MOAN," 1930

Crying, canned heat, canned heat, mama,
Crying, sure, Lord, killing me.
Crying, canned heat, mama, sure, Lord killing me.
Takes Alcorub to take these canned heat blues.
TOMMY JOHNSON, "CANNED HEAT BLUES," 1928

The practice of drinking neat rubbing alcohol, branded Alcorub, as a respite from drinking strained methanol or "canned heat" showed the desperation of some hard-drinking musicians like Tommy Johnson and other poor people in Clarksdale. But come Saturday night, when most workers received their pay, there were other distractions. The many saloons, juke joints, brothels (or boogie houses), and variety theatres in the town's New World red-light district catered to the varied leisure needs of the resident and transient population. New World also provided lucrative and regular work for self-accompanied singers like Son House and Tommy Johnson as well as small bands, as explained by Handy. "Big nights, occasions when social and political figures of importance were expected to dine and dance with their favorite creole belles. . . . This led us to arrange and play tunes that had never been written down and seldom sung outside the environment of the oldest profession. Boogie-house music, it was called."

The proliferation and juxtaposition of high- and low-life entertainment alongside wealth and abject poverty gave Clarksdale the feel of a border town. You could have a lot of fun there but also get into a lot of trouble. Get into *a lot* of trouble and you could find yourself locked up at Clarksdale's nearby Parchman Farm.

Judge gimme life this morn-in
Down on Parchman Farm
Judge gimme life this morn-in
Down on Parchman Farm

Oh you listen you men,
I don't mean no harm
If you wanna do good,
You better stay off ol' Parchman Farm
BUKKA WHITE, "PARCHMAN FARM BLUES," 1940

The prison system established in the Southern states after the Civil War relied on notorious prison farms like Parchman, Cummins, and Angola, "the bloodiest prison in America." They played their own part in contributing to the musical culture of the region and were themselves the subject of many songs. Angola was one of the prisons where convicted murderer Huddie "Lead Belly" Ledbetter was incarcerated, spending his second term in the prison for "assault to murder," having previously sung his way to a governor's pardon in 1925 for two earlier, similar convictions. Lead Belly was an engaging storyteller as well as a consummate songster, ably accompanying himself on the twelve-string guitar. During his years in prison, he had collected many songs, building up a huge repertoire of not just the blues but also cowboy ballads, comedy songs, and even a little light opera. In the 1930s, Library of Congress archivist and folklorist John A. Lomax toured Southern prisons with his teenage son Alan collecting prison work songs. On that trip he discovered Lead Belly, who was only too willing to demonstrate his repertoire. It included "Midnight Special," an archetypal prison song describing jail life and promising freedom from it for every prisoner blessed by the light of salvation from the steam engine—although the "light" could equally signify the release of being run down by the train:

Well, you wake up in the mornin',
You hear the work bell ring,
And they march you to the table
To see the same old thing.
Ain't no food upon the table,
And no pork up in the pan,
But you better not complain, boy,
You get in trouble with the man.

Let the Midnight Special,
shine a light on me,
Let the Midnight Special,
shine her ever-loving light on me

Lead Belly's undoubted performing skill with this song and with "Rock Island Line," another train song, was allegedly used by Lomax to parlay a second governor's pardon. The (once again) reformed prisoner went on to perform at Governor Oscar K. Allen's mansion many times, no doubt as a shining example of the state's ability to show mercy to prisoners who reformed, although he was often dressed up in prison fatigues to demonstrate that even a hardened murderer wasn't beyond redemption. Lead Belly was happy to go along with play-acting and dressing up for a while, but he soon realized he was being used so that others could profit. He became suspicious of Lomax, whom he drove for, wondering if the folklorist took more than his fair share of record and ticket sales.

People have always visited the South to see what they can take, and in the 1920s music was a rich local resource, often seen by archivists and record companies as another cash crop to be harvested. To locate their musical bounty, the big, predominantly Northern music publishers and record companies sent scouting parties across the South to see what music was popular locally and what could be borrowed, reworked, and recorded outside of copyright.

• • • • • •

Big record companies like Columbia, Victor, and Paramount were not just interested in the blues or race records. They were keen to mine any seam of music that had regional or local appeal and developed separate catalogues that allowed their retailers to order "white hillbilly," "string band," or "old-time singing" records. White hillbilly music proved its popular appeal as early as 1924, when the Victor release "Wreck of the Old 97" sold over a million copies and became the first hit record of a genre that would become known as country music. It was also one of the first white hillbilly records to feature a singer accompanied by solo acoustic guitar. The vocalist, Vernon Dalhart (born Marion Try Slaughter), started out as a local hillbilly singer in rural East Texas, gained professional classical training in New York, and went on to record over five thousand 78s. Across his career he employed numerous musical styles and used any one of a hundred pseudonyms. But in 1925, he used his regular stage name, Vernon Dalhart, to record a country song and his second hit, "The Runaway Train." The accompanying guitarist was another professional, Frank Ferera. Better known as a Hawaiian lap-steel player, he recorded Hawaiian songs as well as blues, including W. C. Handy's popular "St. Louis Blues." Both artists were studio musicians, precursors of session players, and relatively expensive commodities. The record labels knew that local artists would be cheaper once they had been located, and to do that meant sending people out into the region where the music was already popular and was being played in public.

When record company scouts planned to visit a town, they advertised in local newspapers to stimulate word-of-mouth that they were looking to record new talent. With promises of a recording fee of $50 for each side cut—and in the case of one scout, Ralph Peer, royalties for each record sold—the response often ran into dozens of local musicians queuing from early morning. Peer, credited with first coining the term "race record," had originally been employed by the OKeh label, recording Black blues and gospel alongside a few professional white hillbilly singers. But it's well cataloged that he had little personal liking for either Black music or its artists. He recorded them because they sold records, and his pay was directly linked to record sales. But he was clearly successful in what he did, quickly defecting in 1927 from OKeh to the larger, and still dominant, Victor label. Peer and his engineers set up their Western Electric mobile recording equipment in a disused hat factory in the Tennessee town of Bristol. In choosing Bristol, a major regional Appalachian town, Peer was trying to attract primarily white local folk artists who might appeal to a similarly white, God-fearing audience across the region.

Can You Sing or Play
Old-Time Music?
Musicians of Unusual Ability
Small Dance Combinations
Singers
Novelty Players etc
All Invited
This is an actual try-out for the purpose of making records

Musicians who were accustomed to playing to small local audiences, often just friends and family and whoever was around to come to a farm dance, flocked to wherever the recording sessions were held. The idea that "foreigners" from forty or fifty miles away might be interested in their music, as well as willing to pay good money to hear it, was big news.

• • • • • •

Ralph Peer had been sent to the Southern mountains by Victor Records in the hope of finding a locally sourced repeat of "The Wreck of the Old 97." It had been the best-selling record for over three months in 1925–1926, and by 1927 the song was well on its way to selling a total of seven million units, making it one of the biggest records in the first seventy years of recording. The stakes were high, but Peer didn't disappoint; the sessions he held in Bristol became a landmark in country music. Not only did these early field recordings give white hillbilly and old-time music a wider audience, but they had a huge impact on the entire music industry, helping create the concept of the three-minute pop song.

The Western Electric recording lathe required a flatbed truck to transport it. Nevertheless, the bulky machine was the first mobile recording device, enabling record companies to cut the master wax disc on site from which thousands of copies could be made and sold. Popular mythology holds that the three-minute length was dictated by the amount of music that could fit onto the first ten-inch 78 rpm discs. While it seems reasonable, it isn't totally accurate—early 78s could carry up to four minutes of music per side. The three-minute pop song was primarily due to how the cutting turntable was powered.

The field studios were often rented church halls or hotel rooms, and the unreliability of rural electricity meant the mobile recording lathes needed a mechanical power source. The solution was a heavy weight pulling a flywheel as it fell to the floor. A pulley and governor controlled the speed, spinning the heavy platter of the cutting turntable at a constant 78 rpm. The one-hundred-pound counterweight took about three-and-a-half minutes to descend from the top to the floor, so artists were told that they had a maximum of three minutes recording time.

Many folk songs typically had dozens of verses, but artists quickly cut them down to three or four, with a middle chorus or instrumental break to fit the newly imposed time restriction. The typical session allowed time for one rehearsal and microphone check and then one take, a process that acted as a kind of quality control, sifting out the enthusiastically hopeless from the talented semiprofessionals.

The resulting recordings were often huge sellers, and their popularity influenced the convention of the three-minute pop song with three verses and chorus, a structure that has persisted to the present day.

Over the course of ten days (and nights), Peer—using the Western Electric recording lathe fitted with the new, more sensitive electric microphone—recorded dozens of individuals and groups in Bristol. But two artists, recorded on the same day, made up what are now known as the "Bristol Sessions." They constitute white country music's Big Bang moment and influenced decades of popular music. Through these two sessions, Jimmie Rodgers became the first guitar-playing "pop" star of the period and Maybelle Carter the pioneer of a style of guitar playing still revered and used today.

Rodgers created the blueprint for contemporary country music; he recorded songs in which you also can hear the embryonic style and structure of rock 'n' roll. The early death of his mother led to an itinerant childhood working alongside his maintenance foreman father on the Mobile & Ohio Railroad. These circumstances gave him all the insight and credentials he needed to write authentic songs about hard work, hard living, lost love, despair, and an inevitably lonesome life. The onset of tuberculosis at twenty-seven forced him to quit the railroad and turn his natural singing and guitar-playing talents into a meagre living playing both solo and in string bands in local bars, juke joints, vaudeville, and blackface minstrel shows and tent dances. His band auditioned for Peer in Bristol, but squabbling over their recording name and what to sing led to Jimmie recording his session as a solo artist. His first two cuts were both minor hits, but Rodgers's subsequent recording, "Blue Yodel" (aka "T for Texas"), with a yodeling chorus "borrowed" from the style of blackface minstrel Emmett Miller, was the song that transformed him into a national star. Two years after its initial release, it had sold five hundred thousand copies and went on to sell over a million, with each sale earning Rodgers a few cents in royalties.

Rodgers massaged his backstory, becoming the first nationally recognized musician to create a public persona (or possibly two, given he was initially the railroad's hard traveling "Singing Brakeman" and then the lonesome "Blue Yodeler"). In 1930, he moved to Texas and started appearing onstage in a fringed buckskin jacket and cowboy-style clothes, thereby becoming the first popular cowboy crooner. Over the next five years, Rodgers recorded dozens of country classics, including "Why Should I Be Lonely?," "Daddy and Home," "In the Jailhouse Now," and "Miss the Mississippi and You." In these simple twelve-bar blues, and in his many sequels to "Blue Yodel," we hear the very essence of early rock 'n' roll. Rodgers would have known the term as Black slang; he would have heard it from Black blues singers like Trixie Smith in "My Man Rocks Me (With One Steady Roll)" (1922), who sneaked the sexual innuendo past the censor.

Influenced by Black blues, gospel, hillbilly, and early jazz, Rodgers also pioneered the crossover of musical styles. In 1928, he released "Waiting for a Train," featuring the Hawaiian steel guitar of Ellsworth T. Cozzens, and in 1930 recorded "Blue Yodel No. 9 (Standin' on the Corner)," which featured Louis Armstrong on jazz trumpet.

Whether as plain Jimmie Rodgers, the Blue Yodeler, or the Singing Brakeman (having starred in a short movie of that name), Rodgers was as popular as many bona fide movie stars of the period and sold over 20 million records in his six-year career. In true country music style and taking a storyline from what could have been one of his own songs, Rodgers, having just completed a recording session in New York, collapsed in the street and, two days later, finally succumbed to tuberculosis. He was just thirty-five. The world had lost a great songwriter and singer but also an idiosyncratic and original guitarist. Rodgers combined rural folk, early blues, syncopated jazz, and ragtime in his subtle guitar style. His bass runs, punctuating the chords, gave his accompaniment a bouncy lope, a style copied by many later players, including Johnny Cash.

Bob Dylan has long recognized the influence that Jimmie Rodgers had on him and his 1960s folk revival peers: "He was a performer of force without precedent, with a sound as lonesome and mystical as it was dynamic. He gives hope to the vanquished and humility to the mighty."

Dylan likewise recognized the influence of the Carter Family, the second music pioneer that Ralph Peer recorded in Bristol on that same day in 1927.

• • • • • •

Maybelle Carter had been born into a large family in an area of rural western Virginia known as Poor Valley. By sixteen she was married and singing and playing guitar in the Carter Family trio with her first cousin (and sister-in-law), Sara, and Sara's husband, A. P. Carter (who was the brother of Maybelle's husband). The Carters were already well known across rural Appalachia, singing in churches and at various social events. But when word reached them that a Victor Records scout was auditioning and recording new talent, the group and their young children made the fifteen-hour car trip to the town of Bristol, Tennessee, to audition for Ralph Peer. Maybelle Carter, then eighteen years old and seven months pregnant, later recalled the visit: "They just had an old building that we recorded in. It wasn't a regular studio; it was just an old warehouse. We did everything we did on one mike. They cut on a big wax. About so thick, and if you make a mistake they shave it off—you couldn't erase it like you do a tape."

Sales of the first three songs the Carters recorded exceeded even Peer's expectations. But he knew when he first set eyes on them never to judge a book by its cover, or a singer by how they look. "They wander in. . . . He's dressed in overalls, and the women . . . they're country women from way back there. They looked like—well, later I called them 'hillbillies' and that's what they looked like. . . . But as soon as I heard Sara's voice, that was it."

Two years later, Peer recorded more songs with the Carters, including "Wildwood Flower," which sold 120,000 copies within a few months of its release—ten times the usual sales for a popular rural record. "Wildwood Flower" is today still a country and bluegrass standard and a must-have in any country guitarist's repertoire. More importantly, the style of guitar playing, what became known as the "Carter Scratch," that Maybelle used on this and most other Carter Family recordings, influenced the way guitars sounded and were used in country music for decades.

Maybelle gave the Carter Family their new and unique sound by intuitively playing the melody line on the bass strings with her thumb while her fingers strummed or "scratched" a hybrid rhythm on the first three treble strings. It is the opposite of the way most people played the guitar up until then—traditionally the thumb was used to keep a steady bass rhythm going while the fingers played the treble melody line. The Carter style sounds relatively simple, but done well—and her raw style was perfection—it's both deceptively rhythmic and hard driving. It led the way to many future country guitar styles, from Merle Travis's "Travis picking" to Chet Atkins's "Atkins's finger-style" technique, and it is the root from which Mark Knopfler of Dire Straits derived his trademark twang. Maybelle in essence was the lead and rhythm guitarist combined, while her cousin Sara and brother-in-law A. P. sang and played support rhythm. The Carters were hugely popular for over fifteen years, but when the family group finally split up in 1943, "Mother" Maybelle Carter formed a group with her three grown-up daughters and played on into the '70s. One of her last TV appearances was on *The Johnny Cash Show*, her daughter June having married Cash a few years earlier, continuing and ensuring the Carter family influence on country music across the decades.

The Carter Family had a huge repertoire of songs. A few were original compositions, but most were reworkings of traditional hymns or tunes that the English and Irish settlers of Appalachia had brought over from the old country. This tradition of reworking and rewording was also a legacy that the Carter Family passed on. Their recording of "The Wayworn Traveler" was put to new words and performed live by a young Dylan as "Paths of Victory." A few years later, he changed the time signature and wrote yet newer lyrics to the original tune to give us "The Times They Are a-Changin'." In fact, many of the songs Dylan worked on with the Band in the 1960s, later released as *The Basement Tapes*, were adaptations of songs and arrangements that the Carter Family regularly played.

• • • • • •

As both Carter and Rodgers came from relatively poor backgrounds, it's no surprise they both started out with modest guitars. However, when they achieved stardom, they pioneered a trend followed by countless players to this day. They chose to buy the most expensive guitars available from the most celebrated American makers of their time. Their choices had a marked effect on the guitars that fellow professionals and keen amateurs played.

While Jimmie Rodgers did have an itinerant upbringing, staying with various relatives while his father's railroad work took him all over the South, he was not the dirt-poor child his songs often suggested. By the time he reached Bristol in 1927, he was a thirty-year-old, road-tested performer playing a steel-string Martin 00-18; albeit a budget model in the Martin catalog, it was nonetheless a good guitar. But such was his meteoric rise that just a few months after his first record came out, he ordered direct from Martin a 000-45, the most expensive guitar in their catalog. He also seems to have been the first artist to have his name inlaid in pearl along the neck of his instrument. Jimmie went on to sign an endorsement deal with Weymann, another Pennsylvanian-based German immigrant luthier, who built a similar-sized guitar, the Weymann Jimmie Rodgers Special, which now resides in the Country Music Hall of Fame. But it is the two Martins that continue to be revered in the rarified world of celebrity-owned instruments.

Early photographs of the Carter Family show Maybelle playing a Gibson L-1 flat-top, and we know she played a low-priced Stella on the first Bristol Sessions. Both instruments were relatively cheap, but they were still respectable guitars as befitted a local, semiprofessional musician. But as the financial rewards of becoming country music's first star trio began to hit, Maybelle quickly acquired something special—the most expensive guitar Gibson made, the L-5, bought by her husband Ezra (A. P.'s brother), who also managed the family group.

Maybelle took delivery of her Gibson L-5 sometime in 1929, just a few months after "Wildwood Flower" had become a nationwide hit. It was an expensive guitar, retailing at $275 (a few dollars more than a brand-new Model T Ford). Today an L-5 archtop, what many would consider a jazz guitar, seems a strange choice for a hillbilly or country artist like Carter. String-band players tended to favor cheaper, flat-top guitars, but in the late 1920s and '30s, the L-5 was popularized by the influential jazz guitarist Eddie Lang. He had also developed his own unique playing style, combining rhythm and lead in his immensely influential and highly popular jazz recordings. By the time Maybelle received the L-5, the Carter Family were, like Lang, often playing in front of electronic microphones—whether broadcasting live on the radio or in recording sessions—and the L-5 worked well in that environment, regardless of the player's style.

The L-5 had been introduced by Gibson in 1923 as an extension of their mandolin range—and possibly a final attempt to rescue mandolin orchestras from imminent extinction. Gibson had started business riding the mandolin craze that gripped both Europe and America at the turn of the century, creating a family of mandolins in different sizes. Gibson mandolins, mandolas, and mandocellos employed unique, violin-style carved arched tops, and the wonderfully majestic-looking archtop guitars in the same style were intended to be used by Gibson enthusiasts in mandolin orchestras. The guitars sound markedly different than most flat-top guitars, having a loud, crisp, penetrating tone with very fast decay—meaning that the individual notes don't blur into each other. But unlike classical guitars with complex overtones and sustain, they didn't initially catch the imagination or match the expectations of most regular guitarists.

While Gibson enjoyed early success as *the* mandolin specialist during the mandolin boom, after World War I things didn't go so well. Their business fortunes were not helped by a leaden management who didn't seem to understand much about making instruments or what the market and musicians now wanted. As the eight-string mandolin's popularity waned, to be replaced by the tenor banjo utilizing the same fingering on just four steel strings, Gibson shifted to tenor banjo production. The move laid some important foundations for the development of the bluegrass banjo of the 1940s, but the tenor banjo gave them nowhere near the sales success they had had with the mandolin.

Which brings us to Lloyd Loar, under whose direction the Gibson L-5 was developed. There is some credence to the view that salvation for the Gibson company came in the shape of Loar and his development of a range of superlative master model instruments that transformed the fortunes of Gibson in the 1920s. Unlike the company management, Loar played the mandolin and guitar to a professional standard, was a serious student of music theory, and was accomplished in the evolving science of acoustics. He also had a personal passion for making the Gibson range sound significantly better.

Loar joined Gibson in 1919, primarily as a design consultant and "acoustical engineer," although he went on to hold many roles within the business. He set about taking Orville Gibson's already innovative designs and construction techniques and "tuning" the various components of the instruments so that they worked as a sonic whole. He experimented with thinning the fronts and backs of the body and lightening and graduating side panels and top braces (tone-bars) so they resonated harmoniously.

The instruments developed during his time at the company were launched and marketed as master models and cataloged as Style 5. The range embraced mandolins, their larger variants, and the L-5 archtop guitar. Cosmetically, the Loar Style 5s were given a unique sunburst finish, developed by the Gibson finish department and designated "Cremona Brown" in homage to the town in Italy where the legendary Stradivarius had his workshop. Each instrument carried a paper interior label personally signed by Loar stating that "the top, back, tone bars and air-chamber of this instrument were tested, tuned and assembled instrument tried and approved." Loar is an almost mythical figure for many Gibson enthusiasts, but there is debate over exactly what he did and how hands-on he actually was. There is evidence that he batch-signed and dated labels that were applied to instruments when they were shipped, sometimes long after Loar had in fact left the company.

But Loar as savior of Gibson is an attractive and convenient myth—the gifted maverick who did not get on with an uncharismatic management. The development of the Mastertone and master model ranges was almost certainly a team effort—during Loar's time at the company the workforce numbered over sixty, and a whole team of people worked in engineering and research. The master model instruments were time-consuming to build and something of a pain for a high-volume instrument factory like Gibson to produce. More importantly, they were slow sellers; in fact, Loar's period with Gibson was something of a financial fiasco—the company was taken close to insolvency.

The refinements that Loar and his team introduced in the Style 5 series included violin-style f-holes that replaced the round or oval sound holes of conventionally designed fretted instruments; the scroll body outline; carved backs and tops; and tuned body components. Professional players at the time heard how the louder, more focused sound that f-holes projected was ideally suited to playing into a microphone and being heard above a big, acoustic orchestra's brass section. In a time before postproduction and studio mixing, Maybelle was aware that her signature guitar style—the blend of lead and bass lines—had to cut through the vocals and other instruments. Whether she realized that the L-5 was precisely the right instrument to do just that is unknown—she primarily had the most expensive guitar that Gibson made at the time because she was a star. But there is no doubt that the guitar was the right guitar for her music.

There is equally no question that the L-5 and the instruments of the Loar period are superlative.

It was the Loar-inspired F-5 mandolin that was "rediscovered" by Bill Monroe in the mid-1940s to give him his unique sound. First introduced in

1922, it had a longer neck than standard at the time and a raised fingerboard to accommodate the introduction of f-holes. These features helped the top vibrate better and improved tone and volume, and Monroe knew that it could embrace his new style of bluegrass music. Such was the success of his sound in the late '40s and '50s that bluegrass players began actively searching out Loar-labelled and post-Loar (so-called Fern) F-5 mandolins. Their improved projection, longer necks, and distinctive "bark" enabled players to reach more muted chop chords, thereby emulating Monroe's sound and style of playing.

By the 1960s and '70s, F-5s were considered "legendary" by a new generation of bluegrass players. In 1969, prewar Gibson F-5s sold for about $1,500, triple the price of the equally legendary prewar Herringbone D-28 guitar. They had also reached the notice of instrument collectors and speculators, and by the 1970s the very best examples were selling for $100,000. In 2004, the Country Music Hall of Fame also acquired Maybelle's L-5 for $575,000 from Gruhn Guitars, while in early 2007 a couple of Lloyd Loar F-5s reached $200,000 before the market took a severe downturn. The recession and stock market crash meant that speculators had neither true collectors nor utility players to sell to. The market for F-5s has yet to fully recover.

Loar left Gibson in December 1924 and effectively went missing from the instrument business, only to reemerge in 1933 to set up a company with a former Gibson general manager. He had been experimenting with a solid-bodied viola with an electric pickup as early as 1923, and he later patented designs for an electric piano, so he must have realized the potential for an electric guitar. While it was no surprise that the Vivi Tone Company of Kalamazoo was established primarily to produce electric instruments as well as to develop some of Loar's more unconventional acoustic ideas, it was surprising that he didn't get it right. (He strongly advocated that an electric guitar didn't need an acoustic body or any form of sound chamber.) Yet whatever Loar's talent with acoustic instruments, he certainly didn't have a similar genius for electric guitars—or he didn't bring it to Vivi Tone.

The company was not successful, and the electric instruments it produced in 1933 were poorly designed, not especially loud, and were manufactured at nowhere near Gibson master model standards—something that supports the view that while at Gibson, Loar wasn't singlehandedly responsible for all the many things he is credited for. While Gibson featured Loar in some promotional literature, he was just one member of a talented team that produced some remarkable instruments in the early 1920s. Perhaps it is a shame that he left the company without developing his ideas for the electric guitar: with the Gibson team around him, the title "inventor of the modern electric guitar" could have been added to the Lloyd Loar legend.

It is another Gibson legend who is regularly credited with inventing the modern, solid-bodied electric guitar—the guitarist, multitrack pioneer, and amateur inventor Les Paul. But while Les Paul was an inventive player of the electric guitar, he was not its inventor. That credit lies with an ex-vaudeville performer turned entrepreneur, George Beauchamp. In the late 1920s, Beauchamp was experimenting with ways of amplifying guitar strings, which eventually led him to create the instrument that brought a new, different sound to music: one that became a driving force for numerous musical forms. The birth of the electric guitar might easily have sounded the death knell for the acoustic model, but instead it spawned a whole new era of music that thrives to this day.

Gene Autry playing a 1933 Martin D-45 Custom.

The Depression and the Emergence of the Modern Flat-Top

The decade of the 1930s was shaped by the Great Depression and marked the era when popular music usurped "serous-minded" or elitist music. But what was the music that was so "popular," who was producing it, and who was listening to it?

The musical and movie show tunes that became "standards" of the Great American Songbook and sold in the millions were created by the professional songwriters and music publishers of Tin Pan Alley, who largely controlled the music business in the United States. The jazz music that young city folk seemed to be dancing to was mainly created by popular bands and dance orchestras and was effectively controlled by the radio and record industries. Both genres intermingled but generally produced material focused on a narrow range of topics: looking for love, finding love, falling in love, being in love, being cheated on while in love, falling out of love, falling back in love . . .

But another type of popular music created in the 1920s and '30s came from the grassroots—folk music (in its broadest sense), including hillbilly, country, and the blues. This music was popular with poor Black and white people living in the rural South or the urban North and was often written by, about, or for the nation's most oppressed. It expressed the joys but also the issues and concerns of people who didn't spend all their time falling in and out of love.

Helping to express the travails of everyday life was the six-string acoustic guitar—providing both accompaniment and inspiration. It sat fixed at the heart of these uniquely American songs. The best were made by Martin and Gibson, but many more were made in large instrument factories and sold through the numerous mail-order catalogs. As all these makers responded to the challenges of the Depression, the types of instruments they produced shaped both the guitar industry and popular music.

• • • • • •

There is a well-drawn analogy that if Martin guitars were the Mercedes Benzes of their time, then Gibsons were Cadillacs. Certainly, the conservative, meticulously documented, quality-first German aesthetic that Martin brought to guitar design, manufacture, and even branding contrasted with the entrepreneurial, market savvy, slightly flashy, all-American brand that is Gibson.

Martin guitars had sold well in the '20s but were not selling so well by the early 1930s. The Depression was taking its toll on the company, as it was on the whole musical instrument industry. But there was another reason for lackluster sales: Martin's largely outdated product range. The company still offered many obsolete models, little-changed since the late 1800s, using smaller bodies and traditional, wider, twelve-fret necks; they were unsurprisingly not considered "modern" guitars. Even in 1931, when it launched the Martin-branded version of the large dreadnought guitar it had first started making for the Ditson company back in 1916, it was as a wide-necked, twelve-fret model with a slotted headstock. These features, seen as old-fashioned, slowed down initial sales. Only after the company transitioned to a longer and narrower fourteen-fret neck in 1934 did sales of the iconic dreadnought finally start to improve.

When the instrument was first produced in 1916, it was never entirely clear for whom the original Ditson III model was intended or what style of music they played. It was fan-braced, so it could have been designed for Hawaiian steel slide players, or, as was the case for the later Martin Dreadnought, it may have been targeted at professional musicians who were asking for guitars that could be heard alongside the banjos, fiddles, and the occasional brass instruments in their bands. Martin literature called it a "bass" guitar because its greater size gave it a lot more bass response and a boomy sound, something of an anathema for a company that had spent the previous one hundred years carefully creating guitars with a finely balanced tone across the whole sound spectrum. Professionals working in the first recording studios knew that the early mechanical microphones (a large horn driving a diaphragm and exciting a cutting needle) couldn't pick up the finesse of a finely balanced instrument, but they could "hear" the loud thump of a big, bassy guitar. But by the 1920s, the newer electric microphones used in modern studios and radio stations could pick up both the higher frequencies and the bass. After a short run of prototypes, Martin cataloged two versions of the Orchestra Style D (dreadnought) guitar: a plain, mahogany-bodied D-18 for $65; and the D-28, made with Brazilian rosewood and featuring much fancier appointments, for $100. Despite their higher price points in the Depression years, they achieved some success with both professional as well as better-heeled amateur players.

Unsurprisingly, Gibson quickly copied Martin in 1934 with their first large-bodied flat-top guitar, the jumbo. It was initially produced in small numbers, but as the market for larger guitars started to gain momentum, Gibson heavily promoted an expanding range of advanced large-bodied models. These were powerful-sounding guitars with, according to the Gibson catalog, "a bass so deep, rich and full that it can be 'felt' as well as heard." Despite the moderately successful sales of these advanced models, it was still Gibson's budget brands and instruments made under contract supplying basic, own-label guitars to mail order companies like Montgomery Ward that kept the business afloat in the Depression years.

But Gibson had been a late entrant to the flat-top guitar market. Martin had been making guitars for over ninety years when in 1926 the Gibson Mandolin-Guitar Company brought out its first two Gibson-branded flat-tops. The plain and soberly named L-0 and L-1 guitars were both well-made midsize guitars, and while Gibson priced them significantly below their mandolins and early archtops, they were still relatively expensive compared to most mail-order instruments. Only the more successful professional hillbilly players and Black blues musicians were able to adopt them as everyday working instruments.

A small, dark-bodied guitar that looks a lot like one of the early Gibson L-0s or L-1s appears in perhaps the most iconic picture in the history of Black blues music. The photograph, taken around 1935 at the Hooks Brothers Photography Studio on Beale Street, in Memphis, shows twenty-five-year-old Robert Johnson wearing a snappy hat and a pinstripe suit and holding what is widely accepted to be a Gibson L series guitar. But experts differ in their opinions. Guitar aficionado George Gruhn believes that while the guitar looks like a late 1920s L-0 rather than a Gibson L-1, he questions whether it is even a Gibson at all. Nonetheless, over the years various Gibson L-1s have turned up purporting to be "Robert Johnson's guitar from that photo," but, as with most things Johnson, fact and fiction blend. A Gibson L-1 offered at $6 million in 2005 by a US memorabilia dealer as the "Johnson guitar" was quickly shown to be very little like the one in the Hooks Brothers photo, and its dealer promptly crawled back into the ether. In 2015, much media fuss was made over a Florida businessman who claimed he had found "Johnson's lost guitar." The claim proved ridiculous, though, because it had no provenance other than the guitar was the right date and "looked like" the one in the Hooks Brothers photo. Well, it had sounded vaguely credible until the Florida man revealed that a few years earlier he had sent the guitar back to Gibson for a complete refinish, thereby erasing any hope of authentication.

While any guitar directly traceable back to Johnson is the Holy Grail of guitars, it is only such for memorabilia hunters. Guitar collectors want more, as George Gruhn points out. "Collectors of fine instruments care about who made it, the year of production, the model, and its condition cosmetically and structurally—as well as whether it is fully original with no alterations and the historical significance of the model."

But what makes the search for the Robert Johnson guitar somewhat academic is that Johnson's contemporaries never recalled him playing anything as expensive as a Gibson, which in the '30s retailed at around $30. At that time, a farm laborer earned just $5 a week. The guitar Johnson is holding in the photo could have been a studio prop (possible but unlikely given its cost) or, more likely, lent to him by a musician friend especially for the photo. However, his contemporaries do recall him regularly playing both a Stella and a Kalamazoo KG-14, a Gibson budget brand; both cost around $12 and were instruments much more consistent with an itinerant musician's financial means.

Both Gibson and Stella guitars, made by the Jersey City–based Oscar Schmidt Instrument Company, distributed their cheaper instruments throughout the rural towns of the South via general stores, gas stations, and the furniture stores that sold early phonographs and the records they played. The furniture stores were also where many Delta blues guitarists listened to records and auditioned for record company scouts. Alongside the Stella brand was Kalamazoo, just one of over forty brand names that the Gibson company used to differentiate its budget models from the premium Gibson brand.

There is a view among modern collectors that Kalamazoo-branded instruments, which took their name from the city where the Gibson factory was situated, were better-made and therefore superior to Gibson's other contract brands. Made in the thousands, Kalamazoo-branded guitars were no better or worse than the guitars produced by Gibson with Cromwell, Kel Kroydon, or Martelle on the headstock. In fact, Gibson was known for making a large batch of a particular model guitar and only stenciling the brand name on the headstock as the batch neared completion and wholesale orders were confirmed. Most of these guitars were ladder-braced rather than X- or fan-braced. Using four heavy transverse braces meant a quicker and simpler, and therefore cheaper, build process that produced relatively durable guitars. Their sound is less complex than an X-braced instrument, delivering crisp rather than boomy bass notes and sustained mid and high notes. These guitars helped create the trademark blues guitar sound—crunchy bass and precise lead notes—a sound that dominates not just the Johnson recordings but the playing of Charley Patton, Skip James, and Son House.

Regardless of what instrument Robert Johnson played, or was photographed with, he is now widely celebrated as both "the King of the Delta Blues Singers" and "the greatest blues guitarist who ever lived." Both sobriquets are still the cause of heated debate, but Johnson is certainly the greatest blues guitarist who ever *died*. He was the founding member of the exclusive "27 Club": subsequent members include Brian Jones (a founding member of the Rolling Stones), Jimi Hendrix, Janis Joplin, Jim Morrison, Sandy Denny, Kurt Cobain, and Amy Winehouse, who all died forlorn and messy drug- or alcohol-fueled deaths aged just twenty-seven. Maybe it was coincidence, or maybe, like Robert Johnson, they all did deals with the devil for their extraordinary talent?

But Johnson's is the name that usually springs to mind when describing an archetypal Black blues guitarist and singer. And that's partly because his dark, romantic life story is as mysterious, confused, and fuzzy as his music is influential.

Even confirming something as basic as the birth dates of Robert Johnson and Charley Patton isn't easy because, like most blues players, they were itinerant musicians for most of their careers. Even in their relative heydays—for Patton the early 1930s, for Johnson the mid-1930s—they made relatively few recordings. Those they did make were mostly done in makeshift hotel studios without the benefit of the modern custom of recording logs. Moreover, they were playing before the widespread growth of radio and the advent of national artists, so they were little known outside their local stomping grounds of juke joints and barrelhouses. They are thought of by modern enthusiasts as "popular," but they rarely played in front of crowds bigger than fifty people. For all these reasons, little was written about them during their lifetimes, and what was known at the time had been long forgotten by the early 1960s, when blues music finally began to have an enthusiastic following again.

Therefore, sorting the facts of their lives from myths has been their life's work for many blues enthusiasts. Gayle Dean Wardlow was twenty years old in 1960 when he started collecting blues records. Frustrated at the lack of biographical information about the makers of his favorite blues recordings, he developed an interest and skill for sorting through public records and city directories and in locating birth and death certificates—he was the first to find Robert Johnson's. In the mid '60s, Wardlow became a blues researcher and investigator, researching what would become his magnum opus, *Chasin' That Devil Music: Searching for the Blues* (1998).

When playing in juke joints or at a picnic or barbecue, a player like Johnson would have played whatever songs were popular at that moment, usually a bit of everything from show tunes to popular ballads. But when Robert Johnson was finally recorded, his producer would have wanted original songs, which were unencumbered by the need to pay a writing royalty. Therefore, his recorded songs were often derivative of many of the great blues players who went before him—those he copied via contemporary recordings and the few he learned from directly—such as Delta musicians from Tutweiler, near Clarksdale, like Willie Brown and Son House.

Despite inauspicious beginnings, it's the originality of Johnson's guitar playing that makes him stand out. In 1930 Johnson was just a young harmonica player who followed Son House around the local juke joints. House, speaking in the 1950s, remembered Johnson's early, crude attempts to play guitar while he and Brown were on their breaks between sets.

> And such a racket you never heard! It'd make the people mad, you know. They'd come out and say, "Why don't y'all go in and get that guitar away from that boy! He's running people crazy with it!" I'd come back in, and I'd scold him about it, "Don't do that Robert. You drive the people nuts. You can't play nothing. Why don't you play that harmonica for 'em." But he

> didn't want to blow that. Still, he didn't care how I'd get after him about it. He'd do it anyway.

There is evidence that Son House taught the rudiments of playing guitar to the twenty-year-old Johnson before he left the Clarksdale area in search of his father around 1931. But that is overshadowed by the myth: his transformational trip to "sell his soul to the devil at the crossroads" in exchange for his guitar-playing skill. The story was that he had been away only a few months before he returned playing the guitar like a demon . . . or the devil. The reality behind the myth was that Johnson was away from Clarksdale for well over two years. Some of that time he lived with guitarist Isaiah "Ike" Zimmerman and his family, and some of that time he locked himself away to practice intensively, perfecting his technique and trying out his stage act two hundred miles from his original base of Coahoma County. (The latter custom is known as "woodshedding.")

Given that Johnson started playing in earnest when blues guitar records were in relatively wide circulation, it is possible that he had holed himself up with his guitar and a $10 wind-up "suitcase" gramophone and studiously listened and built on the work of the masters.

On his return to the Clarksdale area, he went back to see his idol and mentor, Son House, who was still playing juke joints alongside Willie Brown. House, again speaking in the 1950s, recalled:

> When he came back . . . me and Willie Brown was playing out and he walked in. . . . "I want you to see what I learned." . . . So I said to him "Alright you better do something with it too," and I winked my eye at Willie. So he sat down there and finally got started. And man he was so good! When he finished all our mouths were standing open. I said, "Well ain't that fast! He's gone now."

He wasn't only fast but accurate, able to play in a variety of styles, particularly an upbeat boogie-shuffle, where his playing imitates a strong left- and right-hand piano accompaniment. Notably, his guitar-playing style varies, even within a single song, showing the interplay of his many tricks and rhythmic licks. This, together with his plaintive hummed intros and other-worldly falsetto vocals, made up his trademark sound. Many modern guitarists hearing his recordings for the first time believe they are hearing two guitars playing and one man singing. But it's all Johnson, recorded live across just two sessions by the English producer Don Law for Brunswick Records, a division of Warner Bros. The first session was recorded in 1936 in the corner of room 414 of the Gunter Hotel in San Antonio, Texas; a year later, in 1937, he was recorded in the Warner Bros. film exchange building at 507 Park Avenue, Dallas.

The recordings are among the most famous of all blues guitar recordings; but Robert Johnson, along with the devil at the crossroads story, arrives relatively late in the history of the recorded country blues and at a time when the Delta blues style was going out of fashion. Having cut his first sides in November 1936, his landmark recordings happened just two years before his death—a death variously reported to have been caused by strychnine slipped to him by a jealous lover or husband, congenital syphilis, an arterial aneurysm, an excess of bad moonshine, or pneumonia (or possibly all five combined). Whatever the actual cause, a few hours after playing at the Three Forks juke joint in Greenwood, Mississippi, Robert Johnson was retching uncontrollably, running a burning temperature, and had to be carried home. A few days later, and—according to (fellow musician) Robert "Honeyboy" Edwards—just after "getting on all fours and howlin' like a mad dog," he fell down dead. The Robert Johnson legend was born.

During his lifetime Johnson was neither a widely known live musician or a successful recording artist. He played occasionally in West Memphis and St. Louis, but he was mainly known around his local area of Clarksdale and just across the Mississippi in Helena, Arkansas. He sold relatively few records; of the twenty-nine songs he recorded, his best seller was "Terraplane Blues," a minor regional hit that sold just five thousand copies. It wasn't until 1961, when *Robert Johnson—King of the Delta Blues Singers*, a compilation of his early sides, appeared that he found real fame. Released during the folk and blues revival in America, it's now an essential for every enthusiast's collection. Back then, it was possibly the first time that people like Dave van Ronk, Bob Dylan, and a few British blues players had heard of him. Even after these lo-fi recordings had been cleaned up for modern ears, they required concentrated and repeated listening to yield their full promise.

Despite spurious theories that the recordings were speeded up, the rapid-fire guitar licks and artful tempo changes inside the rigid twelve-bar pattern are all pure Johnson. His repertoire contained well-structured, complete songs, often with inventive double-entendre lyrics. "Terraplane Blues," "Come On in My Kitchen," and "Kind Hearted Woman Blues" are all composed and performed for the age of the three-minute record. It's also easy to hear how Johnson's playing style carried into the sound of the early electric guitar in urban Chicago blues, particularly in the playing of Muddy Waters. We know the songs were rigorously studied, and often shamelessly reworked, by generations of contemporary blues players who admired Johnson. Eric Clapton, Keith Richards, and Jimmy Page were yet to discover that the Johnson repertoire was itself a reworking of songs released by artists Johnson admired. "Walking Blues" is closely based on "My Black Mama" by his mentor Son House; "I Believe I'll Dust My Broom" on Kokomo Arnold's "Sagefield Woman Blues"; "Sweet Home Chicago" on the same man's "Old Original Kokomo Blues"; "Come On in My Kitchen" on "Sitting on Top of the World" by the Mississippi Sheiks. The list goes on and on.

Besides the power of his music, part of Johnson's contemporary appeal (and the brouhaha over Johnson's actual guitar) is undoubtedly linked to the fact that white, middle-class blues fans and aficionados like their blues legends to conform to a stereotype: Black, poor, possibly blind, and to have recorded a couple of hard-to-find 78s before returning to the family farm and dying a miserable death in poverty. The Mississippi Delta was certainly the right place for those things to happen. In 1935, seventy years after the end of the Civil War and the abolition of slavery, the American sociologist Rupert Vance called the Delta "the deepest South," a place that he judged was still "cotton obsessed, Negro obsessed.... Nowhere but in the Mississippi Delta are antebellum conditions so nearly preserved."

When the eminent Southern historian James C. Cobb called it "the most Southern place on earth," he wasn't describing its geographical location but the extremity of its sheer "Southernness." The phrase connotes a brutal place. The Delta lynched more Black people per square mile than any other part of Mississippi, and, despite most counties having 80–90 percent Black residents, many towns explicitly forbade Black people being "abroad on the streets" after dark. "N—— don't let the sun go down on you" was a sign prevalent in many parts of the South until well after Johnson's death.

• • • • • •

The blues music that Johnson was playing in the mid-thirties had evolved from its raw roots as field hollers and the songs regularly sung by enslaved people into a synthesis of looser, syncopated jazz and ragtime. Ragtime was created by piano players mimicking the complex, syncopated sounds of brass and banjo bands heard in the bars and streets of New Orleans in the late 1870s.

Delta blues music of the 1930s shared some of the rhythmic patterns of ragtime and early New Orleans jazz. But it also had a relaxed, irregular style and was often more mournful, accompanied by vocals telling stories of hardship or lost love; it was also rich in sexual innuendo soliciting or celebrating love of a different kind.

Across the South grueling, long work hours, shanty accommodations, and subsistence pay gave many amateur blues singers a life that was bleak and full of the sort of anger and frustrations worth committing to song. Recordings of these dark, plaintive songs are what many modern enthusiasts see as the authentic sound of the blues. But the touring or "walking" musicians of the time, playing clubs, boogie houses, and juke joints, were expected to entertain, not just empathize. The early recordings of the same Black blues musicians who influenced Robert Johnson—players like Charley Patton and Son House—singing "Oh Death" or "Death Letter Blues" give listeners only a glimpse of their performing repertoire. To make a living, professional musicians played what their audiences wanted to hear. Even in the deep South, Black audiences wanted the popular hits of the day and whatever else Tin Pan Alley was serving up, often comedy songs and romantic ballads. But when Black blues singers got into the studio, it was a different story. The record companies wanted them to play original blues, not previously recorded popular songs encumbered with a copyright. Even the blues sides they cut weren't necessarily seen by local audiences as "the blues"; for many they were just working-class Black pop songs of the day or tunes the juke joint crowd could dance to.

Something recognizable as the blues had circulated in Black America thirty or forty years earlier, when blues songs were mainly work songs, usually called "ditties," and were uncatalogued and unrecorded. W. C. Handy's 1912 "Memphis Blues" was the first blues known to have been written down, and "Crazy Blues," recorded in New York in 1920 by Mamie Smith, is accepted by many ethnomusicologists as the first proper blues recording by a Black singer. It was also hugely popular, selling 75,000 records in its first month and over a million copies in its first year. While "Crazy Blues"—an intoxicating blend of brass, syncopated piano, and Smith's plaintive voice—marks a turning point in American popular music, it was not the first blues to be recorded. Like the early jazz recordings, white musicians were recording blues songs as early as 1915, sometimes as their musical specialty but more likely as part of a vaudeville turn and then often as a curiosity or amusement aimed at their white audiences.

Black female vaudeville blues singers like Ma Rainey and Mamie and Bessie Smith, who played the lucrative East Coast tent-show circuit, dominated the early years of popular recorded blues singing in the early 1920s. Male singers appeared in greater numbers only in the latter part of the '20s. The sexually explicit lyrics of "Black Snake Blues" and "No More Jelly Roll Blues" were well understood for what they were, and, according to Henry C. Speir, who owned Mississippi record stores in the '20s and '30s, 90 percent of these recordings were bought by women. Perhaps the single or double entendres were just more acceptable when sung by women for women. Black women who held down a regular job and earned a weekly wage cooking or cleaning for white people would completely get a song like "My Handy Man" and its lexicon of sexual euphemisms involving greasing *her* griddle, whipping *her* cream, or trimming *her* front lawn.

• • • • • •

The blues recordings of the 1920s and '30s also have a definite North-versus-South, urban-versus-rural divide. More musically sophisticated blues came out of Chicago, while the deep South produced more personal, raw, pained expressions of the hand-to-mouth life experienced by many Black rural communities. While city blues utilized more complex arrangements and ensemble playing, the Southern blues sound was typically one person accompanying themselves on guitar. And very often that one person played a guitar that modern audiences recognize less from the South of the 1930s and more from the United Kingdom and the United States of the mid-1980s. The cover art of Dire Straits's multimillion-selling album *Brothers in Arms* centers on a photograph of Mark Knopfler's 1937 Style O, fourteen-fret National resonator guitar.

Martin, Gibson, and Oscar Schmidt, the makers of numerous guitar brands but especially Stella-branded budget instruments, all produced traditionally built, wood-bodied guitars. But some blues players in the 1930s were playing a revolutionary style of guitar made with a metal body—a guitar not only louder than anything heard before but with a sound, according to its inventor, that "flowed like a river." Working in Mississippi in the '20s and '30s was the Jackson-based record company scout Henry Speir, the man who discovered, auditioned, and first recorded Charley Patton, Son House, Skip James, *and* Robert Johnson. Speir told blues researcher Gayle Dean Wardlaw in the 1960s that while most bluesmen "played the old, cheap Stella guitars," he had also stocked in his store "the big jumbo metal-bodied guitars that he sold for $32.50." The price suggests that these would have been National duolians, the cheapest of their guitars, which featured a frosted matte "duco" spray-paint finish. According to the National catalog, duolians were "priced so anyone can afford to own one." Despite the claim, very few local bluesmen in Jackson, Mississippi, could have afforded such an expensive guitar. But players who had recorded a few sides would have been impressed with the look and sound of these metal-bodied National guitars, which were invented and first produced in 1926. Tampa Red and Son House (the slide guitar player whom Muddy Waters had heard "all over the Delta") achieved much of their plaintive, whiny sound playing slide or bottleneck on National resonator guitars.

Both the metal body and the unique resonator technology inside the Nationals were developed by the DOpyera BROthers, who used a derivation of their family name and kinship when they later formed the Dobro company. Immigrants from Slovakia who on arrival in America first set up a cabinetmaking business in California, the Dopyera family were drawn there by the mass rebuilding following the 1906 San Francisco earthquake. The two brothers, John and Rudy, were keen amateur musicians and even keener inventors, regularly registering various patents. Alongside cabinetmaking, they also repaired musical instruments and in the early 1920s started manufacturing "National" tenor banjos utilizing some of their patented ideas. In the late '20s, they met George Beauchamp, a vaudeville singer and Hawaiian steel guitar player looking for someone to make him a much louder guitar, one that could compete with the brass and woodwind instruments of the vaudeville orchestra. The Dopyeras initially built an instrument based on Beauchamp's own ideas for a wood-bodied guitar mounted on a stand and equipped with a gramophone-style brass horn that amplified the soundbox. Beauchamp apparently did use the ungainly setup in his act, but the Dopyeras knew it wasn't the solution. After experimenting with some ideas initially developed for their metal-bodied banjos, they built a prototype instrument using three super-thin aluminum cones resonating inside a metal, guitar-shaped body. Each metal cone vibrated like the paper cones in a modern loudspeaker.

From the outset, their "tri-cone reso-phonic guitar" created a sound that was both loud and liquid, especially when played with a metal slide. Its keening sound sat somewhere between the sonic brilliance of a banjo and the full-bodied midrange of a guitar. John Dopyera patented the design, and the brothers started producing guitars by hand under the National brand in 1926.

In 1928, the two brothers—now joined by their flamboyant ex-client, the vaudevillian Beauchamp, sitting rather uneasily as their business partner—assembled backers, set up the National String Instrument Company, and began full-scale production. National tricone models were available as Spanish-style guitars with standard, rounded necks and were played like the traditional guitars favored by blues players, but the majority were built for playing flat on the lap, Hawaiian steel–style. The "steel" in the name refers both to steel rather than gut strings as well as the steel knife or bar that was used to stop or "fret" the strings. The craze for Hawaiian music had continued unabated since 1916, and many of the top Hawaiian musicians now based in California were close to the Dopyeras' original workshop in Los Angeles. National guitars were adopted by many of these Hawaiian guitarists, including the most famous of them at the time, Sol Hoopii. Aside from being the most influential of the Hawaiians, Hoopii, whose style blended jazz and blues, influenced both country music as well as western swing dance music. Jazz and white hillbilly performers from Duke Ellington to Jimmie Rodgers were soon adding the unique sound of Hawaiian steel to their recordings.

When blues guitarists on the other side of the country heard about the power and tone of these new superloud guitars, those with the funds were soon making recordings using National tricones. Slide guitar master Tampa Red used the smooth-sounding National Style 4, with its rich sustain, for instrumentals like "Denver Blues." Blues player Johnny Temple, who lived in Jackson, remembers Memphis Minnie and her husband and singing partner Kansas Joe McCoy returning from a recording date in Chicago in 1929 with a pair of brand-new Style 1 tricones in the back seat of their equally brand-new car. These early, entry-level Spanish-style instruments with their silver-nickel finish, designed for picking rather than lap-steel, cost $250 for the pair and were the first metal-bodied guitars ever seen in Jackson. The fact that they looked amazing was no doubt a bonus for working musicians like Memphis Minnie and Kansas Joe. Also looking to stand out was Tampa Red, who used the soubriquet "the Man with the Golden Guitar" after National allegedly made him a "gold-plated" special.

But by the late 1930s, the arrival of a viable electric guitar quickly led to a decline in sales of the expensive steel-bodied Nationals. Sol Hoopii deserted his National tricone and switched to an electric Rickenbacker lap-steel. The electric guitar and valve electronics would give professional musicians a guitar with a balanced tone and amazing sustain that was even louder than the heavy-to-handle National. It was therefore no wonder that National and the Dopyeras' later Dobro resonators gradually lost out to the rise of the electric guitar.

But as leading players switched to electric, their discarded Nationals made their way into the hands of local blues players. Soon many street and touring musicians were able to afford this now-cheaper, secondhand precursor of the electrically amplified guitar; compared to Stellas and Gibson Kalamazoos, they were both loud and extremely durable, essential qualities for a hard-playing touring musician in what was for many still a largely unamplified world. Son House, whose first recordings in 1930 didn't earn him national success, was another locally popular musician who had a second career following his rediscovery in the 1960s folk music revival. On virtually all his recordings, Son House played stinging slide guitar in Spanish tuning on a National—a Style O, duolian, or triolian. The singlecone Style O instruments, with their sharper, attacking tone, worked perfectly alongside the ex-preacher's sparse bass slaps and gravel voice. His emotional intensity is staggering as his guitar slips, slides, and growls around tunes like "Death Letter Blues."

National's success was fated to be short-lived given that the company started production at about the same time that numerous inventors and guitar makers were trying various electro-mechanical ways of amplifying the guitar. However, it is George Beauchamp, the vaudevillian and catalyst behind metal-bodied National resophonic guitars, who can rightfully lay claim to being the father of the electric guitar. Ironically, having inspired the invention of the resonator, he was the architect of its near-demise.

In the late 1920s, guitar companies like Vega and Stromberg-Voisinet experimented with transducer pickups, amplifying the soundbox of the instrument, often by utilizing components from early telephone mouthpieces. Beauchamp uniquely focused on something that amplified the individual strings, what he called a "string driven magnetic pickup." He set up Ro-Pat-In (ElectRO-PATent-INstruments) with an engineer, Adolph Rickenbacker, and after some early prototypes using a frying pan shape made of wood and cast aluminum, they mounted a coil pickup onto a wooden, Spanish-style body.

Their first production model, from the company that eventually became Rickenbacker Guitars, was sold in 1932 to Gage Brewer, a Wichita bandleader and guitarist. Brewer advertised his new electric guitar sound as "a combination of natural personal technique and electrical perfection" and announced that he would be using it at an upcoming Halloween dance. The instrument used a fourteen-fret neck and Beauchamp's new pickup fitted to an existing tenor guitar body. There are no reviews of the evening, so we have no way of knowing how it went down with the audience. But regardless of how it sounded that night, the electric guitar as we understand it today had been invented and premiered, although for most players it was still somewhat of a novelty. Its time would come in the next decade, when the instrument would become an integral part of electric blues and country music. In the 1930s, the Ro-Pat-In frying pan–shaped Electro was a lap-steel guitar suited to the still popular Hawaiian steel sound. Although the first electric guitar was premiered on the radio by another inventor-guitarist, Alvino Rey, the first electric guitar recordings were made in 1933 by Joseph Lopes with Noi Lane's Hawaiian Orchestra. The sound of steel amplified by electricity was quickly picked up by western swing bands, not least "the King of Swing"—the wise-cracking ex-blackface fiddling minstrel and medicine show performer Bob Wills. Wills recruited the steel guitar of Leon McAuliffe into his band, the Texas Playboys, in 1935. Their early recordings in 1938 included "Ida Red," the musical inspiration for Chuck Berry's "Maybellene" (1955). But when Wills added a hiccupping, double-stopped steel guitar to their later recording, "Ida Red Likes the Boogie" (1949), you get the prototype for Berry's signature guitar sound. Beauchamp's invention had let the electric genie out of the bottle. But back in the '30s, the blues music that was being recorded and sold across the rural South was still acoustic.

• • • • • •

Record company producers and early A&R agents from New York and Chicago had been active since the '20s "discovering" rural players until major companies like Columbia, Victor, and OKeh began using local scouts. These were often record retailers who owned and ran furniture stores in Mississippi where the early phonographs and the records they played were stocked. Men like Frank Limbo in the town of Itta Bena and Henry Speir in Jackson began scouting for talent. Speir reckoned that on "good spring and summer days" in the '20s he would sell between three and six hundred records at 75 cents a disc, all pretty much exclusively to local Black people.

In an age before "sale or return" (i.e., unsold stock returned to the company), retailer-scouts had to know what sold and which players were up-and-coming or had fallen out of fashion, so naturally they were tuned in to distinctive local styles. While many songs may have been categorized on the record label simply as "vocal blues with guitar accompaniment," the scouts were mindful of the different styles that sold in their areas. The often mournful, percussive Delta blues style was distinct from the bouncy, "ragged time" and syncopated East Coast "Piedmont picking" of Blind Blake and Blind Boy Fuller, often a more cosmopolitan sound. The more improvisational and strident "Memphis" picking of Furry Lewis is as distinct from the talking Texan slide played by Blind Willie Johnson as it is from the vocally driven Chicago hokum of Big Bill Broonzy and Tampa Red.

The Delta blues players knew that the scouts were men with musical knowledge, discerning ears, and, most importantly, connections with record companies. Because Henry Speir had already "discovered" Delta players like Son House, Skip James, and the Mississippi Sheiks in the 1920s, he was the first person Robert Johnson sought out when he was ready to record in 1936.

Once this essentially local music had been captured in the studio, released on record, and broadcast on radio, cross-synthesis of the various regional styles was inevitable. Throughout the 1930s, blues, jazz, gospel, ragtime, and hillbilly fiddle tunes intermingled in many singers' repertoires, resulting in musically diverse players recording the same songs. Both the Black blues player Blind Blake and the white hillbilly singer Jimmie Rodgers released versions of "In the Jailhouse Now" (its composition often, but incorrectly, credited to Jimmie Rodgers rather than to Blake). And while jazz became a style regularly played by white and Black musicians, the early blues will always be associated with Black players, as rural old-time or hillbilly music will rightly be seen as something akin to white man's blues.

• • • • • •

But everything was unsettled and changed by the Great Depression. The once-booming radio and record industries were equally affected by the fallout from the Wall Street crash of 1929. Record companies were doubly hit: many people were no longer able to afford even 75 cents to buy a record, and the increasing reach of radio broadcasts (at least for those who could afford a radio) entertained listeners for free. With the greater broadcast range of powerful radio stations, the weaker, less financially secure ones were literally overwhelmed by their more powerful neighbors.

The guitar industry, which had weathered declining sales by making mandolins and ukuleles during their respective booms in popularity, went into downturn mode. Many instrument companies, including Lyon & Healy, were wiped out by the financial crash, and those that survived did so only by quickly introducing cheaper, stripped-down models or by switching production to other products. Gibson made, among other items, wooden children's toys. Martin had experimented making wooden jewelry to keep going, but what in fact saved them was their ability to quickly simplify the complexity of design and manufacture and level of decoration on their guitars, thereby reducing prices. The decline in popularity of the banjo, superseded by the more musically versatile guitar, also played its part. In the late '20s, Martin had started producing four-string tenor guitars, effectively a banjo neck on a smaller guitar body. With a similar tuning to the tenor banjo, the transition for banjo players was easy. Martin's production of tenor guitars and small-bodied, minimally decorated guitars increased during the Depression: at one point both became their bestselling instruments. But the record, radio, and guitar industries had another competitor calling on their customers' limited budgets.

• • • • • •

As often happens in hard times, people looked to the entertainment industry to take their cares away, if only for a brief couple of hours. By the time the Depression hit, the burgeoning cinema industry had progressed from silent films to "talkies." But the cinema's natural, working-class audience was living through tough times, and attendance and revenues were down. By the peak of the Depression in 1933, ticket sales were half what they had been in 1928, even though cinemas had drastically dropped admission prices. Many movie houses had closed as theater chains rationalized and tried to recoup the heavy investment in equipment required to screen talking movies.

What audiences were watching during the Depression era were often pure escapist pictures, but there was also a strong audience for films rooted in social realism. *I Am a Fugitive from a Chain Gang* and similar titles were based on some of the despairing headlines of the day, while ostensibly humorous films like the Marx Brothers' *Duck Soup*, Mae West's *Goin' to Town*, and any number of W. C. Fields's shorts often took a comedic poke at lax government, self-serving public institutions, and contradictory moral codes.

The election of Franklin Roosevelt in 1932 and the New Deal programs he enacted from 1933 to 1938 brought about a renewed optimism; films were produced that presented Americans as "breezy, likeable, sexy, gallant." These traits were evident in the emerging, escapist "Westerns with music" that featured heroes who were handsome and wholesome, kind to children, and romantic with the ladies. And none more so than Gene Autry, the archetypal singing cowboy.

After an unsuccessful attempt in 1928 to break into New York radio as a hillbilly singer, Autry sharpened his act and, like future country music stars Hank Snow and Ernest Tubb, relaunched himself as a Jimmie Rodgers imitator, even borrowing Rodgers's early cowboy look. If you listen to Autry's first recordings between 1929 and 1931, it's often impossible to tell the difference between Autry and his idol. Performing as "Oklahoma's Yodeling Cowboy," he joined *National Barn Dance*, a highly popular syndicated radio show. After cowriting and releasing the somewhat syrupy "That Silver Haired Daddy of Mine" (1931), Autry became the hottest star in a radio show that focused on white rural music.

He did so by slightly modernizing what Jimmie Rodgers had pioneered just a few years earlier. A couple of lucky bounces, in the shape of performances in front of influential agents alongside the right business connections, presented him with a short hop to Hollywood and global fame.

There had been singing cowboys accompanying themselves on guitars in the movies before Autry, but they often played just one song loosely related to the plotline. These brief musical interludes were played around the campfire or under the lady's bedroom window before our hero returned to righting a wrong, chasing bad guys, or rescuing a child from a mineshaft, disused well, or burning homestead. Hollywood found in Autry a tall, handsome, clean-cut, competent actor who could sing well and play guitar in the emerging movie-cowboy style. The movie *Tumbling Tumbleweeds* and the song from which it took its name were both big hits, as was the rereleased "That Silver Haired Daddy of Mine," selling a further five million copies. Autry's blend of Jimmie Rodgers–style yodeling with his down-home, steady voice effectively invented easy listening country-pop. His appeal and success as a singing cowboy film star proved to be hugely important to both the guitar and country music industries, not only by giving the guitar visibility but also because Autry was one of the first professional guitarists with an obsession for acquiring high-end acoustic guitars.

And acquire he did. Even when he was fresh into his first job as a telegraph operator, he bought two Martin Style 42 guitars, expensive instruments at a time when the company was mainly selling plain, low-end models. As soon as he was making real money in the early 1930s, he continued acquiring the best flat-top acoustic guitars that Martin, Gibson, and even the small Larson company had to offer, sometimes returning standard models that he owned for the companies to fancy up by adding pearl inlay. In 1933, and exactly like his idol Jimmie Rodgers, he approached Martin to make him a custom guitar. He wanted the fanciest, largest, and most expensive guitar they made, and, like Rodgers, he wanted his name inlaid in pearl script along the length of the neck. Maybe it was fate that in the company's one-hundredth year, one of the most famous artists of the period had ordered a bedazzled version of the recently introduced Martin Dreadnought.

In 1933, a Dreadnought with Style 45 appointments was a custom order. Autry's new guitar, with pearl ornamentation on all edges, a slotted headstock, and twelve frets clear of the body, was the first D-45. Because Autry, like many other professional players, used a plectrum to give increased volume, his guitar also came with a faux-tortoiseshell pickguard to protect the wooden top from being scratched.

Autry appeared onstage and in many of his ninety-three cowboy movies playing his fancy Martin D-45, resulting in other singing cowboys copying his style. Many of these artists were looking to stand out, so fancy guitars and full Western stage clothes soon became the custom for most cowboy singers, whether singing ballads or playing western swing with a cowboy group in Texan dancehalls. Autry had in the space of just a few years migrated from being a regionally popular singing cowboy to a globally recognized film star. His popularity and status also brought prominence and glamour to the music he played; only a few years after his rise, *Billboard* magazine stopped using the term "hillbilly" to classify white rural music and started using the more dignified classification "country and western."

Although the fanciest flat-top guitar from what had been the most expensive guitar maker in America was priced at $200, it was still cheaper than Maybelle Carter's Gibson L-5 archtop. This price disparity was partly because archtops used more materials, often took longer to produce, and generally required different craftsmen than flat-tops. But most probably the price difference was because Gibson felt they could command that price from their professional customers. Cheaper flat-top guitars were associated with Black blues players and hillbilly musicians, who were reckoned to have limited means that wouldn't stretch to an expensive archtop even if they wanted one. The archtop guitars that Martin and Gibson were making were aimed at white professionals playing in hotel jazz and dance bands, far more lucrative gigs than those of poor rural musicians playing in church halls or bars. However, professional musicians generally only provided a showcase for makers like Martin and Gibson. Most instrument companies knew they would fail if they relied solely on selling to professionals—then as now, it is the lucrative and higher-volume amateur and enthusiast market that keeps their businesses going.

Across the '20s and '30s, jazz orchestras and dance bands had become popular in upscale hotels and city dancehalls and were therefore broadcast on the radio. Most of these orchestras and bands had a tenor banjo, played with a plectrum, as a key rhythm instrument; its sharp, loud tone cut through the brass and woodwind sections. However, by the late 1920s, bands were adopting a smoother, silkier sound that was a long way from the harsher, syncopated Dixieland music that had brought the banjo into jazz bands only ten years earlier. Banjo players were being asked by their band leaders to double-up on banjo- and guitar-playing duties. While four-string tenor guitars had gone some way to help tenor banjo players make the transition, they still lacked the silky, smooth sound that bands were aiming for, the precursor of swing dance music. Banjo players knew that they had to make the leap to six strings and the mellow, woody sound they offered.

The transition wasn't just a case of learning the notation of what was effectively a completely new instrument; the physical transition wasn't easy either. In modern terms, it's the equivalent of a contemporary rock guitarist trying to move from a Fender Telecaster (with a slim, "fast" neck and a curved radius on the fingerboard) to a classical guitar (with a much wider, fatter neck and a flat fretboard). They may both be guitars, but they are a world apart in playing style and technique. Although it meant learning a new tuning and chord shapes different from the banjo, professional players were soon asking for guitars that were really fit for their purpose.

Perry Bechtel was an accomplished and highly influential tenor banjo *and* guitar player from Atlanta who promoted himself as "the Man with Ten Thousand Fingers." Bechtel wrote a letter to Martin asking them to design a guitar tailored to his singular style and playing needs. He added a heavy hint for a hefty discount, suggesting it would be "something he could recommend to his *many* musician friends." C. F. Martin III took the bait, but what began as a custom order turned into a testy collaboration. The demanding Bechtel's desire for Martin to make a flat-top guitar that suited a plectrum-banjo player eventually resulted in a guitar that became known as the OM (or Orchestra Model, to signal its intended users). In the end, it was not a completely new model but an adaptation of a standard Martin 000-28 with a neck that was narrower and longer than usual. "Longer" allowed players to reach notes higher up the fretboard, and "narrower" (with strings closer together) allowed faster picking with a plectrum.

The OM-28 that Bechtel received in September 1929 influenced guitar design well beyond the jazz age. Longer, narrower necks—with fourteen frets clear of a shorter body, solid peg-heads, and teardrop pickguards—became the norm at Martin and were quickly adopted by many other flat-top guitar makers. Bechtel's original guitar used banjo-style tuning pegs on a solid peg-head to tune the steel strings. A feature familiar to a plectrum banjo player, the pegheads were primarily fitted as an easy, expedient, off-the-shelf solution. Banjo pegs were soon replaced by the more familiar, but strengthened, right-angle tuning machines used today. The transition to steel-string guitars was complete, and to this day Martin only produces a few nylon-string classical guitars. The future direction of the flat-top guitar was heavily influenced by a man better known as a banjo player than a guitarist.

Martin probably hoped the OM would attract more professional East Coast dance band musicians like Bechtel. But the design never really caught on with jazz and orchestral players, who preferred the sound and tone of the archtop guitars with f-holes pioneered by Gibson. But the easy-playing OM flat-tops did achieve some success with players of other musical styles of the time. Roy Rogers, the other big-name singing cowboy film star, bought a secondhand OM-45 Deluxe from a pawnshop. Rogers and other Western cowboy bands, who were now invariably playing with plectrums to improve volume, adopted the guitar, which stimulated amateur plectrum players to buy as well. The unique features of the OM and other subsequent modifications to fret type and scale length were quickly incorporated into Martin's 000 model, and the OM name disappeared from the Martin catalogue in 1934.

Despite this premature withdrawal of the OM designation, the model is again today a massively popular guitar for Martin and many other makers. In the contrary world of guitar styling, OMs are now regarded as the perfect guitar for finger-style picking and are played by guitarists who wouldn't dream of picking up a plectrum.

Martin in the 1930s had, in the OM and the Dreadnought, launched two groundbreaking guitars to once again dominate the flat-top market, although Gibson continued to dominate as the premier archtop guitar maker throughout the Depression. As Maybelle Carter used her Gibson to pick out her signature melodies, the jazz player Eddie Lang used his to create the modern jazz-band guitar sound: chord melodies interplayed with smooth, single-string melody runs. The sound is bright and lively when played with a plectrum but smooth and mellow when played with bare fingers.

Lang's jazz style always had a distinct, reedy, acoustic blues feel to it, possibly an overlap from the years when he recorded under the pseudonym Blind Willie Dunn with blues guitarist Lonnie Johnson. The L-5, launched in 1923, was way ahead of its time, appearing a decade before big-band jazz and the need for a loud, percussive guitar had really emerged. As the big-band sound took off, Gibson, still mindful of the Depression, introduced cheaper variants of the expensive ($275) L-5. This was in part to compete with the Epiphone Company, which, in an attempt to steal Gibson's crown, introduced in 1931 a full range of archtops, each marginally cheaper but slightly bigger than the comparable Gibson model. Gibson responded in the battle for volume, tone, and dominance with the eighteen-inch-wide Super 400. Taking a leaf out of Martin's original price-based naming policy, the Super 400, complete with a genuine leather case, cost an eye-watering $400.

Epiphone (today a budget brand owned by Gibson offering affordable versions of the Gibson range produced in the Far East) was, in the '30s, an independent company and a force to be reckoned with. Initially primarily a banjo company, Epiphone had correctly forecast the end of mass popularity for the banjo and switched to producing guitars. The business was started by the Stathopoulos family, immigrants who escaped oppression in the Ottoman Empire. The eldest son, "Epi," renamed the company and led its expansion into archtop guitars. Epi also had a flare for marketing, naming his biggest and most luxurious guitars with big, luxurious names: De Luxe, Broadway, and the biggest, at eighteen-and-a-half inches wide, the Emperor. The advertisements it ran for these new, wider-bodied models demonstrated how big they were by showing how much of a naked woman's body one of their new guitars covered . . . the answer was just enough!

Perhaps because its ornate design was so over the top, the Gibson Super 400 attracted not only jazz players but also country and western artists looking for a guitar that made them stand out onstage. Gibson took encouragement from the styling and size of the Super 400 to really expand the look into the flat-top market. The company saw the free publicity and subsequent success that Gene Autry's custom-ordered D-45 had brought Martin; in a game of "my hat's bigger than yours," they furnished Ray Whitley, another singing cowboy from the movies, with his own custom guitar. This one-off guitar was soon launched to the public as the Gibson Super Jumbo (or SJ). Significantly bigger than the dreadnought, and showcasing many visual cues from the lavishly decorated advanced model L-5 archtop, it was the same price as the D-45 at $200. If the D-45 was glitzy in an understated Martin way, the SJ, eventually to be the J-200, was big and blousy—the visual blueprint for Gibson flat-tops of the future. If you examine Martin and Gibson flat-tops built today, you can see that their general look and feel were pretty much laid down at this point in the 1930s—influenced variously by the banjo, orchestra, jazz, and cowboy swing bands.

Woody Guthrie playing a 1940s Gibson L-00.

8

The Most Popular Fretted Instrument

By 1940, hillbilly string bands were playing what was known as "old-time music." Usually consisting of guitar, fiddle, five-string banjo, and mandolin, many string bands had started to brush up their technique and repertoire to advance into the more commercial country and western market. The Sons of the Pioneers, with Roy Rogers on guitar, had made the crossover from radio to early cowboy movies to become one of America's most popular singing groups.

Their success with original songs like "Tumbling Tumbleweeds" (written by band member Bob Nolan) inspired many country artists to dress up as cowboys, but the addition of "western" to country music was not just about Western-style stage outfits or singing cowboys in the movies. It referred mainly to western swing: up-tempo dance music popular in the Southwestern states since the early '30s and played by slick strings bands usually augmented with percussion, piano, and lap-steel guitar. The music had diverse musical roots, including blues, gospel, and even Dixieland jazz, but popular bands like Milton Brown and His Musical Brownies catered to young dancers and were influenced by dance-band hot jazz. Movie cowboys did have an important part to play in country and western's popularity, but only as the Hollywood invention of the singing cowboy continued to grow in prominence and appeal.

Another variation of up-tempo country music, honky-tonk, arrived on the scene in the early 1940s via Ernest Tubb, whose take on country music also featured the electric lap-steel guitar. Tubb, like many country musicians, learned his stagecraft in the rough, noisy "honkatonk" bars of Texas, Tennessee, and Oklahoma. Centered on the two-step, a dance rhythm with a characteristically sharp backbeat, Tubb accompanied his Jimmie Rodgers–inspired nasal singing style with an acoustic guitar. But when he came to record what was to be his first hit record, "Walking the Floor Over You," his producer recalled a conversation with a record company salesman: "Bar owners are asking all the time for records that can cut through the noise of a rowdy, crowded bar."

Record company salesmen—who monitored song popularity by reading the counters in the Wurlitzer jukeboxes installed in bars and diners—were worth listening to. In the early '40s, 250,000 nickel-in-the-slot machines operated across the United States, each holding twenty 78 rpm shellac discs (the vinyl 45 rpm single didn't arrive until 1950), and each helped promote and generate the sale of 13 million records a year. The sonic "cut-through" bar owners were requesting came courtesy of the electric steel guitar featured on many western swing discs.

Only a year before Tubb's recording session, an article on the future of the guitar in *Downbeat*, an industry magazine popular with professional musicians, ran the headline: "Guitar Men—Wake Up and Pluck! Wire for sound; Let 'em Hear You Play." It clinched the deal. Tubb's producer, Dave Kapp, teamed him with Fay "Smitty" Smith, a radio station session guitarist with an electric steel guitar that he played in western swing dance bands. Country music's first electric steel guitar was added to Tubb's acoustic string band, and when Tubb and his Texas Troubadours played the *Grand Ole Opry*, the audience shouted for more. Driven by the needs of the record industry and its record buyers, country music got slicker, louder, and much more commercial, echoing the mood of a bigger, brassier, more self-confident post-Depression America.

During the '40s country music also got much more formulaic, as tends to happen when professional performers, looking for success and a regular living wage, develop their own version of what was selling and playing on the radio. But there were still artists trying to keep country music "authentic," by which they meant "acoustic." The Monroe brothers, the youngest brother Bill on mandolin and Charlie on guitar, started out as a harmony duo. In 1938, after four years together, Bill renamed the band Bill Monroe and the Blue Grass Boys, thus signifying who was in charge as well as referencing the silvery-blue flowers on the meadow grass pastures near the Monroe home in Rosine, Kentucky. The music they were playing in the early '40s was as progressive as acoustic music got at the time, and their style was on its way to becoming what we would recognize today as bluegrass. With clear roots in traditional Appalachian old-time mountain music and crossbred with some blues sounds that had floated up the Mississippi, the music also offered a rhythmic nod to the then-popular European polka. Some early recordings even included an accordion. But its truly unique ingredients were a combination of high-energy acoustic playing under two-, three-, and four-part vocal harmonies and a real sense of swing. As Bill leans into the microphone to sing "Rocky Road Blues," you can hear the embryonic sounds of rockabilly and Bill Haley's "Rock Around the Clock," recorded nine years later.

The Monroe band's sound further evolved in 1944 after Lester Flatt joined the group. Flatt was a lead singer with a sedate lyrical style who also played traditional, old-time rhythm guitar. When twenty-one-year-old Earl Scruggs was recruited in 1945, everything stepped up a notch. Scruggs brought a new, high-impact style of banjo playing using three picking fingers. It was fast, lyrical, and highly syncopated, and it complemented Flatt's rhythm guitar with his signature thumb-picked "Flatt" bass runs. They both played in the relatively simple style of Maybelle Carter, except they played a whole lot faster, producing what Alan Lomax called "folk music in overdrive." Together they created what Flatt described as a whole new realm. He recalled: "When we got Earl, it was really the first time a sound like that had been heard. . . . There may have been a similar sound, but we then had what was to become known as bluegrass music."

They had created the defining blend of banjo *plus* guitar, a style that we recognize from "Dueling Banjos" from the Southern backwoods movie *Deliverance* as well as the upbeat musical soundtrack scoring *Bonnie and Clyde* and *The Beverly Hillbillies*. Bluegrass was different from everything before it, as new and as radical as acoustic string-band playing had ever been.

Despite carrying Flatt's name, the bluegrass G-scale bass run—the signature bass riff at the heart of much bluegrass and country music—was almost certainly the invention of Bill Monroe's brother Charlie rather than Flatt. And this signature sound led one model of Martin to become *the* guitar for bluegrass pickers, primarily because it had both increased volume and strong bass tones that could compete with the other instruments in the band. Bill Monroe had bought a Martin Herringbone D-28 in 1939 and played it on "Muleskinner Blues" during his *Grand Ole Opry* debut later that year. So influential was the Monroe band that the rosewood-bodied Martins he recommended to the many guitarists who served their musical apprenticeships with him became the authoritative guitar sound of bluegrass players. To this day, the D-28 (and its many copies, whether cheap factory knockoffs from the Far East or deluxe American handcrafted tributes) is still the preferred picking guitar—and the ultimate instrument for many flat-top enthusiasts.

Although the first early 1930s Dreadnoughts, the predecessors of Monroe's D-28, were not initially a financial success for Martin, the design evolved into just what Martin and professional musicians needed. Guitarists in multi-instrument bands craved a guitar with a deep-toned bass and the volume to compete, but they also wanted a "modern" instrument, which meant a narrower, fourteen-fret neck. In 1934, to get the extra neck length, Martin shortened the body and squared off the upper bout, thereby creating the modern dreadnought shape.

Beyond this new shape, Monroe's D-28 had two further essential modifications that gave it the smooth bass and increased volume that band players wanted: an Adirondack spruce top and forward-shifted scalloped braces. Although in fact Martin had moved the sound hole back toward the braces from the very beginning, by lessening the top braces' mass (by scalloping, or scooping out, wood), the top vibrated more freely. It seems only a minor change, but it was highly effective in improving the overall tone and volume of the instrument. But by the late 1940s, many guitarists either were putting heavier gauge (i.e., thicker) strings on their instruments or were tuning the guitar up to an A scale to further increase the volume. However, the increased tension risked pulling the bridge off, and fearing an avalanche of warranty claims, Martin discontinued scalloped braces. Nobody much talked about it, and even if people did notice the change in tone, they carried on buying regardless. Ironically, the thing people did notice—that the original herringbone border decoration was missing—had no effect on sound as long as it was executed delicately, as it was on Martin designed and built guitars.

The herringbone on the D-28, while part of its signature look, also helps identify prewar, so-called golden era instruments. The delicate herringbone-

Herringbone binding detail on a Collings guitar. (Courtesy of Joe Bastura with Collings Guitars)

pattern inlay around the outside top of the guitar is a fancy marquetry strip inserted between the hard, protective ivoroid (celluloid plastic) binding and the soft spruce top of the guitar. The decorative strip, called "purfling," was premade by specialist producers, and in the early 1940s Martin still imported all their herringbone strips from makers in Germany. All went well until World War II, when supplies from Germany understandably dried up. Herringbone D-28s were still being produced from existing stocks of purfling until 1947 when, unable to get an American manufacturer to stray from munitions duties, Martin changed its purfling to simple, tasteful, alternating black-and-white stripes, echoing a similar pattern that used stained pear wood and pale poplar first used by the Amati family of violin makers in 1564.

Martin kept making D-28s after the war, and people kept buying them—but gradually players started to notice that the new ones didn't just lack the herringbone; they didn't sound nearly as good as the old ones. Bluegrass players like Monroe were the first group to start actively seeking out prewar D-28s, but folk players and other discerning acoustic musicians also caught on. By the 1970s, all prewar D-28 prices had increased; the bluegrassers were followed by bands like Crosby, Stills, Nash & Young performing with the instruments onstage. Prices for a prewar D-45 peaked at around $8,000 by the mid-seventies, after which the market stagnated. But it recovered in the mid-eighties, when baby-boomer investors were paying even bigger premiums for prewar, golden era Herringbone D-28s. Prices started to escalate, which moved the instruments out of the reach of most bluegrass players.

Part of the appeal for many collectors of the prewar D-28s are the myriad myths surrounding precisely what part of the aural jigsaw makes these the best-sounding Martins. And like so many things in the world of vintage guitars, many *are* just myths, with little or no foundation in fact.

For the casual enthusiast, there was a sense that *any* old guitar sounded better because it was old. But most collectors knew that the superior tone was down to more than just the age of the guitar; they knew that the structural differences between certain golden era guitars and most postwar guitars played a role. There has always been a search for a magical ingredient: Could it be the composition of prewar lacquer? Or the hot-hide glue used at the time? Or a special batch of Brazilian rosewood Martin had in stock in that era? There was even daft talk that the density of the herringbone purfling made a difference, or that very cold winters in Nazareth during the 1930s and '40s affected the stiffness of the spruce used to make tops.

The reality is that every part of the guitar and its construction can make a sonic difference—glue, neck material, thickness of the top, type of spruce, and so on—but the consensus among experts like George Gruhn is that it's primarily the combination of Adirondack spruce and the forward-shifted scalloped braces that gives the prewar instruments superior sound quality. These two elements in the hands of skilled makers are pivotal.

The role of craftspeople leads to the rather maudlin suggestion that postwar Martins were lesser guitars because many skilled crafts*men* failed to return from the war in Europe and the Pacific. While the exact numbers of Martin employees who went to war and failed to return aren't known, we do know that there was natural attrition in the Martin workforce as older skilled workers were retiring or dying off. Some stories have circulated that production at both Gibson and Martin was taken over by women when the men went to war or left to work in armament factories. Before the war, Gibson certainly had women working in guitar finishing, quality inspection, packing, and winding guitar strings, but it seems fanciful to believe that all the males, especially experienced guitar makers, many of whom would have been over forty-four years old and therefore exempt from the draft, left the industry. There is no reason why women couldn't make guitars, but what is difficult to believe is that a group of women *or* men could be trained up so quickly to make instruments. (In the case of Gibson, what are known as Banner Era guitars, carrying a decal with the legend "Only a Gibson Is Good Enough" on the headstock, are believed to have been made primarily by a new group of female guitar makers.)

The creation of a wartime workforce of female luthiers at the Gibson factory isn't impossible, but vintage guitar enthusiasts, interested in why a particular model evolved in the sometimes poorly documented history of a maker, like finding a quirky story or individual to build a story around. One such man was undoubtedly John Deichman, one of the older, German-speaking immigrant journeymen working at Martin who was still capable of building a complete guitar from scratch. Deichman appears to have been responsible for building many important prototype models during his long career at the company. Although he is often referred to in Martin historical literature as *the* Martin shop foreman, there is no record that he ever held that post, and the Martin company had many departmental foremen rather than just one. Having joined the company in 1912, Deichman made the dreadnought prototype for Ditson back in 1916 and the first OM in 1929. Working closely with Frank Henry Martin, the last Martin family member who was a trained luthier, Deichman helped design and build many guitars before and during the war.

Older, more experienced workmen like Deichman were too old to go to war, but they do provide another theory as to why Martin prewar and wartime guitars are so good. These older craftsmen did their best work before and during the war using the best wood that Martin had in storage. By the golden era, the company had been making guitars continuously for close to a century, and across that whole period Martin always bought the best quality tonewood it could find. Martin records and correspondence often refer to trips to select and buy timber from the best sources and detail the care with which that wood was cut and stored in Nazareth. As the Great Depression and then the war reduced demand for expensive guitars, it is likely that the D-28s were built using only the best wood the company had stored away. In the hands of Martin's best journeymen builders, that wood enabled someone in a room listening to a prewar D-28 owned by guitar maker and champion picker Wayne Henderson to be lost for words . . . or at least left breathless after he had completed writing this paragraph of sonic hyperbole:

> It sounded like the gates of heaven had opened. The tone was demonstrative, but it was controlled, balanced. Its voice was stately, regal, Olivier playing King Lear. But you didn't have to be a world-class flat-picker to appreciate this magnificent instrument. I strummed a simple E chord and in an instant, I was enveloped in a blanket of harmony, each note blended yet distinct. And the wave went forever—thirty-five, forty seconds later I could still hear faint overtones dying away. Playing this guitar, or hearing it played . . . was a sensory explosion, a great Bordeaux, a stolen kiss.

But back to Bill Malone and the Blue Grass Boys. It was more a case of a goodbye kiss when Flatt with his D-28 and later Scruggs left the band. Both publicly claimed that they had no intention of making music together, that they were just exhausted from the relentless touring schedule Monroe kept them to.

Rough sleeping between the series of one-night stands—with each member of the five-piece band taking a turn driving the "Bluegrass Special," the converted station wagon the band used as a tour bus—must have been tough.

There was also resentment that Monroe kept his band on paltry wages. But whatever the reason, Flatt and Scruggs deserted the highly dictatorial Bill Monroe in 1948 to form the Foggy Mountain Boys. Still an acoustic string band essentially playing what they termed "country music" with guitar, banjo, and violin, Flatt and Scruggs would soon embrace the plaintive, slide sound of electric lap-steel guitars being used in honky-tonk and western swing. But they didn't want to "go electric." To achieve their desired sound, they added a new "old" instrument into their mix: the Dobro resonator guitar. These successors to the early National metal-bodied guitars were made by the Dopyera brothers from 1928 until the outbreak of World War II. Essentially a standard wood-bodied, flat-top acoustic with a thickened top, the Dobro could support a revolutionary "spider leg" metal resonator to mechanically sustain and amplify the sound. They were cheaper to make and lighter than the metal-bodied resonator guitars originally adopted by Delta blues players like Son House and Bukka White. But as fewer rural blues guitarists continued to play the National and Dobro into and beyond the 1940s, many instruments were relegated to attics, and the resophonic guitar that briefly bridged the gap between acoustic and electric was all but forgotten.

However, in 1949, when the Foggy Mountain Boys were looking for that something extra to make their acoustic sound richer, they revived the Dobro rather than the heavier metal-bodied National. Rather than playing sitting down in the Hawaiian lap-steel style, and given that all his fellow band members were standing, their first Dobro player, "Uncle Josh" Graves, strapped on the much lighter Dobro and turned it through 90 degrees to play it horizontally across his waist. He used a steel bar to press the strings along the fretboard, a technique still used by bluegrass resonator players today. The other guitarists in the band were now all playing Martin Dreadnought or Gibson jumbo guitars, giving themselves the best possible chance of being heard above the resophonic slide guitar, mandolin, and fiddle in the band.

Guitars were now officially bigger, to the point where even solo artists were using the wider-bodied dreadnought "bass guitar," as Martin literature at the time categorized it. From this point through to the modern day, what has been considered the "normal" shape and size of the acoustic guitar is the dreadnought or jumbo.

Much of what would become guitar-led "good-time" country and western was being played primarily in the Southwestern states, where the western swing music of Bob Wills and Tex Williams, old-time country, and the emerging subgenre of bluegrass were the popular musical genres that filled the Southern airwaves. And, thanks to the syndication of the *Grand Ole Opry* on 140 NBC affiliate radio stations, country music was becoming a national phenomenon. A full year before the attack on Pearl Harbor prompted America's entry into the war, there was no reason why good-time country and western music should reference the realities of a war that was happening thousands of miles away in Europe and still farther away in the Far East. However, in New York, there was a resurgence of political sensibility in folk music that put traditional acoustic instruments, including the guitar, center stage.

• • • • • •

Socially and politically aware urban folk music was born in the early 1900s with the labor union songs of Joe Hill and the International Workers of the World. It was given fresh impetus in 1940 with a simple introduction made at an aftershow party.

"Here. Woody Guthrie, I want you to meet Pete Seeger."

Seeger was just twenty years old and making his first concert appearance. Guthrie was twenty-seven. The introduction was made by twenty-five-year-old Alan Lomax, who was following in his father John's footsteps as a song collector and archivist for the Library of Congress. Lomax had already introduced

Seeger to his father's "discovery" Huddie "Lead Belly" Ledbetter, then an "old man" of fifty-one years, who in turn had shown Seeger how he played twelve-string guitar. Lead Belly's style often involved playing partial chords or just bass notes to provide a sparse accompaniment that didn't get in the way of the melody or mask the lyrics. Throughout his career, the words were always the main thing, especially when he was writing songs that sought to right (or just draw attention to) a wrong.

In 1937, Lead Belly had been invited to Washington by the Lomax family to record for the Library of Congress folk music archive. On the night of his arrival, having been turned away by numerous whites only hotels, he and his wife quickly discovered that Jim Crow was as present in the capital city as it was in their native Louisiana. Perhaps he was not that surprised that Washington was only "the home of the brave and the land of the free" for white people.

In "The Bourgeois Blues," Ledbetter spells out that even in the country's capital city, whites called a "coloured man a n—— just to see him bow" and charges that he doesn't "wanna be mistreated by no bourgeoise."

While things had always been tough for most Black Americans, at the turn of the decade in 1940, and despite the best efforts of Roosevelt's New Deal, unemployment and economic depression across the United States made life bleak for all the working classes. Furthermore, the years of devastating drought and dust storms across the plains of Oklahoma, Texas, Kansas, and Colorado created a natural disaster that prompted the largest migration in American history. Over three million people from the Great Plains states moved away, including thousands of farmers abandoning their barren homesteads. Many migrated West in search of work in the promised land of prosperity, California. But the state, still recovering from the Depression, did not welcome them. Local farmers were positively hostile to the migrants, while public police forces and the landowners' private police, the vigilante men, were not averse to extorting a little cash, or "dough," from them. The extortion of *do*ugh is at the center of one of Guthrie's most popular songs, "Do Re Mi." Its cautionary tale warns migrants that while California may be a garden of Eden, they better go back home to "Texas, Oklahoma, Kansas, Georgia or Tennessee" if they don't have the necessary "do re mi."

The government had been slow to fully appreciate the level of poverty and malnutrition; the migrants felt not only unwelcome but forgotten and voiceless. But through the dustbowl photographs of Dorothea Lange and the writings of John Steinbeck in novels like *The Grapes of Wrath*, the dustbowl refugees were about to find a voice from someone who looked and sounded just like them.

Woody Guthrie was a self-styled itinerant troubadour who chose to live in the style of the many Okie migrant workers displaced by the crisis. He had toured the country, allegedly riding boxcars with his guitar on a string over his shoulder, singing in migrant camps like the guitar picker in Steinbeck's *Grapes of Wrath*. In his typical "aw shucks" persona, he often referred to himself as "a little one-cylinder guitar picker," but he was a whole lot more. Throughout his travels he wrote dozens of guitar-accompanied songs describing the plight of the working class. Guthrie's most famous song, "This Land Is Your Land," is still the unofficial American anthem of the dispossessed, celebrating and affirming American freedoms and opportunities. A seemingly simple folk song saluting "a land made for everyone," it actually describes an America that, in Guthrie's eyes, was a place where only the rich and privileged were able to enjoy its bounties. Released in 1940, "This Land Is Your Land" was a bitter protest against Irving Berlin's massively popular "God Bless America," first recorded in 1938. As World War II took hold "far across the sea" in Europe, it became a patriotic anthem for peace. But Guthrie despised Berlin's song, sickened by its syrupy lyrics and unrealistic view of America. He felt that it was all right for Berlin to ask Americans to be grateful for a "land so fair" (and so it was, as long as it was viewed from the swish 5th Avenue apartment of a privileged Broadway songwriter), but Guthrie knew the view from outside the relief office was far from looking like a land "made for you and me."

Guthrie borrowed the melody for "This Land Is Your Land" from an old Carter Family song and wrote lyrics that intentionally parodied the sweeping geography of Berlin's lyrics. The song, or at least its first few verses, are well known, having been recorded by everyone from the New Christy Minstrels to Trini Lopez, and those lines are still taught in schools across America today.

But Guthrie had included a couple of left-leaning verses when he first penned it in 1940. Originally called "God Blessed America," this more pointed title questioned whether "God blessed America for me," or at least for working people like him. His original final verse, describing people "as they stood hungry" outside the relief or unemployment office, was omitted from his first recording of the song in 1944. The omission was probably because these were difficult times in America for a left-leaning activist songwriter with a family to support. The irony in Guthrie's persona as a committed and passionate champion of the beleaguered and dispossessed is that while he certainly witnessed hardship and spent time with the poor who stood in line at the relief office, he had a better start in life than Irving Berlin, whom he so despised.

In 1893, Berlin arrived pretty much penniless at Ellis Island in New York Harbor as a five-year-old with his parents and seven siblings. The Beilin family name was entered as Baline by immigration officials, and for his first years in America "Izzy Baline" worked and lived in Manhattan's Lower East Side, initially selling newspapers and later busking on street corners. Eventually, as a teenager, he got a regular job as a singing waiter in the infamous Pelham Café, the haunt of numerous uptown celebrity slummers. By the time he was plugging and finally composing songs in Tin Pan Alley, his name had been anglicized to Irving Berlin.

Guthrie, on the other hand, had been born into a prosperous upper-middle-class family whose patriarch was a local political chancer, property speculator, and sometime slumlord. After their property empire and fortune were wiped out by the crash at the end of the Oklahoma oil boom, young Guthrie found socialism and went on the road in search of a socialist utopia. Guthrie the hobo, street singer, general "hard travelin' man," and voice of a dispossessed generation of Okies was his own invention. (In a wonderful piece of irony, Guthrie's persona was what young Bob Dylan based his *own* invented persona on when he arrived in New York fresh from his equally middle-class upbringing as the son of a store owner in the upper Midwest.)

When Alan Lomax presented Woody Guthrie to Pete Seeger in that New York apartment, he not only introduced two activist folk singers and guitarists, he also introduced two sons of prosperous upper-middle-class parents. They had both known entitlement, but both chose to more readily associate themselves with the underprivileged, the labor movement, and the Communist Party of America.

Born in 1919, Seeger's father was an avant-garde composer and his mother a concert violinist. Charles Seeger came from a wealthy East Coast family, and despite his own social democratic politics, he dispatched his young son to a variety of smart boarding schools in preparation for his intended entry into Harvard as a scholarship student. The young Seeger's career trajectory took a sharp left turn when he developed an interest in the four-string tenor banjo. A subsequent trip with his father in 1936 to the Ninth Folk Song and Dance Festival in Asheville, North Carolina, hosted by the five-string banjo player Bascom Lunsford, was the young Seeger's epiphany. "I discovered there was good music in my country which I never heard on the radio. I liked the strident vocal tone of the singers, and the vigorous dancing. The words of the songs had all the meat of life in them."

Seeger and Guthrie both had a passion for social justice and shared a mission to use song to highlight continuing racial injustice and the problems of the working classes. Their firm belief that popular song could motivate both white and Black working-class people to organize, and to take a stand, continued a musical tradition adopted in the early 1900s by the Wobblies (the common name for members of the labor union the Industrial Workers of the World) and their pioneering activist protest singer Joe Hill. A mythical hero for both Guthrie and Seeger, Hill wrote numerous songs designed, as he put it, to "fan the flames of discontent." But Hill is best known through the poem celebrating his life and mourning his early death by firing squad: "I Dreamed I Saw Joe Hill Last Night," by Alfred Hayes. Set to music in 1936, it was to reappear in 1969 sung by Joan Baez at the Woodstock festival.

Together in New York in 1941, Seeger and Guthrie became close friends. They helped establish a Popular Front collective, the Almanac Singers, often singing material that could have come straight out of the Wobblies–Joe Hill songbook. Guthrie, just flesh and blood but with a mythological persona, became the iconic legend of the '40s folk revival, while Pete Seeger became folk music's most prolific and ardent popularizer. As a group player and soloist, he encouraged audience singalongs to get people to actively engage with the music. Adopting a version of call-and-response singing called lining out, Seeger taught a nation the words and tunes to "We Shall Overcome" and "If I Had a Hammer." In "Talking Union" (1947), he explained why and exactly how to set up a union.

Closely connected with the unions, the Communist Party of America, and the American Peace Committee, Guthrie, Seeger, and the Almanac Singers used song to promote an agenda that was antiwar and antiracist, that supported unions and promoted religious tolerance. When Germany invaded Soviet Russia in July 1941, they adopted a more strident antifascist stance. After writing "Talking Hitler's Head Off Blues," Woodie Guthrie, for the first time, scrawled across the face of his guitar the words "This Machine Kills Fascists," a slogan borrowed from the lathes of munitions workers. He was to write, scratch, or paint the same words across the dozens of Martins and Gibsons he owned, borrowed, and lent to aspiring songwriters across the '40s and '50s. He wasn't the first person to use the guitar as a weapon of peace, but he was certainly the most important.

Seeger, who had scrawled an alternative slogan ("This machine surrounds hate and forces it to surrender") on his banjo, was uncompromising in his stance as both pacifist and patriot. Releasing "Dear Mr. President," a talking blues that recognizes "we've got to fight," so that when the time comes, he will stop playing the banjo and swap it for something that "makes more noise."

Ever the pragmatist, Seeger recognized that "we got to lick Mr. Hitler, and until then other things will have to wait"; but in the same song he reminds FDR that while he is prepared to put his pacifist principles on hold, he won't fail the civil rights cause. His list of things that need fixing in America was long and inclusive. He tells FDR that American people want better laws, better homes, better schools, better jobs. And he wants them for everyone, not just the privileged. He wants no more Jim Crow, no more segregation through race or religion or because a worker decides to be in a union.

Seeger and the Almanac Singers (and their later, more commercial, manifestation, the Weavers) were using the stage as a soapbox and popular song as their megaphone. Their big impact on the popularity of the guitar was their intentional use of the folk instruments favored by Appalachian hillbilly string bands in the early part of the century: acoustic guitars, banjos, and fiddles, along with autoharps and dulcimers. Affecting a folksy style in manner, dress, and instrumentation, like Seeger the other members of the group were anything but simple, down-to-earth folkies. Sophisticated, highly literate, and persuasive performers, their material was pro-union, antiwar, antidraft, and often supportive of Black leaders campaigning against racial segregation in the army and the exclusion of African Americans from defense contract work. The group was commentating on a world order that, thanks to the Nazis, was rapidly changing. In a pre–Pearl Harbor America, their politics veered from isolationist to gung ho warmongering and touching every stop in between.

> *I started out to write a song to the whole population*
> *But no sooner than I got the words down,*
> *Here come a brand new situation*
> UNPUBLISHED SONG BY WOODY GUTHRIE

Despite the shift, the Almanac Singers were ultimately judged by the establishment (and Army intelligence and the FBI in particular) as seditious, and the group eventually disbanded in the early '40s, primarily to protect themselves from the beginnings of McCarthyism and the Red Scare. When the war ended in 1945, out of the embers of the old group emerged the Weavers, a more popularist quartet interested in playing more than the music of rural white Americans—their repertoire included Black blues and gospel as well as Latino and Eastern European music. During their heyday, they achieved a uniquely broad appeal, selling large numbers of records to a popular audience while still satisfying an urban, middle-class, left-leaning intelligentsia. Seeger was convinced that this pluralistic approach helped all Americans "learn about ourselves, and . . . learn about each other"; he went on to ask, "How many white people have discovered their own humanity through the singing of American Negro songs?"

The '40s had seen the Almanac Singers and the Weavers—together with Lead Belly, Guthrie, and Seeger as solo performers—establish folk music ("the music of the unlettered") as popular entertainment and make the guitar (the instrument of the untrained musician) most readily associated with the protest movement and songs calling for social change.

But 1941 was a milestone year for the guitar and acoustic guitar-based music. It was the year that the guitar finally came of age in terms of sales. From being the lesser cousin of the banjo, mandolin, and ukulele, in 1941 the guitar became the most popular fretted instrument in the United States.

• • • • • •

While this first guitar-driven folk revival achieved a level of popular appeal for a music with both Black and rural white roots, it was still only a small part of what most Americans were listening to: popular music. And at this time, popular music was still largely segregated in terms of players and audiences.

The white pop music of the '40s, with its lean toward Tin Pan Alley's "Moon, June, Spoon," consisted of big-band jazz, close harmony singing groups, and stylized crooners. The big bands were, for the most part, white musicians providing crisp, white jazz and dance music, from Glenn Miller and Tommy Dorsey to the giant of them all, Benny Goodman. Harmony groups like the Andrews Sisters and the Ames Brothers were just two of dozens of similar groups. In terms of solo singers, none was more accomplished, or more popular, than Bing Crosby, the first crooner of the microphone age. Although mainly remembered now as the pipe smoking, cardigan wearing, affable bass baritone who sang "White Christmas" and who played the straight man alongside comedian Bob Hope, Crosby's singing ability and musical credentials were impeccable.

Crosby's formative years were firmly rooted in the informal jazz of the 1910s and '20s, and his partnership with the pioneering jazz guitarist Eddie Lang in the '30s resulted in some of his best performances. Early recordings like "Some of These Days" are a masterclass in precision, pitch-perfect scat singing. But Crosby's popular singing style—soft, intimate, unhurried, and ranging from baritone to high tenor—was a product of the electronic microphone, and this was its decade. Its coincidence with the explosion of American popular song, and the Great American Songbook in particular, both shaped American music and made it a global enterprise.

In the '40s, Black artists were still performing primarily to Black audiences. Back in the Mississippi Delta, KFFA, broadcasting from the town of Helena a few miles east of Clarksdale, was the only radio station that played music exclusively by and for African Americans. *King Biscuit Time*, featuring the blues harmonica player Sonny Boy Williamson, was broadcast daily at 12:15 p.m. to coincide with the lunch breaks of African American rural workers in the Delta. The show still broadcasts its thirty-minute slot to this day and gives its name to the annual King Biscuit Blues Festival, which began in 1986. Like Clarksdale, Helena was home to many blues musicians, including Little Walter, Robert Nighthawk, and James Curtis, but, as with Clarksdale, the town is further evidence of the exodus of many African Americans from the Delta up to Northern cities. In its day, Helena became something of a regular musical stopover for musicians like guitarist B. B. King on their way to the blues clubs of Chicago.

Most white jazz players, keen on pleasing a white audience, may have been listening intently to Black jazz but usually it was done to bleach the color out of that year's jazz recipe. While Dizzy Gillespie was playing fast-tempo bebop in songs like "Salt Peanuts" and the Duke was creating a jazz standard in "Perdido," white musicians were making their versions palatable to the thousands of couples flocking to their shows to dance. Over the next decade, Black music was adopted, adapted, and incorporated into the broader white musical landscape, albeit one where more white people had now begun to listen to Black performers.

The acoustic guitar played a fundamental role in this transition and in the development of the popular music that dominated the next four decades. The primary instrument of the blues, hillbilly folk, and country and western music, it was also in the hands of many of the musicians who were sowing the seeds of rock 'n' roll.

In 1926, the Texan blues guitarist and singer Blind Lemon Jefferson released "That Black Snake Moan":

Mama, that's all right, mama that's all right for you
Mama, that's all right, mama that's all right for you
Mama that's all right, most seen all you do

By 1946, the overall theme, meter, and lyrical refrain of "Black Snake Moan" had been very slightly adapted by the Delta blues player Arthur "Big Boy" Crudup into "That's All Right" (1946). One of the first rhythm-and-blues hit records, it was covered again in 1954 (after another slight adjustment to the words to avoid copyright royalties) by Elvis Presley, giving America one of its first rock 'n' roll hits.

Billboard magazine had started publishing its Hot 100 record chart in 1940; by the end of the decade the separate race records chart was renamed, by a hip young reporter named Jerry Wexler, the Rhythm & Blues Top 10. Electric rock 'n' roll didn't formally arrive until 1951 with Ike Turner's "Rocket 88," but across the '40s, players like T-Bone Walker, Johnny Shines, John Lee Hooker, and Muddy Waters were pioneering the use of the electric guitar and in doing so creating the electric blues. Performers like Howlin' Wolf had been singing songs like "Smoke Stack Lightning" since the late '20s, but his propulsive electric version didn't appear until 1956. But while electric blues had been bubbling under the surface for quite a while, among the first electric players was Memphis Minnie (born Lizzie Douglas), whose performance at a New Year's Eve party in the early 1940s was reported by writer and poet Langston Hughes in the leading Black newspaper, the *Chicago Defender*.

> She grabs the microphone and yells, "Hey now!" Then she hits a few deep chords at random, leans forward ever so slightly on her guitar, bows her head and begins to beat out . . . a rhythm so contagious that often it makes the crowd holler out loud. . . . All these things cry through the strings on Memphis Minnie's electric guitar, amplified to machine proportions—a musical version of electric welders plus a rolling mill.

We know from that review that the diminutive Memphis Minnie was wearing high heels and a neat ball gown while standing on top of an icebox at the 230 Club in Chicago. But we *don't* know what guitar she was playing. What exactly was, in the words of Langston Hughes' "making the guitar strings so hard and loud"? By the early '40s, Minnie had moved on from the metal-bodied acoustic National tricone resonator she had played back in the '30s. But despite the electric guitar still being in its relative infancy, things were moving fast, and Minnie needed a guitar that worked for her style of playing and the raucous places she played in.

The Stromberg-Voisinet and Kay guitars using the early, crude transducer pickups were old technology by 1940. The George Beauchamp–designed Rickenbacker Electro, while capable of sounding like "an electric welders rolling mill," had a bulky pickup that meant it had to be played flat on the lap, and that wasn't Minnie's style. She needed one of the new electric Spanish guitars capable of being held and played like a regular instrument. That night in Chicago she was almost certainly playing a National New Yorker Spanish Electric, a guitar that looked like an archtop but with no f-holes in order to limit feedback. For a country-blues player who wanted her guitar loud and clear, the National was almost perfect. Almost, because what Minnie really needed for her style of playing was a solid-bodied electric guitar, but they were yet to be developed by the companies that would perfect and dominate the electric guitar over the next fifty years, Fender and Gibson.

Today the Gibson company is almost synonymous with the modern electric, but it had been slow to realize its potential. In 1935, the ever-cautious management at Gibson finally understood they could no longer ignore the market and started producing what was an unsuccessful range of Hawaiian instruments, effectively copies of Rickenbacker and National lap-steels.

They might have stopped their involvement in electric guitars right there had it not been for the insistence of mail-order giant, and Gibson's biggest customer, Montgomery Ward. Due to that client's insistence, Gibson employed an ex-radio ham to develop its own electro-magnetic pickup. The company built the plywood-bodied Montgomery Ward 1270 to test the technology and to gauge market interest. And the interest was there: over nine hundred of the plywood-bodied instruments sold in the few years after its slow launch in 1936.

Emboldened by the success of the 1270, in 1936 Gibson mounted the same bar pickup on a solid, spruce-topped archtop guitar with solid maple back and sides. The ES-150 had arrived, and it has been in continuous production, in various manifestations, by Gibson ever since. It's a guitar that deserves to be lauded as the one that really started the electric revolution. In the hands of jazz player Charlie Christian, it helped shape not only guitar jazz but the musical possibilities of the electric instrument.

With a long, slim, single-coil bar pickup that kept out of the way of the player's picking hand, it might have been a perfect guitar for a hard-working travelling musician playing a party in a sweaty club. But while its hollow body and f-holes allowed it to be played acoustically, it couldn't be played raw and loud the way Memphis Minnie wanted.

Nonetheless, Gibson sold a few hundred ES-150s almost immediately, but they didn't really catch on until the young Black jazz guitarist Charlie Christian realized the potential for the electric guitar to become a solo instrument in a jazz band. Playing a superior ES-250 with the Benny Goodman Sextet in 1941, Christian released "Solo Flight," the blueprint for the sort of single-line solo playing only trumpets and saxophones had previously been capable of. The ES had the new pickup mounted close to the neck, which gave the guitar a warmth and richness but also an ability to punch its weight when the player wanted to ramp things up.

Just a year after the release of "Solo Flight," Christian was to die of tuberculosis at age twenty-six. In his short career, he laid down a style of amplified guitar playing that was initially copied and then further developed by jazz guitarists from Wes Montgomery to Joe Pass to Barney Kessel. He also achieved something else—he was a Black musician from Oklahoma City employed by the most popular jazz bandleader in the United States, a white man who until he heard Christian play didn't see the point of having a guitar in his band at all. Charlie Christian not only converted Goodman but accelerated the adoption of the electric guitar in all types of music. Such was the speed of change that acoustic guitar makers Harmony, Vega, and Gretsch were soon all making electrics. However, by 1946, Leo Fender, a young radio and electronics enthusiast, stood in a newly rented steel-frame building in Fullerton, a city in Southern California. Having started out making lap-steel guitars and amplifiers, he was about to industrialize guitar manufacturing. In 1949, the first prototype solid-bodied guitar from the Fender Electric Instrument Company looked set to make the craftsman-luthier redundant. The electric guitar, in its many manifestations, enabled the guitar per se to be heard in big jazz bands, in the hands of solo blues players, and in country and western lineups. It would also help inspire electric rock 'n' roll. It seemed likely that the days of the acoustic guitar as a stage instrument might be numbered.

Ken Colyer playing a 1950s Hofner six-string.

Skiffle and a Guitar Craze in Britain

The popularity of the acoustic guitar during the first half of the twentieth century was very different in America compared to Great Britain. Factories in Chicago and New York had produced multiple thousands of instruments every year of the 1930s and 1940s, and the Sears and Montgomery Ward catalogs each had many pages of guitars, some as cheap as $3. There were literally hundreds of thousands of acoustic guitars distributed across the whole of America, augmented by a fast-growing number of the relatively new electric guitars.

But Britain, in the period between the first introduction of the steel-string acoustic guitar in the early 1900s and its ubiquity in the popular music of the 1960s, never seemed that interested. The guitar was largely an instrument for professional dance-band musicians using plectrum jazz guitars, a minute number of professional classical players, and a small band of schoolchildren and amateur enthusiasts playing classical pieces on low-quality imported Spanish guitars. But a musical phenomenon in Britain brought about a sea change in both the global popularity of the acoustic guitar and who chose to play it.

Between 1954 and 1959, a new type of music brought about a forty-fold increase in the number of guitars purchased annually in Britain.

Forty-fold!

In 1950, around six thousand guitars were sold in Great Britain, virtually all foreign made; the British domestic guitar-making industry was limited to a few makers of high-quality archtop jazz guitars. Just seven years later, annual imports exceeded 250,000. Ben Davis, the head of Selmer, the UK's largest importer and distributor of musical instruments, remarked that by Christmas 1957, "People were wandering London's Charing Cross Road music district with bunches of pound notes in their hands looking to buy any guitar the music shops had."

That Christmas, Davis told the press that his company had "6,000 on order and wish I could get more." In fact, he was organizing his own charter flights to ship instruments from Europe to London, resulting in fanciful headlines in British newspapers, including "The Guitar Craze Hits Fortissimo." There was even a story going around that more music shops than jewelers were broken into that year.

Guitars were, in all senses of the word, HOT.

This unprecedented demand for guitars was fired by the craze for raw-edged, guitar-led skiffle music that had started sweeping Britain in the early 1950s. By 1957, the majority of the 250,000 guitars flooding into the country were destined primarily for the hands of an estimated forty thousand amateur and semiprofessional skiffle groups, marking the height of the skiffle craze. The guitars being played to the rhythm accompaniment of homemade tea-chest string basses and washboards played with thimbles were all from European makers. A combination of postwar austerity, a shortage of US dollars, and a balance-of-payments crisis meant that import restrictions on American goods coming into the United Kingdom were still in force. Even if American guitars from companies like Martin, Gibson, and the newly formed Fender had been available, they would have been beyond reach anyway, far too expensive for the young amateur skifflers of a chronically hard-up Britain.

The instruments young skifflers *were* able to afford ranged from a cheap (often barely playable), 25-shilling flat-top acoustic (c. £30 [$40] at today's prices) to a basic archtop guitar for £15 (c. £360 [$450]). To put these prices into perspective, the average weekly wage at the time was £15. With few affordable British-made instruments available, the guitars in music shops in the '50s included decent Hagstrom and Levin guitars from Sweden, cheap guitars from communist Czechoslovakia, and relatively poor quality Rosetti and Egmond folk guitars from the Netherlands. However, most instruments were coming from southern Germany, marginally ironic given that World War II had rendered Germany an economic and manufacturing wasteland only a decade earlier. The main German guitar makers, Hoyer, Hofner, Klira, and Framus, were all companies set up and staffed by immigrant violin makers from the small Bohemian town of Schönbach.

This small town was known in the seventeenth century as the Austrian Cremona, at a time when Bohemia was part of the Austro-Hungarian Empire. Following World War I, it became part of the newly formed country of Czechoslovakia until the largely German-speaking border area was annexed by the Nazis in 1938. Germany claimed that what they called the Sudetenland was historically and rightfully German; the annexation helped trigger the declaration of war between Britain and Germany.

Seven years later and following the end of World War II, the old Czech borders were redrawn and the town of Schönbach fell under communist rule. German-speakers in the area were hated by the new Czech president, Edvard Benes, who talked about seeking the "final solution to the German question" in his country. Times were terrifying and brutal for all German-speaking civilians, and Schönbach's 1,600 violin makers were forcibly absorbed under state control. By 1949, following a Russian-backed communist coup d'etat, every person of German ancestry was expelled from the country, but not before many thousands had been beaten, raped, or murdered in bloody reprisals that mirrored, and in many cases rivalled, the brutality the Nazis had inflicted only a few years earlier.

Among the many escaping the violence was the Hofner family, including violin makers Karl Hofner and his two sons, Josef and Walter. Like many, they had packed their tools and a few belongings and made the arduous trek west into southern Germany where they sought resettlement in Bavaria, then still under US administration. Karl's granddaughter Gerhilda remembers the difficulty her family had trying to set up their workshop: "You couldn't buy anything, everything was done by bartering. So many screws for a sheet of glass, that sort of thing."

However, by the early 1950s, and with help from the Americans who had initially given the embryonic companies old military barracks to work in, the craftsmen had created instrument workshops in and around the town of Bubenreuth in Erlangen-Höchstadt. Businesses grew and basic workshops soon turned into small factories. In the 1950s, when orders from Britain for guitars started to outpace those for violins, many of the makers, including Hofner, shifted production accordingly. Jazz-style archtop guitars share many construction techniques with violins, so the transition was not that difficult. Hofner, as far back as the 1930s, had been producing a few steel-string Schlaggitarren guitars with arched tops and backs, modelled on the archtop guitars produced by the Gibson company in the early 1920s.

Given the extraordinary demand for guitars in Britain by 1957, it's difficult to comprehend why there wasn't a substantive British guitar industry in place to satisfy that demand. The explanation involves several factors.

Although there had been a lively interest in the banjo in Britain from the 1840s, when American blackface minstrel players like Joel Sweeney visited the country, there wasn't a subsequent interest in amateurs playing the guitar or the mandolin when the banjo fell out of fashion in the 1920s. Unlike in America, where playing the parlor guitar thrived, Britain didn't seem that interested. The portability of the banjo, mandolin, and guitar suited the United States, a nation whose population was on the move for the whole of the nineteenth century. In contrast, Britain in the nineteenth and twentieth centuries was a physically settled nation. Few people lived more than a couple of miles from the town or village where they were born. There were no mass migrations, no open plains or a vast, expansive West beckoning people to try ranching, farming, or even gold prospecting—and therefore British folks felt no need to pack a portable instrument for company or family entertainment. The immobile, solid piano became the popular home instrument, and even working-class homes in Britain could occasionally afford a secondhand "joanna" (Cockney rhyming slang for a piano). If you didn't own a piano, you could always find one in a pub. If you were wealthier and you went to a hotel for an evening's entertainment, there would be a band or orchestra. Learning the guitar just wasn't a relevant or obvious option.

On top of this, in the period from 1900 to 1950, while there were Spanish-style classical guitars being imported into Britain (from Spain, Austria, and France), they were for playing a classical repertoire. There was little music in Britain that sounded like the popular country blues, folk, or old-time music played on steel-string flat-tops, and there were no guitar factories like Lyon & Healey to satisfy demand and sell to the nation through a multiplicity of mail-order catalogs. Some steel-string flat-tops and acoustic Hawaiian guitars were produced by British banjo makers who had started making archtop jazz guitars in the 1920s . . . but very few.

Furthermore, after World War II government measures channeled raw materials like wood and metal into reconstructing Britain—purchasing luxury products was restricted. Bizarrely, an item like a new guitar required a government-issued permit that only professional musicians could obtain. In addition, and up until 1959, guitars were classed as luxury purchases and carried a one hundred percent tax surcharge.

Finally, even without the tax surcharge on imports, good-quality British-made guitars were still expensive and out of the reach of most amateur players. Postwar, reasonably well-made archtops from Emile Grimshaw or Abbott-Victor, who were deadly rivals but two of the only brands building guitars for professional players, would cost around £50 ($200 at 1948 exchange rates), similar in price to a much superior Gibson or Martin.

The British guitar industry after the war, stifled by permits, supertaxes, and limited demand, never got a chance to develop beyond a few small-scale builders of dance-band style archtops. Postwar Britain was on its knees, and therefore guitars were a very low priority. By the time skiffle boomed in the mid-1950s, it was too late for a guitar industry to establish itself, so instrument importers like Selmer turned to Europe. And by the time Britain returned to real economic growth, America had cornered the premium guitar market, and German, Italian, and Japanese makers were fighting for the mid-price and budget segments. The only affordable British acoustic brand around for the mid-1950s skiffle boom was Antoria, a Leeds-based company, but even it was having its guitars made abroad—initially by Framus in Germany and then by Guyatone in Japan.

By the time the US luxury goods import ban and 100 percent luxury tax were finally lifted in mid-1959, skiffle music was fading in popularity and electric beat music was on the rise. Young electric players were either putting basic pickups on an existing acoustic skiffle guitar or buying cheap knockoffs of American solid-body instruments made in Czechoslovakia and Japan. Or, if they wanted the same guitar as those played by McCartney and Lennon while in Hamburg, an entry-level Club 40 hollow-bodied electric from Hofner.

The first British company making solid-bodied electric guitars specifically for British beat players was Supersound, which produced a small range of crudely built guitars designed by Jim Burns, including the £66 "Ike Isaacs" Professional. In addition, Emile Grimshaw Jr.—who had started in the '20s playing banjo in British dance bands and with his father had established a banjo- and guitar-making business—was still around. By the early 1960s, he was producing a small range of solid-bodied electric guitars. The Grimshaw Short Scale of 1959 was a well-made but poor-sounding instrument, and its prosaic name and plain styling gave it little chance against guitars with superb looks and sound further enhanced with futuristic names—think Stratocaster in Fiesta Red—even though at £100, the Fender cost was almost twice that of a Grimshaw.

Regardless of price, most British beat guitarists in the know really wanted an American guitar, and ideally a red Fender Stratocaster like the one Hank Marvin of the Shadows played. But Fenders were very few and far between in Britain. British guitar legend Jeff Beck recalls that in 1959, when he was a guitar-obsessed fifteen-year-old, even information about American guitars was scarce. "I remember travelling for a whole morning on the bus to go and see a guy who had a Fender catalogue, with a red Stratocaster on the front cover—I stood outside his house while he showed it to me, I wasn't even allowed to touch the paper brochure."

That 1958–1959 brochure was the same one Cliff Richard had requested from Fender in California, ahead of his first visit to the United States with his manager. When he showed the brochure to Hank Marvin and asked what guitar he wanted him to bring back, Marvin pointed to the red Stratocaster with gold-plated fittings on the cover and said, "That one!" Had Fender decided to put a different guitar on the cover—perhaps the Telecaster (without a tremolo arm) that Marvin's guitar hero played, rockabilly picking legend and Elvis's guitarist James Burton (a member of the legendary "Wrecking Crew" session group)—things might have been so different for the look and sound of British rock 'n' roll in the '60s.

Meanwhile, back in the mid-1950s, demand for guitars in the UK was so strong that the German makers had trouble keeping up. Importers like Ben Davis at Selmer, with specially chartered cargo planes sitting at the Frankfurt airport waiting to bring the guitars to Britain, couldn't wait for wood varnish or paint to dry. To speed things up, many makers started covering their basic flat-top guitar bodies in red, sticky-backed plastic, mimicking the red Fenders.

Most of the German producers focused on producing the easier and quicker to construct flat-top guitar, but Hofner kept archtop styling in their model lineup. Which is why, in 1961, at Hamburg's Steinway music store, the uniquely shaped guitar that caught Paul McCartney's eye was the Hofner 500/1 violin bass, to be known thereafter as the Beatle bass.

McCartney's choice was pragmatic. There were very few, if any, left-handed guitars made, so most lefties turned the standard right-handed guitar upside down and restrung it accordingly. That's a flipped, right-hand Fender Stratocaster we see Hendrix playing at Woodstock; it looked odd, but it worked. However, McCartney was looking for something better than a makeshift solution. "I found this Hofner violin bass. To me it seemed, because I was left-handed, that it looked less daft because it was symmetrical. So I got into that. That became my main bass."

What happened to the German guitar industry just after the war was incredibly important in shaping contemporary popular music around the world. Had it not been for the forced migrations during and after the war, the comfortable, conservative violin makers of Schönbach would never have been forced to leave their small, Bohemian town and seek safety and a fresh start in postwar West Germany. Their ability to fulfil the demand from British skifflers by mass-producing cheap but playable acoustic guitars meant that John Lennon's mother Julia could afford to buy him a guitar. That enabled sixteen-year-old Lennon to form a skiffle band and thereby meet fellow guitarist Paul McCartney at a local church fete.

If you ask anyone in Britain who invented skiffle, they would probably say Lonnie Donegan. Skiffle was the music that brought the Beatles together: Lennon, McCartney, George Harrison, and Ringo Starr all starting out as teenagers in amateur skiffle bands. All four later credited Donegan with inspiring their first musical steps and noted the critical importance of skiffle as the sound that inspired not just the Beatles but thousands of young people across Britain to make rather than just listen to music. But while Donegan was a big skiffle star, he didn't invent it, nor did he introduce it to Britain. Those accomplishments lie with someone few people have ever heard of.

• • • • • •

Skiffle had evolved out of, and then grew alongside, the British traditional or "trad" jazz revival that emerged postwar in the late 1940s. This British revival of early New Orleans jazz featuring Black jazz musicians like Louis Armstrong, Joe "King" Oliver, George Lewis, and Bunk Johnson attracted an audience younger and more carefree than the older and academically inclined bebop and improvisational jazz connoisseurs of the period. Its infectious, fast-paced, carefree rhythms encouraged duffle-coated youths of both sexes to dance rather than sit with serious-minded, bearded aficionados sagely nodding their heads and tapping the odd toe.

One Dixieland revivalist (or trad jazz) group started adding to their performances what became a uniquely British practice—a more relaxed interval set. According to Ron Bowden, the band's drummer, "We used to break down the band and they'd do a skiffle set between sessions. We'd go off and have a fag and a drink." The breakdown would perform four or five songs, allegedly to give Ken Colyer, the trumpet-playing leader of the band, a chance to rest his weak lip and "to put down his horn and accompany himself on guitar." Alongside Colyer was the band's banjoist, Tony (later Lonnie) Donegan, and Chris Barber, the trombonist, on stand-up bass. They played a mix of old American folk and blues songs in the style of 1920s "skiffle" parties popularized by Black Southern immigrants in the Northern industrial cities of the United States. Tenants in the crowded apartments in poorer, predominantly Black areas of Chicago and Philadelphia hosted parties to raise money for their rent. A few cents allowed entry and the opportunity to buy cheap booze and dance.

The music that accompanied the drinking and dancing was provided by a piano or guitar backed by a homemade rhythm section of washboard, tea-chest string bass, and saucepan drums. There were various local terms for these parties: a "percolator," "boogie," or "parlor social"; a "skiffle" or a "shake." In the '20s, "skiffle" was not a description of the music or even a style of music; it just meant a rent party. In 1925, Jimmy O'Bryant and his Chicago Skifflers cut a record, and other bands produced songs like "Hometown Skiffle" and "Skiffle Blues," but the music they were playing—a mix of ragtime, piano blues, jug-band hokum, and guitar-led country-blues—wasn't skiffle. The word "skiffle" wasn't used to describe a style of music until 1953, when a BBC engineer in London asked the self-appointed manager of Ken Colyer's amateur jazz band how to label the recording of a few songs by the band's breakdown group.

Bill Colyer was only the part-time manager of his younger brother's band, the Ken Colyer Jazzmen. Ken was the uncompromising, intransigent leader, guitarist, and singer. Bill knew what they were playing was authentic, but that it was also the blues. As a highly knowledgeable jazz and blues enthusiast, he was uneasy about telling the British Broadcasting Corporation that a bunch of young, white, middle-class, suburbanite Londoners were playing the music of authentic Black players like Lead Belly, Blind Lemon Jefferson, and the Memphis Jug Band. "Skiffle" was a word he knew from the American records he had in his extensive collection, and the rough-and-ready music his brother's group was playing was not dissimilar. Henceforth, "skiffle" officially described a uniquely British style of American country-blues.

Ken Colyer was a largely self-taught trumpeter obsessed with Dixieland and

New Orleans jazz and what then was being called "revivalist jazz." A year earlier, in 1952, the amateur jazz trumpeter, unable to read music, had rejoined the Merchant Navy purely to get to New Orleans where he could hear in person musicians from the spiritual home of traditional jazz.

His first trips in "the merch" in 1947 had taken him to Italy, to the Middle East, and eventually to Montreal, but he went nowhere he could hear any jazz. He eventually reached New York, where (according to an interview with his biographers Ray Smith and Mike Pointon) he finally found some live jazz: "This was living. These men had only been names on records and personnels in HMV and Parlophone catalogues, and here they were in the flesh: Bobby Hackett, Lionel Hampton, Cliff Jackson and probably many I didn't recognize. I stayed until the band finished for the night. It was about 5:00; I was still on cloud nine."

His experience in New York jazz clubs made Colyer even more intent on getting to New Orleans, and despite his initial misgivings, he signed on to a beat-up cargo steamer that at least travelled to the Southern states and around the Caribbean. He spent months on the slow, rickety steamer, still not going anywhere near the US South, but he used the long trips to improve his skills playing trumpet and guitar.

When the *S.S. Empire Patrai* finally docked in Mobile, Alabama, on October 8, 1952, Ken Colyer decided that while the ship took on fresh cargo for the next leg of its journey, he would slip off to New Orleans and scout out opportunities for an extended stay. Before leaving the ship, he wrote home to his brother Bill, telling him that his eventual plan was to "pay off here or somewhere on the coast and ease my way down to 'Noo Awlins' and find my own way home."

The New Orleans part of his trip hadn't been totally left to chance. Before leaving London, Colyer had visited Westminster Reference Library. Having found a New Orleans telephone directory, he wrote down the telephone numbers of all the New Orleans jazz musicians he could find listed. With the little money he had—not much more than few dollars, since merchant seaman were only paid off at the completion of their contract—he made the 160-mile trip from Mobile to New Orleans by Greyhound bus. Equipped with a pocketful of nickels and dimes, he started dialing the numbers he had. His simple plan eventually bore fruit; he connected with Edmond "Doc" Souchon, a medical doctor, journalist, and leading light in the New Orleans jazz revivalist movement.

In his letters home to his brother Bob, Colyer was delighted to report that he had connected with a more-than-welcoming Souchon. To his further delight and admiration, the good doctor had met both King Oliver and Jelly

Roll Morton in the 1910s and went on to introduce Colyer to his jazz heroes George Lewis and Kid Howard. Colyer had just enough time to get back to Mobile and rejoin the *Empire Patrai* hours before it departed for various ports in the Caribbean.

In November, the creaky ship, with Colyer as assistant cook, returned once more to Mobile. Having been given a twenty-nine-day visitor's visa by the immigration authorities in Mobile, Colyer returned to New Orleans with no intention of returning to either Mobile or the galley of the *Empire Patrai*.

Back in New Orleans, he reconnected with Doc Souchon, George Lewis, and the other musicians he had met on his earlier scouting trip. Now equipped with his trumpet, Colyer impressed his heroes enough to let him occasionally sit in with them.

From his letters home, Colyer seems to have spent most evenings through late November in various jazz clubs watching bands, sitting in when invited, and joining after-hours jam sessions that lasted to the early hours. By December, he was running short of money and registered for a US Social Security card that allowed him to get a job laboring as a roofer for a dollar a day. The combination of spending all night in jazz dives and repairing roofs from seven a.m. to six p.m. must have been exhausting, even for a twenty-four-year-old.

Colyer's US visitor's visa expired just before Christmas, and he was late returning to the Immigration Office to renew it. Realizing that getting another visitor's visa was unlikely, he casually asked for an extension "until he could sign onto a ship leaving New Orleans." To Colyer's shock, he was arrested on the spot under new immigration regulations. Merchant seamen who overstayed their visas became federal detainees and were normally kept under house arrest at the local seamen's mission until papers were arranged. But the New Orleans authorities had decided that all detainees would be handed over to the local sheriff and kept in the local prison with regular criminals until things were sorted out.

Despite protestations, Colyer was detained for thirty-eight days, spending all day in an overcrowded holding pen and from six p.m. to six a.m. locked in a shared cell. Colyer could not initially understand why he was being treated like a common criminal. Seven weeks into his time in detention, a local New Orleans newspaper, *The Item*, ran a story alleging that his treatment was race-related. It was rare for white musicians to play in colored bands, especially in a segregated state like Louisiana. Colyer had been warned that this might catch up with him, and while nothing was formally said, he *had* been warned.

After many letters to the local British consul, who explained that he was largely powerless to intervene, and after attempts by local musicians and well-connected friends to get his visa sorted, he was finally released, sent to Ellis Island in New York, and formally deported.

His fate had been reported weekly in the various British music newspapers and on the BBC jazz program. *Melody Maker* magazine carried Colyer's exclusive "New Orleans Newsletters" every week. As a result, the jazzman eventually returned home a minor celebrity and something of a hero for the cause of jazz.

According to jazz critic George Melly, Colyer had originally "emerged" in the late 1940s as something of a "joke," or at least a somewhat dubious figure within the revivalist jazz community. By the early 1960s, Melly, in his own biography, *Owning Up*, had revised his view.

> Ken invented British traditional jazz. . . . It was he who established the totems and taboos of traditional jazz . . . , but he was too uncompromising, too much a purist. A great many people made a great deal of money out of this, but not Colyer. Awkward as an old bear, often too drunk to blow properly, he has played as he wanted to since the very beginning.

But along with the celebrity, Colyer also returned from America with a headful of country-blues songs ready to be introduced to the trad jazz band consisting of Chris Barber and banjo player Tony Donegan that he was rejoining to lead. In early 1953, a six-piece band dubbed Ken Colyer's Jazzmen travelled to Denmark to effectively rehearse in front of live audiences and hone their act, including the three-piece breakdown sessions. Having initially established the breakdowns with Colyer sitting down to play guitar, Donegan occasionally swapped the banjo for a guitar, and now (as Lonnie Donegan) made sure he was the guy standing up in front of the microphone. It probably marked the first time the guitar moved from being just part of the rhythm section to the instrument the lead singer and star of the band played. He probably didn't know it, but in just three paces Donegan revealed to millions of hormonal teenagers their true destiny.

Many of the songs they played were those Colyer had brought back from New Orleans. "Freight Train," "Mama Don't Allow," and "Midnight Special" were simple, easy-to-play, three-chord tunes; in fact, a few could be played with just one chord. The music was raw, infectious, and easy to emulate, but even Colyer was skeptical that it was something that would last more than a few months.

Brian Nicholls, a writer for *Jazz Journal,* was present when Ken Colyer's Jazzmen first appeared back in London in April 1953, and his review is reminiscent of how a visitor in February 1961 to Liverpool's Cavern Club might have felt on first seeing the Beatles.

> The Skiffle Group which takes over during the intervals at the London Jazz Club is obviously going to be the success of the year. It's getting so that more people flock into the club for the interval than for the rest of the session. The group varies in personnel, but is always based on the guitars, banjos and vocals of Ken Colyer, Alexis Corner [*sic*] and Lonnie Donergan [*sic*]. . . . The repertoire includes such numbers as Trixie Smith's "Freight Train Blues," "Long Gone John" and Woody Guthrie's "New York Town." If you don't believe that kind of music could be a draw in London . . . drop in and feel the electric atmosphere that builds up during Lonnie Donegan's version of "John Henry."

Within weeks, amateur skiffle groups were springing up like wildfire, and for the first time young people were making and playing music for people of their own age. When Donegan was asked to explain the success of skiffle, he said, "In Britain we were separated from our folk music tradition centuries ago and were imbued with the idea that music was for the upper classes. You had to be very clever to play music. When I came along with the old three chords, people began to think that if I could do it, so could they. It was the reintroduction of the folk music bridge which did that."

Lonnie, via his fan club and through his many appearances across the country, encouraged the formation of more local skiffle clubs where teenagers could listen to records and hear local amateur skiffle groups play. The idea of teenagers, rather than "responsible adults," organizing themselves was novel and led to the mechanism that would blossom into the many folk clubs that opened in the 1960s.

Skiffle quickly equaled trad jazz in popularity, and the release of "Rock Island Line," sung by Lonnie Donegan, cemented the popularity of the music in both the UK and the US. In a "coals to Newcastle" turnaround, the record reached number 8 on the *Billboard* charts and influenced American musicians, including a young Buddy Holly, to (re)discover the primarily Black blues tunes from their own musical heritage.

Donegan—with his new, adopted first name appropriated from visiting American bluesman Lonnie Johnson—now struck out on his solo career. For

"Rock Island Line," his record company had also assumed, perhaps without Donegan's total understanding, the writing credits of what became, in 1955, his first hit record. When the musicologist Alan Lomax, who in 1934 had discovered and first recorded the song among the Black chain gangs of Arkansas, saw the writing credit, he was furious at what he knew was copyright theft. Lomax's protege, the murderer and convict-turned-entertainer Lead Belly, had recorded his own arrangement of the song in 1937, and Donegan's whole delivery was slavishly copied from Lead Belly's. In fact, if you slow down Donegan's 45 rpm single to 33⅓ rpm, you could be listening to Lead Belly's original recording—every gasp and nuance is there. When Donegan toured the United States to promote the hit, his agent even approached Moses "Moe" Asch, who ran Folkways Records, the imprint that had released many of Lead Belly's early recordings, suggesting that Lead Belly had been "singing a lot of songs that his artist Lonnie Donegan *owned*, and that money was owed." The forthright Asch suggested he should come and visit and offered to insert the offending discs where the sun didn't shine.

Add '50s American rock 'n' roll to British acoustic skiffle and the result was an explosion in young people's music in Britain. In July 1957, the Quarry Men, the skiffle band formed by then-schoolboy John Lennon, hooked up with Paul McCartney at St. Peter's Church fete in Woolton, Liverpool. Both George Harrison and Richard Starkey (Ringo Starr) were also playing in separate skiffle groups in Liverpool, and all four Beatles cite Lonnie Donegan, "the King of Skiffle," as the musical star that made a real impression on the kind of music they wanted to play. Starr, looking back on the period, recognized that "a lot of us got out of the factory thanks to Lonnie!" Ironically, the Beatles would steal Donegan's popular crown, forcing him out of the limelight and off the record charts and into the relative obscurity of the British and American cabaret circuits.

Donegan might have been the most famous skiffler of the day and highly influential on both sides of the Atlantic, but his bid to continue his career post-skiffle fell flat. Recording songs like "My Old Man's a Dustman" and "Does Your Chewing Gum Lose Its Flavor (On the Bedpost Overnight?)" soon turned him into a vaudeville and novelty song act.

But Donegan and skiffle awakened a generation, showing them they could have their own voice, do their own thing, be more than clones of their parents, even have their own music. The craze also changed the image of the guitar in the UK, transforming it from a rather worthy classical or dance-band instrument to a symbol of youth, rebellion, and a good time. In place of the soft, mellow sound of a classical guitar piece played on nylon strings came the raw, driven strumming of a steel-string guitar. Donegan always seemed to play at a furious pace—as a tenor banjo player he was used to playing in an enthusiastic, percussive style. Donegan as singer *and* guitarist helped promote the notion of the guitar-toting lead singer standing center stage and in the spotlight. But as important as Donegan and skiffle were for "lighting the blue touch paper," the real credit—as the driving forces behind what evolved into the British blues scene and the subsequent British Beat music revolution of the 1960s—should go jointly to jazzers Chris Barber and Ken Colyer.

Ken Colyer had already made an early dig at his old bandmate Donegan in an article in a British music paper in the late '50s, where he accused him of "lack of talent, little musical taste and being no stranger to plagiarism." By many accounts, the uncompromising Colyer, obsessed with listening to and playing "authentic" music, was a difficult, truculent, and often resentful character. In his biography, his wife Delphine recalls attending a party where she asked Ken, who had been playing his guitar most of the evening: "What's the matter with you? You haven't said two words to me all night." Colyer replied: "Well here's two: fuck off!" "Whack!—the guitar was over my head."

A lack of compromise wasn't atypical for a willfully intransigent music purist who tried to keep the roots of skiffle true to its blues and Black folk music origins. In the sleeve notes of his 1964 LP *Wandering*, he wrote, "Skiffle often highlighted the spurious more than the authentic, but the authentic always manages to survive."

Another decisive figure in the emerging British blues scene was Chris Barber, a talented jazz musician and bandleader. His residency in the late 1950s at London's influential Marquee Club and the various young jazz, skiffle, and blues guitarists who passed through his band are enough to make him the *grandfather* of British blues. Barber was as interested in early blues as he was jazz and brought the young Alexis Korner into his band as guitarist and as mandolin player in Colyer's breakdown skiffle group. Korner, with romantic, gypsy looks from his Turkish-Greek-Austrian Jewish parentage, had, with Barber, been a schoolboy at St. Paul's, *the* private, fee-paying school for the sons of doctors, lawyers, and the gentrified middle-class in West London. (Like Seeger, Guthrie, and Dylan, so many "discoverers" of the music of the so-called downtrodden and uneducated were middle-class boys with privileged backgrounds and educations.)

As the *father* of British blues, Korner sang what Ray Davies of the Kinks described as "posh Kensington blues" with a gravelly West London accent.

He went on to form Blues Incorporated, an incubator for many young blues enthusiasts, from singers Mick Jagger and Long John Baldry to guitarists Keith Richards, John Mayall, and Jimmy Page to drummers Charlie Watts and Ginger Baker. Chris Barber, along with Korner, was also instrumental in regularly bringing Black American artists like Big Bill Broonzy, Muddy Waters, Sister Rosetta Tharpe, and Sonny Terry and Brownie McGhee to play in the United Kingdom. However, conflicts between the US and UK musicians' unions meant that most of these visiting stars travelled without their regular bands. Barber's Dixieland jazz band was often brought in to provide a rather bizarre backing band.

• • • • • •

While in the mid-fifties bebop and modern jazz were all the rage in America, back in Britain, revivalist jazz was still growing in popularity, although it was mainly played by homegrown British enthusiasts.

The Black blues and R&B artists tempted over to Europe were glad of bookings to play in front of enthusiastic audiences, in Britain in particular. Many were suffering the same fate as Chicago blues legend Muddy Waters. At the start of 1954, Waters was at the height of his fame. His biggest hit to date, "Hoochie Coochie Man," was riding high on the *Billboard* charts. But coming straight down the tracks at him was white rock 'n' roll. Carl Perkins, Jerry Lee Lewis, and Elvis Presley were playing white-man's music with what Sun Records producer Sam Phillips called "the black man's spirit and soul." In the course of three months, Muddy Waters's record sales in America dropped by 30 percent. Waters realized he was suddenly playing yesterday's music, and like many Black R&B artists, he was having a hard time getting regular work at home. He knew, as the title of his own song says, "the blues had a baby and they named it rock and roll."

But there was one acoustic blues guitarist and singer, tragically now little more than a footnote in contemporary music history, at the vanguard of what became a '50s mini-invasion of Britain by Black American Blues artists.

Josh White's achievements mark him as something of an American music superstar of the late '30s and the '40s. He was the first African American to have a million selling record; he was America's first Black male sex symbol; he appeared in Hollywood movies (most notably playing an equal to his white costar Randolph Scott); he appeared on Broadway alongside Paul Robeson. In the 1940s, he and white singer Libby Holman were the first male and female artists to record and perform together in a mixed-race band. He was the first Black singer to give a White House command performance, subsequently becoming a regular at the Roosevelt White House, during which time Eleanor Roosevelt became godmother to his son. He also was lead performer at New York's Café Society in Greenwich Village, the first openly integrated nightclub in the United States, where Black and white patrons sat, drank, and danced in the same room—this at a time when Black men were being lynched in Jim Crow Mississippi for looking the wrong way at a white woman. And, pertinent to this story, he was the first professional African American blues and folk artist to tour Britain.

When White first arrived in London in 1950, he was not widely known outside of the jazz and blues cognoscenti, although he had broadcast on the BBC a few times via the US Office of War Information. His music was also featured on a variety of V-Discs, records produced for the use of US troops posted overseas that in Britain inevitably got into public circulation. As welcome and rare a sight as he was, for traditional jazz and blues enthusiasts, White's smooth delivery and polished performances were often deemed "inauthentic" and "insincere." Enthusiasts in Britain had, in the early '40s, been able to access imports of the early race records, and the imperfect recordings of raw, single-take performances on shellac 78s became the default sound of the "real blues." The British Brunswick record label released in 1946 two of White's signature songs, "Strange Fruit" and "House of the Rising Sun," the latter a minor-key version of the Carolina Tar Heels' 1933 waltz-time recording. These highly accomplished performances, while perhaps confirming to aficionados that White was not raw enough for their tastes, helped make his first public appearances sellouts. Snobbish aficionados aside, for the average music fan, White was something else and the real deal. Dennis Preston, the jazz critic for *Melody Maker* magazine, reported: "On Monday night I saw the impossible happen. An artist on his first appearance in this country, and not even a name . . . held an audience spellbound with a twenty-minute selection of unfamiliar folk songs and ballads sung in a most unfamiliar manner."

White returned many times to the UK and continued to tour Britain throughout the '50s. Just as important, he recorded numerous records and several radio programs for the BBC, including the highly regarded *Negro Anthology* series featuring his spiritual and gospel repertoire. For many British audiences, White was their first experience of African American folk and blues. His performances were also the first time many had seen a popular guitar virtuoso outside of the classical school. His early experiences in the 1920s as a "lead-boy" (a poorly paid guide employed by blind street musicians to be their eyes) gave him exposure to many guitarists that he described as "frammers" using the guitar to provide simple chord accompaniments to their singing. As he subsequently met and heard talented fingerpickers like Willie Walker and Blind Blake, he saw the possibilities of a more lyrical accompaniment style, which by the '40s he had made his own.

The cabaret singer Eartha Kitt worked with White in the '40s and realized that he was doing much more than reaching her ears when he played guitar. "The sound of his guitar stirred me sensually. It was irresistible and enchanting and seductive. It tantalized my senses and wined my bitter blood. I watched his hands as they caressed the guitar."

Langston Hughes, the African American essayist and early jazz poet, wrote in the '50s of White's guitar style: "The guitar that Josh White plays is as eloquent, as simple and direct as are his songs themselves. His guitar keeps a heart-beat rhythm that makes you feel his songs in your heart. His guitar has in it at one and the same time, sadness and gaiety, despair and faith. Sometimes his guitar laughs behind a sad song. Sometimes it cries behind a happy song."

In his live shows, it wasn't just White's playing that captivated audiences. He employed enormous stagecraft—the simple act of tuning the guitar at the start of his act was a spellbinding performance in itself, as was his ability to integrate the changing of a broken string and bringing it into tune into his rendition of "Summertime." Many contemporaries at his regular Café Society performances in New York believed that White arranged to break a string on purpose to show off this and other stage tricks. He was so much more than just a singer accompanying himself with a guitar; usually billed as "Josh White and His Guitar," it is unsurprising that he was also the first Black musician to have a signature instrument made in his name.

The Zenith Josh White guitar was produced in 1957 and based on White's steel-string Martin 00-21, its wider neck suited for a finger-style player. There is no record of how many were sold, but we know that the Zenith was the first proper guitar that teenage Bert Jansch bought, perhaps stimulated by the advertisement for the £25 ($30) guitar in the back of *The Josh White Guitar Method* book. (An actual Martin 00-21 bought in 1957 cost around three times the price of the Zenith.) The guitar was produced at the request of Ivor Mariants, a London-based jazz guitarist, teacher, and owner of one of the first specialist guitar stores. It was made in Germany by the small Oscar Teller Company (another Bubenreuth-based maker). It was conceived in 1956, after Mariants had worked with White to create *The Josh White Guitar Method*, the first blues guitar instruction book ever published. Realizing that like White himself, very few guitarists could read music, Mariants wrote the tutorials using both standard musical notation and the cifra system, which was popular among the Spanish flamenco community, whose players also rarely read music. Rather than the five parallel lines of the standard musical stave, cifra used six lines representing the six strings of the guitar, a notation system that with a little application translated directly onto the guitar fretboard. Cifra was later adapted into guitar tablature (TAB), which is used by the majority of non-classical guitarists today.

Popular on both sides of the Atlantic, White's book introduced two young guitarists, John Renbourn and Stefan Grossman, to blues guitar and showed them how to emulate White's characteristic style. It was a style that, in the words of Mariants, featured "some of the most delicious blues phrasing ever recorded." It taught a whole generation of guitarists the rudiments of White's idiosyncratic blues guitar style and even showed how a blues take on traditional English ballads was possible. White had long included traditional British folk songs like "Molly Malone" ("Cockles and Mussels") in his repertoire, delivered with a blues phrasing.

The generation who discovered how to play the blues from White's book applied his blues-tinged fingerpicking to reimagine other English ballads. John Renbourn and Bert Jansch, both individually and together at the heart of the '60s folk-jazz group Pentangle, arranged songs like "Jack Orion" and "Lord Franklin" in White's style. White's trick of reworking traditional ballads with a blues tinge was continued in the 1970s by folk-rock pioneers Fairport Convention.

But what was an American singing and guitar superstar doing in Britain in the early 1950s anyway?

Born in Greenville, South Carolina, as World War I broke out, White had been compelled to leave home after the death of his father to work as a lead boy for an itinerant blind street musician, John Henry "Big Man" Arnold. White's father, a tailor and lay preacher, had allegedly "disrespected" a white rent collector, after which the local police dragged White's father out of the house and through the streets behind a horse. Following a near-fatal beating, White Sr. was committed to a mental institution where he spent much of the rest of his life. The family was thrown into poverty, and with a promise from Big Man Arnold that young Josh's earnings would be sent home to his mother and remaining five siblings, the boy left for a life on the road only two months later. He was just eight years old. As lead boy, he guided the musician, collected coins from his street performances, and would, according to White, "generally dance, sing and beat the drum."

Over the subsequent ten years that White spent on the road, he absorbed the various guitar styles of the numerous street players Big Man Arnold loaned him out to for leading duties. He eventually broke free from a life that was close to servitude, and by the late 1920s, he had established himself in the Black Bronzeville area of Chicago as a singer and guitarist in his own right. Like many Black artists pigeonholed as limited to playing blues, White was equally adept at gospel, Broadway songs, spirituals, ballads, jazz, traditional folk songs, and urban blues as well as his local Piedmont and country blues. However, his experiences travelling across the South as a child and teenager soon taught White that "separate but equal" for Black people in practice meant that lynchings, floggings, and rampant discrimination were commonplace. These experiences clearly informed and fueled his social conscience and led to the introduction of songs into his act decrying the treatment of Black Americans.

After a successful performing career in a variety of cities across the 1930s, he settled in New York in the '40s, teaming up with Lead Belly, Pete Seeger, and the Almanac Singers. Through his own experience, and with their influence, he started adding more social protest songs to his repertoire, decrying segregation and championing human and civil rights. His social engagement and protest lyrics even drew the attention of the president and first lady, who were fans of folk music. Eleanor Roosevelt in particular saw that through folk music "you could hear the people speaking to you." Following his many appearances at the Roosevelt White House, he earned the sobriquet "the Presidential Minstrel."

Although not overtly political himself, like many liberal, socially aware folk singers, White found himself playing benefits and fundraisers. Given the times, it was quite common for anything left-leaning to be linked to the Popular Front (also called the Communist Front). White was perhaps a little overgenerous in his willingness to lend his voice to any cause that identified with social or civil rights. His enormous celebrity as the president's favorite singer, and his undoubted sexual magnetism, proved to be a double-edged sword. After FDR died, it was clear that the conservative, right-wing political elite and the powerful "Dixiecrats" of the Truman administration saw White as a threat: a Black man who'd "risen above his station."

While during the FDR years he'd been protected, the postwar administration was less enthusiastic about a Black liberal with free rein to use his songs to preach his progressive political message. While on a postwar tour of Europe in 1950 with Eleanor Roosevelt as a presidential goodwill ambassador, White heard that he had been named in the *Red Channels* pamphlet as a subversive and a communist sympathizer. *Red Channels*, published by the right-wing anti-communist journal *Counterattack*, was to become the de facto official blacklist of the entertainment and media industry. Performers, actors, and writers who were named in its pages were duly investigated and hounded both by the FBI and the Joseph McCarthy–led House Un-American Activities Committee (HUAC).

White, against Eleanor Roosevelt's advice, immediately flew back to New York "to clear his name," but upon stepping off the aircraft, he was arrested by the FBI, interrogated for hours, and held at the airport pending "deportation to Europe," rather an odd threat to an American-born citizen with a wife, family, and home in New York.

White was not deported but chose to appear in September 1950 before HUAC in Washington, unrepresented and with only his wife Carol beside him. He used the opportunity to tell the committee of his lifelong experiences of racial discrimination and hatred. Specifically, he related how, at the age of ten, he had witnessed a double lynch mob hanging and then burning and mutilating two Black men. The hearing started to get more difficult after he finished reciting the lyrics of his signature song, "Strange Fruit." The song's "pastoral scene of the gallant South" is today more closely associated with Billie Holiday, who often suggested that it was written specifically for her. But back in the early '50s, White had been singing it almost nightly for over a decade, and his 1942 recording was as well-known as Holiday's.

Ahmet Ertegun, the head of Atlantic Records, later called the song "a declaration of war . . . the beginning of the civil rights movement," but reciting the lyrics in front of an already hostile committee had an incendiary effect for White. The questioning got tougher, and he was forced to condemn the Communist Party; only the judicious use of selective memory enabled him not to name any members he may have known. His subsequent and somewhat naive testimony, where he volunteered that he had been "duped by Communist front organizations and some fellow musicians," not only alienated his Greenwich Village left-leaning friends but also was duly used against him. He was officially blacklisted and remained so until 1963. Not many months after his HUAC testimony, and with little paid work in prospect, he left for London, where he based himself through much of the 1950s.

America's loss was Britain's gain. Because White had started leading and performing when he was just a child, he was still a relatively young man with a direct physical link to the blues legends of the '20s. British blues enthusiasts may have had their old 78 rpm records, but in White they found a man who had met, led, and listened to Blind Lemon Jefferson and Blind Blake as well as lesser-known but highly influential Greenville players like Willie Walker. (Both White and Rev. Gary Davis rated Walker a better player than the legendary Blind Blake.)

Josh White's now largely unappreciated influence on the acoustic guitar was in making it much more than just an accompanying instrument. His enduring legacy is in pioneering a hybrid style of blues playing and taking it to a new generation of American and British players. He also made the concept of the solo singer with just an acoustic guitar not just cool but downright sexy, something that wasn't lost on that '50s generation of budding solo guitarist-singers.

The presence of Josh White and, a year later, Big Bill Broonzy touring Britain and Europe stimulated the embryonic British blues scene and paved the way for the next wave of Black blues singers to visit—many of whom were singing a style of blues music that was out of fashion in their own country.

• • • • • •

While Black American blues and folk artists were having a tough time finding domestic audiences in the '50s, what *was* taking off in the United States was a revolution in country and western music. That revolution came in the shape of one man—Hiram King "Hank" Williams.

Hank Williams created his own idiosyncratic style by borrowing the bits he admired in others. Taking the honky-tonk sound that Ernest Tubb had pioneered, he perfected Tubb's faltering, breaking vocal style, brought the electric steel guitar a little more center stage, and added a bit of Jimmie Rodgers yodeling. The result contains the key components of Williams's first number one hit, "Lovesick Blues."

But Williams was much more than a copyist—he brought unique ingredients to the mix, primarily catchy melodies married to a new, intimate style of lyrics that spoke directly to women. Legend has it that he studiously read the agony columns in women's magazines to get into the mindset of his audience. However, he didn't need to look much farther than his own front door. The themes and heartfelt lyrics of his songs came almost verbatim from his own chaotic and troubled life. He was a twice-married, semi-functioning alcoholic who managed to father a child with a girlfriend he had in the two weeks between the end of his first marriage and the start of his second. However poor a husband and father he might have been, it didn't dent his popularity.

In October 1952, he married Billie Jean Berlin in New Orleans. For good measure he married her three times. Once in private and twice more the next day in two public ceremonies, his manager selling tickets at $2 a head to a combined audience of 14,000 fans.

His messy, mysterious death and subsequent funeral early the next year equally reeked of show business. The funeral was attended by over 25,000 people and rivalled the Hollywood-style "fan funeral" laid on for matinee idol Rudoph Valentino.

While being driven between gigs by his sleep-deprived teenage driver, the twenty-nine-year-old Williams, dead drunk in the back seat of the Cadillac, had a heart attack after overdosing on a cocktail of legal and illegal drugs administered by his quack doctor. His lyrics often carry a tinge of self-pity, but he was clearly under no illusions about his general direction of travel; feeling that the only kind of luck he ever had was bad, he knew he would "never get out of this world alive."

Hank Williams was a prototypical guitar-playing singer-songwriter and possibly the United States' first modern-age pop star. By the late '40s and early '50s, his record sales were huge, partly because of his personal appeal, and that of his songs, to women, a newly emerging record-buying audience. From this point and to this day, the country music industry judges all records on their ability to appeal to a notional "thirty-seven-year-old housewife with two children," the audience that back then, and now, attracts the most valuable commercial advertising dollar.

While he was country music's first superstar, he was also the last major country artist promoted as being as "hillbilly as korn liquor." In the '50s, country was smartening its image and becoming an industry interested in the business of making music *and* money—or rather making money *through* music.

Williams was born to a poor family in rural Alabama in 1929. The third child to survive, Williams was born with spina bifida. When Hank was just six, Williams's father was permanently hospitalized, and he was largely brought up by his mother, Lillie. His own illness also meant that Williams was by all accounts a lonely child and poor student. He was drawn to music, and Lillie bought him a $3.50 acoustic guitar when he was eight years old and sent him to shape note, or Sacred Harp, singing lessons at the local Wesley Chapel. Raw and gutsy, shape-note singing, a nineteenth-century form of unaccompanied congregational song, no doubt gave Williams the confidence to sing loud and in tune from an early age.

But by the time he was eleven, he was tagging along with a Black street musician, Rufus "Tee-Tot" Payne, who earned a few cents giving Williams guitar lessons. At thirteen years old, Williams performed on the local Montgomery, Alabama, radio station, and the "Singing Kid," encouraged by his doting and domineering mother, formed a band playing hillbilly country songs. Hank Williams and His Drifting Cowboys (the use of the possessive "his" formalizing that Williams was the star and they were just his backing band) played local hip-hops, dance marathons, and school dances, with audiences remarking on Williams's clear, tuneful voice and ability to charm a crowd. However, having started drinking alcohol at the age of ten, by sixteen Williams was binge drinking, allegedly to numb his chronic back pain. But the Drifting Cowboys were already suffering because of his drunken performances. Felton Pruit, a member of the Drifting Cowboys, remembered his time supporting Williams: "Drunk or sober, it didn't matter. Funny thing was, his time was right on. If you could just get him out there and prop him up, he'd do the show."

By eighteen, Williams was playing regularly on local radio and had achieved real fame in the Montgomery area. When war broke out and his band members left to join the forces, he seemed to lose impetus. Without a band and ineligible for service due to his back problems, he gave up all hope of making it big and went to work in the shipyards of Mobile for the duration. However, once again pushed by his mother, who had booked some dates in bars and dancehalls for him, he returned to Montgomery, where he joined a travelling medicine show and met his first wife and future manager. Audrey Sheppard replaced Lillie as the provider of the drive that Williams lacked, and before long, they had formed a new version of the Drifting Cowboys and were performing regularly on an even bigger radio show.

The *Louisiana Hayride* was broadcast weekly on KWKH, a powerful clear channel radio station based in Shreveport that reached millions of listeners across the South and the Southwest. It was known as the *Grand Ole Opry*'s nursery, and Williams and the ever-ambitious and protective Audrey saw it as a stepping stone to Nashville and the big time. By 1948, Williams had signed a music publishing deal and had released two successful records, "Move It On Over" and "Honky Tonkin'," but the *Grand Ole Opry* had already heard of Williams's reputation for drinking and missing shows and wasn't interested in giving him a slot.

Roy Acuff, an *Opry* stalwart and a hero to Williams, somewhat prophetically told him, "You gotta make a choice boy . . . drinking or making a living out of music. But if you carry on as you are the good Lord will make the decision for you anyway."

Williams had his first number-one record in 1949 with "Lovesick Blues." The tune was not self-penned, an irony since he had over three hundred songs published and claimed to have written over a thousand. Despite it being an extremely ragged, out-of-meter recording, the *Opry* could ignore him no more. At his first performance, he mesmerized the audience and became the first *Opry* performer to get six straight encores. Williams had reached the big time and hit after hit followed.

Despite the ever-present electric-steel guitar of Don Helms in his backing band, Hank Williams was still primarily an acoustic performer. He played many guitars throughout his career, but a Martin D-28 dreadnought was a favorite and appears in most stage photos from this 1949–1951 golden period. He was soon more popular than his heroes Ernest Tubb and Roy Acuff, producing big hits like "Your Cheating Heart," "You're Gonna Change (Or I'm Gonna Leave)," and "Cold, Cold Heart," written immediately after visiting his wife Audrey in the hospital.

Unbeknownst to Williams, Audrey had contracted an infection following an illegal home abortion, and he arrived with a clearly inappropriate gift of a mink coat. When he bent over Audrey to kiss her, she pushed him away saying, "You sorry son of a bitch. . . . It was you that caused me this suffering," blaming his playing around for her own infidelity and subsequent abortion. His housekeeper recalls a confused and distraught Williams coming home from the hospital saying, "That woman has a cold, cold heart" and then sitting down and writing the lyrics in twenty minutes.

Williams is not strictly in the mold of the confessional singer-songwriters who would come along in the 1970s, but there is no doubt that many of his best songs were directly influenced by the dramas happening in his own helter-skelter life. Despite limited formal education, he had a wisdom and way with words that he found easy to set to music and thus directly touch his audience. He was also proud to be a hillbilly singer and was scornful of singers and bands who "only play our hillbilly songs when they can't eat any other way." His many hits and style of delivery influenced the shape of popular music to come. "Move It On Over," his first recording, is clearly early rock 'n' roll, while at the other end of the radio dial both Tony Bennett and Dinah Washington had hits with "Cold, Cold Heart" in 1952, the same year that Williams's version reached number one on the country charts. (Singer Norah Jones had a hit with the same song almost fifty years to the day later.) Despite the country music establishment's dislike of Williams's philandering and drunkenness, he pretty much created the mold for generations of troubled country artists from hillbilly or poor urban backgrounds living their lives and loves in the public eye—from Dolly to Loretta and George to Johnny.

The stylized vocal gymnastics of Williams's "Lovesick Blues" have been copied a thousand times by rock 'n' roll singers across the decades—just listen to Buddy Holly's borrowed vocal tricks and licks from Williams on his first hit, "That'll Be the Day" (1957). Of course, Williams wasn't the only influence on rock 'n' roll. Hank Snow's recording of his own twelve-bar blues, "I'm Moving On" (1950), spent twenty-one weeks at the top of the country charts and went on to be recorded by the Rolling Stones, Led Zeppelin, Rory Gallagher . . . all only having to slightly pick up the beat to turn it into rock 'n' roll.

Across the whole of the 1950s, guitar-playing hillbilly country artists like Elvis Presley (Oh yes, he was!) made their transition to the mainstream roots of easily digestible and predominantly white rock 'n' roll via country music. Within that transition came the gradual shedding of the acoustic guitar (or its relegation into the backing band), with the emergence of electric guitars and the lead singer.

One song that exemplifies this transition (the shift from acoustic to electric and from country to rock 'n' roll) is "I Gotta Know," by Wanda Jackson, an all-too-rare female artist at the time. Like Elvis, she started out in country music playing a cheap acoustic guitar, although she started much younger, when she was just six. Her father, a keen amateur musician, bought her a guitar from the Sears catalog and taught her to play.

He had brought his family from Oklahoma's dust bowl depression to Bakersfield, a relatively prosperous California town where many Okies settled. The immigrants were an unfairly despised underclass who had brought with them a raucous style of country music: a blend of blues, hillbilly, and honky-tonk that featured fiddles, twangy guitars, and the drums despised by Nashville producers. This amalgam became known as the Bakersfield Sound, and this was the music Jackson was brought up on and started to mimic when she played for her father at home and later entertained her friends.

While still at school, she performed on local radio stations and was picked up as a singer by a touring swing band, its leader unaware that the growly voice and stage appeal came from a girl too young to sign a recording contract. A recording deal eventually followed, which led to her appearance at the Grand Ole Opry, where she played "I Gotta Know" (1956), her first hit record. Songwriter and rockabilly producer Billy Poore writes that it "starts out like a sad, sappy country ballad, and then all of a sudden, Wanda just roars into the meat and potatoes bopping rockabilly sound." As an eighteen-year-old she toured with and dated a young Elvis Presley, who taught her how to play in the same single-stroke style that he used. Jackson continued recording in various genres from country to swing to rockabilly. She covered Nashville Sound ballads, middle-of-the-road pop, and the nascent sound of early rock 'n' roll, but without finding much chart success. Bizarrely, her first number-one hit was in Japan with "Fujiyama Mama." While the song's lyrics show dubious taste—"I've been to Nagasaki, Hiroshima too! The things I did to them baby, I can do to you!"—a hit is a hit. Known as the Queen of Rockabilly, she was belatedly but correctly inducted into the Rock and Roll Hall of Fame in 2009, while still regularly performing live.

• • • • • •

In 1956, Elvis, having made just a few earlier country records, recorded "Heartbreak Hotel," a song he played the previous year during his appearances on the *Louisiana Hayride* radio show. On the RCA recording, he's still accompanying himself on his Martin D-28 acoustic, backed by the Blue Moon Boys featuring the legendary Scotty Moore and Chet Atkins on guitar.

While "Heartbreak Hotel" may not have been the *first* rock 'n' roll song, it was the first Elvis single to chart in the UK. There were good omens when the record was released in Britain: the BBC, which held a near monopoly on broadcasting, didn't think a song inspired by a suicide note was fit for family entertainment (the only kind of entertainment being broadcast by the stiff-necked British Broadcasting Corporation in the 1950s) and put it on its "restricted play" list. Fortunately, the American military's Armed Forces Radio and Radio Luxembourg, the "Station of the Stars" (the equivalent of a commercial border-blaster station beamed into a rock 'n' roll–starved UK from mainland Europe), did play it and helped popularize both Elvis and the record.

Alongside Chuck Berry's recording of "Maybellene," Elvis's voice and delivery on "Heartbreak Hotel" mark a standout moment in rock 'n' roll history. He sounded like a Black singer; he knew all rock 'n' roll was about sex; and he knew how to arouse an audience. As Bruce Springsteen says about Elvis's role in the growth of rock 'n' roll, "Elvis didn't see it coming; he was it coming."

It was Bill Haley's "(We're Gonna) Rock Around the Clock"—or rather its addition at the last minute over the credit titles of the 1955 film *The Blackboard Jungle*—that put rock 'n' roll in the news headlines. Haley, originally a country artist (at least nominally), and the likes of Elvis, Little Richard, Chuck Berry, Carl Perkins, and Jerry Lee Lewis, turned up-tempo country and R&B into

American rock 'n' roll. The transition was helped in no small part by the advent of the electric guitar and the lead singer. This first wave of raw rock 'n' rollers was quickly overtaken by a bunch of clean-cut, all-white artists that played well on national TV: Bobby Darin, Pat Boone, Paul Anka, Neil Sedaka, and Ricky Valance, among them. Their highly sanitized interpretations of rock 'n' roll were pale imitations of what Elvis, Chuck Berry, and Little Richard were doing—and what Trixie Smith was talking about in her 1922 recording "My Man Rocks Me (With One Steady Roll)."

TV was growing fast in the US and had a hugely positive effect on the popularity of rock 'n' roll in its many forms. *American Bandstand*, a popular national TV show hosted by the clean-cut Dick Clark, played the sort of rock 'n' roll that mom, dad, and their teenage kids could watch together. Those mothers and fathers would have had little problem with their daughters dating Bobby or Ricky; perhaps they even would have had a little dance to "Dream Lover" and "Tell Laura I Love Her." This family-friendly version of rock 'n' roll worked fine in a regimented, still socially constrained US, but another UK musical phenomenon was coming that would change everything forever. It created a seismic shift between teenagers and adults, put American-produced pop music on hold, and threatened to kill the acoustic guitar.

Bert Jansch playing a 1960s Yamaha FT150.

10 British Blues, American Guitars

In the 1960s, popular music helped shape the way a generation of freshly minted teenagers dressed, looked, behaved, and talked. The distinctly rebellious "bad boy" rock 'n' roll of Elvis, Jerry Lee Lewis, and Bill Haley—the alleged "music of delinquents" and "rhythm-crazed teenagers"—served to wake up and mobilize the youth of America and Britain. But a decade after World War II had ended, America and Britain were two very different nations. Sleepy, conservative, middle-aged, and middle-class Britain had not welcomed the arrival of American rock 'n' roll in 1956 via the soundtrack of *The Blackboard Jungle*. Rock 'n' roll was soon being vilified by the establishment press, which reported "riots" in cinemas playing the film. The "riots" were mainly teenagers dancing the jive (commonly known in the US as swing) in the aisles at a time when young jivers in dancehalls like the Palais de Danse were marginalized and herded into a small, roped-off area to keep them away from "proper" dancers. In addition, most young people had never heard rock 'n' roll at the volume produced by cinema speakers.

With the encouragement of the establishment press, the older generation hated everything about a music they probably had yet to hear. In 1956, the *Daily Mail*, the voice of conservative "Middle England," reached out to its four million readers in an editorial under the headline "Rock 'n' Roll Babies":

> Dig folks, you're in for a rock 'n' roll session that will send you. Or will it? Our purpose is to not work up but to play down, to enquire into the high-pitched screams of the saxophone and the maddening, monotonous, compulsive rhythm of the jazz drums. These are the main elements in rock 'n' roll, this sudden "musical" phenomenon which has led to outbreaks of vandalism. Under its influence youths and girls jive in the gangways of cinemas and tear up the seats. It is horrible. It is tribal and it is from America! It follows ragtime, blues, dixie, jazz, hot cha-cha-cha and boogie woogie (which must surely originate in the jungle!). The music has something of the African tom tom and voodoo dance. We sometimes wonder whether this is the negro's revenge?

Ironically, the American public was just as fearful of their teenagers being led astray by rock 'n' roll. *Blackboard Jungle* had been banned the previous year in numerous American cities—including the home of rock 'n' roll, Memphis—due to its depiction of juvenile delinquency, "teenage savages," rock 'n' roll culture, and possibly the presence of Sidney Poitier playing an intelligent but rebellious student ringleader who also happened to be Black.

The Britain that emerged from the '50s was radically different, both socially and economically, from an America that had mostly prospered financially during the war. But unlike an America marching toward musical egalitarianism, the British upper classes of Cold War Britain seemingly had the upper hand—and all the fun.

As writer Andrew Cracknell recounted in August 2005 in the *Financial Times*, under the headline "Under the Bomb," "For the rest of us it was bed by ten under lumpy eiderdowns, it was prefabs, contemptuous politicians in homburgs and heavy tweed overcoats and thick brown tea served with your tinned spaghetti on toast."

Even as Britain's postwar gloom and financial austerity began to fade in the early 1960s, and money finally began to appear in people's pockets, it could be a glum place for the majority.

In 1964, when twenty-something tour manager Joe Boyd arrived from Boston to help organize the Blues and Gospel Caravan, a variety tour of Black American musicians that included Muddy Waters, Sonny Terry, and Sister Rosetta Tharpe, he noticed a Britain rich in opportunities for comparison and contrast with his American home.

> For a start, the British didn't seem to own anything. The most poverty-stricken folk singer in Cambridge or Greenwich Village had at least a record player and a refrigerator. . . . In England, pilgrimages would be made with a newly purchased LP to the flat of someone with the means to play it. Milk bottles on the window ledge brought hurriedly inside on winter mornings were a reminder that kitchen appliances—and central heating—were rare luxuries.

But despite, or perhaps because of, the everyday deprivations, a new liberalism sparked a profound and extraordinary change in British society. Restlessness was overtaking the public, and young people in particular. They were no longer prepared to take their lead from their "elders and betters" and no longer willing to be considered and presented as socially and morally inferior. The arts mirrored what was happening in society and doing so in ways that were intended to fire the imaginations of the young: the angry theatre of John Osborne and Harold Pinter, the literature of disillusionment from the likes of John Braine and Alan Sillitoe, and the gritty monochrome "social problem" films from Britain's New Wave film directors.

Cracknell's 2005 article "Under the Bomb" continues: "Early in the '60s, four things happened: those under 25 came into the majority for the first time ever, that cohort had money in their pocket for the first time ever, an element of choice came into the shops—and the pill."

Young people, now less inclined to be restrained by the moral and social mores of their parents, threw themselves into the new scene of drugs, sex, and rock 'n' roll. Although not necessarily all at the same time or in that order.

American rock 'n' roll music of the late '50s and early '60s was losing its initial appeal, as was the distinctly British craze of skiffle. The largely acoustic-guitar-led craze was fading almost as quickly as it had started, replaced by electric British beat music.

• • • • • •

Amateur skifflers, still keen to carry on making their own music, found themselves at a musical crossroads. Traditionalists understandably rejected the emerging British beat scene as too mainstream and were not drawn to American-influenced electric rhythm and blues. They thus found a renewed interest in British folk music.

Its original proponents historically had been upper-middle-class men, for the most part, including Harvard professor Francis James Child, who had a passion for English ballads, and the Edwardian music teacher Cecil Sharp. In Britain, folk music's original epicenter was a 1930s redbrick building situated in London's Camden Town. Cecil Sharp House, the London home of the unpromisingly prosaic English Folk Dance and Song Society (EFDSS), was the spiritual headquarters of the first British folk revival.

For real enthusiasts, the mother lode of British folk sat on the shelves of its ornate sheet music library. Sharp's sheet music archive stood tall among the treasures of early British folk music. Active in the early 1900s, during the first British folk revival, Sharp was an upper-middle-class music teacher and folklorist. He was also an avid collector and archivist of traditional folk songs and dances, his work a precursor to that of American rural song collectors John and Alan Lomax. Collecting at a time when many folk songs existed only in the memories of a few ageing rural singers, Sharp had scoured the British Isles before travelling in 1916 to America to collect material. Then in his mid-fifties, his age and ill-health excused him from the horrors of the trenches, so he swapped the Somme for the oppressive heat of rural Tennessee, from where he reported: "It is strenuous work. . . . There are no roads in our sense of the word. . . . I go about in a blue shirt, a pair of flannel trousers with a belt, a Panama hat and an umbrella. The heat is very trying."

Working vigorously between 1901 and 1920, he lacked the advantage of electronic recording equipment and painstakingly recorded songs in written musical notation in a series of field notebooks. Unlike the Lomaxes, who often claimed their own copyright on songs they collected, Sharp carefully noted where he had collected a song and the singer who had sung it for him. His notebook recorded that in 1918, he collected a version of "Barbara Allen" from "Aunt" Maria Tomes, an eighty-five-year-old former enslaved woman who lived in a log cabin in Nellysford, Virginia—adding a footnote that she smoked a pipe.

He was searching for purer, unadulterated versions of British songs and found that many had been preserved by the descendants of early settlers living in the remote hollows and isolated rural communities of southern Appalachia. In his diary entry for September 10, 1916, he noted: "I have now taken down 250 tunes, and am realizing that the field here is even richer than that which I have been investigating for fifteen or more years in England—a most unexpected fact!"

But, unlike the Lomaxes, he was only interested in white music; on his American travels he only collected two songs from Black singers. In one of his later journals, he described a trip through rural Kentucky: "We tramped—mainly uphill. When we reached the cove we found it peopled entirely by n——!! All our trouble and spent energy for naught."

Sharp's hope was to find English folk music preserved in a historical aspic in rural Appalachia. The endemic, odious racism and language of the time notwithstanding, it obviously never occurred to Sharp that there may have been cross-cultural and cross-racial music making happening. The idea that hillbilly or old-time American music was exclusively white was as ignorant as imagining that only Black musicians played, or felt, the blues. The exchange of musical ideas has always enriched music, but Sharp's mission was to establish the idea that the British Isles, and England in particular, had a musical heritage and that it was neither "a land without music" nor populated by "an unmusical people," as Oskar Hermann Schmitz, a German music critic, had claimed in 1904 to the chagrin of Britain's musical elite.

Sharp's many notebooks, which recorded close to five thousand songs as well as traditional Morris and sword dancing, were bequeathed to the EFDSS and rest in the library of the house built to commemorate both Sharp and his work. Mike Yates, the editor of the EFDSS's *Folk Music Journal*, credits him as a musical giant, "a man who, with unbelievable dedication, had almost single-handedly preserved a whole tradition that would otherwise have vanished under the indifference of a rapidly changing world."

Other song collectors were working during this first revival of British folk, but they were largely a classically inclined group. Composers like Ralph Vaughn Williams and Percy Grainger went on song-collecting trips across the country, noting and transcribing songs from rural workers. Like Cecil Sharp, they were earnest in their endeavors to record the history of British song from what they viewed as the bottom up. "Folklore," a term first coined in 1846 by antiquarian William Thoms, was in many ways an academic construct focused on "the traditions . . . of the uncultured masses." But in tidying up melodies and cleaning up ribald lyrics, those who sought to save rural songs changed many of them into material suitable for being sung by a group of urban enthusiasts in dinner jackets and evening dress. Largely due to this propensity, by the end of World War I, English folk music had become a dry, academic pursuit.

However, in the lead-up to the brief skiffle boom and its focus on American folk songs, a renewed and parallel interest in indigenous traditional song emerged. Whereas skiffle employed the tough, romantic themes of American songs set on prison farms with chain gangs or featured stories of hobos hitching rides across the Great Divide, the English folk revival embraced traditional British pastoral themes. This mix of styles meant that in the 1960s, the music heard across a typical evening in a British folk club was often a heady blend of British, Irish, and American material.

Unaccompanied, finger-in-the-ear songs like the Irish air "She Moved Through the Fair," sung by earnest young men and women in chunky sweaters, would make up half of the evening. The other half might include a guitarist who had mastered Davey Graham's 1960s adaptation of the same melody but with an Indian-Arabic tinged DADGAD tuning and renamed "She Moved thru the Bizarre/Blue Raga." Contemporary British and American songs often juxtaposed rural plainsong against adaptations of traditional songs that romanticized the lives of the working class in the industrialized cities. Despite the incongruity, it seemed to satisfy most of the performers and their audiences. Much like the Greenwich Village folk revivalists, most British folk enthusiasts, drawn to songs about downtrodden farm laborers or exploited steelworkers, were well educated, urban, middle-class, and usually strangers to either plough or blast furnace.

The 1960s British folk club scene was, like that in America, also characterized by the political nature of much of the music and many of the club organizers, audiences, and players. The founding fathers of the second British folk revival, Bert Lloyd and Ewan MacColl (the latter born James Henry Miller), were active in left-wing politics. Through the Workers' Music Association, the folk movement had strong links to both the Ban the Bomb movement (later the CND [Campaign for Nuclear Disarmament]), the Socialist Workers' Party, and other left-leaning activists. MacColl in particular wore his politics on his sleeve, having written both "The Ballad of Ho Chi Min" and "The Ballad of Stalin."

The opening verse of the latter tells how "Old Joe" had led the Soviet people on the road to victory. Listeners expecting the next verse to contain a witty sting will be disappointed: there are another eight verses of adulation before the song's conclusion. MacColl was unflinching in his regard for Stalin while failing to mention gulags and Stalin's Great Purge. Ignoring the deaths of millions, he focused on proselytizing that the workers' state was "the best that the world had ever seen." Little wonder, really, that most folk clubs were rumored to have had members of the UK security services mingling among the audience. When visitors enquired as to how to spot them, regulars warned, "Watch out for anyone tall wearing white socks." With Young Communist leaflets and the odd protest march banner on hand, if you spotted anyone wearing an old blue duffle coat, you could be moderately confident there would be a CND badge pinned on it somewhere. The iconic design contained the semaphore letters for *N* (nuclear) and *D* (disarmament) and appeared on numerous folk club guitars, a cold war update of Woody Guthrie's "This Machine Kills Fascists." (Even by the late '60s, thick, woolen World War II navy surplus duffle coats, or "convoy coats," redundant after the Battle of the Atlantic, were still in plentiful supply.)

At these CND marches, acoustic guitars were always present, accompanying antinuclear protest songs and providing entertainment. In fact, some people's first experience of seeing an acoustic guitar played in person would have been on these marches or at these gatherings, thus steering many listeners to the folk clubs.

These elements helped cement the guitar as the universal instrument of youth. While the enthusiasm of singers and audiences kept the idea of traditional British folk music alive, by the late '50s, acoustic guitar players had started appearing between a cappella renditions of "John Barleycorn" and group singing of "Spencer the Rover." Meanwhile, folk clubs were multiplying. In 1961, the British folk magazine *Sing* reported that there were thirty-six across Britain. Ten years later, it was estimated that London alone boasted four hundred—albeit many were impromptu affairs held in the upstairs rooms of pubs or in the back of coffee bars, often emerging from the embers of skiffle clubs. In the early days of what was a real revival of folk music, some clubs even encouraged "guitar play-alongs," with the singer on the stage shouting out the chord changes to an audience populated by budding guitarists. The contemporary music in many folk clubs, still influenced by the largely amateur skiffle bands, was often rough and ready. Perhaps too ready, and sometimes very rough, for a young audience whose pop sensibilities were beginning to be shaped by beat groups.

American folk singer Peggy Seeger, half-sister of folk legend Pete, had been swept up by the British skiffle movement on a visit to England and had stayed on. She remembered trying to "put a stop to everybody bringing a guitar and having to tune the entire front row." Jimmie McGregor, half of the popular folk duo Hall & McGregor, recalled, "At the time there were very few (. . . really competent . . .) guitar players around. I always reckoned if you could play three chords in the late fifties you were employable—if you could play five you were a virtuoso. If you could play any more you were a bloody show-off."

Often, Jimmie McGregor's show-offs were visiting American guitarists who had started touring Europe, and especially Britain, in the early '60s. Some, like Tom Paxton, came over regularly for a few dates, but others—singer-guitarists like Ramblin' Jack Elliott, Paul Simon, and Jackson C. Frank—stayed for extended periods. Many were hoping to gain a paid residency at the Troubadour in West London, a coffeehouse-style club tucked in a basement on the Brompton Road. American folk players who had been scraping a meagre living passing the hat in Greenwich Village venues heard of a warmer, more lucrative welcome for their kind of music in Britain. Other visitors to the UK were starry-eyed teenagers coming to Europe to escape the conformity of the Midwest and the prospect of an equally conforming job. They found British folk clubs not just in London and other major cities but in most towns. And they were busy most nights of the week, playing to audiences enthusiastic to hear the original writers of popular songs like "The Last Thing on My Mind" or guitarists who had not only seen but also knew and had played with legends like Woody Guthrie and Lead Belly.

Guthrie's and Lead Belly's old sparring partner, Pete Seeger, visited in the early '60s to play at the Royal Albert Hall. That gig was followed by a tour of the independent folk clubs that had financially sponsored the London concert. Playing a fundraiser for his legal fees (incurred following his indictment for contempt of Congress by the McCarthy-led HUAC), Seeger found Britain to be both welcoming and a haven, a place where he could sing without fear of being imprisoned for promoting communism or accused of trying to overthrow the government through the power of song.

Seeger, like many of the Americans who came to Britain, was just a better, more technically advanced player. He was also a more experienced performer, albeit sometimes he seemed a little too showbiz slick compared to many of the regular British "gentlemen amateurs" playing the club circuit at the time. The American players also had more direct experience of the early Black blues guitar styles that had flooded Greenwich Village during these years and echoed in the playing of the mainly white male players.

Rather than just listening to the live appearances of players like John Hurt and Skip James or devouring old country-blues records, by the late 1950s, young middle-class disciples could pay $5 an hour for lessons from once-forgotten

Black country blues guitarists like Rev. Gary Davis. Stefan Grossman, who had some success in Britain, and Woody Mann would both later set up businesses to teach country, Texas, and Delta blues as well as ragtime to baby boomers, first using instructional LPs, then more convenient cassette tapes, and finally CDs and videos.

It seemed that American players coming to the UK from the established New York and Chicago folk scenes of the early '50s knew they couldn't get away with just strumming a few chords and knocking out the same fare of traditional singalongs as a lot of British singers on the folk circuit did. Paul Simon had spent a few years in the early '60s trying to break into the Tin Pan Alley–dominated music business, as both a songwriter and recording artist. He made demos for successful Brill Building writers like Burt Bacharach and husband-and-wife team Gerry Goffin and Carole King and even had a couple of minor hit records. But after hearing Dylan's first two LPs, Simon decided to try his hand at folk music and teamed up with his old high school singing partner Art Garfunkel, but the duo found little success in the Greenwich Village clubs. "Hello darkness, my old friend"—the opening line of "The Sound of Silence," which would become the duo's first major folk-rock hit in late 1965—was initially ridiculed for being a little too contrived and inauthentic by the likes of Dave van Ronk, Bob Dylan, and others in the close-knit Village folk scene that still revered Woody Guthrie.

Discouraged, Garfunkel returned to Columbia University, but Simon, having heard about Dylan's positive experience playing folk in Britain, where he had befriended Martin Carthy, left to try his luck as a solo artist in London. Once there, he also connected with Carthy as well as Roy Harper and other accomplished British folk guitarists who realized that Simon not only was an extremely accomplished fingerpicker who could play most of Dylan's popular songs but also someone who knew how to perform. One popular club guitarist from the period, who gave Simon free bed and board when he played a residency at the Brentwood Folk Club, noted: "He really knew his way around the fretboard. The better club players were beginning to stumble on some advanced chord shapes, but he knew the actual names of really complex chords. We might know *how* they went together but Paul knew *why*!" The British folk singer Harvey Andrews had also seen Simon perform during this period: "The first time I saw Paul Simon, I couldn't believe how brilliant he was. I can remember what he sang . . . 'A Church Is Burning,' 'He Was My Brother,' . . . and 'Sound of Silence.' His guitar technique was like an orchestra to us. We'd not seen or heard that type of playing."

It also appears, from conversations with British guitar enthusiasts who attended Simon's first gigs in Britain, that part of his appeal was due to the fact he played a Martin guitar, no doubt bought with the proceeds of a minor Everly Brothers–style hit record, "Hey, Schoolgirl," that he recorded in 1957 when he and Art Garfunkel first played together as Tom and Jerry. So rare were sightings of expensive Martins in Britain that amateur and professional players would travel miles to catch a glimpse of the legendary instruments.

But it was these American performers who first introduced British folk guitarists to what had become, by the 1940s, the two main styles of guitar accompaniment in America: the picking styles of Maybelle Carter and Merle Travis were more sympathetic and interesting ways for a solo singer to accompany themselves with a guitar than just crudely strumming chords.

Of course, neither Maybelle Carter nor Merle Travis invented the picking styles that carried their names. Maybelle had been taught what became known as the Carter "scratch" or "lick" by Lesley Riddle, a Black banjo player who used to play clawhammer-style banjo and travelled with A. P. Carter, the leader of the Carter Family band, on his various song-collecting trips. Merle Travis certainly developed and popularized the syncopated thumb-picking style still immensely popular today, but he learned it as "Muhlenberg picking," after his home county in Kentucky. But both Bill Monroe and Travis made no secret that they knew the technique had first come from Arthur Schultz, a Black guitar and banjo player and teacher who toured Muhlenberg County. Schultz also taught Ike Everly, father of the Everly Brothers, who lived in the coal-mining community there in the 1930s.

But the arrival of better players from America in the mid-1960s helped accelerate what had been a growing shift away from crude guitar strumming into a unique, British style of playing. British progressive folk had at its heart a distinctive form of finger-style picking, as initially exemplified by traditionalist Martin Carthy. Apart from befriending and teaching both Bob Dylan and Paul Simon many traditional ballads, including his arrangement of "Scarborough Fair" (which both would record without crediting the British player), Carthy had taken both players under his wing, and they were clearly influenced by his style of playing. His percussive playing and idiosyncratic arrangements of traditional songs had also influenced a whole group of young British players, including Nic Jones and Richard Thompson. Carthy was himself influenced by his contemporaries: the gentle jazz and baroque playing of John Renbourn; the aggressive string-snapping of the gruff Scot Bert Jansch; and the maverick playing of musical polymath Davey Graham, a mythical figure of the British folk revival.

Graham stood out as a hip and culturally mystical character. Of mixed Indo-Guyanese and Scottish descent, he had from the age of fifteen devoted his life to playing and exploring the guitar in all its manifestations. By his late teens, Graham had already travelled extensively in Morocco and the Middle East, soaking up the influence of what became dismissively known as World Music. In 1962, aged just twenty-one, he made his first commercial recording, the now highly collectable EP *3/4 AD*, featuring British blues pioneer Alexis Korner, late of the Chris Barber and Ken Colyer bands.

This influential record included both the finger-busting "Angi" and a duet with Korner that was more than a nod to the modal jazz of "All Blues" by Miles Davis. In 1962, this Davis track, from the landmark album *Kind of Blue* (1959), was still a rarity, found only in the hippest of British bed-sits. Graham, following a brief national TV appearance in a Ken Russell documentary, *Hound Dogs and Bach Addicts*, had cemented his reputation as one of Britain's most eclectic acoustic guitarists. And in the tradition of many guitar legends, he was difficult, arrogant, and—due to a dedicated consumption of alcohol and heroin—notoriously unreliable. Despite his undoubted talent, promoters were unwilling to risk booking him. When he was short of money, and with no prospect of being booked for paying gigs, he would take guitar students looking to learn from the legend's erratic flame. Bert Jansch recalls Graham taking a student's £5, putting on a Ravi Shankar record, and telling them to listen. Graham then popped down to the local pub to spend the £5 on beer, only interrupting his drinking to return and turn the LP over. When Graham talked about the *3/4 AD* recording and the role of Alexis Korner, his much more established playing partner, he remarked, "I had the facility, he had the intensity—passion compensating for technique."

It's the combination of technique and innate passion that makes a guitar hero, and Jansch ably demonstrated that he had both in equal measure. He had grown up in the traditional folk club scene of Edinburgh, and while there he was heavily influenced by his contemporary, Graham. In fact, Jansch was first taught guitar by Graham's half-sister, who, it can be assumed, lent her student *3/4 AD*. Once Jansch had discovered that Graham was using alternate tunings (primarily DADGAD, which Graham had adapted from the tuning of the Middle Eastern *oud* and Indian sitar), he picked the tunes apart and synthesized them into the unique Jansch guitar style.

Bert Jansch's other early influence was Annie Briggs, an enigmatic young Nottinghamshire folk singer with a technical understanding of how some of the great British folk tunes were constructed. She and Jansch briefly became lovers and then long-term collaborators: Briggs helped him discover and deconstruct the Irish folk song "Down by Black Waterside," a totem of progressive folk-rock, subsequently allegedly "borrowed" by Led Zeppelin and lightly reworked as "Black Mountain Side" (although wrongly assuming Jansch's use of an alternate DADGAD tuning). On Jansch's own 1966 recording, the writing credit on "Black Waterside" lists "Traditional"; by 1969, the writing credit on the Led Zeppelin track reads "Jimmy Page." Page is alleged to have pulled the same stunt on his Yardbirds "composition" "White Summer," which he "borrowed" note-for-note from both Jansch's and Graham's arrangements of the traditional Irish ballad "She Moved Through the Fair." Page even wrote Graham's discovery cum invention, DADGAD tuning, out of his version by renaming it CIA (Celtic-Indian-Arabic) and effectively claiming it as his.

It's said that if a guitarist's left hand shows what they know, then the right shows who they are. The logic behind the maxim is that the left, fretting hand is selecting the notes or the chords, and that is a matter of memory, of knowing where the notes are. The right hand is the personality and style of the player. Not just whether you strum, fingerpick in a fixed pattern, or pick in a free, more intuitive way, but the way you do it. The various nuances become your signature sound. Professional guitarists talk about Jansch having a "dancing left hand" and a "highly syncopated, free-flowing right." The dancing left hand not only refers to his unerring ability to select the perfect notes from along the length of the fretboard but also signals how he added personality by using his left hand to bend strings, add delicate vibrato, mute strings, or slide into and out of notes. His free-flowing right hand demonstrates his seamless ability with rhythm. Many players took many months trying to replicate Jansch's placement of notes, but it took them countless years to come close to his complex rhythmic tricks and off-measure time signatures. Jansch, like Davey Graham, was influenced by folk, jazz, blues, and both Eastern melody and time signatures. But unlike Graham, in Jansch the influence is a subtle undercurrent rather than any overt inlay or pastiche. His repertoire, a blend of American folk-blues and fresh arrangements of traditional British and Irish songs, resulted in Jansch surpassing his early influencer to become the guitarist du jour of the London folk-blues scene headquartered in the Les Cousins club in London's Soho.

Les Cousins, an all-night folk club opened in 1965 on Soho's Greek Street, occupied little more than a basement corridor below a Greek bistro. Despite its diminutive size, anyone who was anyone in the '60s guitar-driven contemporary folk scene played there. It thrived initially because many established folk clubs doubted the worth of nontraditional folk and wouldn't host it on their stages. Les Cousins opened at 10 p.m. and ran until 7:30 the next morning. Many performers started their professional careers there, using it to try out new material before an often sleep-deprived audience as well as to swap ideas and guitar techniques with other players. Jansch, John Renbourn, and Wizz Jones, all stalwarts of the scene, were virtually resident players from the first few weeks of the club's opening. Many guitarists, from visiting Americans Paul Simon and Bob Dylan to Brits Cat Stevens, Ralph McTell, Roy Harper, John Martyn, and Nick Drake, all passed through, and a little of the place rubbed off on each of them. Ian A. Anderson, a popular '60s folk club musician and later editor of *Roots* music magazine, recalled that "the music got so exciting because everybody listened to everybody else. So although you might choose to play one thing, at the same time, you had an open mind for something else."

For most of his playing career Jansch played a relatively basic, Japanese-made Yamaha version of the classic Martin dreadnought. Despite his legendary status and enduring influence, it seems unlikely that Jansch ever made big money from his craft, and it's easy to speculate that this was why he settled for a relatively modest guitar. Celine Camerlynck, the luthier who made a series of repairs on Jansch's Yamaha, explained that he liked the large profile neck Yamahas have, the larger body of a dreadnought, and the unfussy way it suited a working musician. Across the '60s Jansch was known for turning up to gigs and borrowing a guitar to play. In later years he prided himself in rarely buying guitars, and clearly Yamaha would have gifted him his guitars from some point. But it's also fair to say that the Yamaha sounds pretty good, and we could romanticize that, as a modest man, Jansch wasn't seduced by Martin's classic original version.

But it wasn't just the tone that Jansch squeezed out of whatever guitar he had to hand that makes him so important—it's his blend of techniques that delivered the emotion in his playing. He recalled that in his teens he saw Big Bill Broonzy on a black-and-white Scottish TV documentary and noticed how Broonzy's "big, white thumb-pick popped out of the TV screen," mistakenly assuming that was the root of his highly percussive playing. But like many British players influenced by Broonzy, he eventually realized that the "rhythms were held down by the thumb" while the fingers picked out the melody. Players refer to Big Bill's "dead thumb" playing totally independently from the fingers.

The footage he recalled was from *Low Light and Blue Smoke*, a deeply atmospheric seventeen-minute film made in 1956 at the instigation of Belgian couple Yannick and Margo Bruynoghe, Broonzy's occasional promoters and managers in Europe. The film, made by a college friend of the Bruynoghes, twenty-six-year-old Jean Delire, was a stylized documentary set in a smoky Belgian cellar bar and made to showcase and promote Bill, then in his mid-sixties but looking twenty years younger. It went on to influence a generation of British guitarists across the early '60s. Although little-seen upon its initial release, after winning a few awards, it came to the attention of celebrated Scottish documentary filmmaker John Grierson and featured in his series *This Wonderful World.*

The five songs captured on the film highlight Broonzy's rhythmically driven playing, marked by bass runs and a thumping but heavily dampened monotonic bass. Like Robert Johnson, he often sounds like two guitars playing at once. In showing the Broonzy film, Grierson had reached an unlikely audience: the many teenage wannabe guitarists waiting to be shown the light in a still bleak Britain. Decades before video recorders or play-on-demand, and despite ITV broadcasting for only eight hours a day, the program is recalled by at least four music legends-in-waiting. Keith Richards, only twelve or thirteen at the time, recalls that in the film Broonzy "encapsulated everything I wanted—to sing, to play guitar and to be Black."

An equally prepubescent Eric Clapton apparently remembered: "The music alone would have been tremendously captivating, but to see Bill as this solo bluesman, cigarette smoke curling around him, under a bare lightbulb, just him and his guitar. I felt like I was looking into heaven."

Songwriter Ray Davies, who would found the British pop group the Kinks, back then was just another North London teenager trying to learn guitar and sing. He remembers seeing the film and knowing that "what I saw and heard changed my life." He was probably speaking for all working-class aspiring pop stars when he opined: "It didn't matter to me that he was Black and from Chicago. What mattered was that he sounded like me. He had rough edges to his music. There was nothing contrived about it, and he sounded working class. He didn't seem to be anything other than what he was."

Broonzy, like Josh White before him, already had a long and varied career before he arrived in Europe, and, like White, he was to die young. Both men also achieved a level of popular fame that brought the true voice and character of Black folk and blues to a popular white audience. They performed to entertain, of course, but they also shined a spotlight on the endemic racism toward Black people in America. They also had an enormous influence on

British musicians through their songwriting and guitar playing and subsequently on the development of modern folk and blues music in the 1960s. Both men reconstructed or embroidered their life stories to suit personal circumstances, whether their marital status, career aspirations, or the mood of listening audiences. Studs Terkel, the American author, broadcaster, and oral historian, knew Broonzy well. Looking back over various interviews Broonzy had granted, Terkel noted with a slight barb that "Bill is always telling the truth . . . his truth." Broonzy was a whole lot more interesting and multilayered than their standard musical fare to fans like Ray Davies, Keith Richards, and Eric Clapton.

In 1951, Bert Wilcox, an English folk club promoter who had seen Broonzy perform to much acclaim in Paris, booked him to appear at the 1,500-seat Kingsway Hall in London to just a few dozen folk and blues enthusiasts. A few months earlier, Josh White had given his UK farewell concert in the same room to a capacity crowd. Given that Bill had yet to officially release any records in Britain, the audience huddled together in the old Methodist chapel were enthusiasts of the raw country-blues that Broonzy had returned to, a sound rarely heard in postwar Britain. According to the review by the respected jazz journalist Max Jones, writing in the weekly music newspaper *Melody Maker*, Broonzy "found here an audience receptive to the best songs in his extensive repertoire and to his finest feats of guitar-manship, an audience that regarded him as a combination of creative artist and living legend."

Having left behind him the guitar of his Chicago years, a 1920 Gibson Style O artist model archtop, Broonzy adopted a Martin 000-28 flat-top that he played until the end of his life. The country-blues singer was enamored with Europe, a place where he was adored and celebrated, a place where Jim Crow racism didn't exist and where he would not be arrested for being a Black man. In fact, he was so comfortable in France, Belgium, and Britain, that despite periods at home in the US to tour and see his wife and family, Broonzy regularly returned to Europe to play and also to visit the child he fathered with his longtime Dutch girlfriend, Pim.

He was a popular fixture on the British folk circuit in the '50s (folk clubs were where early blues enthusiasts tended to congregate), liking both the touring life in Britain and the undoubted appreciation of audiences who may never have seen a Black performer live before. He also had a liking for whisky and the company of women. Hosted by the Waterson folk dynasty, he played a one-night gig well off the beaten blues track in Hull, Yorkshire, only a couple of years before his death. The British folk guitarist Martin Carthy was there, and as well as being impressed at seeing an actual Martin guitar for the first time, he vividly recalled Broonzy's urgent need for "a big drink" after the show. They took him to the Gainsborough, a local fish-and-chip restaurant and the only place open after eleven p.m. in the port town. Broonzy, looking at the menu of fish and chips and potato patties and chips enquired, "Do they serve Whisky & Chips?"

Broonzy was a charismatic, imposing, and attractive figure in the monochrome Britain of the late '50s. Val Wilmer, a photographer and music writer who met most visiting jazz and blues musicians during the period—from Ellington to Coltrane to Muddy Waters to Hendrix—was not easily starstruck, but she clearly recalled the impression Broonzy made when she met him during his last visit to London in 1957. "He was this huge man coming into the room. . . . I don't think there is any other meeting I've ever had with somebody like that . . . who was so important to me."

Broonzy's advantage over Josh White, his immediate predecessor in Britain, was that the jazz and blues cognoscenti were much more willing to see him as the authentic, "real" blues man. For them, Broonzy was the link between prewar players and postwar guitar music—a Black man born into an enslaved family with a troubled past and an aggressive, raw guitar style to match. He was the natural bridge between the often hard to listen to but authentic country-blues singers of the '20s and '30s and the "slick and effete" Josh White. Broonzy had worked out that both white American and European audiences wanted their blues singers rugged and unpretentious. The version of Big Bill he presented played up the slightly problematic stereotype of a hard-travelled Black man from the Mississippi cotton fields, accompanying himself with a simple guitar and singing the songs that he learned as a child on the cotton plantation or picked up on the road.

Broonzy had been born in rural Arkansas in 1903, a date that he usually massaged back to 1893, which allowed him to talk with authority about his time serving in the US Army in Europe in World War I. Initially a corn-husk or cigar-box fiddle player, in 1923, twenty-one-year-old Broonzy (like Josh White, Louis Armstrong, and so many rural Southern players at the time) became part of the Great Migration, moving north in search of opportunity in the thriving Black metropolis of Chicago's South Side. Opportunity for Broonzy came in the shape of Papa Charlie Jackson, the man who in 1924 first popularized the concept of recordings featuring a solo singer accompanied by guitar. Jackson taught Broonzy to play guitar, and they went on to appear together in minstrel and medicine shows. It may seem odd, but it was not unusual for Black musicians to appear in blackface minstrel shows. Success was far from instant, but Broonzy just plugged away for the next ten years, playing solo and in a variety of bands and writing songs for other Chicago players. During this time, he developed a unique R&B guitar style and a "virile yet mellifluous rooster crow" of a voice. That voice got him invited, in 1935, into the studio to record a few sides for the prestigious Vocalian Records label.

In December 1938, he got his big break by filling in for the recently deceased Robert Johnson at the "From Spirituals to Swing" concert at Carnegie Hall. The show, billed as "An Evening of Negro Music," was produced by John H. Hammond, the man who had recorded Bessie Smith's last sessions and Billie Holiday's first. Hammond would later recruit and record Aretha Franklin, Bob Dylan, and Bruce Springsteen. That evening, in front of a capacity audience and on the same bill as the Count Basie Orchestra, Sidney Bechet, Benny Goodman, and Sister Rosetta Tharp, the largely unknown Broonzy walked out onstage with only an acoustic guitar and premiered "It Was Just a Dream," a song he had recently written but was yet to record.

The song sets up the idea of an African American being welcomed as an equal into the White House, even being offered the opportunity to sit in the president's chair—a brave if not audacious song choice in front of a primarily white New York audience before the civil rights movement. The subject of the song was especially surprising since most of what Broonzy had been writing and singing before he found himself booked to play in front of what was his biggest audience to date was hokum—double (and sometimes single) entendre songs like "Tight Like That," "How You Want It Done," and "I Want My Hands on It."

A few years later, after Broonzy realized that he could probably be more successful with a white, city-dwelling audience, and through involvement with Pete Seeger's postwar People's Songs initiative, he wrote "Black, Brown and White Blues," a song that he played and carried with him for the rest of his life. The song explains that if you were white, you were "alright." Even if you were brown, you could probably "stick around." But if you were Black, you needed to "Get back, get back, get back."

It was a courageous act for a Black man to have written and performed such a song, as it predated the popular politicizing of folk songs that happened during the '60s folk revival. His subsequent involvement in the touring folk music revue "I Come for to Sing" completed his transition from urban Chicago blues player to solo folk blues guitarist and singer. It was this version of Broonzy who first arrived in Europe in 1951 and subsequently appeared in *Low*

Light and Blue Smoke. His performances in the film show the enormous sound that he got out of his guitar and why reviewers of his first London concerts refer to "the immense sound and swing of the guitar playing, the dexterity of the solos, the richness of the accompaniment and the wonderful relationship between the vocal and instrumental parts."

• • • • • •

So it was that among the many young British guitarists of the late '50s and '60s whom Broonzy influenced, there was Bert Jansch. And it was Jansch who picked up the baton and further inspired the next generation. Jansch's confusion over Broonzy using "a white thumb pick" was probably the result of the usual luminous ghosting on early British black-and-white televisions. Broonzy rarely, if ever, played with a thumb-pick, preferring bare flesh from which he was able to create his driving style. Folk guitarist Martin Carthy, who had helped fund Broonzy's "whisky and chips," commented, "Whatever Bill played, it just swung like hell."

To get his own signature swing and sound, Jansch combined the exaggerated but muted bass enabled by a thumb pick with a subtle left-hand technique. His technical and stylistic influence is still quietly present in today's acoustic and electric guitar music from Britain and America, as it has been for the past forty years. Neil Young revered him: "As much of a great guitar player as Jimi (Hendrix) was, Bert Jansch is the same thing for acoustic guitar . . . and my favorite."

Young admitted that his own "Ambulance Blues" leaned heavily on Jansch's "The Needle of Death." Young recorded his own version of the latter song for Jansch's memorial concert in London at the end of 2013. Unable to attend the concert in person, the ever-idiosyncratic Young sent instead a film that in its own way spoke to Jansch's ability to reach back to folk songs from hundreds of years earlier while projecting himself forward into the later guitar styles of British electric players like Johnny Marr and Bernard Butler. Everyone in the audience that night was moved when Young ambled into frame on the film, picked up an old Martin 0-21 guitar, and squeezed into a vintage Voice-O-Graph record-cutting booth, a piece of equipment no bigger than a telephone box, to "cut" a one-take 45 rpm acetate. By choosing to sing an unadorned version of "The Needle of Death," he seemed to be paying back a debt on behalf of every guitarist who directly stole or unknowingly borrowed from Jansch. As the *Guardian* newspaper reported the next day, "It was a great act of respect, a little ancient, a little modern."

The acoustic guitar music of the late '60s was also "a little ancient and a little modern"—a time when Delta blues, traditional folk, and modal jazz were at the center of an era of genre bending in serious contemporary music. It's easy to see the influence of Delta blues and traditional folk in much of the acoustic music of the time, but the influence of the modal jazz recording "All Blues" spanned both sides of the Atlantic, whether sitting at the heart of Tim Buckley's "Strange Feelin'," or of "Hear My Call" from British folk-jazz fusion group Pentangle.

Pentangle was the coming together of two extraordinarily talented guitarists: Jansch and his English contemporary John Renbourn. Rather than being supported by a modern, modal jazz rhythm section, they worked alongside Danny Thompson's freely inventive, trippy upright bass with Terry Cox delicately brushing his way across a full drum kit.

• • • • • •

In the late '50s, those amateur skifflers not lured into the folk scene but still driven by the "let's get a group together" culture that skiffle had generated looked either to the British blues scene or the more rock 'n' roll–orientated beat sound. The more professional picked up the guitar-led style of Chuck Berry and added the rhythmic template of Buddy Holly to create a big-beat, danceable rock 'n' roll music of their own. Beat, and Merseybeat in particular, was also an antidote to the British versions of Elvis (Cliff Richard, Tommy Steele, etc.) who were now performing largely dreary ballad-based music.

British groups modified the established skiffle group format—a singer with acoustic guitar out front supported by a second guitarist and a rhythm section of tea-chest or string bass and washboard. They adapted it to feature an electric lead guitar supported by a rhythm guitar, with electric bass guitar and drums playing four-to-the-floor with a backbeat. With minor variations, this lineup remained the essential blueprint for most popular groups for the next fifty years.

The Liverpool groups played a rock 'n' roll softened by tight male vocal harmonies and were immediately popular. Their numbers grew exponentially. Estimates are that in 1960 in the Mersey-Liverpool area alone, there were over three hundred Merseybeat groups that saturated the local clubs (so-called jive hives). As there were relatively few venues to play outside Liverpool and only a few clubs in London were willing to book them, the Mersey groups had to look further afield for places to play.

Germany once again provided an important catalyst. The country that supplied the cheap, accessible guitars used by the skiffle groups that had in turn helped create British rock 'n' roll was only a bilious ferry ride across the North Sea from England.

The port city of Hamburg had a lively club scene to entertain its many foreign visitors. The crowds were a combination of merchant sailors and tourists, all looking for a good time in the shape of alcohol, sex, drugs, and someplace to hear loud, lively, modern music. This made for a combustible mix. Because the rock 'n' roll scene had been slow to get started in Germany, the clubs looked to Britain for talent, and a steady supply of British bands made the trip to Hamburg. There the clubs didn't want bands simply to keep the drinkers, prostitutes, and their clients inside by playing continuously for several hours; they also had to *mach schau*, to make a show. Essentially, they had to kick up a noise and do more than stare at their shoes. Thus, many British groups, including the Beatles, used their time in small, sweaty Hamburg cellar clubs (like the Top Ten and Indra) to develop and perfect their acts. The Beatles' first booking in Hamburg was to play forty-eight consecutive nights at the Indra Club; their second was a fifty-six-night run at the Kaiserkeller. When they returned from Hamburg after months of playing up to ten one-hour sets across a day, seven days a week, in front of noisy crowds, it is no wonder they returned as a highly fluent five-piece unit. In the extensive sleeve notes to the Lennon box set *Anthology*, an extract from a '70s interview notes:

> It was Hamburg that did it. That's where we really developed. To get the Germans going and keep it up for twelve hours at a time we really had to hammer. We would never have developed as much if we'd stayed at home. We had to try anything that came into our heads in Hamburg. There was nobody to copy from. We played what we liked best and the Germans liked it as long as it was loud.

It was woodshedding inverted. It was playing to rowdy, receptive audiences instead of going to a secluded hut in the garden or backyard, someplace where you wouldn't be disturbed or disturb others, to work at a song or musical part repeatedly until it either drove you mad or you achieved perfection.

Woodshedding is the primary reason why the Beatles, by 1962 pruned down to just four members and with a new drummer, were so good in the studio from the outset. It obviously helped that they had two talented songwriters who could both sing and harmonize, an inventive lead guitarist in George Harrison, and a left-handed drummer (recently poached from another Hamburg group) with a unique musical style and perfect sense of tempo. Ringo Starr, although not a jazz-trained drummer like the Rolling Stones' Charlie Watts, influenced a generation of pop and rock drummers. He was definitely much better than the acerbic description of him allegedly given by Lennon when an enthusiastic journalist asked Lennon if he was the best drummer in the world: "Ringo's not even the best drummer in the Beatles."

Although their new manager, Brian Epstein, had no prior experience in talent management, he handled them wisely over the subsequent twenty-four months. While they had immediate success in Britain, none of their first three records, "From Me to You," "She Loves You," and "Please, Please Me," had made much of an impression on the *Billboard* chart. Before the Beatles, British bands just didn't trouble the US charts overmuch. Epstein knew that to break into America, they needed a number-one hit in the US, and he set Lennon and McCartney the task of writing one. Midway through October 1963, the pair sat at the piano in the basement of Paul's girlfriend's parents' house. They came up with the line "Oh you, got that something," and in just under an hour they had penned "I Want to Hold Your Hand." A week later, they spent the day recording it in Abbey Road Studios, along with two other tracks.

In December 1963, Epstein visited New York to broker the Beatles' first appearance on American TV. While there he gave an interview with the *New Yorker* magazine, recounting their success in Britain. The magazine noted that Epstein spoke "with an air that we associated more with an English drawing room than with Tin Pan Alley." His sober delivery stood in sharp contrast to the natural braggadocio of the cigar-chomping showbiz manager. The twenty-nine-year-old Epstein told his and the Beatles' story with the cool understatement of a man who knew "I Want to Hold Your Hand" was about to be released. He quietly talked of "minor TV appearances," "teenage girls weeping in the streets," and "riot scenes taxing the strength of the British police," all while "selling over five million records." Sounding like an accountant, he was assured in his subsequent predictions for geographic expansion and the future prospects for the business when he told the interviewer: "I think that America is ready for the Beatles. When they come, they will hit this country for a six."

Epstein didn't sound like Tin Pan Alley because he wasn't part of it. In fact, he was about to be instrumental in taking it apart. It's unknown whether the US music business, the *New Yorker* magazine, its journalists, or their readers were cricket fans and knew that hitting something "for a six" was the equivalent of hitting one out of the park. But they were about to find out. The timing of his visit was not by chance. On Boxing Day (December 26, 1963), the day "I Want to Hold Your Hand" was released in the US, it was number one in the UK.

Bob Dylan playing a 1930s Gibson Nick Lucas Special.

Gone Electric

"I Want to Hold Your Hand" reached number one on the *Billboard* Top 100 charts in America on January 17, 1964. The Beatles were poised to lead what the "most trusted man in America," CBS newscaster Walter Cronkite, termed "the British Invasion," bringing Beatlemania to the attention of the mass American audience. In the weeks leading up to their first appearance on the *Ed Sullivan Show*, much of the American press was writing about the Beatles. Even the sober-minded *Washington Post* ran a precursive foreign news story under the headline "Thousands of Britons 'Riot'—Liverpool Sound Stirs Up Frenzy."

It's impossible to overstate the scale and effect of the British Invasion on America. Thanks to the press coverage, when the Beatles first played the *Ed*

Sullivan Show on February 9, 1964, they pulled a record-breaking audience of over 73 million viewers. Nearly half the nation watched the band play that Sunday night, the adults no doubt appalled at the sight of the young teenage girls in the studio audience losing control and screaming hysterically. But while the Beatles led the invasion, the scale of the whole British musical juggernaut needs putting into perspective. Even the well-liked, but less groundbreaking, British pop band the Dave Clark Five was the star act on the weekly Sullivan show an extraordinary seventeen times. Such was the power of these British bands that the popularity of American pop genres from the late '50s and early '60s declined, including vocal groups like the Paris Sisters, the Blossoms, the Shirelles, and the Everly Brothers. The latter's unbroken run of thirty-five Top 100 hits came to a halt with the arrival of the Beatles. Phil Everly obviously recognized that the Beatles' close harmonies bore deep similarities to the brothers' own, and while he couldn't say anything too negative, he was sourly dismissive of the group. "I was listening to the music and to me it wasn't revolutionary . . . [but] they knew we were from the '50s . . . [and] you had to be English. It was 'in' to be English. Music quit being something you could earn your living by, it had to be a social movement." The irony was that both Lennon and McCartney adored the Everlys. "When John and I first started to write songs, I was Phil and he was Don," McCartney recalled.

It wasn't only close harmony groups that suffered; the hugely popular guitar-based instrumental surf music from groups like Dick Dale & the Del-Tones and the Ventures started to fizzle out almost as soon as it had begun. Even the career of Elvis Presley, a teen idol, was temporarily stalled. Some American bands even took to using faux English names and putting on English accents to gain popular traction and fans. Riding this wave of Beatlemania, and "guitar-and-drum" beat groups in general, was a domestic amateur guitar boom inspired by the social cachet and hormonal roller-coaster ride on offer for guitar heroes like John, George, and Paul.

All over the world, whether playing bossa, folk, or Merseybeat, the guitar worked the same magic. Brazilian beat journalist Ruy Castro, the "biographer of Brazil," wrote about the simultaneous rise in the popularity of acoustic guitar–led bossa nova and young male guitar players: "They all believed that their chances with members of the opposite sex would increase if they could duplicate what they heard on certain records they played until they wore out."

Pictures of the Beatles playing Gretsch Country Gentleman guitars and Epiphone Casinos were everywhere, so it's easy to see them as just an electric guitar band. But from the early '60s to the early '70s, George and John were often playing matching Gibson J-160E acoustic-electric guitars. The guitar sound on early recordings such as "Please, Please Me" and "Love Me Do" and on later songs such as "Norwegian Wood" were from these Gibsons, as was the first recorded instance of intentional guitar feedback at the head of "I Feel Fine."

The J-160E was not a particularly popular model when Gibson first introduced the concept of a flat-top acoustic, with a pickup installed under the top of the body, in 1954. The converted dreadnought-shaped instrument was primarily designed as a plug-in stage guitar and never sounded great acoustically. The plywood top, rather than solid spruce, and the ladder bracing didn't help the sound. For most working musicians, the J-160E was an acoustic workhorse at home and on the road, but when players plugged it in at gigs, they liked its punchy, percussive stage sound. The brittle, jangly tone sounds great when Lennon plays it on the recording of "Norwegian Wood," double-tracked alongside George Harrison's newly learned sitar part. Once the Beatles had used the instruments, sales picked up hugely. Lennon had seen these exotic imports in Rushworth's Music House in Liverpool in late 1962 when the band was yet to make any real money but needed new guitars. Their cautious manager Brian Epstein bought them for £161 each on "the never never" or hire-purchase credit. One of the two guitars was stolen in 1963 when the Beatles played a London Christmas show. It resurfaced in a US junk shop in the late '60s and was bought by a man named John McCaw, who initially didn't know what he had found. A little research and a few decades later, in 2015 the "Lennon guitar" sold at a Beverly Hills auction for $2.4 million. However, it is generally accepted, and supported by Beatles' guitars aficionado John F. Crowley, that the guitar that was stolen in 1963 was the instrument registered to George Harrison. He and Lennon apparently swapped the identical guitars quite often, but exactly whose or which guitar sold for $2.4 million seems to matter little. Lennon used the remaining J-160E extensively in both songwriting at home and studio recording, while Harrison more regularly played lead on electric guitar. Lennon acquired another J-160E in 1964 and managed to hang on to it. Following a psychedelic repaint in the flower-power era (carried out by Dutch artists Simon and Marieke Posthuma, known collectively as "The Fool"), it was stripped back down to bare wood and reappeared as the guitar Lennon strummed on "Give Peace a Chance" during John and Yoko Ono's 1969 "bed-ins" for peace.

• • • • • •

But Beatlemania wasn't the only factor that rapidly accelerated the popularity of the guitar. The earlier folk revival and subsequent rise of the contemporary folk scene in America had a huge influence on amateurs picking up acoustic guitars and the growth of the global guitar industry. Folk music had been largely underground from the late '40s through the mid-1950s, mainly as part of the politically aware beatnik scene. By the late '50s, it was emerging as a more popular mindset, and not just in Greenwich Village. There were parallel folk movements in Chicago (at the University of Illinois Chicago, the famous Old Town School of Folk Music, and numerous North Avenue clubs), Berkeley, Boston, Milwaukee, and in numerous college towns across America. While guitarist-singers like Bob Dylan and Joan Baez were important, for some folkies they were not sufficiently "authentic"; many enthusiasts preferred the rawer look and sound of groups like the New Lost City Ramblers or the "high lonesome" sound of singers like ex-miner and farm laborer Roscoe Holcomb and guitarist Doc Watson, who specialized in playing old-time fiddle tunes on acoustic guitar. But whatever complexion of folk you preferred, the five-string banjo and acoustic guitar were usually at the heart of it.

In 1961, Martin & Co. sold just over five thousand guitars. By the mid-1960s, demand for their guitars spiked due to a combination of the popularity of traditional folk followed by the Beatles boom and subsequent interest in folk-rock. Such was the demand that Martin dealers were waiting for up to three years to receive orders, with stores keeping what few Martins they had in glass display cases, further building waiting lists. In fact, the company was unable to take full advantage of the boom; the North Street factory just couldn't produce enough guitars to meet demand, and in July 1964 Martin finally opened a new production facility to answer what looked like insatiable demand. Production continued to steadily climb throughout the late 1960s. Annual sales reached a record 22,637 instruments in 1972. However, even with the new factory, demand continued to outstrip supply. The acoustic guitar had moved from something that professional musicians and enthusiasts played to something that every teenager and young adult had to have. Many American retailers were not only back-ordering Martins but any affordable, entry-level guitar from US makers. They were looking for something cheaper than Martin or Gibson but still of a quality they could sell to teenage players.

Cheaper American brands like Harmony, Kay, and Favilla also prospered during the '60s guitar boom, but most couldn't maintain quality when they stepped up production to meet demand. The guitars they produced were barely utilitarian—fine for campfire singalongs but not much else. Badly shaped and poorly fitted necks made them difficult to play, and truss rods (steel bars embedded in the neck to help keep it straight) that should have improved playability were often fitted but impossible to adjust. Poor-sounding and difficult-to-play guitars were fine as wall hangings, but such inferior instruments put many beginners off for life. While even a bad American-made guitar could be sold when there was nothing else available, when good-quality Japanese acoustics started arriving in big numbers and at good prices, those substandard makers were in trouble.

In the late '50s US importers and music stores, desperate for any stock at all, had often purchased cheap, and equally poorly made, "export grade" student guitars from Japan. With anglicized names like Kingston and Marco Polo, they obviously didn't quite serve, but they did provide an opportunity the premium Japanese manufacturer Yamaha quickly grasped. The company had been manufacturing classical guitars for the Japanese domestic market from just after World War II, building quality instruments in their small factory in Hamamatsu, Japan's "City of Music." In the mid-1960s, Yamaha finally introduced America to their first steel-string dreadnought-inspired models. These sold for around $99 and were of a far superior quality than American-made guitars of the same price. It was the making of the Yamaha brand, now a respected and dominant global guitar maker, but it was also the death knell for US makers like Harmony and Kay.

European, mainly German, manufacturers were already geared up, thanks to the British skiffle boom of the '50s, to take advantage of the subsequent acoustic and then electric guitar boom of the '60s. But two new names appeared from an unlikely quarter. The Hagstrom company in Sweden and Pigini in Italy were major piano accordion manufacturers, satisfying a postwar boom in polka dance music.

Polka music and the folk dance it accompanied were said to have originated in Poland in the 1840s. The dance itself, in speeded-up waltz time, was all the rage in East Coast beer gardens in the latter 1800s, where the boisterous couple's dance scandalized conservative middle-class Americans. Its popularity among eastern and southern European immigrants, "so-called 'hyphenated Americans,' German-, Polish-, Czech-Americans," led to it being seen as something that descendants of the first English Protestant settlers should avoid right up to the 1930s.

After World War II, a wider definition of "whiteness" emerged that now included groups like Polish and Italian Americans. Elements from these cultures, including pizza and Americanized pasta dishes from Italy and the polka from northern and eastern European countries, were slowly being accepted across the nation. In the decade between 1945 and 1955, Frankie Yankovic, using the bigger, louder piano accordion rather than the typical button accordion, was christened America's Polka King after he introduced an Americanized version of the polka with English lyrics and a jazz-influenced rhythm section. While Britain was crazing over skiffle, America was in the midst of its own polka dance craze.

Interest boomed in the music's signature sound, the piano accordion, and their makers set up strong distribution deals and a network of tutorial studios across America. But the craze faded in the early '60s with the arrival of the Beatles and the popular triumph of rock 'n' roll. When accordion sales fell, Hagstrom and Pigini decided to switch to manufacturing the more-popular guitar. While Hagstrom focused on rather sparkly electric guitars, echoing the bright plastic bodies of their accordions, Pigini decided to build electrics, archtops, and acoustics for the global market. Their plan was to undercut the prices of domestic American manufacturers and established German manufacturers, who at the time were still riding high on the back of the British skiffle boom.

Oliveri Pigini was something of a chancer. When he set up Eko (eek-oh) Guitars, he had absolutely zero experience in making guitars. To solve this problem, Pigini hired the services of an experienced German jazz guitarist and luthier, Wenzl Rossmeisl, to help establish production. Within a few years, and using industrial-scale manufacturing processes, Eko became the largest-volume guitar maker in Europe. From its factory in Recanati in the Italian Marche region, Pigini produced half a million classical, acoustic, and electric guitars every year across the 1960s.

Wenzl Rossmeisl and his son Roger had both graduated from the Mittenwald School for Instrument Making in Bavaria. The carving skills involved in violin making translate directly to the carved back and front of archtop jazz guitars, and both Rossmeisls specialized in making these complex carved instruments.

The younger Rossmeisl, Roger, moved to the US and initially joined Gibson in Kalamazoo. He later joined the guitar company started by a fellow German, Adolph Rickenbacker, and designed a number of legendary semi-acoustics, including the 330, in the distinct, angular "German school" style. These guitars were popularized initially by the Beatles and the Searchers in Britain and then the Byrds in the United States. Roger Rossmeisl left Rickenbacker after a falling out—melancholia and studious drinking were allegedly the drivers of both his creativity and his tricky personality. He subsequently moved to California to join Leo Fender, where he designed several archtops and Fender's first acoustic guitar range before he returned to Germany in the 1970s, something of a broken man.

Meanwhile, back in the mid-1960s, the British Invasion, and the Beatles in particular, had not only kicked off the guitar boom but had served to make American rock 'n' roll look like last year's model and effectively stifled what had been a growing revival in American neoethnic folk music.

• • • • • •

The successor to Pete Seeger's politically outlawed and blacklisted group the Almanac Singers was the Weavers. Significantly more mellow, the group had a string of number-one hits until even their softer-edged but still politically aware folk music was once again pronounced un-American. Surviving the savagery of McCarthyism, a more mainstream version of folk emerged, from smiley, optimistic ten-piece ensembles like the New Christy Minstrels to close harmony groups like the Kingston Trio and the Tarriers. These groups had polished and prettied-up old murder ballads like "Tom Dooley" and presented them on stage, radio, and TV. The Tarriers were more uncompromising in their choice of music and led the way, but they were soon overtaken in popularity by the Kingston Trio. The latter group's success was the result of tutoring by publicists and professional voice coaches, and their polished close-harmony singing, interlaced with carefully scripted stage banter, won over popular audiences, although not the serious folkies. The group featured a six-string and a tenor guitar, plus a banjo, and sported impossibly neat hair and matching costumes; the act was an immensely popular television favorite. But compared to four young, long-haired, irreverent Liverpudlians with unscripted beatnik personas, they suddenly appeared decidedly uncool.

By 1965, not only had the popular audience largely abandoned folk music for British beat groups like the Beatles and the Dave Clark Five, but so had many US folk musicians. The British groups that thrilled young audiences into screaming hysterics had inspired a whole generation of young American musicians.

It wasn't only the Beatles' music but also the instruments they played that influenced the American music scene. In 1964, Rickenbacker had given the very first electric twelve-string the company made not to a US group or musician but to George Harrison, who was immediately featured playing it on the title tune for the first Beatles film, *A Hard Day's Night*. Many of the next generation of American groups had been folk music fans, including guitarist-singers David Crosby and Roger McGuinn, who joined up with singer Gene Clark to form Jet-Set, later rebadged as the Byrds, with McGuinn as the notional frontman. Together the group went to see the Beatles' film, and McGuinn recalls how they were all taken with the jangly twelve-string guitar sound pioneered by Harrison on the Rickenbacker 360. The next day McGuinn, a dedicated folk singer, traded his acoustic guitar and five-string banjo for the Rickenbacker and put its distinctive sound at the center of his group's music on songs like "Mr. Tambourine Man" and "Turn, Turn, Turn." A now-long-forgotten San Francisco–based group, the Beau Brummels, took the sound and close harmony of the Beatles, the Searchers, and the Hollies to start the so-called San Francisco sound with songs like "Laugh, Laugh." Both groups laid the foundations of American folk-rock and led directly to the formation of groups as diverse and musically influential as the Lovin' Spoonful, Buffalo Springfield, and the Mamas & the Papas.

But while the electric folkies were tripping out to the chiming, jingle-jangle sound of the electric twelve-string, urban folk fans were wondering what all the fuss around this "new" guitar sound was about. The sound of the twelve-string acoustic guitar was well known to the musicians and audiences frequenting the folk clubs and coffee bars of Greenwich Village and Chicago's Old Town. The '30s blues musician Lead Belly made an acoustic Stella twelve-string his signature instrument, as did country-blues players Fred McDowell and Blind Willie McTell. Lead Belly almost singlehandedly carried the instrument from the '30s, where its considerable volume helped street and juke joint musicians make themselves heard, into the '40s and '50s. By the 1960s, when Lead Belly had been dead for over a decade, his legend was still burning bright, thanks largely to Pete Seeger and the Weavers rerecording his "Goodnight, Irene" and "Rock Island Line" and making them even bigger hits than he had.

The twelve-string guitar has six standard strings paired alongside strings tuned in unison or an octave higher. This created a sound that Pete Seeger, a signature twelve-string player himself, described as "clanging bells." The bells clang in a discordantly nice way, though. The pairs of strings vibrate out of phase, so while they are technically in tune, the ear reads the in-and-out phasing as pleasingly out of tune. The twelve-string is the sound of Lead Belly's "Rock Island Line," the Rooftop Singers' 1963 number-one hit "Walk Right In," most tracks by the Byrds, and, in years to come, Led Zepplin's "Stairway to Heaven" and the Eagles' "Hotel California."

It's thought that the twelve-string has its origins with itinerant Italian craftsmen working in the many guitar factories in the American Northeast. Italian instruments like the mandolin had always had double-courses of wire strings. Thus, in the constant search for "louder," Italian luthiers easily alighted on double-stringed guitars. Lead Belly custom-ordered his wide-bodied twelve-string from Snr. Pardini, a luthier working for Oscar Schmidt Co., the Jersey City makers of budget-priced Stella guitars.

The '60s folk revival crowd were familiar with Lead Belly's guitar sound. His popularity went way beyond his earlier champions: the folk revivalists of the '40s and '50s, British skifflers, and Kerouac's beat generation counterculturalists. But despite this relative fame, Lead Belly was the notable omission from a six-album set that all true 1960s American folk fans and musicians kept close at hand: the *Anthology of American Folk Music*.

In 1952, Harry Everett Smith, a twenty-something boho mystic, amateur anthropologist, musicologist, and obsessive collector of old 78 rpm folk and blues records, quit a dull maintenance job at Boeing and moved east to New York to try his luck in the music business. Within a few weeks, and down to his last few cents, he was trying to persuade Moe Asch, head of the influential Folkways Records imprint, to buy his complete hoard of vintage discs for cash. Asch wasn't interested in owning such a large collection of largely unknown, rural folk music but offered Smith $200 for the use of the discs on the condition that he pulled together a manageable selection that might have appeal to his general folk music audience. Smith already knew the records intimately, but $200 was enough to fund and inspire him to make a deeper, forensic analysis of his discs. After weeks holed up in a small, rented office, he compiled a collection that made up a six-disc collection of LPs that became the *Anthology of American Folk Music*. Its accompanying handbook, with its blend of weird engravings and "discographical references," only increased the mystique of the package.

The eighty four recordings selected by Smith were singular choices, featuring only rural music recorded between 1927 and 1932, the period between the invention of the electric microphone and the height of the Great Depression.

The anthology's importance, as vital today as when it was released, is that the 78s Smith selected were what real people in rural communities of the American South were buying during this five-year period. Smith excluded field recordings collected by academics like John and Alan Lomax or by the Library of Congress because his criterion was that every recording in the anthology had been commercially released, albeit in numbers as low as five hundred copies for an artist with limited local appeal. Smith excluded Lead Belly because, after having been discovered by John Lomax, he was promoted and displayed, initially often like a freak-show curiosity, for the white intelligentsia. The point of Smith's curation was that his choices were recorded, pressed, and bought because they were popular music, the "seven-inch singles" of their day. Smith appreciated that these were rarely casual purchases. Many of these 75-cent discs were advertised in newspapers and bought by money orders sent directly to the record company, or they were purchased in a store when a rural family ventured into their local town.

By the early '60s Smith's idiosyncratic anthology had attained the status of a mystical vinyl Bible for folkies from Peter, Paul and Mary to Dave van Ronk, who brought the collection to the attention of his disciple, a young Bob Dylan. Although many of the artists featured in the anthology are beyond obscure, and some songs are a very hard listen indeed, its overall influence—part sourcebook, part talisman—was immense. While half of the recordings had been made only thirty years before the '60s folk revival, listening to these essentially live performances of what music writer Greil Marcus terms "Old, Weird America" must have felt like listening to the music of another time and country altogether. But much of its appeal lay in its very weirdness, comparable to today when owning (and displaying) your 80g of Miles Davis's *Kind of Blue* or Coltrane's *A Love Supreme* implies coolness and an informed retro musical taste. (When old, revered vinyl LPs are reissued, editions that weigh 80 grams signal for vinyl collectors a quality remaster.) There was a sense that just having it, with all its complex, overwritten, arcane packaging, would bestow upon the owner not just coolness but a visceral connection to the true roots of American folk music. It would be interesting to know how many people actually listened to the complete collection—at the time of its original release and after subsequent reissues.

But in between the obscure recordings of Congregational church choirs, Sacred Harp singers, popular jug bands, and Cajun accordion groups are string bands. Featuring the guitar, fiddle, and five-string banjo, they dominate the collection. And it's the guitar, accompanying a vocal solo or as part of a group, that features on sixty of the eighty-four selections. What you can hear in the scratchy recordings, captured on the early electric microphones, are the sounds of Stella, Harmony, Kay, Regal, National, Gibson, and Martin guitars, although it's virtually impossible to distinguish which instrument is being played. Only the National and Dobro resophonic guitars have a telltale sound discernible on what are quite crude recordings. They often sound banjo-like, with their sharp, keening tone. But the guitar's predominance across the recordings is more evidence that by the late 1920s, the guitar was no longer the instrument of the parlor played by young ladies of leisure—it had become the way rural America entertained itself. Smith's anthology created a direct link between '20s rural music and the folk revival, influencing the shape of the folk music recorded or created by Baez, Dylan, Paxton, and their compatriots.

For those owners who found the scratchy tracks, sometimes recorded directly from Smith's worn original 78s, too challenging, there was an alternative way to connect to the past. Contemporary "old-time" bands like the New Lost City Ramblers quickly incorporated long-forgotten songs from the anthology like "Henry Lee" directly into their repertoire, which is where people like Dylan would have likely heard them. It also influenced the choice of guitar the Greenwich Village folkies used.

Joan Baez had been taken as a thirteen-year-old to see Pete Seeger and was soon using Seeger's songs, both his own compositions and traditional ballads, to entertain friends and family with her otherworldly soprano voice. When Albert Baez, the family patriarch, got a faculty position at MIT, the family moved to the Boston area, which at the time was very much at the heart of the burgeoning folk movement. While her mother came from Scotland, the paternal side of Baez's family had come from Puebla, Mexico, and with her Hispanic looks, she had encountered racism at primary and secondary schools and at college. She had flirted with the idea of Anglicizing her performing name but decided to retain Baez, and as such she became a well-known player in the area. Her big break was an appearance at the first Newport Folk Festival in 1959. Baez was a relative unknown in a lineup that included big names in the popular folk scene: Pete Seeger, blind bluegrass flat-picking pioneer Doc Watson, recent chart-toppers the Kingston Trio, and Odetta. The latter was folk and gospel royalty, whose guitar-playing style, classically trained voice, and perfect diction would influence Baez. From that gig soon came a recording contract and a meteoric rise as something of a folk superstar. In 1962, she released her third album, *Joan Baez in Concert*, which included a live recording of her first Bob Dylan cover, "Don't Think Twice, It's Alright."

By now Baez had put aside her simple Gibson flat-top and was playing a fancy slot-headed Martin 0-45, a guitar that she would play for much of her professional career. Because of the classical guitar style slot-head many people assumed it was a gut-string Spanish guitar, but in fact she had chosen a style of steel-string guitar popular in the early 1930s. Other musicians and bands were picking up old instruments, sometimes to lend them old-time authenticity but mainly in the knowledge that older instruments sounded better. Both

Martin and Gibson saw the trend and launched folk singer guitars aimed at the growing desire to be a "folky." Martin introduced their twelve-fret slot-head New Yorker models in 1961, based loosely on a 1920s Style 00-21. The New Yorker name was a nod to pre-1898 Martin guitars stamped "Martin & Co., New York" on the headstock. Their guitars were stamped this way because the company's main distributors were still based in the city; Martin and his small team of builders had left New York a good fifty years earlier.

• • • • • •

Long-forgotten tracks on the original LPs that made up Smith's selection included a 1928 recording of "Spike Driver Blues" by Mississippi John Hurt, one of only a few artists accorded the honor of having more than one recording in the anthology. Hurt played a guitar bought for him by his mother for $1.50, an instrument he referred to as "Black Annie," but it was of such poor quality that on the recording he is playing a guitar loaned to him by the OKeh recording engineer. By the 1930s, he was a relatively mainstream player on the blues circuit and was known simply as John Hurt. By the early '60s, when he had long retired back to the rural South, a group of East Coast college musicologists, inspired by the Harry Smith anthology, tracked him down to a two-room shack where he was living rent-free in exchange for looking after a farmer's handful of cows. The group had done an enormous amount of public record and census searching and had interviewed many of Hurt's contemporaries to find his whereabouts. On the verge of giving up, the guitarist and record collector Tom Hoskins looked again at the lyrics of Hurt's song "Avalon Blues":

Avalon's my hometown, always on my mind
Pretty mama's in Avalon, want me there all the time

True to his name and the song's words, Mississippi John Hurt had been minding his own business or perhaps hiding in plain sight, living with his "pretty mama," now his wife, in the Mississippi town of Avalon all the time.

In 1963, he was brought to Washington, DC, where at seventy-one he started a second career playing primarily to white, middle-class, college-educated blues fans. Legend has it that when classical guitar maestro Andrés Segovia heard Hurt's solo recording of "Frankie," he couldn't accept that it was just one guitar playing rather than two. Regardless of his talent, Hurt had sold his only guitar many years earlier, and as part of his fee for playing, he was instructed to go to Fretted Instruments in Greenwich Village. The original owner, Marc Silber, recalled telling him, "You can have anything in here and they'll pay for it." Ignoring the expensive Gibsons and Martins, he settled for a relatively modest Guild F-30 Sunburst because "it's two colors at once." Hurt, together with other near-septuagenarian singer-guitarists Son House and Skip James, went on to perform on the same playbill as Dylan at the 1965 Newport Folk Festival.

It was at the same festival, on the night of July 25, 1965, that Dylan first publicly "went electric," backed by a four-piece band led by Paul Butterfield on guitar. The night when, for many folkies, he betrayed the already fragile folk music scene. A year later, in Manchester, England, backed by a four-piece band led by Robbie Robertson on guitar, he was branded a Judas as he emphatically cast aside the sound and image that he was most readily associated with—the folk-hobo, the singer with a simple acoustic guitar.

Anyway, that's how history tells the story. Or how the papers told the story. They say that large sections of the Newport crowd booed an electric Dylan offstage. Al Kooper, who played keyboards that night, explained that the hastily assembled band had only rehearsed three songs and that the booing started only after Dylan left the stage. He calculated: "If you travelled from god knows where and paid god knows what to see Bob Dylan, and sat through music you didn't relate to for three days, and then he came out and only played for 15 minutes, what would you have done?"

But Dylan, or the press, or the writers of music legend, in reporting their version of "Dylan Goes Electric," had created another musical crossroads for guitar-based music.

Dylan had actually "gone electric" three years earlier. Much taken with the British beat sound and subsequent "invasion," Dylan released "Mixed-Up Confusion" in 1962. With a prominent skiffle backing track, it featured a tiny Martin 1-21 acoustic fitted with a Gibson electric pickup played with fluidity by Bruce Langhorne, the original "Tambourine Man." According to Dylan, Langhorne had also brought a "gigantic tambourine . . . as big as a wagon wheel" to the session. In fact, it was a Turkish *daire*, an ancient tambourine about three feet in diameter with interconnected bronze discs in the rim.

In 1964, the British group the Animals released an electric version of the traditional folk ballad "The House of the Rising Sun," leaning directly on Dylan's own 1962 acoustic reworking of the tale of a ruined girl who ended up in a brothel in New Orleans. (Far from being an original American folk song, as the Animals had supposed, the ballad was almost certainly of English origin. "Rising Sun" was a popular name for English taverns or pubs from the mid-1600s, and by the 1700s many taverns had a bawdy house, or brothel, using their upstairs rooms. Entries for "Rising Sun" appear in libertines' directories, and a number of eighteenth-century broadside ballads warn about the perils of catching syphilis by frequenting "bawds," or prostitutes. The song has a similar theme to another Anglo-American cautionary tale, "St. James Infirmary Blues." The original tune for "Rising Sun Blues," as sung by the Carolina Tar Heels string band, has, like "St. James Infirmary," its roots in early British ballads "The Unfortunate Rake," "Matty Groves," and "Little Musgrave and Lady Barnard.")

Dylan had been taught "Rising Sun Blues" by Dave van Ronk—whose own rearrangement of Josh White's minor-key version of the song introduced the enduring descending bassline. With the US success of the Animals' version, Dylan's producer at the time, Tom Wilson, overdubbed a Fats Domino–style drum and electric guitar backing track onto Dylan's original acoustic recording, releasing it to a few radio disc jockeys, but to little interest. It was, however, noticed by Dylan's hardcore fan base, many of whom were outraged that their underground folk hero was flirting with the electric guitars of commercial rock 'n' roll. Perhaps that dissent delayed his immediate shift to electric, but later that same year Dylan heard the demo version of the Byrds' cover of his "Mr. Tambourine Man" ahead of its release; it was the only Dylan-penned song to ever reach number one on the pop charts. His regard for the Beatles' electric beat music was probably shaded with envy at its mass popularity; it now only required him to be excited by the incendiary Chicago blues of Mike Bloomfield to convince him to make the switch to electric for his upcoming appearance at Newport.

A Fender Stratocaster was a controversial replacement for the small Martin guitar he had borrowed from his then-girlfriend Joan Baez to first play "Mr. Tambourine Man" at Newport the previous year. The small, top-of-the-range Martin 0-45 that Baez played had its own story. It was, even back in the '60s, an expensive guitar to use onstage, but by 1998, after thirty years on the road, she'd retired the guitar. A band member told her that given its provenance and history, it probably had a conservative value of $100,000. Martin offered to restore the guitar to its former glory as a gift to Baez and by way of a "thank you" for being a loyal Martin player. Guitar technicians were using an inspection mirror and an intense light to examine the inside of her instrument for signs of structural damage when the repair department at Martin discovered a message written in thick black pencil on the underside of the top: "TOO BAD YOU ARE A COMMUNIST."

No doubt during a previous service, repair, or simple restringing, a disgruntled guitar technician, possibly offended by Baez's prominent left-wing politics and anti-Vietnam stance, had taken the trouble to carefully write the words backwards inside the guitar—knowing that only another technician with a mirror could read them. The '60s were a time when the definition of a "loyal" American was difficult to figure, and "reds" were clearly thought to be both in as well as under many folksingers' beds.

Newport in 1965 saw a changing of the guard in the world of folk and traditional music. In 1963, Baez had proudly introduced a twenty-two-year-old Dylan to the festival audience for the first time. In 1964, Pete Seeger and Dylan played in the same offstage guitar workshop at the festival, where the elder statesman proclaimed that "Dylan may well become the country's most creative troubadour—if he doesn't explode." But in 1965, Seeger, a board director of the Newport Festival, was the one who exploded, literally trying to pull the plug on Dylan's amplified guitar.

Dylan's journey from playing a simple folk singer's acoustic guitar to an electric Fender Stratocaster took a little less than five years. He had arrived in New York in early 1961, fresh from Minnesota and carrying a plain but still classy Martin 00-17 guitar. The notion of a young Dylan blowing into the big city with a beaten-up thrift-store guitar carried across his back on a piece of string makes a great image, but it's a myth. The same myth paints Dylan as the young, parentless roustabout hobo riding a boxcar into New York's DeWitt freight depot like a modern-day Woody Guthrie. But it was the story that Dylan told in his first interview with Billy James, the Columbia Records public relations point man detailed to write the backstory of their new signing.

"How did you get here?"
"I rode a freight train."
"You mean like a boxcar."
"Yeah, like a boxcar. A freight train."

Dylan had in fact "rode" a '57 Chevrolet Impala sedan into New York "across the country from the Midwest . . . straight out of Chicago" and was dropped off right by the George Washington Bridge in Manhattan. The folk singer who had left Minnesota knew he couldn't bill himself as Robert Zimmerman. "Can you imagine Zimmerman up in bright lights? It would burn you to death!"

Dylan borrowed the quote above from the Broadway star Ethel Merman (née Zimmerman, but no relation), who knew her name was too long and probably too ethnic for public use. Back in Minnesota, Robert Zimmerman had already become Bob Dillon. He was never particularly fond of the Welsh poet, but as a teenager Dylan was a big fan of Westerns—particularly the long-running 1950s TV Western series *Gunsmoke* featuring Marshal Matt Dillon. Figuring out that Westerns weren't hip in the bright lights of New York, and attracted to a more interesting spelling, his Columbia contract is signed "Bob Dylan."

Neither were Dylan's parents "long gone," nor had he been "kicked out" of home. The well-educated son of a successful electrical store owner, Dylan had always played quality guitars. He had started with the simple Martin guitar way before he arrived in New York or got a record deal, but when he started recording, he seemed to favor Gibsons. The guitar on the cover of his first album, *Bob Dylan*, is the Gibson J-50 that he also used on *The Freewheelin' Bob Dylan*. After the J-50 was "lost in action" in 1963, he acquired, from Marc Silber's Fretted Instruments in Greenwich Village, his most famous acoustic, a blond 1930s Gibson Nick Lucas Special. It's the main guitar he played in *Don't Look Back* (1967), D. A. Pennebaker's documentary portrait of the artist as a young man, covering Dylan's 1965 "Judas" tour of Britain. The Gibson, with an extra-deep body and a thirteen-fret neck, combines the bright balanced punch of a smaller-bodied guitar with a deep, throaty bass. The 4¼-inch-deep body makes it as deep as that of a dreadnought, hence the strong bass. The unique design of thirteen frets clear of the body places the bridge at the mythical "sweet spot" on the top and gives the instrument a tone, according to one owner, "as sweet as black treacle." For the rest of his career to date, Dylan has basically swapped between Gibsons and Martins, including Baez's Martin 0-45 he initially borrowed at Newport.

Dylan arrived in New York a modestly accomplished guitarist, having learned his skills playing in a number of school bands and as folk singer "Bob Dillon" in cafés in Minneapolis. Singer-songwriter Nanci Griffith, who was always drawn to his more musically challenging songs, noted, "Some of Bob's stuff is really hard to play! Even as a guitarist he's more innovative than he's usually given credit for, especially in terms of voicing. Bob would find an unusual placement for his fingers and create augmentations of a chord that no one else had ever used. Or he'd use a chord you had not heard in that context."

However good the music and the lyrics, neither Baez nor Pete Seeger was enamored by Dylan's change to electric. Both artists were unimpressed and continued to play acoustic for the rest of their long musical careers.

• • • • • •

Seeger's critical place in popularizing and politicizing the guitar-led folk music of the 1960s undoubtedly colored his attitude toward the Dylan phenomenon, making his response something of a roller coaster of emotions and reactions. Seeger initially saw Dylan as the heir to his friend Woody Guthrie and someone who might continue the work he had started in the '40s, using folk, or people's, music as a tool of progressive politics. In particular, Seeger wanted people to participate and, in his own words, "to sing out with confidence." And if what was sung out was aligned with Seeger's politics, helping "the little guy fight for fairness," then all the better.

Given that so much of Seeger's musical career was publicly left-leaning, it was small surprise that he was denounced as a communist during the Joseph McCarthy–led House Un-American Activities Committee hearings, having been identified as such by Burl Ives, a close friend and fellow folk singer. Ives had since the '30s and '40s been an immensely popular and highly regarded liberal-leaning singer and guitarist; at the time he was much more widely known than Woody Guthrie or Pete Seeger. He rather bizarrely volunteered to speak before HUAC, behavior that Seeger later likened to "fingering, like any common stool pigeon, some of his radical associates of the early 40s. He did this not because he wanted to but because he felt it was the only way to preserve his lucrative contracts."

Unlike those he identified—and it is alleged that he named dozens of actors, singers, and activists—he continued to perform and record prolifically. Interestingly, having been known as an avuncular singer of folk ballads and children's songs, including "Big Rock Candy Mountain" and "The Blue Tail Fly" (or "Jimmy Crack Corn"), Ives is better remembered now as a rather corpulent and sinister film actor. Perhaps it was no coincidence that while he was betraying Seeger before HUAC, Tennessee Williams, a social and political radical, wrote the part of the mendacious, corpulent Big Daddy in *Cat on a Hot Tin Roof* specifically for him.

At the McCarthy hearings on August 15, 1955, Seeger refused to follow the easy route by invoking his Fifth Amendment right against self-incrimination. While remaining silent under the protection of the Fifth Amendment would have kept him out of prison, with considerable bravery (or maybe pig-headedness) and to the huge frustration of the committee, Seeger sought the moral high ground by asserting his right to free speech under the First Amendment. He must have known that the Hollywood Ten had used the same plea and had been imprisoned for contempt of Congress. However, keeping quiet was not Seeger's style: "I am not going to answer any questions as to my association, my philosophical or religious beliefs or my political beliefs, or how I voted in any election, or any of these private affairs. I think these are very improper questions for any American to be asked, especially under such compulsion as this. I would be very glad to tell you my life story if you want to hear of it."

The committee declined his repeated offers to tell them about his life and the songs he sang. Seeger was ultimately, and unsurprisingly, indicted for contempt of Congress. Subsequently sentenced to ten one-year terms in prison (to run concurrently), he never actually served time but did have to keep the federal government informed anytime he left his district of New York. Although he successfully appealed his case in a fight that lasted until 1962, he was, in consequence of his contempt charges, often banned from playing at events unless he signed an oath that he would not use his performance to "promote communism or overthrow the government."

Who would have thought that a single man and a guitar could be so threateningly powerful? But Seeger was one of the very few activist singers who genuinely suffered for using song to preach about civil and workers' rights, racial and religious equality, international understanding, and antimilitarism. Perhaps what most offended Seeger about Dylan strapping on a Fender Stratocaster at Newport in 1965 wasn't just the noise (rendering his all-important lyrics inaudible) but that he seemed to be using his freedom of speech not to protest, persuade, or preach but purely to excite and entertain. It's easy with the hindsight of history to know that Dylan was not deserting the cause, but at the time it must have looked like betrayal to Seeger.

In the United States of the mid-1960s, McCarthy was long gone (disgraced by Senate censure in 1954, he died of alcoholism in 1957 at the age of forty-eight), so Dylan had little to fear, whatever he sang about. But around the world, protest singers with guitars continued to play an important part in an unarmed struggle against poverty, inequality, despots, and dictators. They realized that they might not change the world, but maybe their words and songs might shed a little light into the dark places where oppression and injustice lie.

Dylan's friend Joan Baez often talked about the power of music. "People say music changes the world but the guitar, of all the instruments, is played everywhere. Under every dictatorship there is some dilapidated guitar and the local 'Blowin' in the Wind.' . . . The guitars in these countries have been the most wretched things but they've served their purpose of uniting people."

Baez, a life-long activist, pacifist, and champion of civil rights and social justice, may have been thinking of Chile's folk scene, especially Víctor Jara. Two associates of Baez's from the Greenwich Village scene, Phil Ochs and Country Joe McDonald, had visited Chile to meet with Jara when the first freely elected Marxist head of state, Salvador Allende, was in power. Jara was seen by many left-leaning internationalists as a cross between Woodie Guthrie, Bob Dylan, and Martin Luther King, but after Augusto Pinochet's coup in 1973, Jara was detained in Chile's Estadio Nacional along with five thousand other supporters of the deposed Allende. Shortly afterward, the singer's body was found riddled with bullets on the street outside the stadium. The guitarist's wrists and each of his fingers had been broken, and severed, as a postmortem message from the junta to all musicians tempted to use song in protest against the new regime.

• • • • • •

Meanwhile, in the relative sanity and sanctuary of Abbey Road Studios, and as Dylan was infuriating and "betraying" his folk fans as he went electric, Paul McCartney was rather perversely recording the completely acoustic "Yesterday" (1965), serving to further underline the latent power of the acoustic guitar in a world now largely dominated by the electric. "Yesterday" was written solely by McCartney and recorded on an Epiphone Texan flat-top lent to him by producer George Martin; it is the Beatles' most financially successful song (although primarily because of its 2,200-plus cover versions). McCartney's other major self-penned acoustic song, the civil rights commentary "Blackbird," was recorded a few years later on his own Martin D-28 and is also in the top ten of the Beatles' most financially lucrative songs.

It's misleading to label either of these McCartney-penned compositions and performances as "by the Beatles," and the group, and in particular the ever-truculent Lennon, was annoyed that "Yesterday" was even being proposed for inclusion on a Beatles album. It belongs to a genre of highly personal songs performed by their composers, a genre categorized in record stores by the 1970s as "singer-songwriter." But many earlier artists—from Blind Lemon Jefferson and Lead Belly, through Jimmie Rodgers and Hank Williams, to Josh White and Woody Guthrie and ultimately Bob Dylan—had explored songs in which complex imagery and veiled metaphor hid real-life events or their writers' true emotions. Regardless of era, it was a concept that was only possible with the acoustic guitar and a genre that, while rooted in 1960s folk music, only truly came of age in the following decade.

But before the acoustic guitar–playing singer-songwriter generation based in Laurel Canyon would have its decade in the sun, folk music traditionalists were already wringing their hands at the way some modern, "progressive" folkies, weaponized with electric guitars and drum kits, were torturing the authentic canon of their source material. What was being created were often electric takes on traditional songs as well as original compositions that sounded like something that might have been written a hundred years earlier. In the mid-sixties, Dylan adopted as his road band four Canadian rockabilly multi-instrumentalists and a mandolin-playing drummer from the Arkansas Delta. They had been known variously as the Country Squires or Levon and the Hawks, but usually just the Hawks. Whatever they called themselves, they were a great bar band who, having started out on the road in the late 1950s when they were seventeen or eighteen, seemingly came out of nowhere. Dylan had made a singular choice, finding a tight, road-ready band with interests in rock, country, gospel, Delta blues, even soul. As the anonymous backing band on Dylan's difficult world tours of 1965 and '66, they found themselves playing to booing crowds who jeered the acoustic folk Judas who they believed had betrayed them by going electric. By 1968, the group had officially metamorphosed into the Band and created a genre of music that would come to be known as Americana. Although they had tired of touring with Dylan, in 1967 they hooked up with him again in a remote town in the Catskills, woodshedding in the basement of a rambling, broken-down, big pink house and playing something closer to the eclectic roots and primitive music pioneered by guitarist John Fahey—a style he christened "American Primitive." Dylan chose not to release any of the tapes of those basement recordings (at least until 1975), but the group continued honing a collection of songs that in early 1968 became *Music from Big Pink*.

Standout tracks like "Chest Fever" would later be described as "cosmic American rock" by roots music magazine *No Depression*—what they described as music "inventive in songwriting and delivery, cosmic in the sense of being cutting edge . . . but built upon the tried and true." "The Weight," which became the Band's signature tune, is set in the hometown of the Martin guitar company in Pennsylvania. *Music from Big Pink* offered a "physical and psychological journey that touched on everything from railroads, gospel spirituals, getting back to the big city, and Robert Johnson's deal with the Devil in Clarksdale. Most of all their first album shows that all five members of the band knew that whoever wrote the song, they were never there just to play along and keep time."

The songs on *The Band*, the group's second album, conceived later in 1968 in upstate New York, were much more than just another collection of tunes. They formed a concept album that spoke of older, rural themes—the harvest, slavery, and the Civil War. From the studiously rough-and-ready album cover photo that mimicked the daguerreotype Civil War photography of Mathew Brady to the tack piano, accordion, jaw's harp, and loose trombone in the instrumentation, the album was folk-rock's *Sgt. Pepper*, albeit one that sounded like a musical message in a bottle from an earlier time.

The twelve songs on what became known as *The Brown Album* were largely written in the hippy rural idyll of Woodstock in upstate New York, where Dylan had hidden himself away in a wooden mansion near that of his legendary hard-assed manager, Albert Grossman. Hendrix and Van Morrison were fellow residents. (The small town was, confusingly, located many miles from Bethel, where the Woodstock festival was finally held.)

Guitarist Robbie Robertson, who with keyboard player Richard Manuel sang and wrote many of the songs on the album, also shared engineering credits. He was looking for the sort of "woody, thuddy sound" more usually associated with a log cabin halfway up an Appalachian mountain than a recording studio. For *The Brown Album* sessions, he intentionally mimicked the jam-session sound of Big Pink's basement, where the Band's first album had been recorded. Bizarrely, the recording equipment for those sessions was installed almost three thousand miles away from Woodstock, in Sammy Davis Jr.'s pool house. Attached to the rat-packer's old Hollywood mansion on Evanview Drive, it was only a couple of miles from Laurel Canyon and even closer to the bars and music venues of Sunset Boulevard. The studio setup was lo-fi, acoustic and unplugged, forty years before those terms entered the musical lexicon and fifty years before the hot-valve analog technology was repopularized by Jack White and the White Stripes. The Band themselves were in turn revisiting the acoustic recorded sound of the 1920s and '30s. Music journalist Barney Hoskyns described the Band's music as "made organically by men who'd pulled back from the insanity of fame."

The influence of *Music from Big Pink* has been long, wide, and deep, affecting everything from early British folk-rock to new wave and punk. Elvis Costello recalled that hearing the Band for the first time "was like receiving a letter from the other side of the world, a world you couldn't possibly understand let alone visit. It was only later when you knew a bit more about Hank Williams and Bessie Smith that you started to fill in the blanks."

The album also profoundly affected a new band then practicing in a suburban North London living room, a musical collective that basically invented the British version of Americana, electric folk-rock.

• • • • • •

Fairport Convention, which started in the time-honored tradition of "three young men meet in a pub and form a band," was different because that band became the Petri dish of British electric folk. Like the Band, where singing and playing duties were interchangeable, there was no dedicated lead singer or lead guitarist—whoever and whatever was right for the specific song ruled. In 1968, Fairport's first eponymous album had twin lead singers—Judy Dyble (later replaced by Sandy Denny) and Iain Matthews—and two highly competent guitarists in Simon Nicol and Richard Thompson (who initially played a London-made Grimshaw GS30 on covers of early American folk-rock songs like Mimi and Richard Farina's "Reno Nevada").

Originally influenced by West Coast groups like the Byrds and Jefferson Airplane, Fairport Convention found in Denny's arrival (her voice was perfectly described by Australian critic and essayist Clive James as "open space, low-volume, high-intensity") an inspiration to follow in folklorist Cecil Sharp's footsteps and rediscover their own British traditional music heritage.

The Band's *Music from Big Pink*, with its marriage of raw, rustic gospel vocals and multiple instruments intricately interwoven, not only transported listeners to the Deep South but became, for the Fairports, a gauntlet thrown down. Standout tracks like "The Weight" led to a realization that they had little need to inhabit an American musical heritage. By the time they were halfway through producing their third album from 1969, *Liege & Lief*, they had heard the Band's *Brown Album*, the even-better follow-up to *Music from Big Pink*. If *Sgt. Pepper* raised the bar that helped perfect the Beach Boys' *Pet Sounds*, then the Band spurred Fairport Convention to make *Liege & Lief* their own masterpiece. But it was a masterpiece born out of tragedy: amid the creative fervor, the band's original drummer, Martin Lamble, and Richard Thompson's girlfriend died in an auto accident. Somehow the group got back on their feet. They added Dave Swarbrick on violin and Dave Mattacks (the drummer of choice for virtually all the major British electric-folk solo artists and groups) and started afresh. *Liege & Lief*, released in December 1969, artfully entwines traditional and original songs, completing the journey from rural to urban and ancient to modern. But as importantly for guitarists, the album reveals the sheer musical brilliance of Richard Thompson's electric and acoustic playing.

As the decade that had borne witness to so much creative and social change came to a close, there was to be one more throw of the musical dice. On a dairy farm in upstate New York, the Woodstock Music and Art Fair took place.

It was the defining musical happening of the 1960s and the rightful bookend to a period that saw the mass popularization of music aimed at, and played by, young people. But contemporaneous news coverage carried little about either the music or the (counter)cultural significance of the event. News stories in both the US and the UK about Woodstock revolved largely around the traffic jams and health and safety (the *New York Daily News* and *The Times* in England), nudity and skinny-dipping (the prurient, sensationalist British Sunday newspaper the *News of the World*), and "free love" induced by drug taking (the conservative voice of "middle England," the *Daily Mail*). The much-replicated logo for the festival, featuring what looked like a white peace dove sitting on the neck of an acoustic guitar, seemed to suggest that this was much more than a music festival. (The logo's designer, Arnold Skolnick, a Madison Avenue ad guy, points out that his original design featured not the dove of peace but the local gray catbird perched on the end of a flute. The catbird remained, but the strong graphic outline of a guitar headstock was felt by the promoters to be more appropriate for a festival that was to be dominated by the guitar.)

Woodstock is recalled primarily as a rock festival, featuring as it did many electric bands and closing with the iconic Hendrix rendition of "The Star-Spangled Banner." But the festival lineup was a child of its time that featured numerous acoustic bands and solo singers. Two acts gave career-defining acoustic performances: the one-hour opening performance by Richie Havens, and Crosby, Stills, Nash & Young playing only their second live gig at three a.m. on the final day.

As much as Hendrix, the Who, and Ten Years After thrilled listeners with their high-velocity electric pyrotechnics, many artists like Richie Havens, armed with just an acoustic guitar, left an indelible mark on the festival. Havens, the son of a Blackfoot Native American father and a British-Caribbean mother, had started out playing in street corner doo-wop vocal groups near his Brooklyn home, but he soon moved to Greenwich Village to take part in the late '50s beat scene as both a street artist and poet. Only in his early twenties did he pick up a guitar. His improvised, mesmeric rendition of "Freedom/

Motherless Child" at Woodstock showed just what a powerful tool a mere acoustic guitar could be when passionately worked as a percussive instrument. Woodstock propelled Havens's career, and he became renowned for his free reimagining of Beatles and Dylan songs.

Havens's performance and Crosby, Stills & Nash's "Suite: Judy Blue Eyes" (four song fragments combined by Stills about the breakup of his love affair with folk singer Judy Collins) are just two of many standout performances by an emerging group of acoustic guitar–playing, self-composing singers. By 1969, most of the performers at Woodstock were playing their own material, bypassing the very notion of Tin Pan Alley, a metonym for the music industry, with its arrangement of bosses and manufacturers (publishers and professional songwriters) and workers (singers). Dylan, speaking in 1985 for his generation of songwriters as much as for himself, reflected on their impact on the music business: "Tin Pan Alley is gone. I put an end to it. People can record their own songs now."

It was more likely a combination of the Beatles and the British Invasion that started to topple Tin Pan Alley and make the contract writers of the Brill Building (at least those who couldn't sing) redundant. But one singer-songwriter who could very much both write and sing, Carole King, saw what was happening. After her divorce from her longtime writing partner Gerry Goffin in 1968, she moved to Laurel Canyon with her two young daughters. Her first solo album, *Writer*, was not a great success, but her second, *Tapestry* (1971), hit the mark. In the process, she gave herself greater freedom and more control over the creation and presentation of her art.

The song "Woodstock," the anthem of the festival and, in many ways, of the flower-power '60s itself, was written by a Canadian-born poet-composer-singer, Joni Mitchell. As the very epitome of the fragile, introspective singer-songwriter, the twenty-six-year-old crossed into the next decade to define the genre.

John Martyn playing a 1970 Martin D-28.

12

The Singer-Songwriter and the D-28

In the acoustic guitar world, the 1970s was the decade of the singer-songwriter. Vintage Martin D-28s, once the preferred guitar of 1940s bluegrass bands, became the workhorse of this fraternity. Across the decades we've seen professional musicians choose the latest, the most fashionable, the most expensive, or the most innovative guitars. Now, many of this generation of players gravitated to older instruments—and a large number chose Martin D-28s in particular. These trophies of nostalgia appeared in the hands of musicians of many musical persuasions across the era.

Joni Mitchell acquired her 1956 Martin D-28 in 1966, only to have her "dear one" stolen in 1973. Before she owned it, the guitar had travelled to Vietnam and back with its original owner, a US Marine captain stationed at Fort

Bragg. After Mitchell acquired it, she used it on all her early albums, pre- and post-Woodstock (although Mitchell, despite being one of the leading artists of the Woodstock generation, didn't make it to the actual event). However, "Woodstock," the song that best captures both the spirit and cultural importance of the festival, she performed on a Fender Rhodes electric piano. She wrote the song in her New York hotel room while watching live TV news coverage highlighting the chaos surrounding the festival. The details of the event came via the firsthand description given by her then-lover, Graham Nash, who had performed there with Crosby, Stills, Nash & Young.

The coming together of half a million "kids" may have been an insignificant hippy event for the media but not for Mitchell. America after the assassinations of John F. Kennedy, Martin Luther King, and Robert Kennedy Sr. was still embroiled in Vietnam; its economy was geared to benefit big business; and its government was still run by the "good ol' boys." The song offered her an opportunity to reflect on what was happening to her adopted country and to ponder its place in the world. By the 1970s, the divide between America's and Britain's cultural left and their economic right was especially apparent.

Mitchell didn't go to the festival because it clashed with her first appearance on America's only hip prime-time TV show: *The Dick Cavett Show*. Cavett was rock friendly, unlike the older, father-like host of *The Ed Sullivan Show* (who only six years earlier had introduced the Beatles to America). Cavett's show beamed contemporary musicians directly into millions of living rooms across Main Street America. Mitchell had been booked to appear at the festival (which ran from August 15 to 18), but her manager advised her not to go, fearing she wouldn't get back in time—the festival closed on Monday morning, and Cavett's show was recorded on Monday afternoon ahead of a Tuesday-evening broadcast. This advice was understandable given the importance of Cavett's audience. It seemed sound . . . at the time. There was also rampant skepticism about the festival's viability. Led Zeppelin, the Rolling Stones, the Doors, and the Jeff Beck Group had all turned it down. But many acts (and their managers) didn't know about the plans to film the event; that film would deliver the festival performances to a global audience. Before the release of Michael Wadleigh's multicamera documentary *Woodstock* in 1970, few people outside of America had heard of, let alone actually *heard*, acoustic bands and singer-songwriters like Crosby, Stills, Nash & Young, Richie Havens, Arlo Guthrie, and John Sebastian. Even fewer folks, aside from some vets and members of the anti-Vietnam movement on the West Coast, knew of the band Country Joe and the Fish and its lead singer, Joseph McDonald.

His "The 'Fish' Cheer/I-Feel-Like-I'm-Fixin'-to-Die-Rag" was a black comedy song and something of an anthem for those who opposed the Vietnam War. The film and the accompanying triple LP soundtrack forever transformed the careers of McDonald and many other performers.

While Joni Mitchell never made it to the farm outside of Bethel, it turned out her manager's fears were unfounded. Her appearance on Cavett was gate-crashed by returning festival players Jefferson Airplane and two members of CSN&Y. Stephen Stills proudly showed the "real Woodstock mud" on the leg of his jeans, and David Crosby recalled the sight of the festival from a helicopter as looking "like an encampment of the Macedonian Hordes crossed with the biggest group of gypsies."

The Dick Cavett Show aired on Tuesday evening, August 19, thirty-six hours after Jimi Hendrix's two-hour set closed the three-day festival at nine a.m. on Monday morning, August 18—half of the crowd had left the site to return to work. As Mitchell listened to the excited memories of festival survivors, her wistful expression said everything. She realized that she had sacrificed what could have been the defining live performance of her career for a TV appearance. Looking back at it now via YouTube, the fifty-year-old sequence looks cool but quaintly dated. The host is razor-sharp but carefully coiffured and perma-tanned; Cavett wears a pressed safari jacket and a silk neckerchief. But getting the imprimatur of Cavett was a big deal, and, as Crosby later reflected, Mitchell's absence magnified her appreciation of the event. "She captured the feeling and importance of the Woodstock festival better than anyone who'd been there."

Mitchell's song "Woodstock" hit number one on the charts in the US by way of CSN&Y's guitar-driven rock version. It was also a surprising number-one hit in the UK through a pedal steel guitar–affected, country-folk take by Matthews Southern Comfort (the Matthews being Iain Matthews, late of Fairport Convention). Mitchell finally released her own version on her third album, *Ladies of the Canyon*; it was also the B-side on the 45 rpm single of her only truly mainstream hit, "Big Yellow Taxi."

"Woodstock," aside from being a perfectly pitched, insightful, contemporaneous record of the event, is also a highly personal observation. Had it been written a decade earlier, it would have been knocked out to order by a talented songwriting team housed in the Brill Building to cash in on a youth news story. Mitchell wrote it as a personal reflection on an event she had desperately wanted to attend. Playing there would have been doing something she loved more than anything else, but she settled for second best, writing what became an enduring anthem for a generation of which she was at the heart. The success of both the singer and the song was a good indicator that the 1970s might just be the decade of the emotionally *and* politically aware singer-songwriter. And the key to the whole genre's success was the affordable, portable, easy-to-play acoustic guitar. If country music is "three chords and the truth," then singer-songwriters were adding two minor chords and opening up their hearts.

The veteran British music journalist David Hepworth views 1971 as "the Annus Mirabilis of the long playing album": a time when we listened to music differently, often privately at home. For many listeners, it was a largely static activity, often the sole activity, and therefore more intense and all-engrossing. The LP album was usually played with the intention of listening to the whole thing, anticipating the end of side 1 and then flipping it over to finish the performance on side 2. While the '60s had been the decade of the three-minute single, the '70s, and 1971 in particular, was when the LP as an art form hit its stride and truly came of age. In fact, 1966, itself a banner year in the history of pop music, was also the last year that the sales generated from singles exceeded that of LPs.

This change in listening format signaled the shift from transient interest in a three-minute song to a broader, more lasting interest in, and involvement with, the artists who produced an album of twelve songs. Cover art, printed lyrics, and sleeve notes were pored over by listeners looking for clues as to what stimulated the creation of the latest offering from the artist.

British acoustic artists from Cat Stevens to Steeleye Span were in top form, and even David Bowie's fourth album, *Hunky Dory*, had a strong acoustic guitar presence compared to his previous, much harder-rocking *The Man Who Sold the World*. In America, Bill Withers's first album, *Just As I Am* (1971), was written using his small-bodied Guild F-20. His acoustic approach helped bring a folkier and more introspective angle to the soul genre; except for two covers (including an acoustic version of the Beatles' "Let It Be"), the songs were written by Withers.

Hepworth's proof of theory is a list of over a hundred and fifty superlative albums released in 1971 alone. Unsurprisingly, the list includes career-defining albums from dozens of the period's American singer-songwriters: Joni Mitchell's *Blue*, Carole King's *Tapestry*, James Taylor's *Mud Slide Slim*, Carly Simon's *Anticipation*, and Don McLean's *American Pie*. From CSN&Y there was a clutch of excellent solo albums: David Crosby's *If I Could Only Remember My Name*, Graham Nash's *Songs for Beginners*, and Stephen Stills's *Stephen Stills 2*. Only Neil Young is missing, although he bracketed the Annus Mirabilis with masterpieces: *After the Goldrush* (1970) and *Harvest* (1972). It's a collection of music that is largely built around the acoustic guitar and belongs geographically in California—and spiritually to Laurel Canyon.

The center of gravity of the music business since the beginning of the twentieth century had been New York, home to Tin Pan Alley and the Brill Building, where a sixteen-year-old Carole King first plied her trade as a professional songwriter. New York was where the record company bosses, the producers, the A&R men, the studio-session musicians, and, most importantly, the songwriters lived and worked. New York was also where the business of music happened. Even by the late '60s, the record industry still saw the ownership of and rights to the songs as "the business." That mindset stretched back to the 1850s and the days of Oliver Ditson, when owning the publishing rights was, literally, a license to print money. Performers were just the vehicles that put the songs out there, and the industry regarded most performers as interchangeable commodities. It was quite common for the same popular song to be released simultaneously by multiple artists. But the latter part of the '60s had seen the growth of singers who wrote their own songs, including the Beatles and the Rolling Stones, British groups that had quickly grown out of mouthing someone else's words (and paying for the privilege).

The mid-sixties had also seen the growth of artists who wanted to live somewhere other than New York, where record company executives could reach them when they required them to perform. What followed was a gradual shift of influence from the chilly East Coast to a place where everything was warmer. In California, the air was clear, the sea was blue, and even the "suits" were people "like us" rather than older, glossy-haired businessmen in shiny business attire. The musicians were all relatively young. Ninety-five percent of the artists in Hepworth's Annus Mirabilis list were under thirty-two. With the arrival of creative talent came a group of managers and music businesspeople who were more in touch with the music and the artists they were working with. They weren't just people of the same age but people who used the same language, dressed the same way, went to the same parties, even took the same drugs.

Independently minded musicians had started migrating to California, and Los Angeles in particular, in this period. Joni Mitchell, her agent David Geffen, and her manager Elliot Roberts (who were both native New Yorkers) had all been based in the city, but together they moved to California. On being asked why she chose to live there, Mitchell quoted a passage from an old book she bought at a flea market:

> Ask anyone in America where the craziest people live and they'll tell you California. Ask anyone in California where the craziest people live and they say Los Angeles. Ask anyone in Los Angeles and they'll tell you Hollywood. Ask anyone in Hollywood and they'll tell you Laurel Canyon. And ask anyone in Laurel Canyon where the craziest people live and they'll tell you Lookout Mountain.

She bought her tiny cottage on Lookout Mountain in 1968 for $36,000 and owns it to this day. It's the house she returned to following a breakfast with her lover Graham Nash at Art's Deli on Ventura Boulevard, after she had bought a $150 antique vase. Nash suggested she put some flowers in the vase while he lit a fire to ward off the chill of the damp LA morning. According to Nash, it was a rare moment when Mitchell wasn't working at the piano, and he decided to write "Our House," a song "celebrating just an ordinary moment."

Nash was part of the British Invasion, having toured the US numerous times with the successful British close-harmony pop group the Hollies. But he became disillusioned with the group's musical direction and their unwillingness to record his material, so Nash packed the songs "Marrakesh Express," "Teach Your Children," and "Lady of the Island," abandoned his life in Britain, and headed to LA. He left the Hollies on December 8, 1968, and two days later was introduced to David Crosby at "Mama" Cass Elliot's Laurel Canyon house. By early January, Nash, Stills, and Crosby were at Joni Mitchell's cottage on Lookout Mountain. All three were experienced in singing harmony in successful groups: the Byrds (Crosby), Buffalo Springfield (Stills), and the Hollies (Nash). Crosby recalls that they sang Stills's "You Don't Have to Cry" to Nash. When he asked them to play it a third time, he added the top harmony part, and everyone in the room knew that they were going to have to work together. Mitchell vividly recalls that first meeting: "[They] raised their voices together ... [and I] witnessed the joy of them discovering their blend."

The "blend" they discovered included three voices from three very different places: California (Crosby), Texas (Stills), and Manchester, England (Nash). With the subsequent addition of Neil Young's Canadian falsetto, it was a blend that made the CSN&Y sound such an interesting and unique signature in California music. The formula of close vocal harmonies backed by acoustic and electric guitars in a folk-rock setting was explored to similar success across the '70s by numerous bands, but notably by the Eagles and the British-based band America, best remembered now for the multimillion selling CSN&Y-esque "A Horse with No Name."

• • • • • •

Laurel Canyon had become a haven for LA's creative community as early as the 1940s and '50s, when many Hollywood actors took to the hills to let loose and invariably get arrested at the numerous marijuana parties. Jazz guitarist Barney Kessel had moved into the Canyon in the early '40s, as had Gerry Mulligan and Chet Baker, as West Coast jazz started to become recognized as a relaxed antidote to the frenetic bebop sound emanating from New York. The Canyon's proximity to jazz clubs like the Haig, Crescendo, and Interlude, just a fifteen-minute drive down the valley road to Sunset Strip, helped cement its attraction. By the early 1960s, singer-writers like Jackie DeShannon had arrived, and new clubs like the Troubadour, Ciro's, and the Trip were hosting pop acts like Sonny & Cher, John Sebastian's the Lovin' Spoonful, and the Byrds, who broke through in 1965 with their first hit record, "Mr. Tambourine Man."

But record companies, funding expensive recording sessions with newly formed bands like the Byrds, often did not trust the bands' ability to deliver a faultless studio performance. The movie business (and allied movie soundtrack industry) had attracted growing numbers of session musicians who chose to make LA their home, and the record company producers employed the best of them in the recording studios.

The best of the best were a group of musicians known as the Wrecking Crew. Members included Larry Knechtel and Leon Russell, who had played alongside Roger McGuinn on the Byrds' first recordings. Other Los Angeles–based Wrecking Crew personnel included guitarists James Burton, Glen Campbell, and Carol Kaye: the latter two played on the Beach Boys' *Pet Sounds*. Kaye was the only woman in the Wrecking Crew and is credited on over ten thousand recording sessions and hundreds of the hit records. She was Quincy Jones's regular bass player on all his film soundtrack work, including *In the Heat of the Night*. His view was that "Carol Kaye . . . could do anything and leave men in the dust."

What made Carol Kaye first choice as a session bass player was that, like Paul McCartney, she started out playing six-string acoustic guitar. Paul, at sixteen, was a very competent guitarist, but he changed to bass because George and John were both guitarists and the group needed a bass player. By the same age, Kaye was playing jazz guitar in her father's bebop band and soon migrated into a leading session player. Tired of carrying a six-string acoustic, a twelve-string, and an electric guitar to those sessions, she noticed that bass players got paid the same union rate and had only one instrument to carry. But it was her sensibilities as a guitarist that made her bass playing much more than a thumping rhythm instrument slavishly following the chords. Listen to her intro on Glen Campbell's iconic "Wichita Lineman"; her bass-driven riffs lie at the heart of Ike and Tina Turner's "River Deep—Mountain High" and Sonny & Cher's "The Beat Goes On." Kaye invented these bits on the fly during the sessions, and they're picked with a plectrum rather than the bare fingers used by traditional bass players. The acoustic guitar's influence is everywhere in popular music.

By the time Joni Mitchell arrived in Laurel Canyon, Roger McGuinn and Chris Hillman of the Byrds, J. D. Souther, Judee Sill (Souther, Sill's lover, was "the Cross Maker" of her most famous song), and the members of the Mamas & the Papas, among many others, had already made it their home. Fellow Canadian Neil Young had an idea similar to Mitchell's and converted an old Pontiac funeral wagon for the journey south from Canada—he lived in the hearse for a while before finally taking a house near Mitchell's on Lookout Mountain. His "Out on the Weekend" clearly records the thought that the environment would allow him as an artist, as the lyric says, to "start a brand new day."

While the musicians most associated with Laurel Canyon were and are white and their music is often negatively characterized as mellow, soft adult-rock, in fact it reflects a rich blend of influences from jazz, blues, and rock to bluegrass, western swing, and British psychedelic-folk. Most of those singer-songwriters were acoustic guitar players, and the nature of their performances put the voice and, importantly, the guitar at the heart of the mix. While some singers did just strum folky block chords to accompany their voices, many had started pattern-picking over the chord progressions (using a series of short, fixed, repeating patterns played with the right hand). The repetition makes them highly rhythmic, holding the song structure together. Early Leonard Cohen songs like "Suzanne" and "Hey, That's No Way to Say Goodbye" (both 1967) are examples of complex pattern picking taught to a young Cohen by a Spanish classical guitar teacher when he was a teenager.

Self-taught players like James Taylor developed much more complex fingerpicking accompaniments, employing a piano-like approach, sustaining individual notes that create fluid transitions between chords. Taylor's guitar arrangements carefully select, as well as delete, notes from a chord and allow him to harmonize the guitar part with the melody. Rather than the guitar forming a backdrop to his baritone voice, as in Cohen's style, the guitar is woven into the tender melancholy of his vocals. Equally, Taylor's almost exclusive focus on songs in the keys of D, A, and E, his single-note phrases that preempt the arrival of the chord change, and his use of suspended chords are all part of his signature sound. These techniques, along with the delicate hammer-ons and pull-offs played on his 1964 Gibson J-50, are used to powerful effect on songs like "Fire and Rain" and "You've Got a Friend," and they changed and influenced the style of guitar playing for many singer-songwriters to come. This style of acoustic guitar playing enhanced the emotional, confessional style of writing and created deeply personal performances. Taylor, and artists like him, made albums that became staples of every cheap apartment or college dorm room. These artists were, as he sang, the ones "up on the jukebox . . . singing this sad song."

Unlike the male-dominated world of rock bands, where the rule seemed to be that the "guys played and girls watched," successful singer-songwriters could be of either gender. Jackson Browne, remembering Laurel Canyon and that era, saw that female artists counted and noted that Joni Mitchell in particular was much more than "another canyon lady." "It was the beginning of very big changes in the way women were regarded by society. It was a huge step forward in independence from religious dogma and there was no hierarchy there. If anything women had more power than they'd ever had."

And perhaps surprisingly, for those who regard Joni Mitchell primarily as a singer and writer, she also stands out as a guitarist. With her unique use of unorthodox guitar tunings and equally complex picking and strumming patterns, she was way ahead of her time and the skill level of many of the male singer-songwriters of the era. Chris Hillman of the Byrds recognized her talent early on: "What Joni Mitchell did was far and above what most of the guys could do as a songwriter *or* guitar player."

Henry Diltz, initially a folk musician, knew everyone in the Canyon and became the semiofficial photographer of the period. His photos provided the cover art of the first Crosby, Stills & Nash album and James Taylor's *Sweet Baby James*, and they appear on over two hundred more covers. But his rarely seen, intimate photographs of the musicians in their downtime are most revealing. One standout shows a scene in a Laurel Canyon garden where Mitchell sits cross-legged playing her Martin D-28 while Eric Clapton and David Crosby look on. Joni Mitchell explains that "Eric is just staring at me playing guitar and David looks proud, like the cat that ate the cream."

Clapton knew every note on the fretboard, had studiously mastered every blues scale, and knew how to channel the best Chicago blues players, but

Mitchell had, from the outset, a unique and prodigious talent. Crosby had always respected her intuitive musical ability and told me when I talked to him in 2015 that "she was the best of all of us, an extraordinary talent."

Mitchell had suffered from polio as a child that resulted in a weakened left hand, and she started to experiment with alternate guitar tunings to help her play traditional songs with simplified chord shapes. What Clapton was trying to work out in Mickey Dolenz's backyard was how she made the sounds she did with such relatively simple chord patterns. He knew about dropped-D tuning, the blues players' favorite, and open-tuning guitars to the basic chords of G and C, but Mitchell was using complicated hybrid versions that she created herself. By the '70s, her guitar tunings and chord voicing defied standard harmony and were extraordinarily difficult to dissect and replicate. She has used over fifty different tunings across her career; add to that her use of a capo to change keys, and it becomes bewildering to understand or figure out. Unlike Britain's Davey Graham, who was using established classical Eastern tunings, or Bert Jansch, with his use of the Celtic-tinged DADGAD tuning, Mitchell tuned her guitar to suit her sense of the song and worked it out from there. She explains: "Once I got the open tunings, for some reason I began to get the harmonic sophistication that excited me . . . [and] once I got some interesting chords to play with, my writing began to come."

She mostly wrote the lyrics first, as free-standing poems, and then added the melody. But unlike other writers, she developed original guitar tunings that reflected the sense of the words as well as designing tunings to mirror her mood or even the place where she was writing. She also developed a picking and strumming style that is unique to each of these tunings, the strumming often like a series of brush strokes. Mitchell wrote much of her 1971 release *Blue* while backpacking through Europe. For easy travelling, she carried a mountain dulcimer, a four-string instrument from Appalachia traditionally picked with a quill and played across the knees, Hawaiian style. Mitchell dispensed with the quill and slapped the strings rhythmically. Without a guitar for over a year, she changed her playing style. She recalled that she had seen Stephen Stills play his Martin dreadnought this way on the post-Woodstock *Dick Cavett Show*, and her break from the guitar awakened that latent memory.

On that Dick Cavett episode in 1969, Joni had played "Chelsea Morning" on the 1956 D-28 she had acquired from the US Marine captain who had taken the guitar on a tour of Vietnam (military rather than musical). According to Mitchell, the guitar had a near-miss "while in Indo-China." Mitchell explained that while the Marine was out on maneuvers, his tent and all his belongings, including a second guitar, were largely decimated by shrapnel. "When they cleared the wreckage all that survived was this guitar. I don't know whether the explosion did something to the nodules in the wood, but that guitar was a trooper, man."

While the Martin "bass dreadnought" was conceived as a guitar to be flat-picked in a string band, just listening to Mitchell strum-picking in open-D tuning on her early songs shows her unique feel and reveals how her loose, irregular, harp-like technique played around the lyrics. On "The Gallery" and "I Don't Know Where I Stand" (from *Clouds*, 1969), the same guitar is simply fingerpicked to magical effect. She described her guitar as a "mini orchestra," with the high strings serving as a horn section and the low strings as her bass, cello, and viola. Her "dear one . . . my beloved" D-28 may have survived Vietnam, but it was eventually damaged on a commercial flight and then stolen from a baggage carousel as she finished *Blue*, her fourth album. But by that time Mitchell had begun to explore an even more avant-garde, jazz-influenced sound palette, using open tunings with added 6ths, 9ths, and 13ths. She started using electric jazz guitars and ultimately chose a guitar specially constructed for her by a friend, Fred Walecki. The Stratocaster-style instrument, fitted with a Martin-style acoustic neck and hooked into a Roland synthesizer, electronically recreated her many alternate tunings at the touch of a few buttons by an off-stage technician.

Lyrically—and unlike Jimmie Rodgers, Woody Guthrie, or Dylan, who channeled the world of railroad whistles, free-spirited travelling men, and hobos to create personas—Mitchell used her music as a confessional. Her lyrics had, by the release of *Blue*, moved from the elliptical, hippie sentimentality of "Big Yellow Taxi" to the writer's refuge of disillusionment, often tracking the sinking of her contemporaries or the sense of bewilderment and isolation that the hippy generation was feeling as the new decade beckoned. *Blue* was an album of songs pored over by her male and female fans—who recognized that these were clearly more than just the musical jottings of a working musician. They seemed beyond real. Autobiographical songs like "Little Green," about giving up her only child for adoption, are self-excoriating, and it is therefore no wonder that her confidantes believed the album to be too raw, too personal, imploring that if she continued to write from the perspective of a butterfly pinned to a cork board, she would burn herself out. *Blue*, as a suite of songs, follows her emotional journey from lonely, hospitalized child in polio leg-calipers who can only dream of a river she "could skate away on"; to pregnant teenager talking to her unborn child, soon to be adopted, a victim of the "nonconformer" who has abandoned them both. She is the "lonely painter," the lover of Leonard Cohen, who is "in her blood . . . her holy wine"; she is the fitful wanderer, whose heart cries out for her adopted home, California. But as a singer-songwriter-guitarist, Mitchell reinvented the guitar as an accompaniment instrument.

• • • • • •

If Joni Mitchell is the female singer-songwriter who pioneered the transparent confessional style during the '70s, Jackson Browne is her male counterpart. Like Mitchell, he is a musician comfortable and highly competent on the piano but rightly admired and most associated with the acoustic guitar. In 2007, Browne, having started his career over thirty years earlier, was still successfully touring, offering his audiences the choice of "really tender song[s] filled with despair" or "really weary song[s] laced with hope." He often played solo, using stripped-down arrangements and intimate acoustic versions of his best material. At one such concert, Browne reflected on his love of guitars, how back in the '70s he made do with just a couple of instruments before revealing to the audience that "Stephen Stills . . . was the first guy I'd met who needed a separate truck to transport his guitars. At the time I thought it was the most decadent thing I'd ever heard of." The audience laughed as Browne, pausing to look around at the twenty or more highly collectable vintage acoustic guitars circling him onstage, went on: "I really didn't understand then . . . about guitars."

His mention of Stephen Stills as his first exposure to professional Guitar Addiction Syndrome was notable, not least because ten years later Browne was hailed by *Fretboard Journal* magazine as the current "fearless leader of the Guitar Geek Nation." And while Stills and CSN&Y helped inspire generations of singer-songwriters musically, they also had an important effect on the fortunes of the acoustic guitar in the modern era. Stills, Young, and Crosby were prodigious guitar acquirers and, unlike many artists, actively toured and played with their vintage acoustic and electric guitars. All three played vintage guitars during what was only their second live appearance—Woodstock in 1969.

Since the '60s players in the know had been paying more for a quality old Martin or Gibson than for a new model. While many casual players still saw them as just nice old guitars, by the '70s they had become "vintage guitars"; a 1937 D-28 easily sold for many hundreds of dollars. While there had always been a market for the more interesting older guitars, when "rock money" entered the vintage guitar market, prices shot up another level and then really started to soar. A prewar Martin D-45 would, by 1976, easily fetch $8,000.

George Gruhn believes that CSN&Y certainly "helped fortify the market. But bluegrass and old timey players were keenly aware that old ones were both superior and cheaper than new ones. Well before Crosby, Stills, Nash & Young were choosing old instruments over new, people in the bluegrass movement were very aware of vintage instruments."

Some of these players had long memories. Guitars played during the golden era that they had heard years before stuck in their heads and were sought out or tracked down years later. One such seeker was Tony Rice, "the flat-pickers' flat-picker," and the guitar was a 1935 Martin D-28 with the serial number 58957.

Rice had first seen the guitar backstage at a radio show in 1960 when he was nine years old and making his first radio appearance in his family band. The owner of the D-28 was Clarence White, the first full-time lead acoustic guitarist in bluegrass. He was playing alongside his brother Roland in the Kentucky Colonels. Rice clearly recalled the guitar White was playing: "I saw that old D-28 and it didn't have a name on the headstock. I asked what kind of guitar is that?" White identified the Martin and even let him play it. "The only thing I knew is that it looked like hell but it sounded like a million bucks to a nine-year-old kid."

While all eighty-three herringbone D-28s Martin made in 1935 are highly sought-after by players and collectors, this one, with the serial number 58957, is the most notorious of them and another trophy to nostalgia.

The first owner of 58957 went unrecorded, but in the late 1950s the guitar, by now badly beaten up, had been traded in at a Santa Monica guitar store by a student at UCLA. The guitar had been played heavily with a pick, and the sound hole had been enlarged at some point to remove the many ragged "pick bites" around its edges. The ebony fingerboard was pitted and coming away from the neck, making it essentially unplayable. What had been back in 1959 just a beat-up, basket-case, secondhand guitar was bought for $25 by the teenage Clarence White. He initially had the guitar cheaply repaired to use as a backup or "second" stage instrument, primarily to play rhythm guitar on.

White played the bluegrass circuit in a variety of bands before becoming a session player and being subsequently recruited into the Byrds by Gram Parsons in 1967. Together they produced the groundbreaking *Sweetheart of the Rodeo* LP and gave birth to the style of music that became alt-country. Before White's early death in 1973 (another victim of an auto accident), he produced enough dazzling music to have reinvented modern bluegrass picking. His style featured beautiful melody runs, often replacing the traditional role of the mandolin in a bluegrass band. Utilizing his trademark technique on classic albums by the Byrds, Jackson Browne, and Linda Ronstadt, he became *the* bluegrass picking legend of the '60s and early '70s. Around 1966, White either pawned or used the D-28 as collateral for a loan to buy an electric guitar.

The guitar disappeared, but nine years later Tony Rice, now twenty-four, was about to become the guitar's next owner. Rice had taken Clarence White's place as the top bluegrass session player. In 1975, he started thinking about "that D-28," but all he could learn of its whereabouts was that it might be in the hands of a liquor store owner called Miller living in California. So he began ringing around California liquor stores and asking if their owners happened to be called Miller. Remarkably he found him and the guitar, which had apparently sat under the Miller family bed for nine years.

Despite its provenance, only a few hundred dollars exchanged hands. Now in Rice's hands, White's fabled D-28 had a new mojo and together they took bluegrass flat-picking to another level, not only playing old-time fiddle tunes but also pioneering what became "progressive bluegrass." With slides, hammer-ons, pull-offs, and high-velocity strumming and using a pick and fingers with speed, precision, and volume, Rice's playing set a new gold standard. The D-28's backstory and Rice's playing just increased the notoriety of the instrument.

The Clarence White D-28 lived a charmed life. When White owned it, the guitar was often close to unplayable, probably the reason he used it primarily as a rhythm guitar—his frustration with it and quick temper once led him to shoot the guitar with a pellet gun. His carelessness also caused him to reverse over the guitar with a tour truck. In Rice's hands, it was submitted to two hours submerged in seawater when his Florida home was hit by a tropical storm. Yet it survived, repaired by every celebrated and legendary repair guy in the US . . . including Randy Wood of Nashville, Richard Hoover of Santa Cruz Guitars, and Ervin Somogyi, now a mystic guitar sage but back then just another guy known for handling complex repairs on valuable instruments. Dick Boak even raided the Martin guitar museum to find an original 1940s scalloped brace for one of the more drastic refurbishments.

While other makes and models of guitar may have survived tours of Vietnam, baggage carousel mistreatment, or tropical storms, it's the Martin D-28s and their stories that have survived and prospered. They are the ultimate trophies of guitar nostalgia and remain at the center of guitar obsession for both acoustic and rock musicians. As George Gruhn observes, another market dynamic changed once rock bands like CSN&Y entered the acoustic market in the '60s and '70s. "Before that the electric and acoustic markets were very much separate entities. But after folk-rock hit things changed. Rock 'n' roll and the now-popular folk-rock musicians were earning and therefore able to pay at a different magnitude than acoustic artists. Many of the acoustic player/collectors were bitter at being priced out of the market."

Gruhn was also at pains to point out that professional performers were much more than just profligate wealthy collectors. The professionals were choosing old guitars because they played and sounded significantly better than most new instruments, certainly in the early to mid-1970s when new guitars from major makers like Gibson were often "very poor."

Martin and Gibson both took a while to notice that the major competition against their new guitars was, paradoxically, coming from their own old guitars. A D-28 Martin made and sold wholesale to a retailer in 1937 for $50 was typically selling in 1970 for $800, increasing in price by 20 percent every year, while a brand-new D-28 then cost only $495. Martin realized that the old designs had to be part of its future, and in 1968 the company hired Mike Longworth, a talented inlay artist who had been making a living adding pearl to fabulous-sounding D-28s to make them look more like the desirable and even more valuable D-45. Originally hired to produce the complicated inlay on the D-45, reintroduced by the company in 1968, in 1976 he played a key role in the design and introduction of the HD-28, a heritage edition of the pickers' favorite. While not a totally accurate replica, it did reintroduce scalloped braces, herringbone trim, and a small maple bridge plate from the prewar guitars and was an immediate success. Martin sold a couple of thousand in its first two years of production and a further thirty thousand over the course of the next twenty-five years. Fans of the hallowed D-28 knew they might never find (or be able to afford) a vintage version and were happy to settle for a reasonably authentic reproduction. The idea was a simple one, but it took a couple of decades for the company to realize its full potential when it started accurately reproducing the old designs. Authentic reproductions of classic designs keep delivering for players and the company alike. The HD-28 continues to sell in huge numbers, remaining virtually unchanged since 1976. In 2018, it was rebooted as the HD-28 "Reimagined," looking and sounding even more like a vintage prewar guitar.

• • • • • •

In the early 1970s, while America was still buried deep in the physical, social, and political horror of Vietnam, Britain was embroiled in the darkest days of the conflict in Northern Ireland. On the mainland, newspaper front pages were reporting on an endless decade of rabid inflation, unsavory far-right politics, and industrial disputes that would, just when the country was gripped by the coldest winters in sixteen years, lead to the Winter of Discontent.

Across the entertainment pages of the popular red-top Sunday newspapers, where naughty vicars and bed-hopping actresses scandalized and titillated the country's parents and maiden aunts, were now male pop musicians in glittery makeup dressed as boys dressed as girls dressed as boys. Glam rock bands Slade, T. Rex, Roxy Music, Sweet, and Wizzard skirted the edges of acceptability, but in 1972, a flame-haired, androgynous David Bowie appeared as his alter ego, Ziggy Stardust, on the prime-time British pop show *Top of the Pops*. Horrified mothers pulled their hair and clasped their teenage daughters close. But when, sixty-five seconds in, Bowie, wearing a skintight multicolored jumpsuit, flirtatiously put his arm around the shoulders of his peroxide-blond guitarist, Mick Ronson, fathers locked up their sons. Lol Tolhurst, drummer with the postpunk goth-rock band the Cure, remembers "sitting at home on the couch with my mother watching this spectacle unfold, and at the point where Bowie sang the line, 'I had to phone someone so I picked on you,' he pointed directly at the camera, and I knew he was singing that line to me and everyone like me. It was a call to arms that put me on the path that I would soon follow." This summoning was delivered by Bowie performing with a bright blue, twelve-string Egmond acoustic guitar. He would continue to play acoustics throughout his career.

Although Bowie would later achieve musical sainthood, in the early '70s no one serious about their music took glam-rock too seriously. In contrast, the style of rock played by the Rolling Stones, the Who, and Led Zeppelin *was* serious. Progressive rock, as served up by Pink Floyd, Emerson, Lake & Palmer, or King Crimson, playing in 11/8 time, was *very* serious. The British breed of singer-songwriters and guitarists, often playing using alternate tunings or Mixolydian or Dorian modes, sat somewhere in between.

The British guitarists of the '60s discussed in chapter 9 (such as Bert Jansch, Davey Graham, and John Renbourn), with their dazzling jazz, blues, and Celtic fingerpicking techniques, were an entirely different breed from the Laurel Canyon crew or longer-established folkies like Tom Paxton, Phil Ochs, and Tom Rush, who had emerged from the Greenwich Village folk revival. While American singers were influenced by blues, rock, and contemporary country music, most British singer-songwriters came out of, and were initially heavily influenced by, the British folk club scene, which had itself experienced a revival in the '60s.

The guitar talents of the folk club virtuosi had spurred many British singer-songwriters to up their game. The simple accompaniment of a strummed guitar may have sufficed in a folk club in the '50s and early '60s, but by the '70s, it was barely table stakes. To get accepted you needed an inventive guitar style, and what better place to start than with some weird or arcane tuning?

Nick Drake (who followed the oft-to-be-repeated cocktail of prodigious talent coupled with an early death) is the Shelleyesque lost boy—the quiet, intelligent, highly introspective singer-songwriter. Percy Shelley's most well-known lyric poems "Ode to the West Wind" and "Music, When Soft Voices Die" could easily be the titles and often were the themes of Drake's songs. Like Shelley, Drake achieved a degree of fame only after his early death: in his case from an overdose of drugs (of the prescription variety). Like Shelley, Drake had a public school, Oxbridge education and came from a comfortable, if not exactly privileged, background. While Shelley used opium to "free his mind," Drake used copious amounts of hash. And like Shelley, Drake's influence on the three generations that followed his untimely death was immense.

As a guitarist, Drake had developed a highly complex picking style, using double-picked rhythms with varying tempos within individual songs. He coupled these with a superb use of counterpoint. In songs like "River Man" and "Hazey Jane I" (both 1971), melodies are harmonically interdependent but rhythmically independent. These guitar parts are immensely difficult to play, yet Drake, a deeply shy person and hesitant performer, could, in the studio, summon them to order. Before digital editing existed, Drake, recording live with a small orchestra or string quartet, would be able to play the tunes with metronomic precision time after time. The highly regarded producer and recording engineer John Wood said he couldn't "think of anybody else I've ever recorded, with that little studio experience and at that age, who had that ability. It was extraordinary."

The twenty-three-year-old also adopted many different alternate tunings, although he seems to have rarely written them down. B-E-B-E-B-E (from low to high), on, among other tracks, "At the Chime of a City Clock" and "Northern Sky"; C-G-C-F-C-E (from low to high) on "Hazey Jane 1" and "Pink Moon"; B-B-D-G-B-E (from low to high) on "Fruit Tree"; and G-G-D-G-B-D (from low to high) on "Black Eyed Dog." I could go on, but at last analysis he regularly employed twelve different tunings. Performing in an age before electronic tuners and lacking a guitar tech and a cache of guitars, it was little wonder that Drake found it testing to perform live.

He had developed his guitar style and range of alternate tunings during time he spent locked in his room at Marlborough College and in the months between school and taking up a delayed place at Cambridge University. Drake spent what would now be called a "gap year" at a foreign-language institute attached to the University of Aix-en-Provence. This time in France was his equivalent of Robert Johnson's pact with the devil. Beelzebub would go on to extract his side of the bargain from Drake at the crossroads only a few years later.

It was in 1967, while busking in the streets of Aix and haunting its many folk clubs, that he met the young American folk singer Robin Frederick. Another foreign "escapee," she recalled how "at a local club I sang the usual blues numbers and . . . after the set Nick Drake introduced himself." They clearly struck up a friendship, and Fredericks recalled various interactions, both personal and musical: "Nick often experimented with tempos, rhythms and the feel in his songs, making them difficult to play along with."

Taking a break from his language course, Drake had driven with two fellow students from France through Spain and then crossed to Morocco, where the group bumped into the Rolling Stones taking a holiday while they awaited the outcome of the drug charges parked back in England. Despite his legendary shyness, Drake was persuaded to play a few songs for the band, but nothing came of it. Maybe they marked him out as one of the many dreamers, loafers, and general lost souls Tangier attracted. Perhaps they were all in a substance haze. At any rate, Drake, who wrote often to his parents Molly and Rodney back in rural England, didn't bother to mention meeting one of the world's most famous rock bands in any letters home.

But it wasn't an entirely pointless excursion; returning to Europe via the bars and nightclubs of Saint-Tropez, Drake developed his little appreciated mastery of the highly syncopated, Southeastern ragtime, fingerpicking blues.

At the end of his gap year and on his way back to England to take up the place he scraped at Cambridge University, he found time to write to his parents from Paris: "Found myself a job, playing in a night club. Not particularly lucrative, but it passes the time."

While he may not have liked performing to a live audience, from his early recordings Drake showed a talent for floating his introspective, intimate vocals over an intricate guitar part picked on the treble strings countered with complex bass lines, mimicking ragtime piano–style melodies. At Cambridge, he had copies of Bert Jansch's and John Renbourn's first albums, and their blended techniques form part of the complex mix that is Drake's unique guitar style. While his technique is much admired, it is rarely copied or even apparent in the playing of his contemporaries, probably because, unlike the much-copied Jansch, his style is impenetrable. As Robin Fredericks found, Drake is not only difficult to "play along with," but his music is difficult to dissect and thus master; Drake's fondness of obtuse open tunings and his unique picking style meant that most folk club copyists left him well alone.

Even today adoring guitarists obsess over the particular tone and precise timbre of Drake's singular guitar sound. Given that he performed live so little, together with a complete lack of film or video of him playing and the dearth of photographs of him with an instrument, there is still great debate and confusion over what guitars he played. What few pictures that do exist that show him playing further confuse players trying to achieve his sound by using the same guitar. The cover photograph on his second album, *Bryter Later* (1971), shows a Guild M20, although the guitar belonged to the photographer, not the guitarist. One blurry black-and-white backstage photograph appears to show Drake playing what looks like the inevitable Martin D-28. In fact, it is a Levin copy of the guitar—in 1973 Martin bought the Swedish maker and alongside making Levin-branded versions of the D-18 and D-28, they made a small number of Martin-branded dreadnoughts in their Gothenburg factory. But if you listen to the first couple of Drake's albums, the guitar's muted bass sound seems to point toward a relatively small-bodied guitar rather than a dreadnought. It is also evident that his string tone is relatively flat, and there is a theory that he intentionally used old, "dead" nickel strings, devoid of the brightness and complex overtones that most acoustic guitarists seek today. Coupled with his muscular classical playing style, few guitarists then or now sound like him.

Drake, finally taking his place at Cambridge, had been signed by Joe Boyd, a twenty-seven-year-old American producer based in London. Drake's first album, *Five Leaves Left*, was released amid the July heatwave of 1969; it was one of three albums Boyd produced and released on the uber-cool Island record label that month.

Boyd's other albums that year, from Fairport Convention and Dr. Strangely Strange, were well received, but Drake's got mixed reviews. Some critics judged it "interesting," while others found it more "restful" than "stimulating." *Disc and Music Echo* was less impressed, finding the songs "uncertain and indirect." It took the influential *New Musical Express* three months to pronounce their verdict. On October 4, 1969, they eventually compared him to a one-hit-wonder of that summer: "His voice reminds me very much of Peter Sarstedt, but his songs lack Sarstedt's penetration and arresting quality." They all rather missed the point of Drake's music.

Enthusiasts interested in music designed for the LP market rather than the saccharine "pop" singles of the '60s and '70s relied on these weekly music papers for information; national newspapers rarely reported on contemporary music. BBC radio devoted only a few hours a day to "serious" popular music, and the one late-night TV program, *The Old Grey Whistle Test*, only started to broadcast in 1971. Thus, *Disc and Music Echo, Record Mirror, Melody Maker, Sounds*, and the ultra-hip *Musical Express* made or broke bands and their records.

No one could have predicted that Drake would be one of those rare artists whose star was to rise decades after his death. In his own lifetime, he was largely unknown; his first two albums *Five Leaves Left* and *Bryter Layter* barely sold five thousand copies each. *Pink Moon*, his intensely intimate final album, recorded in 1971 in the wee-small-hours across two nights, features just Drake and his guitar. The resulting release, barely twenty-five minutes long, fared little better than its predecessors.

Drake, long dogged by depression, was to die from a "massive overdose that could hardly have been accidental," taken in his old childhood bedroom in the family home two years later.

Across the '80s and '90s, his delicate songs, with their exquisite guitar accompaniment, would occasionally resurface on indie film soundtracks and coming-of-age TV dramas when something haunting and emotionally sincere was called for. Each appearance would recruit a new (if small) cadre of admirers and no doubt net a little royalty money for his estate and his long-suffering manager-producer, Joe Boyd.

Drake's big exposure in the United States came in 1999, when Volkswagen chose the eponymous title track from *Pink Moon* as the soundtrack for an American TV commercial. US sales of the album before 1999 had totaled a meagre six thousand. By 2000, they reached 74,000. As of today, it is estimated that around a million Nick Drake albums have been sold.

A tall, dark-haired, romantically attractive man, Drake found friendships hard to sustain, but, on the principle that opposites attract, he gravitated toward the incautiously extroverted John Martyn, who was also managed by Joe Boyd through his Witchseason production and management company. Drake was initially a great fan of Martyn's equally complex guitar style, having seen him play at Les Cousins folk club in London's Soho. As their relationship developed, Martyn was influenced by, and often intimidated by, Drake's use of altered tunings and complex rhythmic patterns. Apart from having the competence to experiment with Drake's style, Martyn was one of the few people to get close enough to have him explain what tunings he was using. But even as Martyn was inspired by Drake's playing, he was troubled by the declining mental health of his friend. In 1973, he wrote and recorded *Solid Air*, almost as an open letter of concern to Drake. Knowing that for most of his adult life his friend had battled with depression, Martyn could probably imagine what was going through his friend's head as he struggled to move through the "solid air" of ups, downs, disappointments, and betrayals of any would-be performer's world. Just twelve months later, the fragile Drake died from what his poor, bewildered parents were always convinced was an accidental overdose of antidepressants.

John Martyn had been christened Iain David McGeachy. The only son of two professional, touring light-opera singers, he was initially brought up in Surrey, a gentle suburban county in southern England. Following a divorce, the young child lived with his Scottish father on the rougher side of Glasgow, spending summers back in genteel Surrey with his mother's family (but not his mother, as she had rejected him). For all of his public life, John Martyn (renamed at the behest of his record label, he took his new name from his favorite guitar maker) had an unsettling habit of flipping between a broad but incoherent Glaswegian shipyard brogue; a genteel, posh Morningside Scots; Cockney "jack-the-lad" rhyming slang; and the refined Queen's English his maternal aunts may have used when he came to stay as a child. He shifted between accents, using them as a mask and a shield so no one was ever sure which version of Martyn they were talking to—womanizing charmer or threatening bully, tousle-haired poet or belligerent drunk.

Martyn had seen both Jansch and Davey Graham in the folk clubs of Glasgow, and by the age of sixteen he was performing in those same clubs, albeit at the unpaid bottom of the bill. Three years later, the nineteen-year-old was playing the London folk club scene, regularly appearing alongside contemporaries like Mike Chapman and fellow Scot Al Stewart and occasionally with well-established guitar legends Jansch, Renbourn, and Graham. He quickly took a liking to booze and the easily available hash and speed. Mike Chapman saw him often and recalled that "John was a boozer and a stoner in his youth. . . . Mostly he was a stoner, but we all were then. Getting stoned was cheaper."

Joining Island Records as the first white artist signed by Chris Blackwell to what had been his exclusively Black Jamaican music imprint, Martyn's first album, *London Conversation* (1967), was recorded across an afternoon in mono on a Revox reel-to-reel tape recorder in a friend's bedroom. It was blues-tinged, yet also full of whimsical, clever rhymes and gently melodic fingerpicking. Within a few years, Martyn had distanced himself from tracks like "Run Honey Run," material that sounded derivative of the traditional folk guitar stylists.

(Another song on this first album was "Sandy Grey," written in '67 by the young American folk singer Robin Frederick, who had shared a flat with, in her words, the "angelic, self-destructive" Martyn. Frederick did not reveal to him at the time that "Sandy Grey" was about Nick Drake, the shy eighteen-year-old boy with the elusive personality she had met, and fallen for, in Aix-en-Provence the previous summer.)

Another British singer-songwriter, Bridget St. John, was also in Aix-en-Provence that summer, and she moved in the same expat folk club and coffee bar circles as Nick Drake and Robin Frederick. Like Drake, the two women eventually returned to England at the end of the summer. St. John returned to London, where Frederick introduced the strikingly beautiful singer to John Martyn, who helped her get a manager and be signed by the esoteric Dandelion label.

Dandelion was started in 1969 by John Peel, a highly regarded and well-connected late-night BBC radio DJ renowned for championing high art, underground, and the kind of counterculture music rarely played even by pirate radio. Peel announced that he was planning to start his own label with the aim of releasing the kind of music he liked. St. John was Peel's first signing. There's every possibility that Peel initially created the label for her, perhaps because he knew that a female singer-songwriter playing such introspective music was unlikely to be signed by a major label. *Ask Me No Questions* (1969) contained fourteen songs delivered in her cello-like voice; accompanied by her own guitar, she played in a style that might best be called "intimate chamber-folk." Her guitar style was influenced by British players like Michael Chapman, Bert Jansch, and her original champion, John Martyn, who played on the album, contributed his song "Back to Stay," and played with her on her live appearances frequently broadcast on Peel's after-midnight show *Night Ride*.

Her playing style was similar to Nick Drake's in that she also used alternate tunings. In remembering an afternoon spent listening to Drake and Martyn, she recalled being "in awe . . . but able to absorb some small portion of their different tunings and fingerings that I would imperfectly remember." But her songs had the same feel as Drake's—what AllMusic recently described as "rainy day folk Baroque." The two artists shared a further similarity. While their first three albums attracted a small cult following, they failed to achieve any noticeable level of sales. Despite her growing popularity on the UK's college and festival circuit and being voted fifth most popular female singer by *Melody Maker* magazine in 1974, St. John would release only one more album in Britain, *Jumble Queen* (1974) on the Chrysalis label, before emigrating to New York and settling in Greenwich Village in 1976.

From this jumbled collective of superlative singer-songwriter guitarists—following Drake's death, St. John's emigration, and Frederick's disappearance from the scene—it would be Martyn who would build his success over the coming decades, releasing twenty-two studio albums and enjoying great popularity on the alternative tour circuit.

In 1969 Martyn released his first independent but professionally produced and recorded solo album. Around this time, he married the singer Beverley Kutner, who was also managed by Joe Boyd and was, back then, the more promising artist. Boyd had initially thought that Martyn would just be a useful backup guitarist for Kutner, then the rising name in Boyd's small portfolio of artists. But Martyn became a cuckoo in the nest, initially providing backing guitar, then writing songs with Kutner, and eventually becoming part of and then leading the duo, John and Beverley Martyn (note the name order). In 1970, Boyd had shipped the pair off to New York to record an album with American producer Paul Harris. Staying at the Chelsea Hotel in New York became too much of a distraction for Martyn, so Boyd rented the couple a small house in rural Woodstock that belonged to folk guitarists Happy and Artie Traum. Thanks to Boyd's connections, the Martyns met various members of the Band. Levon Helm, whom Boyd persuaded to play drums on a few tracks of the pair's subsequent album, *Stormbringer!*, took a mutual liking to the outgoing, irreverent Martyn. Boyd and Martyn were huge fans of *Music from Big Pink* and *The Band*, and both of the Martyn duo's albums are clearly modelled on the Woodstock sound of the Band.

But John Martyn was a difficult human being. A fusion of a bullying thug and hippyesque troubadour, he was attracted to personalities he could either dominate or fight.

He soon relegated his wife to the role of mother and homemaker, and his next album, *Bless the Weather* (1971), was a solo affair in which he managed to shift himself away from being seen, in his own words, as "a twee wee folky." By the time of his next release—the perfect *Solid Air* (1973), which contained what became his signature song, "May You Never"—his playing style had become completely different from traditional folk music and uniquely his. He had also cast aside the £40 Yamaha FG160 he had first brought with him to London and was playing the guitar that had inspired his stage name. A 1970 Martin D-28 dreadnought was now plugged in to a temperamental and complex spider web of cables linking a variety of early analog effects. In Martyn's own words: "Roughly speaking, it goes like this: the note comes out of the guitar's mic and is fed into the fuzz box that I use. Then it goes into a combination of volume and wah-wah pedal. It comes out of there and goes into the Echoplex that then repeats the note. . . . So I can still play between these two moments. . . . It is something very elastic."

Martyn had "gone electric" but in a way influenced more by the saxophonist Pharoah Sanders than by rock 'n' roll. The Echoplex, which had taken Martin years to fully master, was initially just his way of imitating the sustain Sanders achieved, but he then realized the possibilities that electronics could give to his live sound. Although he had bought a Gibson Les Paul Gold Top in the late '60s, rather than just plug it in, he was trying to extend both the acoustic and the amplified possibilities of the acoustic flat-top. His use of two separate pickups for his acoustic guitar was unique. A Barcus Berry contact pickup attached to the bridge fed a pure acoustic signal into one channel of a Fender twin amplifier. A DeArmond pickup, taped across the sound hole, sent its signal through the Echoplex and the other pedals into the second channel of the amp. The two separate signals allowed Martyn to alter the intensity of each and blend a multiplicity of sounds alongside the strictly acoustic tone of the guitar. It's a technique reworked today to great effect by contemporary players KT Tunstall and Ed Sheeran.

Martyn had consistently criticized folk-rock as "mis-matched wrongness," but he was a master in the subtle blending of other musical genres. In the early days of his electro-acoustic experimentation (on tracks like "Glistening Glyndebourne"), he used tape delay layered over real-time chord shifts and Danny Thompson's jazzy upright bass—nods to both the open intensity of Coltrane's *A Love Supreme* and the modal shift heard in Miles Davis's "So What." Having helped pioneer British jazz-folk, with the release of *One World* (1977) Martyn, in one leap, evolved from progressive folk to trip-hop. To record the album, Martyn, fresh from a period in Jamaica, had decamped to Woolwich Green Farm, the English country estate of Chris Blackwell, the boss of Island Records. Installed in a barn at the side of a lake, Martyn used the space as a giant speaker enclosure: the sound of Martyn's D-28 is captured in real time as early morning geese fly across the lake.

Listening to the guitar sound on "Small Hours" from *One World*, you hear a spare and open synthesized acoustic guitar weaving between the ambient live sound of a far-off train and wildfowl calling in the distance. It sounds as if the full power and intensity of his guitar is being squeezed through a pin-prick, like light from a camera obscura projecting its fuzzy, inverted imagery for the viewer/listener to reconstruct and make sense of. In these recordings Martyn had probably taken the acoustic guitar as far as it can be pushed before becoming a fully electric instrument.

Drake's and Martyn's unique skill as guitarists, together with the poetic sensitivity of their music, is the common ground between two very different men, although their capacity for consuming industrial quantities of hash also united them. While Drake could barely bring himself to communicate with a live audience, Martyn was a charmer who cadged joints from the front row and delighted in crude banter with his regular touring buddy, and fellow hard drinker, the jazz-folk bassist Danny Thompson. Women adored Drake but were disappointed that after they made all the moves he often slipped quietly away. In contrast, Martyn's sexual appetite and infidelities were the cause of much heartache for his "residential woman," his wife and now ex-singing partner, Beverley. Both men were always marked by their devils, but so many of the tracks on the three albums Drake completed, and so many of Martyn's compositions from *Bless the Weather* through *One World*, are hypnotic, inspiring works from two dazzling and influential British masters of the acoustic guitar.

• • • • • •

The 1950s folk boom in Britain and America, the advent of Beatlemania in the 1960s, and the growth of folk-rock in the 1970s all together mark an important period for the European and American acoustic guitar industries. Even with the entry into the market of East Asian guitar makers, supply was sufficiently below demand to keep prices up and profits healthy. Comparatively small companies like Gibson and Martin sold relatively large numbers of guitars. Up to that point, 1971 was Martin's historic record sales year, when the company sold over 22,000 guitars, a huge volume for expensive guitars from what was essentially a small, artisan business. However, from the late '70s through the mid-1980s, outside of niche sectors and dedicated enthusiasts, the guitar wasn't that important anymore. It was not just overtaken by a different instrument; it was completely eclipsed by a totally new style of music.

The arrival of new genres of music and the advent of cheap, polyphonic keyboard synthesizers meant that few wooden acoustic guitars got an invite to the party. By 1979, the whole guitar industry was in decline, and by 1982, when Kool & the Gang were topping the charts with "Get Down on It," the Martin company's total production was 3,153 instruments, their lowest figure since the depths of World War II.

What had at the beginning of the 1970s been the best of times for the guitar industry was by the end of the 1970s approaching the worst of times and a period of darkness was on the horizon.

Neil Young playing a 1980 Taylor 855 twelve-string.

Beyond Martin and Gibson

It's the summer of 1988 and London's Wembley Stadium is packed with 80,000 people attending an all-day concert held to celebrate Nelson Mandela's seventieth birthday and raise global awareness of South Africa's apartheid regime.

The crowd has heard speeches delivered by various celebrities and politically aware actors and film stars lauding the much-loved anti-apartheid activist, at the time still held in prison by the South African government. Equally politically aware comedians have punctuated the gaps between the bands while roadies quickly remove and set up each successive performer's equipment.

The hugely popular band Dire Straits will headline at the end of the day, and by late afternoon the vast venue is at full capacity and fizzing with a crowd enjoying themselves and in a boisterous mood. There have been perhaps a few too many speeches, however.

The British reggae band ASWAD has just finished its set, and the roadies are about to load in the equipment for the afternoon's first big-name surprise guest, Stevie Wonder, booked to play a twenty-six-minute set of greatest hits. That is until his stage manager notices that the hard drive that runs Wonder's trademark synthesizer is missing. Having flown in from the US only that morning, the star arrived stage-side pumped but is now in tears. Without the programmed hard drive, he cannot perform, and he walks back to his dressing room, exasperated. The event's organizers have no band ready to play to the capacity crowd in the stadium or the growing global TV audience that now numbers about 600 million viewers across forty-seven countries.

A virtually unknown artist, Tracy Chapman, a twenty-four-year-old African American singer-songwriter, had played a short acoustic set much earlier in the day before the stadium had filled. She'd covered a few songs off her first album, which had been released only a couple of months earlier. The producers need an act that requires little stage setup, and as one of the only acoustic artists on the bill, she is asked if she will play again. A few minutes later, she walks back onstage to play live to half a billion people. Just her and her Martin guitar.

She arrives to a noisy, restless crowd, entertaining themselves by whistling and occasionally jeering, chanting, and randomly yelling. It could have turned awkward as the diminutive folk singer, lost on the huge stage, starts finger-picking the simple looping, lilting acoustic riff of "Fast Car," the first single from the album. She starts singing: "You got a fast car . . ." Initially she sounds breathless; she can hear the "one, two" of the sound crew from behind the hastily erected stage curtain as they hurriedly try to set up the gear of the next band. The crowd is louder than her, uneasy, perhaps not knowing what to make of the hippyish Black girl with short natural hair and an acoustic guitar. But the simple, rhythmic quietness of the song starts to work its magic. The crowd starts to settle. Thirty seconds in, they are beginning to listen. You see a smile cross her face. She knows she has them. The sound and simple appeal of an acoustic guitar and a solo singer work their timeless magic. Between its release in April and the Wembley show in June, her eponymous first album had sold a respectable 250,000 copies. In the weeks after her appearance at the Mandela concert, the singer-songwriter with her socially aware collection of songs sold three million units.

"Fast Car," a song about a person dreaming of escaping poverty and the drudgery of life, became something of an enduring classic, known across generations and regularly featuring on radio playlists. So no great surprise that thirty-five years later, a still-youthful-looking Chapman played it at the 2024 Grammy awards show alongside country star Luke Combs, who had covered the song the previous year. Combs's version had reached number two on the Billboard Hot 100 and number one on the country chart. Chapman won a Country Music Association award and became the first Black woman to receive a sole songwriting credit for a number-one country hit. As of early 2024, Luke Combs's cover had around 500 million streams on Spotify alone, while Chapman's original recording had reached almost 900 million.

• • • • • •

There were only two acoustic performances at the Mandela concert: Chapman and the much more established British Anglo-Caribbean singer-songwriter Joan Armatrading. While Chapman played solo, Armatrading was playing her guitar-led set of jazz, reggae, and R&B-tinged ballads like "Love and Affection" with a full band. Both guitarists needed to "plug in" their acoustic guitars, but they tackled the challenge of overcoming feedback—the bane of acoustic players playing live—in different ways.

Armatrading had been using Ovation bowl-backed six- and twelve-string Legend guitars, with their unique plug-and-play onboard amplification system, since the '70s. They were a rare innovation in the acoustic guitar world and much loved by many touring acoustic players as a neat, trouble-free way to bring an acoustic sound to a large audience. Clearly, they suit Armatrading since she continues to use them today.

Chapman walked onto the Wembley stage in 1988 carrying a Martin dreadnought acoustic fitted with what looked like a lashed-up, home-modified amplification rig. It had two DeArmond single-coil pickups, which could have been borrowed from an old 1950s Gretsch archtop, screwed onto the guitar's body, along with three control knobs and a three-way control switch, possibly from a Gibson Les Paul, drilled into the top.

While looking somewhat crude, Chapman's guitar was in fact a factory-made production model. Martin had produced three hundred D-18Es in 1959, a belated first attempt to capitalize on the electric guitar revolution. However, it didn't play well as an acoustic, electro-acoustic, or solely electric guitar. The heavy pickups deadened the top, and to accommodate the control knobs and associated electrics, the top was crudely ladder-braced rather than X-braced like all other Martin acoustics.

The first production run sold poorly, partially because of their lackluster performance but also because the D-18E and the even more expensive D-28E were, at the time, among Martin's most expensive guitars and twice the price of the latest Fender Telecaster.

Martin discontinued production of the D-18E at the end of 1959 and of the D-28E in 1964; not long after they withdrew from electrics altogether. The guitars were rarely seen before or after Chapman's appearances in 1988 promoting her first album. But in 1993, the grunge band Nirvana appeared on *MTV Unplugged* (a series that ran from 1989 to 1999) with Kurt Cobain playing a Martin D-18E, sparking interest and a price blip in secondhand models of the much-maligned guitar. After Cobain's death in 1994, his battered D-18E sold at auction for $6 million.

Martin's flat-top electrics—the 00-18E, D-18E, and D-28E—would all fail to take the Martin brand beyond the flat-top. When they tried to enter the archtop and solid-body electric markets, the guitars sold in low numbers.

Chapman stuck with Martin dreadnoughts until 2001, when she walked into Gryphon Stringed Instruments in Palo Alto, California, looking for a small-bodied acoustic. Like many smaller-framed players, she had begun to find that playing the large, wide, and deep-bodied dreadnoughts strained her shoulder muscles and joints.

The salesperson had her try a Model A acoustic made by Judy Threet. The Canadian builder had made the small-bodied guitar on spec in 1999, but it had so far failed to find a home. The guitar was a perfect combination of playability, dynamic tonality, and fit for Chapman, and she held on to it, bringing it onstage at the Grammy awards in 2024.

The next morning, Threet was inundated with calls from friends and fans alerting her to the reappearance of the twenty-five-year-old instrument. Although Threet gave up making guitars in 2010, she is still remembered as one of the first of a small cohort of women builders that emerged in the mid-1980s and 1990s. Fellow Canadian Linda Manzer, best known for her decades-long association with Pat Metheny, is still building. Among her most famous creations are Metheny's "42-string, four-neck, two sound-hole" Pikaso guitar and the Manzer Wedge, which she designed and developed to help overcome the neck and shoulder strain guitar playing can cause. Also still building instruments is the much-revered Los Angeles–based maker Kathy Wingert, recognized for her pioneering work building harp guitars and exquisitely detailed flat-tops.

• • • • • •

The fact that only two acoustic performers played across the whole playbill of an all-day festival broadly reflects the place that the acoustic guitar held in popular music in the 1980s. Its uptake and popularity had already taken a battering from the growth of heavy metal and punk in the 1970s. Punk-rock, mainly an Anglo-American phenomenon that burst onto the scene in 1975, was the very antithesis of acoustic guitar music; delicate fingerpicking and technical ability were replaced by three power chords, distortion, and even the faking of technical and musical incompetence to court notoriety.

Furthermore, until the 1980s, the easiest, cheapest, and coolest way to fulfil your musical dreams was to buy an acoustic guitar. With the advent of affordable synthesizers, drum machines, samplers, and other electronic music aids, this was no longer the case. An individual could produce an entire band's worth of music in their bedroom. Not only was this cheaper and easier than forming a band; it also was new and fresh. The acoustic guitar was not the only loser; whole bands, as well as string and brass studio musicians, could be done away with. Dance music, known in the 1970s as disco, went from a group like Chic—a full band plus strings, brass, and so on—in the late 1970s to drum machines and synths in the early 1980s. This did allow for a wonderful flourishing of creativity: for example, house music and hip-hop were born of this technological change, as young producers were able to express themselves via a new medium. British bands like Depeche Mode, Spandau Ballet, Visage, and Human League no longer needed a couple of guitars and a drummer to start playing gigs, as they had in the '60s and '70s. Now, they more typically had a Yamaha DX7 synth and Korg "keytar" at the center of their creation process and a stage persona in themselves.

The now-affordable digital synthesizer continued to challenge the guitar in all other forms of music, including ballads, soul, pop, and R&B. The top-ten single charts of the first years of the decade were dominated by Michael Jackson and a whole variety of dance and funk acts. Review the mainstream album charts for the '80s and you'll find guitars present, but the delicate country-tinged Chet Atkins–style picking of Dire Straits was more often drowned out in the US by the thrash metal sound of Metallica and Eddie Van Halen, while Def Leppard and Saxon dominated in the UK. Even Gibson and Fender were having a tough time. Their classic electric guitars didn't suit heavy metal, and by the mid-1980s "mass-produced fluorescent 'superstrats'" from Kramer were the top-selling electric guitars in America.

Popular music in this decade was more about image and style, a development that can be credited especially to the birth of the music video. The acoustic guitar would not be seen too often in the '80s videos. Most new wave or new romantic groups were as interested in costuming and makeup as creating music. The acoustic guitar didn't fit with the hedonistic partying of the '80s and its upbeat, machine-driven soundtrack. Perhaps the music suited people's need for a distraction from the social and economic difficulties of the times. Britain was caught up in the Falklands War and its aftermath (its worst international conflict since World War II); enduring a long, drawn-out, and violent coal miners' strike; slogging through a recession; and dealing with the AIDS crisis. However, as Boy George, the twenty-one-year-old androgynous frontman of Culture Club, optimistically noted, "The music scene was healthier than it had been for a long time." However, the acoustic guitar was not a part of this world.

The acoustic guitar industry was certainly feeling the pain. It was a period when the flat-top couldn't have been more unfashionable or musically off-trend.

There was, however, one song recorded right at the start of the 1980s that continues to resonate down the decades, and it injected a little Caribbean cool into the acoustic during its darker days. Bob Marley's "Redemption Song" is the final track on *Uprising*, what would become Marley's final album. Like Joan Armatrading, he used an Ovation guitar to record this, for him, rare solo acoustic spiritual ballad. The song lends itself more to a soul or folk style, lacks much of the reggae rhythm, and was recorded when Marley almost certainly knew he was dying of cancer. Released in Britain as a single in 1980, "Redemption Song" would become a standard and inspiration to guitar-playing backpackers and beach-bar playlists worldwide. Like "Fast Car," it has never seemed to age, and linking one of the world's most iconic artists to the acoustic guitar has probably been no bad thing for the guitar's image and appeal.

• • • • • •

Despite shrinking sales, the '80s were ironically also a decade of contrasts for the acoustic guitar. Taylor Guitars, a company formed in 1974 during the peak of the folk-rock boom, led the way in the '80s into high-tech guitar manufacturing. Paradoxically, alongside Taylor, a growing group of individual guitar makers were returning to a hand-building process that C. F. Martin would have recognized from his own apprenticeship.

The flat-top acoustic had gone underground, or at least into the relative shadows of bluegrass, country, and folk. Little wonder that in 1983, when

Martin & Co. was trying to celebrate its 150-year anniversary, it was not just laying off staff but facing closing its doors forever. It had known tough times in the Depression and across two world wars, but whatever the economic climate, people had still played acoustic music.

Martin, although still only a small business in Fortune 500 terms, had relatively recently arranged bank loans to upscale its operation to satisfy the '70s acoustic guitar boom. Whereas downsizing had previously only involved handing out a few pink slips or working a shorter week, this time it had 60,000 square feet of new buildings and other capital resources under-utilized or lying idle. It wasn't alone. Gibson, Fender, Gretsch, and Guild all teetered on the brink, their fragility brought about as much by the mismanagement of their corporate owners over-expanding these fragile businesses as by musical fashions, punitive interest rates, and key foreign markets in recession. In a case of the greedy leading the incompetent, their owners continued to fund businesses that were making neither money nor good guitars. Martin & Co. only appeared to be capable of looking back, printing "150 Years" on anything that stood still. On the other side of the US, in Southern California, the Taylor company, barely ten years old at this point, was at least putting in place strategies that might permit it to one day challenge Martin in terms of volume.

At the beginning of the 1980s, the nascent Taylor Guitars was a hundred times smaller than its Nazareth rival. But as a result of the '80s guitar slump, a now-shrunken Martin was only ten times bigger than Taylor, which in 1986 produced around fifty guitars a week. Taylor, which initially had a tough struggle, achieved its meteoric growth by reinventing the way guitars were made, in the process throwing away the rule book as written by C. F. Martin. When Martin started in America 150 years earlier, he built guitars in much the same way as he had when, as a young man, he worked for Johann Stauffer. Not long after Bob Taylor and his long-term business partner Kurt Listug started, they did something very different in an industry often hidebound by tradition.

• • • • • •

Taylor Guitars had been born out of Sam Radding's guitar store and hippy cooperative based in Lemon Grove, San Diego. Radding had opened American Dream Musical Instrument Manufacturing in early 1970 and had encouraged local independent guitar builders to set up shop in the rear of his California store. Back then, a built-to-order Brazilian rosewood dreadnought with a base price of $360 allowed Radding to keep $180, with any add-ons or priced options going to the individual builder. Some of those builders who would eventually set up shop on their own included banjo maker Greg Deering and guitar builders James Goodall, Larry Breedlove, and Bob Taylor. By 1974, Radding wanted out and sold the business for $2,400 to his three remaining backroom guitar builders, including Bob Taylor, then nineteen years old. After the sale, and no doubt disappointment that the name American Dream was not actually included in the sale, the most active guitar maker got to hang his shingle over the door.

Taylor's early years were tough, with the three owner-employees living a hand-to-mouth existence, rarely able to draw a livable salary. Like Martin & Co. over a hundred years earlier, the small company appointed a single sole distributor only to fire them a few years later as they declined to order any more stock. The business eventually stabilized—or at least managed to sell enough guitars to pay the bills—but Bob Taylor and his partner Kurt Listug knew they had to find a more efficient way to run the small company. Their first breakthrough was to reinvent the way a small factory manages the production of guitars. Taylor's plan was to set a target number of instruments to be completed every single day: Only completed guitars could be boxed, shipped, and, most essentially, invoiced.

Their targets were two-fold: to finish the target number of guitars every day, and to complete large batches of parts that took more than a day to produce. In essence, Taylor was using the Japanese principles of lean manufacturing to create a modern, faster, more efficient version of the repetitious, production-line process that guitar companies like Lyon & Healy had introduced in Chicago in the 1890s.

A renewed and growing popularity of acoustic music resulted in the whole guitar business starting to pick up again in the late '80s. The uplift came from an unlikely source.

• • • • • •

The Wonder Years and *Thirtysomething* were both massively popular, intelligent, and thoughtful American TV programs that, in their different ways, traded on musical nostalgia. *The Wonder Years* was a family show designed to appeal to baby boomers by setting the series in their golden youth, the late '60s, a time of radical change in America. *Thirtysomething* portrayed those same baby boomers, now in their thirties, as they negotiated their transition from singlehood into married yuppiedom. Both shows appeared in the late

'80s, and significantly, both integrated music from across the '60s and '70s into their storylines. Music wasn't just in the background; it was part of the story, a comment on the action or emotional state of the characters. Much of it was written, arranged, or conceived by W. G. "Snuffy" Walden.

Walden, a guitarist born in Louisiana, played in a variety of blues bands in the '70s and, after moving to the UK, even stood in as lead guitarist in the British rock band Free after their star guitarist, Paul Kossoff, died. Returning to the US in the '80s, he continued his career in music, supporting big-name bands and doing high-end session work. Fearing a future as an ageing touring musician "staying in Holiday Inns as a 60-year-old guitarist," he was asked to audition by scoring the 1987 pilot for *Thirtysomething*. The producers wanted a '70s folk-rock sound and had even approached David Crosby of CSN&Y fame to write a theme song. Walden tried something based on a single acoustic guitar riff and it stuck, creating the show's intro music and musical signature. This success led him to being commissioned a few weeks later to try his luck with *The Wonder Years*. Both shows featured acoustic guitar extensively across their soundtracks, opening credits, and as scene-change stings (the short musical phrase, or stab, used as aural punctuation to the narrative).

Eighty million people tuned into the series premiere of *The Wonder Years* in 1988, and many millions stayed tuned for the next five years, watching 115 episodes until the series finale. As with *Thirtysomething*, immersing the show's baby boomer audience in what had become unfashionable acoustic guitar music reawakened something. An audience who had grown up with Dylan, the Beatles, James Taylor, and CSN&Y creating the "soundtrack to my life" started buying the CD reissues of the vinyl LPs they had bought as teenagers.

The shows gave much-needed light of day to the acoustic guitar, an instrument that the boomers had largely forgotten. A few started looking for the old guitars their parents had consigned to the attic or even bought replacements. When a few years later *MTV Unplugged* reinforced the idea, it mobilized that same group of baby boomers, many entering their own midlife crises, and rekindled an interest in playing the acoustic guitar. This interest led, in great part, to a revival in acoustic-based music.

• • • • • •

Despite enjoying the benefits of the uplift, Taylor realized it had only survived by the skin of its teeth and decided that its future depended on building guitars more efficiently and economically. Their mission was not about building cheaply but rather about finding ever-more-efficient, cost-effective ways to build better-engineered acoustic guitars. Taylor's next move was its most controversial and established something of a schism within modern guitar building.

In 1989, Bob Taylor met the owner of Tom Anderson Guitars, who was using a computer-controlled machine called a Fadal to machine-carve the solid bodies of electric guitars. The Fadal, a large, three-axis milling machine, could saw, drill, and rout all the key solid wooden parts of the electric guitar body. All it required was a computer programmer and a human being capable of loading wooden blanks into the cutting bay of the machine. The items it produced were identical every time, and like all machines, it could work uncomplainingly 24/7 if required. Taylor effectively bet the farm, or what money it could borrow, to buy one Fadal and started using it to make the solid parts of the guitar. Most makers view these parts as adding little to the sound of the instrument—necks, headstocks, bridges, as well as parts such as braces that are hidden inside the guitar. The Fadal also enabled Taylor to redesign one of the most critical, skill-intensive, and time-consuming tasks in guitar manufacture: the process by which the solid neck is joined to the hollow body of the instrument. Since the introduction of the guitar and its many precursors going back to the fourteenth century, the neck was joined to the body by various

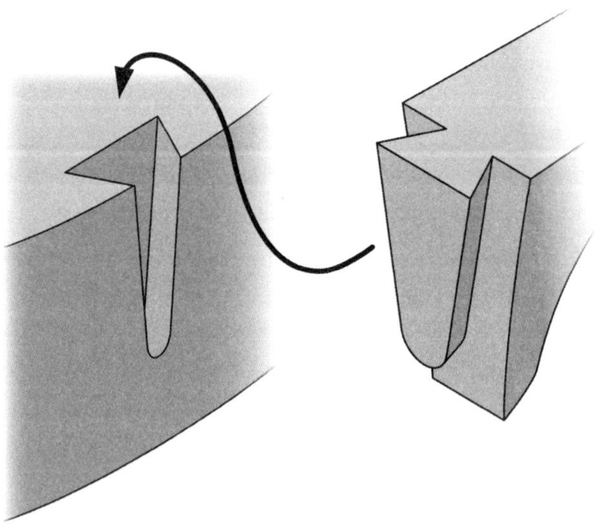

Traditional dovetail neck joint. (Courtesy of Gerry Hayes, Haze Guitars)

traditional woodworker's joints. Martin preferred a strong tapered, compound dovetail joint, invented by ancient Chinese craftsmen cabinetmakers and difficult to execute. They continue to join most guitar necks to the bodies this way. Early Martin antebellum contemporaries like Ashborn and Haynes did not use these complex joints of so-called hidden beauty, using instead a simplified violin-style joint.

Martin's traditional compound dovetail joint is difficult to master and as a result is one of the most daunting parts of making the guitar for an individual builder. It requires cutting a V-shaped, flared tenon on the heel of the neck and a perfectly corresponding mortise in the body's neck-block. Accurately made and fitted, a dovetail joint is very strong and lightweight and requires only a small amount of glue to keep it in place. Because there is a lot of wood-to-wood contact between the neck and the body, it pulls everything together and thereby enhances the overall sound of the guitar. Unlike the Spanish heel joint, used by most classical guitar builders, the dovetail joint allows the neck to be reset over time, another reason for the longevity of many Martin guitars.

However, making the dovetail joint is also one of the most time-consuming processes. Experienced guitar builders say it's one of those jobs that either happens smoothly in a few hours or takes the best part of a day to get right. Essentially, the neck carries the male tenon half of the joint, which fits into the female mortise cut into the body. It demands more than a cosmetic fit because the final angle of the join determines the height of the strings from the fretboard and affects the way the guitar plays, the all-critical "action." Once the joints are cut, you can only make microscopic adjustments. If the action is even a shade too low, the strings will buzz as they oscillate against the frets. A shade too high and the strings require Herculean strength to push down onto the frets. Many cheap, poorly constructed guitars have high action that makes them difficult (and sometimes just plain painful) to play and causes many novice or young guitarists to give up. For all these reasons, using a dovetail neck joint was something that Taylor sought to either simplify or bypass entirely, and they looked at bolting the neck onto the body.

When Leo Fender started making his first solid-bodied electric guitars in the early '50s, he dispensed with any complex glued wooden joints and simply attached the neck onto the body with four bolts: perfectly in keeping with the quick-build, factory style production-line ethos of the Fender company. In 1962, Leo Fender hired the mercurial, cocky Roger Rossmeisl (late of Rickenbacker). He was brought in to design a range of acoustic guitars "for the beach, the coffeehouse and the campfire." Rossmeisl employed the

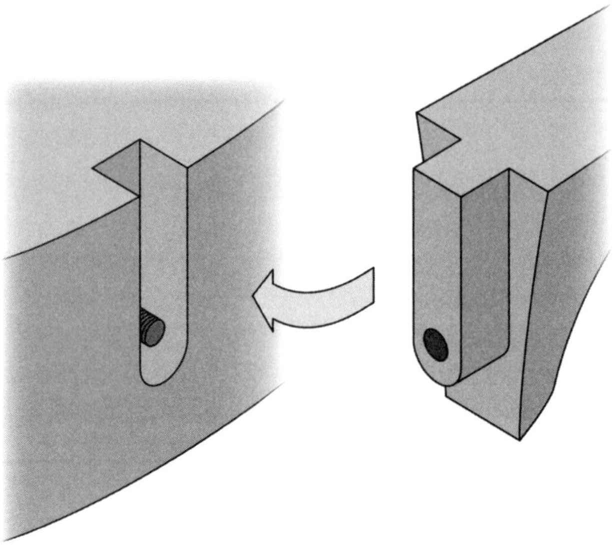

Martin mortise and tenon bolt-on neck joint. (Courtesy of Gerry Hayes, Haze Guitars)

Fender bolt-on approach to attach the neck to the body, given it was a skill the factory already had.

While the Fender-style bolt-on neck from the '50s was efficient, it was also crude. In the late '90s, Taylor was able to create a highly innovative, precision bolt-on design only viable with the use of computer-aided routing, cutting, and drilling. Taylor's modified design, itself based on a method using a glueless mortise and tenon joint reintroduced by builder Stu Mossman in the '70s, is engineered to tolerances of .002 inches, so precise that only a slight error in the application of the lacquer finish can make the neck joint too tight. Aside from simplifying the manufacture process, it also made repairs and adjustments to the guitar's playability very easy. Necks could be simply unbolted rather than injecting steam into the glued dovetail. So efficient is the process that by the early 1990s, even Martin started using an adaptation of the technique in their cheaper models.

However clever Taylor's new neck design was, it represented for many—and not just the purist fringe—a tipping point. It seemed fine when simple, basic parts like braces, the bridge, and even the actual neck profile were machined by a computer. But the introduction of the bolt-on neck marked the point where a critical part of the guitar was being engineered and produced by machine operators and assemblers rather than being the work of craftsmen. People who owned multi-thousand-dollar guitars built by respected low-volume makers like Collings, Bourgeois, Goodall, Breedlove, and others—makers that had subsequently adopted this practice—were often shocked to learn their instruments had a bolt-on neck. While it is sophisticated, modern, and technically sensible, there still seemed to be a defensiveness about the technology among some owners and players of more expensive guitars, many of whom persuaded themselves without evidence that the neck joint affected the sound. The Taylor tone is very forward and bright, sometimes described as techno-pop compared to a traditionally constructed guitar. Owners talk about their cooler, piano-like sound and the easy way a Taylor plays. Martin owners like the bassier but balanced sound of their guitars, convinced that it will only get better with age, and often talk about growing old alongside their Martins. In truth, they both play well straight out of the box, but many players want their guitars to have a soul, a personality, the human fingerprint of the builder.

It is fanciful, but many builders I've spoken to believe that they leave a little bit of themselves in every completed instrument. There is no doubt that Taylor is driven as much by a desire to build increasingly better guitars as it is to improve efficiency and profitability. It shares the desire for "better" with every guitar maker I've ever met. It certainly shares the passion and obsession but also, because of its own struggle during its formative years, its founders know what it's like to work a hundred-hour week producing guitars yet barely make enough money to put food on the table. Taylor represents *a* way forward and freely shares its technological developments with any builder who asks. But many players and guitar buyers question how much perfection delivered through technology we need and actually want. Martin & Co., which today produces a similar volume of guitars to Taylor, uses a fair amount of technology but still considers itself a business rooted in a hand-building culture.

There is a bigger, more fundamental difference between Taylor and Martin. Taylor considers itself a company that uses technology and contemporary manufacturing processes to bring about the affordable American-made quality guitar. Yet where Taylor will modify the design of a guitar so that it can take advantage of high-tech production methods, Martin still insists on using slow, and therefore expensive, handwork if the machine cannot help produce what the company sees as the perfect guitar. So, for example, even though Martin now cuts dovetails using a computer-controlled machine, it retains its trademark headstock volutes even though they require expensive handwork.

Despite the schism between machine versus hand-first construction, it doesn't affect the mutual respect between the two companies. The modernist, industrially focused Bob Taylor readily admits his debt to Martin & Co. First for sharing knowledge as he transformed from an individual builder into the head of a small, struggling guitar company, and then for not foreclosing on his business after he ran out of cash to pay the bill for tonewood he had bought from them. As his business teetered on the brink of financial collapse, Martin wrote off the debt. It's a testament to his decency as a man, and professionalism as a businessman, that many months after Martin had written off the debt, and as soon as he had enough cash in the bank to honor his own check, he repaid the money.

Bob Taylor also goes out of his way to credit independent Canadian luthier Jean Larrivée for coaching him and his business partner through their bleakest times and giving them the confidence to continue.

Larrivée is now one of the few volume builders who still use traditional dovetails. Back in the late '60s, when Larrivée was just starting out, he was no fan of mechanized manufacture but one of a group of builders who sought to return the North American guitar industry to its craft roots. The group's passion was a reaction to big corporations that, following the folk- and Beatles-inspired guitar boom, attempted to diversify into the guitar market. Norlin, with a background in brewing, acquired Gibson; CBS, the entertainment conglomerate, paid $13 million for Fender; and Baldwin, a staid Midwestern piano company, acquired Gretsch.

These corporations had entered a business of which they had little knowledge and with the misguided belief that more volume at lower cost was a winning formula. When demand outstripped supply, as it did in the early '70s, they were financially secure. When demand tailed off and those buyers who remained became more discerning, many guitar companies were in trouble. Their solution was usually to strip out even more cost until many guitars were being assembled at companies like the Norlin-owned Gibson either by experienced but demotivated workers or by low-paid, low-skilled employees. The results were inevitable. These are the guitars that British maker and repairer Dave King had the most difficulty in pricing repairs for: "When you open up a Gibson from the '80s you have no idea whether the guitar was put together by a skilled old-timer or an apprentice who'd started doing the job the previous week!"

Jean Larrivée's cohorts, in the embryonic group of North American guitar builders returning to craft roots, were Michael Gurian, Stu Mossman, and archtop legend James D'Aquisto. They were young men who had matured in the hippy counterculture of the '60s, when there was an upsurge in artisan and skill-based enterprise. Having started building their own guitars in the late 1960s, the small group of twenty-somethings were all, in the words of a near-manifesto written by Mossman in one of his early catalogues,

> disgusted with what has happened to the quality of goods produced in this country. Quality has been sacrificed for quantity. Mass production has gotten out of hand. Craft has almost been completely eliminated from our society. This vile abomination [of plywood] is currently being perpetuated on the unsuspecting guitar playing public on a grand scale. We at Mossman considered plywood briefly one day and unanimously decided that plywood makes the best cement forms available. We do not now nor will we ever stoop to the level of plywood construction, and we apologize for our contemporaries who have lowered the station of our craft by using laminated backs and sides. Mossman considers itself a happy exception to the current trend. We are relatively small and are able to devote all our energies to quality craftsmanship and the selection of fine aged woods. We love making guitars and are proud of our work.

The issue was where they might learn their skills. D'Aquisto, a decade older than the others, had found an apprenticeship in the 1950s with the only archtop builder left working in New York, John D'Angelico, the last of a small group of Italian American archtop builders. But the few hand-builders of flattop guitars left in the US by the '60s were mostly building traditional classical guitars for serious players and concert artists like Julian Bream and Andrés Segovia. Getting apprenticeships was difficult, but classical makers David Rubio and Manuel Velazquez, from whom Gurian learned in the mid-1960s, did take on a few of what they called "creative hippies" and helped them carry the flame of building guitars using their own hands. Out of this small group emerged several low-volume, boutique guitar makers who themselves took on apprentices, wrote the first books about modern luthiery (including Irving Sloane's *Classical Guitar Construction*), and, in the case of Gurian, moved on from building to become the supplier of specialist parts and tools to the next generation of American guitar makers.

These were builders who believed that the "one person, under one roof" ethos allowed the maker to put a bit of their soul into each guitar. And while most builders will use an industrial bandsaw to roughly cut out a neck from a solid mahogany blank, many, like British luthier Dave King, appreciate "the sensation of doing the final shaping of the neck by hand. I can't add much value when I remove the first 95 percent of wood, but I can when I focus totally on that last 5 percent. And only by being directly connected, touching and in control of the wood, can I make those final decisions that make the neck mine."

But much of this must have sounded like heady, naive idealism when in the '80s the guitar industry was on its knees. During the guitar slump of the mid-1980s, Norlin divested themselves of the ailing Gibson company. Figuring that they had neither the financial means nor the stomach to fight the tide of a guitar market ebbing into insignificance, they sold the business for cents on the dollar. CBS did the same with Fender.

Taylor, still small enough to shuffle the numbers on a daily basis, clung on.

They also got a lucky break.

At the time it probably didn't seem like much, but Kurt Listug, one of the original founders and now Taylor CEO, remembers that they were "up for trying just about anything." The artist known as Prince was the unlikely patron who may have helped with a recovery.

Eric Clapton was once asked what it was like to be the best guitarist in the world. He allegedly replied, "I dunno. Ask Prince."

Apart from being a master of funk, R&B, new wave, soul, synth-pop, jazz, and more, and usually playing all the instruments on his recordings, he was also a sensational electric guitarist. But Prince had used a Taylor twelve-string on some recording sessions and liked the instrument. He wasn't alone. Many professional players were picking up Taylor's take on a playable twelve-string. Neil Young had bought a pair of Taylor twelve-strings back in the early '80s and onstage reworked some electric guitar songs using the highly playable guitars. And it was their playability that was building Taylor a reputation as more than just a good-value, American-made guitar.

Twelve-string guitars need to be built lightly to achieve their bell-like chiming sound yet still be able to cope with the tension of the extra six strings trying to pull the guitar apart—equal to the weight of a well-built man hanging from the glued-on bridge. Taylors were known to be light, responsive instruments priced at a point that made sense for road and studio use by working musicians. To suit Prince's "I am not a corporate slave" period, when he did not use any branded guitars onstage, a Minneapolis guitar dealer suggested to Taylor that an unbranded custom twelve-string in "Prince Purple" might catch the musician's eye. They built it. It did catch his eye. He bought it. To everyone's surprise, he even featured it in the 1985 video for "Raspberry Beret." It was just a small act in a market that was still stagnant, but Prince—a respected creative artist popular with a young music audience who were buying large numbers of records—was one artist who seemed to like acoustic guitars again! Things started to bubble in the acoustic world. Then in early 1988 *Thirtysomething* and *The Wonder Years* happened, and the market really began to hot up.

• • • • • •

In the '70s, sitting on the commercial sidelines, watching the guitar boom and subsequent crash-and-burn of many volume guitar manufacturers, was a new generation of guitar makers who were also keen not to lose the skills employed by traditional builders. This new and growing group was different from the '60s hippy cohort of Larrivée, Mossman, and Gurian.

Leading members of this new group included Richard Hoover and Bill Collings, who were running one-person operations or very small teams and making bespoke guitars in small quantities. Many were guitarists themselves, a second cohort of artisan-inclined individuals or established craftspeople discovering an interest in the alchemy of luthiery. While they respected the instruments produced by Martin and Gibson in the acoustic guitar's golden era of the 1930s and '40s, many now had a growing contempt for once-great makers perhaps now resting on their laurels and commanding premium or bespoke pricing for what was a factory-built product. Surely an instrument built by one person with passion was better, more worthy, more soulful, than the output of a guitar factory.

Initially, these low-volume makers struggled financially. Many operated on the brink of insolvency for years. But what united them was their direction of travel. They all had a desire to understand why the guitars made by American makers like Martin and Gibson, especially in the years between 1920 and 1940, played and sounded so good. If they could find out why, then why couldn't they employ that knowledge in making instruments of comparable quality today?

Some, like Hoover, started out repairing guitars. The best achieved significant reputations, often entrusted to repair collectors' treasured guitars from the prewar period. Acoustic guitar manufacturers, even relatively big ones like Gibson and Martin, didn't keep a parts inventory; they made as many bridges, necks, and so forth as guitar orders demanded. If something broke or fell apart, a local repair technician was expected to make the replacement part themselves. As a result, those who really cared about making a proper repair gained a forensic understanding of what made these early instruments so good.

However, when most traditionally built acoustic guitars were originally constructed, they were glued together with little expectation of ever being taken apart. After thirty or forty years of playing, the wood and joints on even an extremely well-made guitar will settle, or the string tension will gradually pull the guitar's geometry out of true, raising the height of the strings from the fretboard. The result is action so high that the instrument becomes uncomfortable, then difficult, and eventually impossible to play. Shaving the bone saddle can help, but we now know that the only real fix is to remove and reset the neck. But if you sent a guitar in need of a neck reset back to Martin in the 1960s, they would have told you that it couldn't be done—because the neck could not be removed. The very notion of removing the neck and then recutting the neck joint to reset the playing height of the strings was, back in the late 1960s and '70s, virtually unknown, even to the company that had made the guitar. Assuming that the bridge saddle had been repeatedly shaved so that there was only a sliver of bone left, to improve the action the Martin factory repair shop would like as not remove the frets, plane the neck down as far they could, and then file the actual bridge down. George Gruhn recalls that by the mid-1960s, the first repairer doing anything like a neck reset was Jon Lundberg. In his workshop in Berkeley, California, Lundberg would loosen the back of the guitar, slip the neck-block back, tilt the neck, and squash the whole thing back in. Gruhn recalls these fixes were known as "slipping the block" or a "California neck reset." Although relatively crude, it rendered an otherwise unplayable guitar playable but at some cost to the integrity of the instrument. Randy Wood, one of a few go-to repairmen in Nashville in the late '60s, seems to have been the first person to actually remove the neck before resetting it—cutting the fretboard where it joined the body and removing the finger-board extension. Dripping hot water into the exposed joint and then heating it to boiling point with the tip of an electric soldering iron softened the glue and eventually allowed the neck to come free.

Around this time proper guitar repair and restoration started to evolve into a profession. Techniques were finessed, transforming the craft of repair into the art that it is today. With no bolted-on components, other than tuners, no readily available interchangeable parts or neat access panels, repairing an acoustic guitar was often more challenging than building a new one. Neck resets and fashioning replacement components not only taught builders what made a great-sounding guitar but often earned them more money per hour than building a new one.

Repair people wanted their work to be invisible. Their aim was to repair the instrument but ideally leave no sign they had been at work. But they needed recognition to prosper. However self-effacing these people are (and many are both modest and hermit-like), who wouldn't want to be known as a great repair technician and from there progress to being the great maker of your age? To this end, technicians like Wood also did work that was meant to be noticed—like inlaying "Elvis Presley" in leaf script along the fretboard of the King's 1969 Gibson Dove. But like many, Wood wanted to originate instruments. He started building mandolins, applying the knowledge gained repairing Gibson F-5 Lloyd Loars to his own, much sought after, multi-thousand-dollar versions. T. J. Thompson, "the Guitar Whisperer"—for many enthusiasts, the repair guru's repair guru—"dropped" his first neck on a vintage Martin OM-28 in 1984 and alongside his reputation for repairing the unrepairable makes just a few Martin-style acoustics with his own name on the headstock. Using an Adirondack red spruce tree he personally selected in 1991, the 217 tops he harvested will last him his lifetime as a builder of guitars. Thompson originals are highly sought after by collectors, with a wait list running at around seven years and prices starting at $40,000.

Like Thompson, many of the outstanding repair techs concentrated on repairing Martins, Gibsons, and other high-end instruments. As golden era models got more expensive and repair techniques evolved, it became both technically feasible and economically viable to invest many days bringing an unplayable Martin D-28 or Gibson J-50 back to life. Builders like Richard Hoover of Santa Cruz Guitars and Bill Collings became hugely respectful of both Martin and Gibson golden era instruments, but rather than continuing to repair or just make faithful reproductions, they started businesses making guitars inspired or very heavily influenced by the very best golden era guitars. But their individual approaches were and still are very different.

Bill Collings, with a metal machining background, developed a modern guitar factory employing CNC machinery and high-end technology to make exquisite instruments. Hoover's low-volume operation in the California coastal town of Santa Cruz started in the late '70s. A modern take on Martin's small North Street manufactory, where the golden era instruments were made, it is today still about the same size and operates with just twenty or so skilled employees.

But despite differing approaches, both of their enterprises served as a wake-up call to Martin, reminding the company what it should have been making in the '80s but often wasn't. The oldest guitar company in America took notice. It started by remembering to respect its own vintage guitars and then by changing the way it designed, manufactured, and marketed new top-end models and the golden era range of instruments.

But there was another, different approach to small-volume guitar building also happening at this time.

• • • • • •

Ervin Somogyi, a guitar builder based in Northern California's Bay Area, first started making flamenco guitars in the late '60s, inspired by and answering a renewed but relatively brief uplift in flamenco playing. A master repairman—he was also one of the select group who repaired the Clarence White D-28—Somogyi was approached by Alex de Grassi, a local guitarist playing finger-style. The guitarist was signed to Windham Hill, a relatively new recording label popular in the '80s and specializing in mellow but serious-minded instrumental acoustic music.

De Grassi and his label mate Daniel Hecht were playing finger-style guitar in a quasi-classical manner. They were looking for a steel-string guitar that delivered the same dynamic range across the whole fretboard demanded by classical players. More prosaically, they also wanted guitars that were comfortable to play when seated on a concert hall stage or in a recording studio. Most steel-string guitars available at this time were based on the Martin dreadnought—guitars that, in the somewhat derogatory words of Somogyi, were "designed to be played standing up with a strap around your shoulders."

Their work, labelled new age music, was also being meticulously recorded on state-of-the-art microphones and studio equipment. The transparency of the recordings showed that the intonation of many vintage and new instruments was often inaccurate above the third fret.

Ervin Somogyi understood exactly what Hecht and his compatriots were looking for, and the resulting instrument, delivered in 1980, was what the builder called simply "the Modified Dreadnought": a guitar that was marginally smaller than the canonical dreadnought but with a deep Venetian cutaway that allowed the player access to the whole fretboard, way beyond that "dusty end." Somogyi lavished time on the intonation, ensuring that every note was pitch-perfect. He also made the waist of the guitar slightly deeper, thereby allowing the guitar to rest comfortably on the seated player's leg. In an early letter to Stan Jay of Mandolin Brothers, the New York guitar dealer, Somogyi remarked that his altered dreadnought was "modified in outline so that the parts are more proportionate and the body lines and curves flow even better."

Somogyi's description didn't sound that radical, but the guitar was more than just a marginal redesign. He was able to voice the instrument for a finger-style player. New age guitar music focused as much on the gaps between the notes as what was being played. Hecht and players like him were recording music that allowed the decay of a note to become part of the piece. Chords played not just beyond the third fret but beyond the twelfth were expected to be true as well as ring out and sustain. Somogyi believed that traditional soundboard voicing needed to be rethought for this new style of playing and set about a radical appraisal of how he built the whole guitar. His approach to this challenge covered every aspect of guitar building, and, given that most handmade guitars involve over three hundred separate steps, his published explanation ran into two dense volumes. There is no doubt his early years making lightly constructed flamenco guitars influenced the lightness of build that he achieved, and he lays great store by an organic approach to voicing. Most volume makers and many individual builders construct their guitars to a set of dimensions or formulas that they were either taught or have arrived at over a number of years of experience. Somogyi's approach is dynamically tailored to each piece of tonewood he employs, echoing the philosophy of the Cremonese violin makers.

There is something of the artisan, the technician, and the shaman, as well as a clever marketing brain, in everything Somogyi does. Unsurprisingly, he is a divisive character in the guitar world, judged as a genius, a possessed madman, and every stop in between. He writes and lectures extensively on every aspect of his approach and philosophy, giving particular attention to the voicing of the top of the guitar.

The search by guitarists focusing on a particular style of music to find the instrument that perfectly fits that style often leads to the reappraisal of existing designs of guitar. In the way the Hawaiian slide guitar was repurposed by western swing and bluegrass players, there is a degree of serendipity in a guitar style coming back into fashion. In Somogyi's original letter to Stan Jay, he says that after the Modified Dreadnought, his second-most popular model was his version of the 1920s Martin OM (or Orchestra Model). Initially designed for jazz and dance band players, the OM was quickly overtaken by the more appropriate archtop jazz guitar. After finding a brief reprieve among western swing players, the OM was effectively renamed the fourteen-fret 000, and the OM name was discontinued from the Martin catalog. It was another fifty years before it was rediscovered, this time by contemporary ragtime guitarists.

• • • • • •

The rebirth of the OM starts in the 1960s, back when a lot of New York folk and blues players had been "raggin' the blues," or incorporating versions of ragtime songs into their repertoire. Alongside the blues, Rev. Gary Davis had played and taught tunes like "Maple Leaf Rag" to middle-class New York kids including Stefan Grossman, who paid $5 an hour for guitar lessons. The so-called Mayor of MacDougall Street, Dave van Ronk, had been raggin' the odd song like "St. Louis Tickle" and the New Lost City Ramblers had played "Dallas Rag" on guitar, mandolin, and banjo. Even Mississippi John Hurt's "Creole Belle" was more ragtime than blues, and the sublime Elizabeth Cotten, she of "Freight Train" fame, had played a gentle guitar accompaniment in "ragged" time.

As the 1970s approached, twenty-five-year-old David Laibman, who had been interested in ragtime music from the beginning of his career, called on his younger cousin, Eric Schoenberg, to realize his ambition to go beyond just "raggin' up" songs. Laibman wanted to do more than just play in a syncopated or ragged style; he wanted "to play complete piano rags, with all the notes and all the sections."

These complete piano rags had been written in the early 1900s by the celebrated ragtime piano players and composers Scott Joplin, Joseph Lamb, and James Scott. Laibman also knew that there were, or had been, guitar arrangements for the piano rags, having seen them advertised on the back of old piano sheet music. Working from what printed music scores he could find, old 78 recordings, and even piano rolls on nickelodeons, he started transcribing the pieces. Laibman had discussed the challenge of playing these complex compositions with Dave van Ronk. These tunes were challenging enough when using two hands on a piano keyboard but nigh impossible for a guitar player who could use only five fingers rather than ten to pick the notes. Van Ronk suggested Laibman find someone to play "the bass part and some of the other stuff," and Laibman chose his young cousin Eric, who was teaching guitar and playing a bit of simple ragged material himself. Eric Schoenberg remembers starting out with Laibman in 1966, practicing for hours every week just to get half a song completed. By the late '60s, they had transcribed, learned, and road-tested enough pieces to approach the legendary Moe Asch at Folkways Records for a recording deal. Folkways was the label of choice for any pioneering folk artist—the young Bob Dylan had somewhat loftily declared that Folkways was the only label that he aspired to be signed to. As far as he was concerned, they were the label that put out "all the great records."

The resulting release from Laibman and Schoenberg was appropriately called *The New Ragtime Guitar*. What they had recorded was a new take on an old form and was in many ways the precursor to much of the complex New York and West Coast finger-style playing in America. It was also the twelve-inch LP that I, as a tentative seventeen-year-old, was "allowed" (by the over-possessive sales staff) to buy in Dobells record store in London more than fifty years ago.

Schoenberg confirms that the fancy guitar he holds in the LP's cover photo was a 1930 Martin 000-45 twelve-fret that he had bought from George Gruhn for somewhere around $600 in 1969. It was purchased before George had a store and was still selling guitars from his apartment or the trunk of his car. Coincidentally, it was pretty much the same 1929-style guitar I had ordered from Martin thirty years later.

After *The New Ragtime Guitar* was released, its relative success meant that Schoenberg continued touring, recording music, and, unsurprisingly, collecting guitars. His particular interest was Martins from the 1920s and '30s. The twelve-fret 000 model had suited his earlier repertoire, but Schoenberg felt that its relatively wide neck, which had only twelve frets clear of the body, meant it wasn't the perfect finger-style guitar.

He found and started experimenting with a couple of the more than fifteen hundred OMs that Martin had made between 1929 and 1933 and discovered that a guitar that had originally been "designed especially for plectrum playing in orchestra work" was ideally suited to ragtime and his finger-style playing. Having fourteen frets clear of the body helped fit seven-octave piano pieces into the almost four-octave guitar neck. Martin did incorporate elements of the OM design into the 000, but the scale length was shortened, which was why, according to Schoenberg, the later 000s "don't do quite the same things as the OM." The longer scale (string length) on the OM gave greater clarity to individual notes across the whole fretboard and greater volume and responsiveness when played sensitively, without a plectrum. The longer scale also made the strings tauter and less likely to slap and bend when he didn't want them to.

By 1977, Schoenberg was the co-owner of a guitar store in Massachusetts specializing in new and vintage Martins. He knew that there was a market for the OM from the level of customer interest and the prices that people were willing to pay for vintage examples, so he tried to persuade the Martin factory to make a couple of OMs as a special order. Initially, they showed little interest (one can assume it was because it interfered with their standardized production), but he already knew they could do it. Schoenberg and Matt Umanov had met while working at Marc Silber's Fretted Instrument Shop in New York, and by the late 1960s Schoenberg was working for Umanov. Together they had written a joint letter asking Martin whether it would make "a few long-scale OM-28s with 1¾" necks." Despite being a model the company hadn't made for over forty years, six guitars, designated SOM-28 (the *S* for Special), duly appeared in Umanov's store. It seems they went almost immediately into the hands of Umanov's friends and NYC players like Roy Bookbinder, although Schoenberg wistfully recalls that despite his involvement, "and typing the letter to Martin!," he didn't end up getting his hands on one.

Fast forward a decade. Schoenberg persisted in badgering Martin, who by 1977 were effectively "the dreadnought guitar company." Wedded almost exclusively to making large-bodied dreadnoughts, it was about to introduce the M series, an even larger-bodied flat-top that was effectively a 0000 based on an adaptation pioneered by Marc Silber and Umanov. During this period, the company made a few attempts at reproducing smaller-bodied guitars from their back catalog, but it met limited sales success. But when you look at its contemporary 1970s reissue of a 1900s 00-45, so many details—things that vintage enthusiasts and collectors of the time recognized and sought—are wrong. The fretboard inlays were oversized slabs of abalone inappropriately borrowed from the much larger D-45. The abalone peghead inlay was the 1930s vertical "C. F. Martin" rather than the traditional torch or scroll that collectors revere. It seemed that Schoenberg almost certainly knew much more about Martins' historic OM models and back catalog than anyone actually working at the company. By sheer persistence, he finally got the company to agree to make more accurate models.

He wanted them to make fancy OM-45 instruments that were "as close as we could get to a 1930s specification" with the longer scale and wider neck he knew worked for finger-style playing. The Martin company had neither the in-house craftspeople nor the set-up to do any volume of fancy, 45-style pegheads or fretboard inlay. Instead, they sent Schoenberg the blank fretboards and peghead veneers, and he got a friend, the vintage inlay specialist Doug Unger from Ohio, to do the work. There is further evidence of this lack of expertise when twelve months later Martin promoted the newly resurrected OM-45 in its catalog as a special-order item. Whereas the Style 45 OMs that Schoenberg offered had appropriate vintage inlay, the factory offering was again slabs of hexagonal abalone on the fretboard and the company name down the peghead. As George Gruhn pointed out when I spent the day with him in Nashville, "During the '60s and '70s, Martin had little knowledge or respect for their heritage . . . [and often exhibited] . . . a 'parts tray' design mentality worthy of the US automotive industry of the same period."

Schoenberg's initial batch of OMs were, according to Martin in-house historian Mike Longworth, effectively the pilot project for what became in 1980 the Martin Custom Shop. Encouraged but not totally satisfied, Schoenberg followed an even more radical route to get as close as possible to his goal, "the ideal finger-style guitar."

His first batch of Martin-sourced OMs were strong sellers. Martin had coincidentally just reintroduced scalloped bracing, true to the original 1930s OMs, which no doubt helped the sound and popularity of the guitars, and Schoenberg continued to order more OM-28s in subsequent years. But he knew the guitars could be even better. One feature Martin had never offered was a cutaway body that would allow adventurous finger-style players even higher fret access. The source for this final evolution of the OM as the ultimate finger-style guitar came in 1984 from Schoenberg's then-repairman, Dana Bourgeois.

Bourgeois, these days a celebrated maker of high quality flat-tops in his own right, was in 1980 doing vintage guitar repairs for Schoenberg's shop. Over a four-year period, he and his apprentice T. J. Thompson worked on or restored many of Schoenberg's prewar Martin OMs. Not only did they both understand what made an OM sound as it did, but Bourgeois also knew that Schoenberg wanted an OM with a cutaway body, one similar to that on a 1930s Selmer-Maccaferri gypsy-jazz guitar he owned. Bourgeois effectively built one on spec, and Schoenberg adored the first iteration of the OM with a modified Florentine-style cutaway. They worked together refining the design and establishing a "classical" aesthetic for the guitar; the result was the first Schoenberg Soloist.

Schoenberg passionately believed he was onto something; a guitar conceived and designed through a cooperation between a finger-style guitarist and a master builder and based on a model created during Martin's golden era. The masterstroke was to approach Martin to build them in the Nazareth factory in cooperation with Bourgeois. Although seemingly a minor event, this was another big-bang moment in the evolution of the flat-top acoustic guitar. Just as significantly, it was pivotal in the survival of the Martin company.

Like all big bangs, countless things, potentially unrelated, must happen at the same time to achieve ignition. Schoenberg and Bourgeois approached the Martin company in 1986, when lots of unrelated things *were* flying around.

Notably, the acoustic guitar market was slack, and with plenty of domestic and foreign competition there was an abundance of good, cheap guitars to choose from. Martin knew how to do good, but not cheap. It wasn't their business model, and sales were weak in an already depressed market. To make matters worse, the family management dynasty of the company was also experiencing a period of uncertainty.

From 1945 to 1986, the company had been run by the nonagenarian and highly conservative president, C. F. "Fred" Martin III. But the old patriarch had just died, and his grandson, C. F. "Chris" Martin IV, succeeded him as head of the company.

Chris's own father—the somewhat feckless, four-times married, racecar and sports team enthusiast Frank Herbert Martin—had been ousted by the board of directors in 1982 after a series of financially and strategically disastrous acquisitions and investments. His eighty-two-year-old father, Fred, was then brought out of retirement, although he did little more than briefly steady the ship while his grandson Chris was readied for the top job. Upon his grandfather's death, thirty-one-year-old Chris quickly realized he needed to be both bold and lucky if the family business, now a barely solvent entity, was to survive. At his first meeting with the firm's auditors, they recommended that he liquidate the failing business. At his second, with the bank, they informed him that they were withdrawing the company's line of credit.

Chris Martin also inherited a largely intact but reactionary management team from his father's disastrous period at the helm. He later recalled that he "worried about spending too much time away from Nazareth for fear that they'd either vote me out of the job or the company simply wouldn't exist on my return."

However, one ally was the buccaneering Dick Boak. A guitar polymath, iconoclast, and restless corporate irritant, he was seemingly predestined to spend most of his career working at Martin. He had already been unfairly fired for going over the head of his unimaginative manager during Frank Herbert's reign, but he seemingly just kept showing up until, during a strike in the late '70s, Chris Martin quietly rehired him. Until his recent retirement and across a forty-one-year career, Boak held a variety of key creative and transformational roles across the business.

In 1986, Schoenberg and Bourgeois visited Nazareth and pitched the idea of a collaboration to Chris Martin. Apart from Dick Boak, who strongly backed the proposal, there was probably no one else at the company who would have taken the meeting or realized what they were talking about. Chris Martin, at that time desperately trying to get the company to think outside the small Martin box, liked the concept. Having been largely brought up by his paternal grandfather, Chris probably knew that the original OM had been one of Fred Martin III's own projects: He had approved, developed, and physically delivered the original OM to Perry Bechtel in 1929. Chris gave approval for two R&D prototypes to be made. Fortunately, given the glacial pace of actual R&D at Martin in those days, the revolutionary approach of a collaboration presented Martin with little to either research or develop.

The Schoenberg-Bourgeois proposal was radical, bordering on the downright disrespectful, to a company that had effectively invented the American flat-top guitar. Dana Bourgeois intended to manufacture key parts in his Maine workshop and then "send partial guitar kits to Nazareth for Martin to assemble." Dana then planned to visit Nazareth to tap-tune or voice each guitar's top and oversee the assembly line to "make critical adjustments to each guitar during construction." After inspecting and playing each instrument, Bourgeois and Schoenberg would sign the label inside the guitar certifying their approval of the Martin-made collaboration.

When I met Schoenberg in 2015, he reflected on his first visit with Dana to Nazareth to meet the production team heads.

He knew that the company was now a modern guitar factory, but not that it had lost all resident knowledge of how the golden era Martins were made. Although "Since 1833" was proudly stamped on the headstock of every guitar and an important part of the Martin brand, it seemed to mean precious little inside the actual company. Production processes that Schoenberg and Bourgeois felt were important to getting the most from a Martin-made guitar were long forgotten. Schoenberg talked about the poorly made pyramid bridges produced by the factory, and I thought of a conversation I had with my own go-to repair person in London.

A few months into 2010, my own trusty Martin 00-42 made an involuntary creak before the bridge dramatically parted from the body. After twenty-two years holding 160 pounds of string pressure, the glue that attached the ebony bridge to the spruce body gave up the fight. It was not an uncommon failing; many older guitars have repaired or replacement bridges . . . some as good as the original, some better, but many are often poor replicas. A common sight is a larger, meatier bridge glued on to cover any minor damage left when the original one came off. Sometimes a DIY guitarist might attempt the repair themselves—usually with a large blob of off-the-shelf adhesive. When repair technicians come across a bridge that's already been home repaired, they usually take a deep breath and see what they might be up against. Unlike the glue used in the original construction, which can usually be dissolved with steam, a superglue or epoxy resin fix is basically permanent. The replacement bridge must be gently chipped off and the rock-like adhesive chiseled away, sliver by sliver. Often it will have penetrated the bridge plate (a piece of thinnish spruce or basswood that sits under the actual guitar top, directly under the bridge), and this will now need replacing as well.

When my guitar tech opened up the case of my 00-42 and gave it the once-over, there was a low whistle. In addition to the bridge no longer being attached to the guitar, it appeared that this was entirely the wrong bridge! I articulated the low whistle. "So is this a replacement bridge after all—put on at a previous repair?"

With a shake of the head, he explained that it *was* the original factory-fitted bridge, but it was "wrong."

"Wrong" meant poorly carved. The pyramid bridge had been made by Martin at a time when they had lost sight of what a proper Martin bridge, with two small pyramids as decoration at either end, should look like. It seemed that by the 1980s, many of the jigs or templates that Martin used to shape body parts were over a hundred years old and worn out. They had apparently been using the same template jigs to shape Martin headstocks and bridges since the 1880s. When Martin introduced the jig that a worker used to quickly shape the headstock or bridge, it created a perfect, sharp-edged repeat every time. But by the 1980s, the jigs had been used many, many thousands of times, and what was once a sharp, perfectly squared corner now had a small radius curve. Every year the sharp edge of the jig had got ever so slightly worn, but nobody had noticed the gradual shift. It reached a point where everyone, including quality control and management, just accepted that Martin produced rounded-corner headstocks or less-than-perfect pyramids.

My tech showed me what a proper pyramid bridge looked like—from a 1920s Martin that was being repaired. It was much more delicately carved, with sharper definition and a more pleasing symmetry.

Dana Bourgeois had noticed the same thing and got his apprentice, T. J. Thompson, to handcraft small batches of pyramid bridges for each Martin-made Schoenberg guitar.

Between 1987 and 1989, Bourgeois produced over 150 Schoenberg Soloist kits for assembly by Martin. Building in batches of ten or fifteen at a time, he adjusted the thickness of the tops and the scalloped braces based on their sound, not a preset specification, as each guitar was assembled. Effectively, the guitars were hand-voiced instruments produced in a factory, albeit the Martin factory. It should be recognized that despite their shortcomings, Martin was still, by a country mile, the best production facility for quality guitars in the world.

Dana Bourgeois eventually left the project, ultimately to set up his own successful guitar business. Schoenberg simply replaced Bourgeois with T. J. Thompson, another guitar-building legend in the making. But back in 1990, Thompson, with Schoenberg, took the refinement of the Martin-made Schoenberg OMs even closer to 1920s specification. This included the reintroduction of hot hide glue along with a greater degree of prebuilding—now to Thompson's standards—before the parts arrived in Nazareth.

The last Martin-Schoenberg guitar was made in the mid-1990s, the three-hundredth instrument made since the project started in 1987. Their importance is immense in the history of Martin and in determining the quality we expect today of a premium, factory-made guitar. A collaboration with a company outsider shook Martin up as a business and in doing so got it back on track. It reminded the company of its heritage. It helped management understand what was possible from a production-line build process. It helped set the benchmark that Martin aspires to today. The presence of Chris Martin IV and Dick Boak was vital as the eyes and ears of the company and as the ones taking the real risk with a venerable business.

But Schoenberg was the project's author. Without his experience and passion, the Martin Custom Shop could not have happened as it did. Neither would the development of the hugely successful Signature Edition models and the golden era and authentic replicas. Eric Schoenberg was not the only expert enthusiast around, but like Richard Hoover and Bill Collings, he brought a passion and understanding of vintage Martins back home to Nazareth.

Schoenberg is still as passionate about OMs as he ever was, working in recent years with several excellent independent luthiers, including Jules Borges and Bruce Sexauer in the United States. They have built small numbers of multi-thousand-dollar OM Soloists, but Schoenberg has also gone on to collaborate with the Recording King company constructing guitars in China to create Schoenberg-inspired 0 and 000s for less than $1,000. His contribution, like those of Bill Collings and Richard Hoover, was fueled not by a desire to wind back the clock or slavishly recreate the past but to learn from the golden era of guitar building in America and apply those standards for the benefit of modern-day makers and players. Anyone owning a Martin guitar made over the last forty years should shake Eric Schoenberg by the hand.

Eric Clapton playing a 1939 Martin 000-42.

Unplugged

While electronically derived music had dominated the 1980s, the 1990s didn't look much better for the acoustic guitar. The decade saw the internet have a seismic impact on the way music was distributed, listened to, and marketed. These changes coincided with an explosion in studio-created sounds as hip-hop and rap hit the mainstream and monopolized the record charts. The decade was also notable for the sheer variety of musical genres in which the acoustic guitar didn't really feature, roughly grouped under the umbrellas of house/dance music, hip-hop/R&B, and various types of rock played almost exclusively on electric guitars. But as Reaganism and the "Greed Is Good" era came to an end, it appeared that at least one group of musicians was using the acoustic guitar to make music: female singer-songwriters.

The music world has always been male-dominated to an unhealthy degree. Since the 1960s and throughout the '70s, rock 'n' roll had globalized and started generating huge amounts of money for artists and record companies, and most often it was created by men, packaged and marketed by men, and focused on a male audience. Band managers, roadies, tour managers, and radio DJs were almost exclusively male. The corresponding received wisdom within the music business was that it was young males who were interested in the minutiae of music: who played which instrument, what sort of guitar they played, who wrote the lyrics, where the music was recorded. Alongside this existed a sexist stereotype that men were not just listeners but often serial collectors of LPs, whereas young women were not overly engaged in the world of long-playing albums, and they tended to buy music in the form of singles.

I recall that at the first live gig I went to in 1969, when I was fourteen, everybody in the room was male. Seeing a girl at a rock gig was rare, probably because most of the venues in the UK were very male orientated, modelled on pubs and drinking halls—rough places, with poor security and drunk men with bad attitudes. In the '70s and '80s, the occasional band had a female singer: prog-rock band Curved Air had Sonja Kristina, who was from Essex in England but played on her Swedish ancestry; blues-rock band Vinegar Joe had Elkie Brooks; while the psychedelic space-rock band Hawkwind, who were very big in the early '70s, were most well known for having Stacia, a statuesque young woman who danced naked for the whole of their live performances, which says it all really. In general, women were rarely made welcome in the industry as musicians, and it's no wonder that few women played rock.

Things have obviously changed. But they've done so very slowly.

The rigors of touring and promoting your music have always been tough on female artists. It was a model designed by and for men, going back to the early 1920s and the beginnings of the blues. Beyond the practicalities of life on the road, women may have been pushed into becoming homemakers. While the Rolling Stones could be touring for a year or more, it was usually because Mrs. Jagger, Mrs. Richards, Mrs. Watts, and Mrs. Wood stayed behind to mind the home and the children and look after the country estate. It goes without saying that female artists were in the minority. So it's surprising, perhaps remarkable, that in late 1999 Taylor Guitars produced a run of one thousand JKSM Grand Auditorium guitars. The letters stand for Jewel Kilcher Signature Model.

Something had happened in the '90s.

I have two copies of *Time* magazine, both dated July 21, 1997. The US edition features a cover picture of the Alaskan singer-songwriter Jewel with the headline "Jewel and the New Women of Rock." The Canadian edition of the same magazine has a cover picture of the Canadian singer-songwriter Sarah McLachlan clutching her guitar, with the headline "The Gals Take Over." The stories are largely the same. According to *Time*, "macho music was out." "Empathy" was apparently "in." McLachlan had, along with a slew of other female solo performers and bands, gotten sick of being told, "You can't put two women on the same bill"; "You can't play two [records by] women back-to-back on the radio." Singer-songwriter Aimee Mann remembers that when she met with record executives at A&M, "They really liked the record, but then they hemmed and they hawed, and finally said 'We can't sign you because we already have a female artist.' That was Sheryl Crow. That was it? One slot?"

Although there were successful female artists like McLachlan and Alanis Morissette selling out gigs and selling lots of records, they almost always were pitched as "alternative," "marginal," or "specialist" acts. It was difficult for women to get consistent airplay or to interest promoters in booking them.

Vanity Fair writer and rock critic Jessica Hopper concluded that it was "sexism passed off as age-old industry logic"—and it was a logic that forced artists like Sarah McLachlan "into competition with other women artists to be the sole exceptional woman allowed opportunity."

So McLachlan and a number of her compatriots decided to do something about it. In 1997, they conceived of and put together a series of large-scale outdoor shows, a touring festival, with a playbill exclusively featuring women. There were big stars and relative nobodies, veterans and newbies getting their big-stage break; they were playing rock, R&B, and country. They called it Lilith Fair, and it ran for three summers across America.

(Lilith, according to myth, was the first wife of Adam, who, having refused to obey the only man on earth, left the Garden of Eden to roam the Earth seeking adventure.)

Back in the summer of 1993, singer-songwriter Jewel Kilcher's search for adventure had taken her four thousand miles from her family home in Homer, Alaska, to live in her van in San Diego. She parked it on a back street, close to the coffee bar where she worked during the day and where she played the occasional night gig. Finally "discovered" in 1995 and signed to Atlantic Records, her debut album *Pieces of You* was slow to gain momentum. She played Lilith Fair, and to her joy, "I went from selling 2,000 records in a year to selling a million every month. It was just crazy how it took off."

Lilith Fair had ambitiously opened at the huge Gorge Amphitheatre in Washington State on July 5, 1997. By the end of its 130-stop tour that year, it had featured lots of musical formats, but initially it was the singer-songwriters playing acoustic guitars who seemed to get real traction. McLachlan, socially aware singer-songwriter Tracy Chapman, New Yorker Suzanne Vega, and Sheryl Crow, still riding high on her breakthrough album *Tuesday Night Music Club*, were the consistent headliners, the ones who drew the initial big audiences. By uniting on one bill spread across a weekend, the artists cross-sold their fan bases. If you understood what Tracy Chapman was talking about, you would probably understand Jewel, Shawn Colvin, and Suzanne Vega, and maybe even Beth Orton's "folktronica." Over three years, the three-hundred-odd shows of Lilith Fair helped acts like Nelly Furtado, Patty Griffin, and Lucinda Williams establish themselves. It also underscored the fact that women will buy music and go to live shows. The sheer number of guitar-playing singer-songwriters who performed at Lilith Fair, during a time when male acoustic guitar acts were not making much headway, drove the visibility and appeal of the acoustic guitar.

Paradoxically, the fate of the acoustic guitar was also resting in the unlikely hands of one of the world's most famous, and respected, male rock musicians. Like many professional guitarists, Eric Clapton had been quietly accumulating vintage and rare acoustics alongside his already substantial collection of electric guitars that he used onstage. In 1992, he was persuaded to film an *MTV Unplugged* concert in England before an invited audience, becoming the fifteenth artist to officially perform acoustically under the *Unplugged* banner. By this point, *Unplugged* had developed beyond a semi-spontaneous singalong with a few band members playing acoustic instruments. Because Clapton wasn't known for having an acoustic repertoire in his regular live shows, the program he put together featured songs unfamiliar even to his longtime fans. Old blues songs that he had first performed as a teenager developing his chops in South London pubs ("Nobody Knows You When You're Down and Out" and "San Francisco Bay Blues") sat alongside the tragic but maudlin "Tears in Heaven." However, it was a rearrangement of his signature rock anthem, "Layla," as a slow, bluesy acoustic number that transformed the show and helped change the fortunes of the acoustic guitar.

Eric Clapton playing *Unplugged* was not just the right person at the right time, but the right person at the right time with the right guitar.

Clapton had commercially endorsed Guild guitars only a few years earlier, in 1986, when acoustic sales were just beginning to pick up again, but he had had little discernible effect on sales of Guilds or any other acoustics. However, a few years later, Clapton's fans, seeing an unfancy, vintage-looking acoustic in the hands of such an iconic electric artist, helped make the flat-top guitar cool again. Turning a rock anthem known by baby boomers from the 1970s into a slow, cool blues number was a real catalyst. It created for that cohort, many of whom were now having their midlife crises, a renewed interest in not just playing but, for some, acquiring acoustic guitars. An instrument that had been seen as a throwback to an irrelevant time of Appalachian hillbillies or Greenwich Village beatniks in black turtleneck sweaters was instantly updated. Clapton's *Unplugged* also played a part in securing the future of the (once again) struggling Martin guitar company for at least another two decades.

It's unclear who invented *Unplugged*, if indeed it was a single person or corporation. It's as pointless as trying to identify the very first rock 'n' roll record. One claimant is Jules Shear, singer-songwriter and host of some of the early *Unplugged* shows. Shear alleges that, after seeing Jon Bon Jovi and Richie Sambora play a two-song acoustic set at the 1989 MTV Video Music Awards, he "came up with the concept . . . when trying to promote my own acoustic record." It's an interesting claim but ironically rather misses the point: The *Unplugged* "concept" isn't about just any artist playing acoustically but about rock musicians from a normally heavily amplified rock band paring down electric songs to their essence—how the writer "usually starts the song." The resulting performances make rock stars "seem more vulnerable; heavy metal groups like Aerosmith are suddenly quiet, almost lyrical." These insights are from a *New York Times* interview with Robert Small and Jim Burns, two senior MTV producers who also lay claim to inventing *Unplugged*. They cite that they were inspired when they saw Bruce Springsteen closing a live show "unplugged, just him and an acoustic guitar."

But before Jules Shear, Bon Jovi and Sambora, or Bruce, and well before Clapton appeared unplugged in 1992, it was an English progressive rock band named after a pioneering seventeenth-century agriculturalist that was the fire-starter for the MTV version of the phenomenon. The original prototype for the MTV series was broadcast in 1987, when three members of the English rock band Jethro Tull played two songs, without any audience, in a casual acoustic setting in the MTV studio—at the time a cramped, badly lit space that resembled a teenager's bedroom. The band was about to play in front of twenty thousand people at Meadowlands Arena in New Jersey, and their promo appearance on MTV was a neat way to get a rock band playing live in the small MTV studio. At the time it seemed so novel, so counterintuitive, to hear heavy rock played with two acoustic guitars and a mandolin. When asked afterwards by the host/VJ Kevin Seal whether the progressive rock band had enjoyed the experience and "ever planned to make an acoustic album," Ian Anderson, the band's front man, dead-panned, "I can see us in another ten years' time doing the cruise ships and really cleaning up."

This early *Unplugged* experience was clearly judged to have ratings potential and much more appeal than pandering to octogenarian cruisers looking for music to dine by. Artists like Bon Jovi and XTC soon followed, and the format settled down to a conventional filmed concert in front of a live, invited audience. However, MTV didn't invent the concept of heavy rock artists performing acoustically.

Electric guitarists have always had acoustic guitars as workhorses. Keith Richards usually worked out early versions of Rolling Stones songs on an acoustic, sometimes going on to record songs like "Angie" and "Wild Horses" as largely acoustic tracks. MTV didn't even originate the idea of filming these relaxed acoustic sessions. Look no further than the filmed Elvis comeback concert in 1968, where the cameras apparently catch Elvis and the band rehearsing acoustically. There are many sequences in the film *Let It Be* where the Beatles are jamming without amplification. In 1979, *The Secret Policeman's Ball* benefit concert featured the Who's Pete Townshend playing acoustic versions of big, muscular electric anthems like "Pinball Wizard" and "Won't Get Fooled Again." These performances all opened up new possibilities for songs that we thought we knew so well. A decade later, Clapton challenged the audience on *Unplugged* to "see if you can spot" his reimagined "Layla."

MTV Unplugged was also building on a gentle upsurge of general interest in acoustic guitar music in the late '80s. Artists like the Indigo Girls, Suzanne Vega, Enya, and the alternative rock band R.E.M. were all developing a nostalgia for the music of the '60s, when acoustic folk of various complexions had been popular. Equally, the original artists from the '60s and '70s were seeing renewed interest in their back catalogue and success with new material. Artists like Paul Simon, James Taylor, Dylan, and even MTV pioneers Jethro Tull, performers who had either started in folk or were influenced by it, were touring again or seeing CD sales increase. Paul Simon had added a twist by bringing the influence of so-called world music into his acoustic mix on his controversial *Graceland* album. After the disco and electronica wilderness of the '70s and early '80s, there seemed to be a glimmer of hope for the acoustic guitar again.

Even country legend Johnny Cash benefitted from the backwash of *Unplugged*. Cash had been "discovered" by Sam Phillips at Sun Studios around the same time that Elvis walked into his studio. Unlike "the King," Cash wrote his own material and had been prolific in the mid-1950s. His career had high spots, including plenty of country hits like the classic guitar anthem "Tennessee Flat-Top Box" (1961) and the iconic prison recordings on *Johnny Cash at Folsom Prison* (1968) and *Johnny Cash at San Quentin* (1969). But he also had his lows. Addicted to amphetamines from his touring years and painkillers for most of his life, by the early '90s he was working the grueling and unglamorous county fair circuit across America, as well as releasing somewhat dubious material like "The Chicken in Black." But in 1994, when Cash was sixty-two, he was approached by music producer and former rap and heavy metal impresario Rick Rubin, who thought Cash had been unfairly abandoned by the music industry.

The old warhorse, who had just been dropped by Columbia, his record label of twenty-five years, was skeptical. Suffering from various health issues and recovering from the cumulative effects of a life of addiction, Rubin's proposal to Cash was simple and insightful. "He said what I would let you do is sit down before a microphone with your guitar and sing every song you want to record."

Cash chose to play Rubin old folk and country songs, none of which Rubin knew. They sat and talked in the thirty-one-year-old producer's Los Angeles house and finally agreed that they would record Cash right here, with just his voice and him playing guitar. No band, no backing singers. "Unplugged" in its purest form. Rubin recognized that Cash "wasn't well enough to tour anymore . . . and his choice was to die or to carry on. And he chose to carry on."

The unlikely pairing created what became Cash's eighty-first album and won a Grammy award in 1995 for Best Contemporary Folk Album. They recorded three more albums together. For *American Recordings IV*, Rubin presented Cash with the Trent Reznor song "Hurt." Cash ignored it multiple times. Rubin explained that "I'd send him a CD of maybe twenty, twenty-five songs. He never chose it. Finally I put it at the top of a new selection."

Cash agreed to record it. Maybe a song that sounded like a young man's suicide note had initially struck a bum chord with the Man in Black. Rubin's logic was that "when you're twenty years old and talking about regret it's heartbreaking. But heartbreaking in a different way, because you've a whole life to figure it out. When you're looking back at your life at the end of your life, with regret, it's brutal."

Looking back at the sessions in 2005, Rubin reflected: "My fondest memories are just of hanging out and hearing his stories. He didn't speak much but, if you drew him out, he seemed to know everything. He was shy and quiet but a wise, wise man."

Unplugged, and the uplift of interest in the guitar-led, stripped-down performances it spotlighted, was what the acoustic guitar world had been waiting for. US guitar makers saw the opportunity and gingerly stepped up production of acoustic guitars. But, to their surprise, guitar stores saw an unfamiliar demographic of customer coming in to buy.

The guitar industry had always targeted thirteen- to twenty-five-year-old males, for the most part. However, when this average twenty-five-year-old male married and started a family, the guitar was usually relegated to the attic, never to be picked up again. This cycle of youthful interest followed by mature rejection had been going on for decades, resulting in the phenomenon of the "Strat in the Attic," explored in Deke Dickinson's book of the same title, which describes a now-classic or rare guitar like a '50s Fender Stratocaster found in a house clearance sale or thrift shop. It's a phenomenon further detailed in guitar hunter Michael Indelicato's *Guitar Man*. The combination of the American baby boomer with an increasing life-expectancy and prosperity meant that buyers not only had more spare time and the prospect of a long retirement but also, importantly, the money to indulge in an old passion.

Seeing an Armani-suited, forty-seven-year-old Clapton on *Unplugged* looking more like a successful tech company CEO than a drug-addled rock god suddenly made picking up a guitar again not just relevant and possible but also fashionably cool to the boomer generation. It didn't matter if a baby boomer had never played guitar—no longer did they need to play air guitar holding an old tennis racquet; they could own the real thing.

Many of this generation of maturing baby boomer were reconnecting with their past and may have bought guitars as part of a midlife crisis, but they were also tuning in to the attractive price escalation of vintage instruments. This made the 1990s a golden period for those guitar dealers who were switched on to the needs and bank balances of this new type of guitar player and buyer. For those American dealers versed in the possibilities offered by the internet, a then-favorable dollar exchange rate also opened up international markets for vintage American guitars.

George Gruhn, founder of Nashville's Gruhn Guitars (in essence the first specialist vintage guitar store), estimates that between 1984 and 1992, the price of quality vintage guitars increased tenfold. "In 1984, a buyer could have acquired a decent prewar Martin D-28 for $2,500. By 1992 they'd have been able to sell it pretty quickly for around $25,000."

It sounds so obvious and simple. So why wasn't everyone just buying vintage? At the time, $2,500 would have seemed a ludicrous amount to pay for what was, back then, at least for the uninformed, just an old guitar that might be about to develop a fault that could cost hundreds of dollars to correct. Especially when a perfect, brand-new Brazilian rosewood D-28, with a lifetime warranty from Martin, was $2,100 in 1984.

Nonetheless, people were taking the risk, and vintage guitars were becoming big business, particularly in America, where many were bought to sit alongside hedge fund managers' collections of vintage French Bordeaux, limited-edition Swiss watches, and classic sports cars.

Gruhn, who literally wrote the book about the vintage American guitar (and banjo, and mandolin, and the other members of the fretted instrument family), had started collecting old guitars when he was in college in the early 1960s.

Sitting in his office in 2015 surrounded by the two things he loves the most, vintage instruments and reptiles, he recounted how he started building an enviable collection of guitars during his university years. "As a young child I had a lively interest in insects. That grew into a passion for snakes and reptiles. At university I studied zoology. Both interests, hobbies if you will, are a mixture of obsession and desire to gain an in-depth understanding of the subject."

When I asked George what drives a guitar collector, he answered, with a knowing twinkle in his eye, that collecting "appeals to folks with obsessive-compulsive disorder. It helps to have a touch of Asperger's syndrome thrown in as well."

Gruhn had started playing guitar in his freshman year at college, possibly driven by the same motivation as many young males before him. However, as one might expect from this self-proclaimed obsessive-compulsive with "a touch" of Asperger syndrome, he started digging deeper into the history of American fretted instruments. "Doing this in the pre-internet age involved reading what few books there were but primarily foot-slogging around pawnshops, thrift markets, as well as mom-and-pop guitar stores."

It's obvious that Gruhn, sitting behind his old oak desk sporting a Howard Hughes–style beard and long grey hair, is an obsessive, hard-assed guitar dealer. But the man has a fine ear and a real passion for the guitar and the music it makes. Without those attributes, he would not have been able to discern the difference between the sound and playability of a '60s Martin and one made in the '40s. He doesn't claim to be the first to spot the quality of the golden era guitar over what were in the '60s relatively inferior modern instruments. But he recalls recognizing that "a good 1940s D-28 Herringbone for $350, was a good deal . . . but no one knew that the same guitar, not that many years later, would easily fetch four figures."

With very little money to his name to actively deal in guitars, his modus operandi was simple. When he spotted something like a late '50s Gibson Les Paul for $100 in a pawnshop, he would shell out a small down payment to secure it, find a buyer from his ever-expanding list of contacts, agree to a sale, liberate the guitar from the shop, and make himself a couple of hundred dollars in the space of a few days. "At the time I wasn't trying to make a living out of guitars, just buying and selling stuff that I knew had a higher re-sale value in order to fund the purchase of better guitars. I was trying to build my own personal collection of great guitars."

This hands-on experience, combined with a zoologist's discipline of classification, meant that soon Gruhn had constructed what amounted to field guides for guitars from the key American makers. Four years at the University of Chicago and one as a grad student studying animal behavior equipped him well for a career as a guitar dealer. But it also meant that "appreciating and cataloging the differences between a 1934 versus a 1949 guitar from the same maker enabled me to understand where the good guitars started and ended."

Soon the collection of vintage guitars filling his student apartment reached the attention of Hank Williams Jr., son of the legendary country singer, who had also started collecting old Martins. "Hank Jr. traded a Martin 000-42 and bought as many guitars from me as his two-seater Jaguar E-type would carry . . . and came back the next day with a bigger car."

Williams Jr., then based in Nashville, offered to set Gruhn up in his hometown, and after only one semester the zoologist dropped out of school in Knoxville and began trading guitars out of a small Nashville apartment. Williams was still a major customer, but so was the young Eric Schoenberg, the New York ragtime guitarist who bought his first prewar Martin 000-45 from Gruhn.

In January 1970, Gruhn finally opened his first proper retail store in Nashville. Two store moves later he was at 400 Broadway, next to the Ryman Auditorium, the spiritual home of country music. The 1,200-square-foot unit opened with an inventory of a couple of dozen vintage instruments. Forty-eight years later, Gruhn Guitars is still flourishing, now located just a couple of miles from the Ryman and in a store spread over three floors and carrying an inventory of over a thousand instruments. It serves the professional musicians of Music City USA as well as anyone with a desire to add to their collection of vintage guitars. It's on every guitar collector's map and is a must-visit destination for any guitarist passing through the South.

When I first contacted George by email, he had offered me "an hour or so" of his time. I arrived at ten a.m. and finally said goodbye at close to eleven that night! During those thirteen hours, we covered a lot of ground.

We talked a lot about what drives ordinary people to acquire extraordinary numbers of guitars. We went out to visit the home of the Grand Ole Opry, the Nashville radio station WSM. Over lunch we ruminated on the nature and future of collecting and whether "kids today still had that collecting gene that is in the heart of every serial guitar acquirer." We exploded a few myths about the vintage guitar industry and discussed the veracity of the recently published book about the manufacture of Gibson guitars during World War II. But most of all we played guitars.

Directly outside George's office, where he spent his days with two cats, twenty-one snakes, and a two-foot-long bearded dragon lizard, stands a forty-foot-long wall crammed with his personal collection of guitars, banjos, and mandolins. As we talked, he would pull an instrument from the wall to illustrate a point. "Just listen to the projective power of this archtop over the balanced tone of the flat-top."

He played a Gibson L-5 archtop from the same year that Maybelle Carter's was made and compared it to a Martin 00 made around the same time.

George is not always easy. Complimenting him on his rendition of Carter's signature tune, "Wildwood Flower," played on the old L-5, I remarked that "Mother Maybelle would have been proud." George retorted, "She would not. I'm using a flat-pick and she never did!," and then fished a thumb-pick out of his pocket to prove his point by demonstrating the classic Carter scratch.

He played an old Regal from the 1920s to show that Martin wasn't the only game in town. To better demonstrate its tonal qualities, we adjourned to an adjacent stairwell with the acoustics of a tiled bathroom on steroids. George directed me to the sonic sweet spot by the bend in the stairwell like an audio engineer demonstrating where the vocalist should stand in a studio.

Together we compared the differences between the Epiphone Olympic archtop, favored by Americana virtuoso Dave Rawlings, and the more expensive Zenith model. We discussed the origins of the nomenclature for the Vega Whyte Laydie banjo. I had it that "white lady" was slang for cocaine or that it was named after the actress Lillie Langtry's famous yacht *The White Ladye*, where notorious parties were held in the 1920s. In fact, it's probably more prosaically named after the white holly wood used for the neck and rim.

The Gruhn Guitars billboard in Nashville at night. (John Stubbings)

For comparison, George pulled down an unprepossessing Gibson banjo from the early 1930s. He gave it a loving look, fingerpicked a few licks and explained, "While it is not fancy looking, it's an extremely good banjo, one of *the* five-string bluegrass banjos, rightly still highly sought-after."

It was priced at a cool $70,000.

We broke around nine p.m. and stepped outside the store for some fresh air and to find something to eat. George continued to explain the nature of guitar collectors between mouthfuls of Vietnamese soup. "Sometimes they are building a specific collection, but often their aim, if they have one, gets distorted and they can often end up acquiring enormous numbers of the same model of quite ordinary guitars."

An hour later night had fallen, and we stood in the parking lot outside of the store. I once again said my thank-yous for his generosity of time.

Looking at my watch I realized that I had almost certainly missed the final set of the bluegrass banjo duo I had marked out as my Nashville evening's entertainment, but I had had an amazing day. I turned to open my car door as George started back to his store when he asked, "You want to see some special guitars?"

Five minutes later we're back in his office above the store and George has hauled out the stars of his reserve collection. First up was "probably the most pristine left-handed blackguard Fender Telecaster on the planet."

Although it was made in 1954, the unique Fender blond finish looked new and made the guitar worth some way north of $70,000. Electrics weren't my thing, but I knew that "Blackguard" referred not just to the color of the pickguard. By 1956 Fender pickguards were generally white, but these guitars, built between 1950 and 1954, also came with ash bodies and AlNiCo pickups that were wired in a configuration that gave them a unique, crunchy, and highly sought after sound. With southpaw Fender players Albert King, Hendrix, and Kurt Cobain lost in action, I wondered if Dick Dale might be interested in buying a guitar built in his heyday.

As I pondered, George handed me a Martin 00-42 from the mid-1930s. Its delicately balanced, bell-like tone left me trying to compare it with my own 1980s Indian rosewood Custom Shop version of the same model. My tone memory was no match for George's, but even I appreciated that an extra fifty years of ageing on Brazilian rosewood delivered a tonal maturity that might be worth paying extra for.

A brown alligator-leather guitar case was pulled out from behind the sofa, just by where the coral snake lived. Inside was a 1959 D'Angelico Excel Custom.

For many collectors and players this, alongside the D'Angelico New Yorker, is the holy grail of the New York archtop jazz guitars. It was made by the legendary New York–Italian builder John D'Angelico in his small Kenmore Street workshop in 1959. The guitar had been made for Henry "Homer" Haynes, one half of the comedy music duo Homer & Jethro. Although known mainly as a variety act, both were top-class musicians, Jethro Burns a dazzling mandolinist and Homer an accomplished rhythm guitarist. George showed, or rather read out to me, original correspondence between Haynes and John D'Angelico. It seems that the custom archtop cost $850 in 1959, about half the price of a reasonable car, and Haynes paid a deposit of $100 in mid-December 1958 to start the build. D'Angelico wrote to Haynes on January 21, 1959, to announce that the guitar was completed. A top-model archtop from the best builder of the time was turned around in a little less than five weeks. I assumed D'Angelico and his apprentice Jimmy D'Aquisto didn't take Christmases off. For a few seconds I contemplated buying it. A couple of years after my Nashville visit, the guitar was acquired by Americana guitarist David Rawlings and provided the signature sound on Rawlings's next album, *Poor David's Almanack* (2017). Rawlings's story is that he was hanging out at Gruhn's store when George

A 1959 D'Angelico headstock. (John Stubbings)

walked in with the D'Angelico and said, "Maybe this could be your new style?" Across the album, you can hear the stark difference between two contrasting archtop guitars. The more utilitarian, factory-made 1935 Epiphone Olympic has a crisp, biting tone that cuts through the sparse arrangements, while the handmade D'Angelico Excel has, according to Rawlings, "more beef in

A 1927 Martin 000-45 headstock and its price tag. (John Stubbings)

the bass." It also has a velvety, honeyed tone, like a rather hip mother singing her baby to sleep.

Finally, I played an astonishing 1927 Martin 000-45, the guitar that my contemporary Custom Shop Martin 000-45 was modelled on. It underscored the appeal of vintage Martins. It also underlined their eye-watering prices.

I left George Gruhn at around eleven that night, having handled examples of most of the landmark acoustic guitars made in America between 1900 and 1960. I was briefly tempted by the 1927 000-45, but if I had taken home everything I had played, my bill would have exceeded $3 million.

• • • • • •

In addition to spending time with George Gruhn during my guitar pilgrimage to the United States, I had visited four of the most legendary guitar stores on the planet. What makes them important isn't their size or the breadth of their range; there were many bigger stores, funded by well-heeled corporate backers. It wasn't how long they had been in business; many very average stores have been operating across a couple of generations, riding the peaks and troughs of demand. What the legendary retailers had in common was that they were usually still run by their passionate and often highly idiosyncratic founders. They are true enthusiasts, who over the past forty-five years have served to shape the American and global guitar market. George Gruhn may be the sort of guy who can put a top player and a new guitar together that gives them a "new style," but he's not the only game in town.

Matt Umanov's on Bleecker Street in New York's Greenwich Village wasn't that big a store, but it was still a station of the cross for the serious guitar pilgrim. When I first began my trip, I had heard how Umanov started in the Village in the early '60s and knew Folk Center founder Izzy Young. I learned how he had run a guitar repair shop or retail store here since the very beginning of the folk revival. Now in his seventies, and a little curmudgeonly, he went on to talk about "Bobby, Dave, and Joanie" with an ease that makes you realize he was more than just there with Dylan, van Ronk, and Baez.

I had participated in a crisp, sometimes brusque, email exchange with Matt for months. He finally agreed to give me an hour of his time on the understanding that he might have to cut that short at a moment's notice as he has "a business to run that feeds me, my kids and my two ex-wives."

Once there he fizzed and faffed, and even hummed and hawed, for around half an hour after I arrived, selling a set of strings to a young mandolin player, scolding his sales guy for not putting a guitar back properly, and taking a call from his accountant. I thought he was going to cry off talking to me, pleading the pressure of work, but finally he led me up to his combined office-storeroom-kitchen and started talking. A few hours later and barring a couple of brief interruptions, he told me that this was just "some of my story in the guitar business."

Matt Umanov outside of his store. (John Stubbings)

On his arrival in the Village, the fifteen-year-old Umanov started hanging out at Fretted Instruments, run by roots guitarist Marc Silber, and soon the hanging out turned into a job. The guitar store's location was variously next door to or within the legendary Folklore Center. There's now the ubiquitous nail bar at 110 MacDougal Street where the Folklore Center used to be. But in the 1960s, it was an informal clearinghouse for the Greenwich Village music scene. Its founder, Israel "Izzy" Young, who also helped start Gerde's Folk City, ran it as a meeting place, impromptu agitprop office for the Right to Sing Committee, and backroom poetry and concert venue. A young Dylan hung out there to listen to records, but his primary objective was to engineer his first meeting with his idol, Dave van Ronk.

When they eventually met one winter's morning, Dylan asked van Ronk if he could play for him, and after hearing him sing "Nobody Knows You When You're Down and Out," told Van Ronk he could perform a couple of songs during his own set at the Gaslight. Van Ronk wasn't surprised to be propositioned by a newcomer: "When Izzy opened that little hole, there was suddenly a place where everyone went, and it became a catalyst for all sorts of things.... There were picking sessions, and Izzy even held a few concerts there to help out singers who needed a gig and couldn't find one elsewhere."

Izzy also took in guitar repairs, many of which made their way to Umanov. "By the time I was nineteen, I was the go-to-guy in New York for repairs or restorations of old acoustic guitars."

By 1969, his once-peripatetic Greenwich Village repair shop was also trading old guitars and had found a permanent home on Bedford Street. It had become the place that all professional and wannabe acoustic players gravitated to for their instruments, and, like Marc Silber before him, Umanov attracted his fair share of young disciples, including the previously mentioned meeting with the teenage Eric Schoenberg.

Umanov was clearly much more than just a jobbing repairman, and his role in the development of the acoustic guitar in the '60s came from his knowledge of instruments and their players.

He had started working as a teenager at the Gretsch guitar factory in Brooklyn and then spent a brief time working under John D'Angelico, the archtop master builder who trained Jimmy D'Aquisto. In 1967, Umanov was approached by a friend, guitarist David Bromberg, who had an old Martin F-7 archtop guitar. The Martin F series was the largest of the company's ventures into archtops. They were an unsuccessful attempt to get a share of that growing market, which in the 1930s was dominated by Gibson and Epiphone. The guitars were a compromise design: They had a traditional carved, arched top sitting on a wider than usual standard flat-top body. In a last-ditch attempt to gain sales, the last models produced used very high-quality woods, including top-grade Brazilian rosewood bodies. Marc Silber had been the first to remove a damaged arched top from an F-7 and convert it to a flat-top, and Bromberg asked Umanov to try the same with the F-7 he had acquired.

Umanov made a new spruce top from scratch and, using vintage abalone and inlays that he had salvaged from other jobs, made the guitar a Style 42 instrument. He started a trend for converting Martin F series guitars, and it became a relatively cheap way to get a 1930s Brazilian rosewood Martin flat-top guitar until the limited number of archtop guitars in circulation dried up. Many years later, Martin made their own version of the Matt Umanov guitar and designated it the M. It was in fact a Martin 0000-sized guitar, but to avoid confusion the company added a new letter in their lexicon. It is unlikely that the *M* stood for Martin; that wouldn't make sense in the ordered world of Martin model designation. Perhaps it was a nod to Matt, whom they credited in the first catalog listing the guitar.

• • • • • •

Gruhn and Umanov and other vintage guitar dealers were helped massively by Clapton's *Unplugged* and the baby boomers, but they were not the only ones who prospered. Combined with a general resurgence in acoustic music, the whole acoustic guitar industry was lifted. The Clapton effect ensured the Martin company enjoyed a fillip that they could never have predicted. Serious enthusiasts and collectors knew about Martin's prewar golden era, but for most casually interested players, Martin equated solely as the maker of the best new dreadnoughts. Suddenly would-be guitarists were seeing Clapton playing a much smaller, differently shaped Martin. It was also clear that these were old guitars. What did Clapton, the man who could buy any brand-new guitar he wanted, know that they didn't? Martin started getting calls from dealers and customers wanting to know what specific models of guitar Clapton had played on the MTV show, accompanying DVD, and platinum-selling CD.

The Martin company had been here before, having watched the vintage guitar boom of the late 1960s and early 1970s, when they had to sit back as old Martins sold faster and for more money than new ones. Guitars that they had shipped to dealers for $50 in 1940 were being traded by vintage guitar specialists like Gruhn, Umanov, and Stan Jay of Mandolin Brothers for $5,000 plus. Guitar-playing baby boomers, seeing bands like Crosby, Stills, Nash & Young playing prewar Martins, wanted one themselves and had the funds to buy. In fact, with a flat stock market, investing in something as cool as a guitar that might well double in price was a lot more fun than holding low-yield bonds or stock.

In the 1960s and '70s folk revival, when guitarists were seeking old Martins, it was vintage dealers who alone benefitted, and Martin didn't want to miss a new opportunity, this one created by Clapton's *Unplugged*. No doubt spurred by the success of their manufacturing collaboration with the Schoenberg OMs, Martin started producing, through their newly opened Custom Shop, limited numbers of "authentic factory replicas" of their guitars from the 1930s and '40s.

Initially these guitars were priced similarly to Martin's mainstream production models and primarily satisfied individual specialist orders rather than being actively promoted as special editions. Martin's first serious foray into the high-value reissue market was to produce a limited run of OM-28s, based on the guitar they had produced for banjo player Perry Bechtel back in 1929.

It was Eric Schoenberg who had noted that used or vintage OM models from the 1930s were becoming increasingly difficult to find. For Martin, it was a chance to test the demand for reissues of classic heritage guitars. And what better model than the OM that had started out the modern era of Martin guitar design.

The ninety-four Bechtel style guitars they produced in 1993 were priced at $4,000 and were quickly bought by players and collectors. (Bechtel's OM was $100 back in the day.) While serious collectors were still seeking out Martin OMs from the prewar years, it seemed that they also had an appetite for reproductions made by the same company as the originals.

A 1993 Martin OM-28 Perry Bechtel. (John Stubbings)

Encouraged by the success of the Perry Bechtel model, the following year Martin proposed making reproductions of the one-off Gene Autry D-45 they had first made in 1933.

The original Gene Autry guitar had taken on something of a mythical status as the "most valuable Martin, possibly the most valuable guitar, in the world." Autry had allegedly turned down an offer of over a million dollars from a Japanese collector, preferring that the guitar remain as the centerpiece of the Autry Museum of the American West. To get Autry on board, Martin brokered a deal to donate to his museum a percentage of the proceeds of each D-45 replica sold. With a Brazilian rosewood body and the same level of ornamentation as the original, they priced the reproduction at $20,000 retail, a cool hundred times the price they had charged Autry in 1933 for the original guitar. It seems that Martin was expecting to produce only a few for very wealthy collectors, but when they announced the project, dealers were more than mildly enthusiastic and sixty-six were made and soon sold.

Luckily, the timing of Clapton's *Unplugged* was such that Martin reckoned it had the measure of the reissue market and some idea of the size of the prize.

The company suggested to Clapton that they make an adaptation of the two different vintage Martins he played on *Unplugged*, donating a percentage of income to his Crossroads drug rehabilitation charity. The guitar it created was an amalgam of his 1939 000-42 and a converted 1960s 000-28 that the factory had previously modified for Clapton to have 45-style decorative fingerboard inlays. The 000-42EC guitar was produced as a signed limited edition of 461 guitars, a nod to the number of the house on Ocean Boulevard where Clapton had lived while recording that eponymous album.

The edition was so oversubscribed that Martin's Dick Boak later remarked that "if only Eric had lived a few dozen blocks up the street." They soon realized they could have sold many thousands of the c. $8,000 guitar.

As a result of the success of the Bechtel, Autry, and Clapton models, Martin responded with more authentic replica and limited-edition signature models, some at even more adventurous prices. It seemed like they had struck the motherlode, a market with a seemingly insatiable appetite and no apparent upper price point. It was selling replica vintage guitars for thousands of dollars more than its standard catalog models, and dealers were surprised by the prices that even relatively new players were prepared to pay for what might be their starter guitar. This success encouraged the traditionally conservative company to be bolder with this new marketing concept. But in many ways Martin was returning to an idea they had first explored back in 1843 when their dealers started ordering de Goñi models that had been named after the celebrated Señora Delores Nevares de Goñi, the first performer to endorse a Martin guitar. It was an idea that other guitar makers took up.

In 1928, Gibson had retained Nick Lucas for the launch of its then-embryonic flat-top guitar range. Known primarily for their mandolins, Gibson knew they needed to establish their reputation as guitar makers, and Nick Lucas was to be their secret marketing weapon. Throughout the 1920s, he was one of the most popular performers in both the US and the UK. With hits like "Tiptoe Through the Tulips," he quickly became known on the radio as "the Crooning Troubadour." He was also among the first to have hits with guitar instrumentals as well as guitar-accompanied singing: "Teasing the Frets" and "Picking the Guitar" were big hits in America and Britain. Gibson initially approached Lucas with a straightforward endorsement deal in return for a significant amount of money. Lucas instead insisted that Gibson make a special guitar designed to his specifications. The resulting instrument, the Nick Lucas Gibson Special, was produced with minor modifications continuously until

1941. Initially costing $125, it was Gibson's most expensive flat-top, nearly three times the price of their other models, and the catalog copy worked overtime to justify the price:

> To play it is to know a measure of the same inspiration that has carried Nick Lucas to great heights. You'll love the feel as it comes to life with the touch of your fingers. Your regard grows like a rare flower watered by the crystal drops of purest melody. It is indeed an instrument by an artist, for an artist. This is the guitar used by many professionals, exclusively for radio broadcasting, recording, and stage. Conducive to amazing progress in the hands of the student or amateur because of its fast easy action.

For this midsized guitar, Lucas had specified a uniquely deep body, which served to give it both volume and depth of tone. As an experienced and gifted player, Lucas clearly knew what he was looking for, and Gibson not only got a huge amount of publicity and kudos from the tie-up but also a guitar that influenced many later Gibson models. The Nick Lucas was the guitar that Dylan used for a lot of his early recording career. Gibson went on to use artist endorsement extensively and, unlike Martin, were relatively happy to supply free guitars and pay artists a small, or large, bonus for "choosing a Gibson."

Maybe initially out of naivety, then perhaps driven by frugality, and finally by a rare arrogance, Martin never overtly gave away guitars or paid for artist endorsement. That was why the evolution of Martin's signature series was so perfect for the company and another win-win for everybody involved. Signature editions fell into two categories: a new original design through a collaboration with the likes of Paul Simon, Keb' Mo', Bob Dylan, or Robbie Robertson, or a retro reissue of a classic catalog model along the lines of the Joan Baez 0-45 (an edition of the classic 0-45 with the addition of her signature on the fretboard). Both approaches clearly communicate, across a broad variety of musical audiences, that Martin was and still is the guitar of choice of the professional. The artist got to keep the prototype or first in the limited edition, and a percentage of the wholesale price went to the artist's charity of choice. Martin benefitted by selling a batch of premium-priced guitars to that artist's guitar-playing fan base.

Gibson was slightly slower to grasp the opportunity post-*Unplugged*, but eventually did, albeit in their own inimitable way. Soon they were producing authentic replicas of the classic Gibson flat-tops produced in the 1930s, '40s, and '50s, enabling enthusiasts to pick up replicas of guitars that were becoming ever-more-expensive on the vintage market. They also jumped on the cobranding market, aiming at fans of rock musicians, Nashville country stars, and even Harley-Davidson motorcycles, in what was little more than slapping a logo on an existing guitar model. This gave nonenthusiasts an opportunity to buy an expensive keepsake or badge of belonging. Many would never be played, but they looked pretty good hanging on the wall of the den.

Celebrity endorsement also proved profitable for the individual luthier trying to gain traction. In fact, it's often the only way a one-man luthier can get the sort of recognition, and thereby charge the sort of prices, that enable them to live above the poverty line. But most single luthiers soon realized that famous guitarists are unlikely to seek them out. The reverse usually has to happen.

• • • • • •

James Olson was a capable, self-taught, but largely unknown luthier when he started making guitars in 1977. By the early '80s, and after many struggles, his handmade guitars were priced at a competitive $900. This was half the cost of an equivalent Martin and a price that left him working for little more than the minimum wage. In 1985, Phil Keaggy, a talented guitarist on the contemporary Christian music circuit, bought a guitar from Olson, who is also a committed Christian. After that, prices began to rise steadily, and a few years on, Olson was able to command a little over $2,000 for a standard model. In 1989, James Taylor started using his guitars, and by the mid '90s, Olson's list prices had gradually crept up to about $3,000, and his waiting list quickly reached three years or longer. He took deposits on every new order that joined the wait list and initially rejoiced in the knowledge that he knew what his future income and workload looked like for the coming few years. However, he soon also noticed that because of the "James Taylor effect," his guitars were appearing on eBay for many-fold the price that he was selling them for. A barely used, often freshly delivered and unplayed Olson was soon selling for $10,000 at online auctions. Olson, perhaps because he was a practicing Christian, took a sanguine view. "I was selling guitars for what I considered a fair price and if owners decided they wanted to trade them, that was their business."

Olson's financial epiphany in the often-fickle world of high-end guitar making came when a guitar that he had made for a young religious youth worker appeared on eBay for $12,500 a couple of days after he had shipped the guitar. Olson had cut him a great deal, only to find that the young man had turned a $9,000 profit on Olson's largesse. Olson closed his order book and spent a few years fulfilling existing orders while watching the vast majority of recipients make a four-fold return on delivery. Then in 2000, he adjusted his prices to match what the market thought an Olson was worth. At that time that was a cool $12,500.

Market equilibrium was restored, and ever since Olson has had a manageable waiting list and sells his guitars for pretty much what a "new-used" one sells for on eBay. Most of his buyers are now collector-players who will hold on to the guitars until Olson goes to meet his maker, when I'm sure they anticipate the price game changes again. Guitar collectors are much like collectors of contemporary art. While wishing no ill, they acknowledge that the death of a successful artist, especially one whose lifetime prices have probably peaked, is the next best thing that can happen to the value of their collection.

But it's interesting to rewind the tape and see what drove the feeding frenzy on Olson guitars and what light that sheds on the whole high-end single-maker guitar business.

Olson was still a relatively unknown guitar builder back in 1985. His workshop was a space loaned to him by the church he joined after coming close to what appeared to be a nervous and physical breakdown, perhaps brought on by a constant eighteen-hour daily build schedule. Like many guitar builders starting out, he was working all hours to deliver guitars at uneconomic prices to a distributor, who after taking their usual margin of around 50 percent, still failed to shift many of his instruments. Early hand-built Olsons at this time could be bought at a discount from a retailer for as little as $400. Olson's prospects for building guitars for a living looked less than rosy, and like many makers he recognizes that his wife pretty much kept things afloat financially for many years. In fact, Olson regularly goes out of his way to highlight that he couldn't have made it without "the best wife in the world. . . . In order to make guitars you don't really need [a wife], but if you plan to make good guitars you better have a really, really good one."

Obviously, things changed when Phil Keaggy bought an Olson.

But did money change hands?

I've spoken off the record to several one-man luthiers whose guitars have ended up in the hands of famous players. Both parties know that the right player's patronage can transform the fate of a little-known guitar maker.

"I love this guitar. . . . Let me take it on the road and see how it suits me."

Such an offer may initially sound like music to a guitar builder's ears, but it's likely to be a cash-free transaction. I met one respected but still struggling guitar maker who was delighted when a middle-ranking singer-songwriter took one of his guitars on trial. He assumed he would be paid for it one day, only to see it for sale a year later on eBay with the player's name as part of its provenance. The bill is still unpaid, and the builder reluctantly accepts that to make a fuss would get him nowhere.

Through a friend, Olson managed to get one of his SJ (small jumbo) guitars placed in James Taylor's hotel room before a concert at a venue close to where the maker lived in Minnesota. Taylor was impressed with the guitar and called Olson to ask what he should do with the instrument. Although Olson's main paying job at the time was as a janitor in the church that gave him workshop space, he swallowed hard and suggested that Taylor could probably afford the $2,500 he was charging at the time. Taylor agreed and ordered a couple of SJs and a dreadnought, along with paying for the guitar he had been asked to try out. Taylor seems to be a decent guy, but with musicians who may also be struggling to make a living, I have no idea if money changes hands. Twenty-five years after Taylor's first order, Olson was completing a limited run of one hundred James Taylor SJ signature models, some selling in excess of $25,000; so for Olson, the Keaggy and Taylor relationships are the gifts that keep on giving.

Either way, the market decided that an Olson guitar was worth $400 in 1980 but $12,500 in 2001. One must ask: Is a 2001 Olson thirty times better than a 1980 Olson?

In the years between 1979 and 2001, Olson made quite a few guitars. He reckons he makes about forty instruments a year, so an Olson made in 2001 was constructed by someone who had made another 880 hand-built guitars since 1979, when his $900 guitars were put in a few local retail stores. Dave King, the UK maker of a small parlor guitar I own, believes that "until you've been making guitars for at least fifteen years, you haven't really got any solid empirical evidence that your instruments really are fit for purpose; that they will last the course; that they won't collapse on themselves, or develop other faults and importantly continue to sound and play well."

Dave recently showed me the very first guitar he made in 1983. At almost forty years old, there is no doubt that it has lasted the course, but back then he didn't know whether he and it would both make it.

Like many one-man luthiers, Olson and King spent their early years making furniture until they were bitten by the guitar bug. Many builders, initially at least, obsessively make the same guitar over and over, perfecting the way they join a particular part, refining the finish of every component, until they are satisfied that they are making guitars that are good enough. In doing this, they are imitating the process undertaken by great masters like Stradivarius.

A Dave King Number 1. (John Stubbings)

Antonio Stradivarius signed his first instrument in 1666, proof that he had completed his apprenticeship. Because his early apprentice instruments are unsigned, it's impossible to know how many he made or how good they were, but it is estimated that he would have carved and constructed nearly a thousand unsigned violins. Like all Cremonese apprentices, he would have been expected to complete two violins each week. Starting as young as twelve years old, apprentices rarely completed their "masterpiece" in under a decade. By the time they were allowed to sign and sell instruments under their own names, they were proven makers.

With the end of the established guild apprentice system, guitar builders were free to follow their own path. Nowadays it's possible for anyone to call themselves a "luthier" after having completed only a couple of guitars. Master builders like Canada's Michael Greenfield are concerned that some raw recruits to the craft set out building ornate and complicated first instruments without the early repetition that he had benefitted from. But most would-be builders enroll in one of the many luthiery courses now on offer and do it the hard way. First guitars are often taken apart and remade. Subsequent, playable attempts are given to friends. As they get better at their craft, they trade or sell their instruments for prices that can make them a real bargain for the canny buyer. That process continues until they are making instruments that they believe in and for which they can charge realistic prices.

But regardless of the name on the headstock, the proof is often in the playing. I've played expensive guitars from big-name makers that just don't sound that good, and Chinese factory-made replicas that play and sound wonderful. As the old antique dealer gag goes, "Well I've looked at what you brought in, and the good news is that you definitely have an original Rembrandt and an equally original Stradivarius. The bad news is that Stradivarius was a terrible painter, and Rembrandt couldn't make a violin to save his life."

• • • • • •

In 2015, I took a meandering two-month solo road trip, essentially making a big loop south from New York to Mississippi before travelling north to San Francisco, taking the long way around. At the start, I added a side trip from New York to Pennsylvania to visit the Martin factory in Nazareth.

I was nearly a week into the journey proper and night had fallen on top of the foggy mountain not forty miles from where the Carter Family first heard, learned, and played "The Foggy Mountain Top." Leaving Charlotte, North

Carolina, that morning, I had been told that the drive through Appalachia and the Smoky Mountains was beautiful. Sadly, it was raining so hard I saw nothing but spray from the semis hauling trailers either side of me.

I was scheduled to meet a yoga master, sometime yogi, and dealer in $20,000-plus custom-made guitars in a curry restaurant in downtown Asheville for dinner. Exhausted after eight hours on the road, I just had time to select some suitable clothes before I went to seek my guru.

I could have easily taken a skeptical dislike to a person whose self-proclaimed mission in life is "to aim for everything I do to be for a higher purpose and to be the best human being I can."

Paul Heumiller is the founder of Dream Guitars, a "salon de guitar" just outside the relaxed, new-age town of Asheville, North Carolina. With long, beached-blond hair, wispy Fu Manchu whiskers, and wearing the sort of loose-fitting clothes that allow him to float around a room, Heumiller has the look of a lifestyle guru. When not teaching yoga, he represents a hand-picked selection of individual guitar makers, most building one-off custom guitars with eye-watering price tags and wait times that run into years. The time I spent with Paul changed my initial opinion of him. Cynically, I started with the view that he had to be a man with a mission to empty the wallets of gullible wealthy guitar addicts. I left dinner believing that his intent is of a higher purpose. He fulfils the dreams of people who want to own a guitar that has been made just for them, but in doing so they also want to support the craft of the artisan builder. Some of these modern-day Medicis are undoubtedly Alpha acquirers: their $30,000 guitars sit alongside the $100,000 watches and $200,000 automobiles stored under their multichambered, temperature-controlled wine cellars. But many also turn out to be regular guitarists who have arrived at the conclusion that one or, perhaps, two great guitars are more rewarding than a room full of modern, factory-made boxes.

We had a fascinating couple of hours discussing the future of the guitar-making industry before agreeing to pick up the conversation again in his guitar store the next evening. Before we part, I ask him to sum up why he thinks so many flat-top steel-string guitarists become serial acquirers. He offered, "Classical guitar players want their guitars to be wives, steel-string players want mistresses."

I pondered on this thought as I drove back to my hotel and decided that I'd better cut up my credit cards and cancel my bank account overdraft facility in preparation for my next encounter with the guitar guru. I knew I had Multiple

Guitar Acquisition Syndrome as a clinical condition and had to take precautions that it didn't get any worse than it already was.

• • • • • •

Over the years I've visited dozens of guitar stores in lots of different states and countries. From soulless guitar superstores to small mom-and-pop affairs as well as the New York legends. But Dream Guitars was a world apart.

It is not so much a guitar store as a high-end gallery, and like any gallery owner, Paul doesn't carry stock. He represents over a hundred individual luthiers. Instruments by mythic masters like Ervin Somogyi, whose guitars regularly sell for north of $50,000, sit alongside those by established craftsmen like Kevin Ryan and Bill Tippin. Most of the instruments he sells start at around $10,000, and their makers have waiting lists stretching up to ten years. There are also hot "new" guys like Jordan McConnell, who, seemingly from nowhere, commands $20,000 for a basic instrument. Alongside the newer builders are the genuine one-offs, player-makers like Wayne Henderson, who had been quietly making guitars for years before being rediscovered and crowned a genius.

A champion bluegrass flat-picker in his own right, Henderson has been making guitars since the late 1970s in his small, chaotic, one-man workshop in the little town of Rugby, Virginia. Alongside guitar building and running his own bluegrass players' competition, he was, until recently, also the mountain town's postman. Back then he was still selling his instruments for around $5,000 directly to people who came to his shop. It wasn't easy to order one, but if you got to meet Wayne, and if he liked the way you played, then you might get on to the handwritten list he kept above his workbench. Some people wait for fifteen years, while others get their guitars in just a couple. What might move your name up the list can be anything from visiting Wayne with something he wants (he collects American Civil War memorabilia) or being Eric Clapton. Clapton got his guitar in a little under three years, and it became the subject of a book, *Clapton's Guitar*. Henderson guitars were regularly trading secondhand for six or seven thousand dollars before the book came out in 2005, when he was only really known to bluegrass players.

After the book things changed.

Paul Heumiller was the first dealer to sell a secondhand Henderson for $20,000. When rumors of the sale started to get out, he got a call from a journalist who wanted to know if the astronomical selling price was true. It turned out the caller was Allen St. John, the writer of the Clapton book. Heumiller asked, "You did buy a Henderson before you wrote the book, didn't you?"

St. John told Paul that he hadn't and was pretty sore about his apparent stupidity.

I spent the rest of my time with Heumiller in a weird state of nirvana. Sure, you can go to a gallery and look at a Hockney or a Bridget Riley but that's about all most people can do. You can talk about it, wonder if it was painted when the artist was sad, happy, or between relationships, even wonder if it's a good investment. But not much more than that. At Dream Guitars, I could do all of that and then play the work of art. And play I did. I held in my hands guitar masterpieces by master builders like Jeff Traugott, Tippin, Petros, Somogyi, and Greenfield. The list and range of guitar styles and wood combinations carried us late into the evening.

Paul then pulled out his own guitar and played me his friend Martin Simpson's arrangement of Richard Thompson's "Waltzing's for Dreamers."

Paul was playing his $30,000 McConnell; the solid blues, blacks, purples, and golds of the fingerboard inlay that continued up into the headstock was a scene from his favorite motorcycle route up into the mountains. The spruce top is made of so-called moon spruce, trees only harvested from the Italian Alps within the last quarter of a waning moon, when the moon's lessening magnetic pull allows the sap in the tree trunk to rest. It was the wood of choice for Stradivarius and is cut only in wintertime so that most of the sap has returned to the roots. According to Heumiller, the violin master's journals from the 1700s show that he believed that moon spruce was stiffer and more resistant to changes in atmospheric moisture. You can smile cynically or just allow the soft, soothing words of the guitar guru to wash over you.

We sang in harmony, we each drank a small glass of the wine I had brought, and then I remembered that it was late, and I was halfway up a mountain and five thousand miles from home with a mystic guitar man.

As I drove back into Asheville and the euphoria of playing so many outstanding guitars began to slowly subside, I wondered about the responsibility of owning any of those instruments. How many were really played once they had been shipped to their new owners? Every successful guitar maker with a waiting list I've spoken to or heard interviewed invariably expresses their fear that, as their instruments become more sought-after, they are less likely to be played and more likely to be locked away in a bank vault. Even makers of more modest guitars from the smaller-volume makers hate the idea of people stockpiling their instruments, waiting for them to increase in value. It seemed that many buyers were making the sometimes inevitable journey from player to collector and then to investor. With the vintage guitar market in some state of flux, many investors have moved on to purchase these masterpiece guitars from contemporary builders, and so the parallels with the modern art market are many. Luthiers emerging seemingly from nowhere to achieve rock-star status. Gallery owners perhaps becoming classic market makers, stockholding or buying-in guitars to maintain prices for the makers they represent.

Gillian Welch playing a 1956 Gibson J50 and David Rawlings playing a 1935 Epiphone Olympic.

Americana and an Acoustic Revival

As the late '90s edged toward the start of a new millennium, Nora Guthrie, the daughter of '50s folk legend Woody Guthrie, was concerned that her father's legacy was all but lost to an MTV generation brought up on a diet of teen pop, electronic dance, and hip-hop. Nora had found a huge stash of lyrics that the Dust Bowl Troubadour had neither recorded nor set to music before he had fallen victim to Huntingdon's disease in 1967. At a Woody Guthrie tribute concert in New York's Central Park, she heard UK singer-songwriter and political activist Billy Bragg perform both the old Joe Hill song "There Is Power in a Union" and a sensitive adaptation of her father's people's anthem "This Land Is Your Land." Following these performances, she saw Bragg as "the only singer I knew who was taking on the same issues as Woody."

Bragg had emerged out of the British postpunk street busking scene that had itself in the mid-1980s grown out of a left-wing political crusade "against everything that Maggie Thatcher stood for, a civil war between two different types of philosophies." Nora Guthrie recognized Bragg's political integrity and gave him the hundreds of pages of lyrics to look over in order to create songs relevant to a younger generation. Interestingly, Bob Dylan, seen by an earlier generation as either the inheritor of or pretender to Woody's crown, relates in his autobiography *Chronicles* that, during one of his many visits to Woody Guthrie in hospital in the early '60s, Guthrie had offered him the same batch of unpublished lyrics. Dylan had apparently visited the Guthrie house on Mermaid Avenue, Brooklyn, the next evening to collect the papers, but Guthrie's wife, Marjorie, was not at home. A twelve-year-old Arlo Guthrie and his babysitter were there but didn't know where the lyric sheets were kept. The nineteen-year-old Dylan apparently just "stayed long enough to warm up" and dry out his boots before slipping back into the cold, wet night.

Using an old Gibson LG-1, Bragg wrote many new melodies to go with the pages of original lyrics, but he also took a page out of Guthrie's own songwriting playbook by adapting existing folk melodies. For example, among the papers was a poem titled "Go Down to the Water" that recalled Guthrie's wartime service in the US Merchant Marine. Finding an appropriate tune eluded Bragg, so he adapted the melody from the Irish air called "She Moves Through the Fair."

The collection had once again reunited Old World music with contemporary New World music. But generating melodies for so many lyrics was an enormous task for Bragg, even with access to the Cecil Sharp House library of traditional songs. Attracted by the work of the Chicago band Wilco and its blend of modern and traditional sensitivities, Bragg co-opted front man Jeff Tweedy to cowrite some of the melodies and for Wilco to act as the house band for the sessions. In 1998, the first batch of Bragg-Wilco "Mermaid Avenue" recordings was issued. The sound of Tweedy's Martin D-28 twelve-string roots the songs in the old-time idyll of Americana and runs throughout the album, indeed opening the standout track from the sessions, "California Stars." The project's stripped-down, spare production of Guthrie's lyrics received a Grammy nomination. Dylan comments, in a sidebar to his recollection of his failed mission to secure the lyrics, that performers who "probably weren't even born when I had made that trip out to Brooklyn" had done a good job in bringing the forgotten lyrics to life.

Bragg and his collaborators reignited an interest in both Guthrie's "voice of the people" style of folk music and in a music that had the simple acoustic guitar at its heart. Their work helped encourage a contemporary reinvention of American roots music that blossomed beyond the first decade of the new millennium. It was a reinvention built on the roots of '90s alternative country that became known as Americana.

• • • • • •

Alternative or alt-country had itself been an attempt to put some roots credibility back into the overly polished style of country music that had dominated the '70s and '80s. Nashville, the Protestant "Buckle of the Bible Belt" (largely the southeastern and south-central states), had also always been a business-first city. By the '50s, it was marketing itself as "Music City USA." It is still a place where socially conservative Protestantism drives business, politics, and society. Since the early '30s, it had been the headquarters of the hugely profitable Bible and church songbook publishing industry and became the center of evangelical hymn writing and publishing, in a country where religious music (gospel, contemporary Christian, and evangelical) is still big business and sells in larger volume than jazz, classical, or bluegrass. With these roots and this expertise, Nashville soon cornered the market for the publishing and production of secular country music too.

From country and western's earliest manifestation, artists have always included gospel and overtly religious songs in their programs and albums. Elvis Presley's only Grammy award was for his *How Great Thou Art* album, produced in the mid-1960s when, suffering from the worst effects of Beatlemania, Presley couldn't otherwise get airplay. Today, mainstream country artists from Dolly Parton to Garth Brooks know it's good business to wear their Christian faith on their sleeves in both their live and recorded repertoires. Country audiences like hell-raisers and have always forgiven their music stars as long as, as the saying goes, they "raise Cain on Saturday but go to church on Sunday."

The first blooming of rock 'n' roll and the broad popularity of modern, TV-ready ballad singers like Pat Boone, Andy Williams, and Johnny Mathis had taken the wheels off country and western's wagon. As part of its modernizing fight-back, Nashville had cleansed itself of old-time and hillbilly music, eager to shed its connotations of inbred, backward people and Hicksville meets *Deliverance* characters. Producers like Chet Atkins and Buck Owens steered away from guitar-led country, lushing up their productions into what became known as the Nashville Sound, with heavy strings and syrupy arrangements that better appealed to its core, "middle-class housewife with two kids at home" radio and TV audience. By the early '60s, country was soon miles away from any guitar-playing folk sensibilities, and artists who weren't guitarists, like Jim Reeves and Patsy Cline (who died in 1963), had won a crossover audience into pop that rebuilt country's dominant position as middle America's favorite music.

But if country was ever truly the "three chords and the truth" that it so often promised to be, Nashville was by the '70s turning into a rhinestone-suited dog-and-pony show dedicated, in the words of Chet Atkins, to "selling records and making money." The music was commercially driven, run by music company executives besotted with knowing not only what sold but also what delivered the right demographic for its radio advertisers. Anything that strayed from the glossy formula just didn't get radio airplay. In a period when being a success was all about big hair and tight pants, being able to sing and play guitar wasn't enough. As a result, many truly talented players, artists like Emmylou Harris and Nanci Griffith, just weren't getting the airplay necessary to secure financially sustaining record deals.

Country music outlaws and never-ending tour-bus die-hards like Johnny Cash, Willie Nelson, and Waylon Jennings had long railed against the rampant commercialism of what started out as fiddle and guitar music. Now so slick it could hardly be recognized as the honest music that Hank Williams pioneered, the band of cantankerous country stalwarts started an outlaw country movement. The songs had substance and authenticity, none more so than Jennings's 1975 song "Are You Sure Hank Done It This Way?" He put into words and music what had been a long-running battle with the "Nashville bean counters" and formula-obsessed producers of Nashville's Music Row. Jennings sang that the industry had to change, possibly to go back to the way it was when Hank had made it—when the talent to write and sing songs was what counted.

Although popular with fans and a country chart hit record, the sentiments of the song were not popular with the record executives at CBS Records who were trying to further cleanse their artist rosters, this time of "unprofitable, old-school country" artists like Merle Haggard and Johnny Cash. CBS, having lured Cash from Sun Records in 1960, dropped him in 1986, something that Haggard resented for a whole pile of reasons. Hanging on to his own recording contract by a thread, he publicly taunted CBS executive Rick Blackburn from the stage at an awards event in Nashville in 2009. "Who do you think you are? You're the son-of-a-bitch that fired Johnny Cash. Let it go down in history that you're the dumbest son-of-a-bitch I've ever met."

Haggard had the sort of badass country music credentials that gave him the authority to rail against the industry. Like Wanda Jackson, who had emerged in the 1950s, Haggard was born in a Bakersfield boxcar in 1937 to Okie parents who had moved to California during the Dustbowl migration. By 1957, Haggard was a twenty-year-old convict sitting in the audience when Johnny Cash played his first prison concert at San Quentin. Haggard, transfixed by both Cash's hard-man persona and gritty performance, set his sights on following Cash into country music, but not before he had been jailed over seventeen times for a variety of petty crimes.

Seeing, and not particularly liking, what they had to do to get back onto the country playlists, many country musicians identified with the outlaws and went back to their own roots. They joined the alt-country scene, where being able to play your own guitar accompaniment actually meant something. Over the next few years alt-country evolved into Americana and a broader roots movement. It even spawned its own magazine, *No Depression*, a quarterly started in 1995 that by 2008, when it stopped printing, had featured cover stars as diverse as Ralph Stanley, Alison Krauss, and Elvis Costello. And as with the '60s New York folk revival that had once more put the acoustic guitar in front of a younger, hip, musically literate audience, alt-country celebrated the roots of American music, however broadly defined.

"Americana," a term initially coined to describe the sort of antique store ephemera that talks to a bucolic vision of old-time American values, took on a new meaning. Now, in the less than crisp words of the Americana Music Association, it embraces "contemporary music that incorporates elements of various American roots music styles, including country, roots-rock, folk, bluegrass, R&B and blues, resulting in a distinctive roots-oriented sound that lives in a world apart from the pure forms of the genres upon which it may draw. While acoustic instruments are often present and vital, Americana also often uses a full electric band."

I'm not sure about the definition. It seems to include just about all styles of music and neatly sidesteps the contribution that African Americans contribute to Americana. Effectively, the AMA was describing the roots-orientated American primitivism that the Band had first pioneered in the late '60s. The 1990s revival of a style of music from a bygone age was a reaction against two things: the industrialized, chart-ready Nashville country and western from artists like Garth Brooks and Shania Twain, and the synthetic, programmed, autotuned pop music of the 1990s. Most of these Americana bands brought contemporary hipness back to the acoustic guitar.

A bunch of Southern US radio station programmers had first started using the term "Americana" to describe a reinvention of the gnarled, "woody, thuddy sound" the Band had been exploring in the late '60s. But this time it was groups like Uncle Tupelo, Whiskeytown, and Wilco who were reinventing and recreating "a distant remembered past."

All three bands had come from similar points on the musical compass. Ryan Adams had moved from a punk rock trio by way of a heavy dose of folk-rock legend Gram Parsons to form, in 1994, the band Whiskeytown in his native North Carolina. The music was described by *Rolling Stone* as "alternative-country's answer to Nirvana." Just before Adams left to become a solo alt-country superstar, the band's sound mellowed to the more sophisticated roots rock as defined by Wilco.

Wilco had also formed in 1994, this time out of the embers of Uncle Tupelo, another short-lived punk band that evolved into an equally short-lived but highly influential alt-country group. The band laced their original music with liberal doses of Carter Family harmony and, on songs like "Whiskey Bottle," Hank Williams–style lyrics. By the time they had morphed into Wilco, they were mixing original songs (mainly written by front man Jeff Tweedy) with covers of old-time country material, including the Ernest Tubb song "The T.B. Is Whipping Me" (1937). Tubb's idol Jimmie Rodgers, who had been whipped and ultimately killed by tuberculosis, might have been proud that contemporary bands were giving a run for its money to the Nashville music business that had spurned the style of hillbilly music he had pioneered.

Many of the Americana artists emerging in the mid-1990s had started out playing that most contemporary of roots music, punk, before discovering the appeal of old-time music. But the artists who, then and now, provide the most perfect expression of acoustic Americana, the duo Gillian Welch and David Rawlings, had different influences.

Welch herself was playing Carter Family and Woody Guthrie songs on acoustic guitar when she was just eight. Her adoptive parents were professional performers and composers for TV, so music was nurtured in the child. While her musical partner Rawlings had developed his prowess on guitar in rock and country bands, things changed after he met Welch, who was a fellow student at Boston's Berklee College of Music in the late '80s. Rawlings's unique style of bluegrass flat-picking soon ascended into the echelon of roots acoustic guitar playing populated only by the likes of Maybelle Carter, Chet Atkins, and Lester Flat. Inspired by the keening, plaintive singing style of Welch, he created a form of lead playing that is so sublime that at times it literally takes your breath away. With echoes of '20s country blues, '40s hillbilly music, and '50s rock 'n' roll sitting alongside the '60s jazz influences of Wes Montgomery's octave playing, Rawlings creates acoustic guitar solos using individual notes and musical intervals that shouldn't make sense but do. Rawlings refers to the often-dissonant notes he favors most as "the ghostly ones." To find and play them, he uses a small-bodied archtop guitar not dissimilar to Maybelle Carter's, although unlike her top-of-the-range Gibson L-5, his Epiphone Olympic was a budget model when it was produced in 1935. But, like Maybelle's archtop, his '35 Epiphone, although made largely from plywood, albeit with a solid carved top, has a sonic punch that works perfectly when played in a group setting into a single microphone. The duo performs onstage, and often in the studio, with a setup not dissimilar to the very early days of recording. Sound balance is achieved by the individual instruments and the singers' proximity to a single microphone.

Both the guitars they use (Welch has from the outset almost always played a 1956 Gibson J-50 flat-top) and their recording style make many tracks seem as though they were cut directly into wax masters by Ralph Spiers in the 1926 Bristol sessions and then lost for seventy years. Equally, the theme and character of the original, guitar-led songs that the duo writes—songs like "Caleb Meyer," "Tear My Stillhouse Down," and "Orphan Girl"—feel like they could have emerged from the deep, dark holler next door to where the Carter Family was producing music in the 1920s and '30s.

Their debut album, *Revival*, emerged in 1996 after a musical apprenticeship in Nashville, "playing everywhere and everything" and hanging out with low-profile but highly influential writers and musicians like John Hartford, Guy Clark, and Townes Van Zandt. Gillian Welch's songs are neither musically nor lyrically from the sunny side of the street. Like the old-time duos the Blue Sky Boys and the Stanley Brothers they obviously admire, they could make "Happy Birthday" sound haunting and sad. They see themselves as "being on the blue team," referencing the words of Van Zandt: "There's only two kinds of music, the blues and Zip-a-Dee-Doo-Dah."

While it's easy to see the pair as just a pastiche of old-time duos from the 1930s, when you look deeper, there is much subtlety, intelligence, and modern sensibility in what they do.

Dave Rawlings's musical ability and musical humility are evident across all their recorded and live work. His backing vocals can be little more than a whisper welded to Welch's quiet alto. While capable of solo pyrotechnics, his guitar usually adds only the lightest three-note phrase to Welch's subtle, steady rhythm playing.

Rawlings's sensibilities as singer, guitarist, and producer came to serve numerous young bands who, in the early 2000s, were exploring the "real, pure, raw power" of string-band music, permutations of guitar, banjo, upright bass, mandolin, and fiddle pioneered in North Carolina in the early 1920s.

Then there are the Avett Brothers.

Often mixing old blues, bluegrass, and jug band music, the Avett Brothers, like so many musicians from North Carolina who also started out in school rock and punk bands in the late '90s, rediscovered acoustic guitars and recorded some impromptu back-porch tracks. Trace elements of neo-bluegrass are at the forefront of their early work, but by the time of their second album in 2002, *Country Was*, their specific blend included Piedmont country blues, folk, and punk united with a heavy strand of Beatle-esque pop melody. By 2008, they had been picked up by uber-producer Rick Rubin, and their style, a popularist Americana, had become more mainstream, with albums charting in the top 5 of the Billboard 200. An appearance on David Letterman in 2015 singing the old 1899 hymn "Keep on the Sunny Side" (coincidentally the first big hit for Gillian Welch's much revered Blue Sky Boys) signaled the popular arrival of Americana. From an acoustic guitar perspective, the brothers were the poster boys for Martin dreadnought guitars: they appeared in Martin advertising, have a signature Martin model made in their name, and exclusively play Martin guitars at their many live performances. But given their North Carolina and bluegrass roots, it's perhaps no wonder they play "the bluegrass guitar."

• • • • • •

With Americana's arrival on late-night, mainstream TV, it's perverse that a genre that in its very name seeks to represent and celebrate the diversity of America's ethnic music seemingly fails to recognize the contributions made by Black and Indigenous blues, jazz, and folk musicians to American roots music. Like the formulaic country and western music it is studiously trying to avoid, Americana is also a genre that is largely dominated by white musicians.

In the plantation days of slavery, Black string bands provided the up-tempo dance music that slave owners and their guests danced to, and Black bands playing to white audiences was a tradition that carried on long after emancipation. So while the modern roots of African American music are most closely identified with the blues, jazz, and R&B, there was also a long tradition of Black musicians playing what was known in the 1930s as old-time music. Blues players across the decades, Blind Blake, Rev. Gary Davis, and Josh White, all had old-time country or hillbilly songs in their repertoires. There were also numerous Black string bands, such as the Tennessee Chocolate Drops and the Mississippi Sheiks, playing classic fiddle and banjo romps like "Cindy Girl" and "Ragtime Annie" at barbecues and private parties in the 1920s and '30s.

At the first Black Banjo Gathering in 2005, held in North Carolina, a young trio of string players and singers formed the Carolina Chocolate Drops and released what would become a Grammy award–winning album, *Genuine Negro Jig*. Both the band name and the album title are a nod to their musical heritage and possibly a small poke in the eye for the AMA and the Americana establishment . . .

Led by guitarist and jug player Don Flemons and banjo player and vocalist Rhiannon Giddens, the band reinterprets early string- and jug-band songs, primitive jazz, and Civil War–era fife-and-drum music. Its purpose is not only to entertain with what *Rolling Stone* describes as "dirt-floor dance electricity" but also to educate and agitate. In their choice of material and the way they present it at live events, every concert is something of a history lesson in roots music. They highlight the central role that Black musicians had in shaping the past one hundred years of rural ethnic folk music. Like much acoustic Americana and, in particular, the recent renaissance of string-band music, they also seek to create music that is "real, raw, pure, plain fun," nothing created or produced in or via a computer.

Rhiannon Giddens has been an outspoken voice in building diversity in American roots music. As the keynote speaker at the International Bluegrass Music Association in 2017, she tackled the elephant in the room: "Why is bluegrass music so white?"

She pointed out: "The question shouldn't be how do we get diversity into bluegrass but how do we get diversity *back* into bluegrass?"

In this book's references to bluegrass banjo music, I've fallen into the usual trope, describing it as the music of *Deliverance* and *The Beverly Hillbillies*. These easy, popular references only perpetuate the myth that old-time string-band music was invented by, or is irredeemably linked to, the Anglo-Celtic white hillbillies living in Appalachia.

Yet . . .

Bill and Charlie Monroe publicly recognized the influence of Black string-band musician Arthur Schultz (1886–1931) on their style of playing. Primarily a fiddler with, according to Bill Monroe, a "bluesy, syncopated style," he was also a talented guitarist whose thumb-picking style predated and almost certainly led to both Travis-picking and the Kentucky-style playing made famous by Chet Atkins.

It'll get sorted but it will take time.

• • • • • •

So are alt-country, Americana, and the growing genre of new folk anything more than a haven for artists not commercial enough to strike it rich in Nashville?

Dylan did an interview in the early '60s where he discussed what had happened to rock 'n' roll. Why it had all but died. He felt that its first phase had started out with good intentions, that it had creative heart, but along the line it had become lyrically bland, with too much "Moon and June" and "I Wanna Be Bobby's Girl." Folk music got its moment in the sun in the '60s revival by using the accessibility of the guitar, which enabled people with something to say (but perhaps limited formal musical ability) to inject content and thoughtful lyrics into the mix. That input reinvigorated what became "a new rock 'n' roll," a new folk music that brought these fresh ideas and blended them with the best bits of what went before: blues, jazz, gospel, hillbilly, field hollers, and more.

The same thing had happened to country music in the '70s and '80s. From the beginning, the genre was never trying to be anything loftier than popular entertainment, albeit entertainment made up of honest, raw content from the people of the mountains and valleys, people who wanted to say something or perhaps just tell their stories. In the 1920s, when urban record companies sent out scouts like Ralph Spier into the countryside to find vernacular music, they found many local people playing their own music—the original version of "three chords and the truth." Over time, it got glossed up by the Nashville business machine to a point where it had become a parody of itself. But that inspired a whole new group of musicians and poets to shake it up and put content, and some kind of authenticity, back in.

Popular music will always be a cycle of creation, burnout, destruction, and reinvention. The cycle regularly encourages a musical phoenix to rise from the embers, as it had with Johnny Cash and the American Recordings. Time after time, musicians find something new, perhaps something they can believe in and take on the road. Success initially breeds success, but an excess of success ultimately breeds contempt, and before long they feel they are in the same dog-and-pony show that they were initially rebelling against themselves. Often, it's their original musical inspiration, the simple acoustic guitar, that they pick up to find that inspiration again. It's the perfect gateway instrument for new musicians and a return ticket for seasoned artists who have lost their way and want to start afresh.

• • • • • •

Americana, and its many derivations and acoustic-led subgenres, has put the acoustic guitar back into the hands of a generation of younger musicians. Through them, it's back in the public eye as the original roots instrument, connecting modern sensibilities with the authentic folk music of America. The same phenomenon has happened in the UK, where roots-derived contemporary folk is also thriving, sometimes on a very low-key and local level, but also with the global appeal of West London band Mumford and Sons.

But this modern revival has its critics, who often challenge its authenticity. It is portrayed as music that is nothing more than a millennial's reimagining of a '70s reinterpretation of a '60s reinvention of a style of music that came to the fore in the 1920s and '30s, which itself borrowed verbatim from the imported folk music of nineteenth-century Ireland, Scotland, Africa, Spain, Mexico, and elsewhere. It is also often pilloried for being faux-rural in its presentation: male urbanites don plaid shirts and grow thick beards to look like hoary-handed sons of the soil; they play alongside young women dressed as though they had just stepped out of a Dorothea Lange Dustbowl photograph.

Most singers and players of Americana today live lives that are very different from those of Jimmie Rodgers and the Carter Family, whose authenticity in writing and performing songs about the hard life of rural America came from personal experience. Unsurprisingly, it's true that very few, if any, contemporary Americana musicians experienced anything close to the poverty or hand-to-mouth upbringing of traditional old-time or hillbilly players or live in the poor, rural areas where these singers usually came from. But does where you were born or live matter? Does the fact that the Avett Brothers were born in rural North Carolina make them any more "authentic" in their playing than Gillian Welch, who was adopted by a successful New York showbiz couple who moved to California to be near Hollywood, while her band partner, Dave Rawlings, comes from prosperous, largely middle-class Rhode Island? In the way that blues aficionados like their heroes Black, blind, and dead, I sense that Americana fans would like Welch and Rawlings even more if they had some physical or familial connection with Appalachia and poverty. The iconic photographs of the Band that Elliot Landy took in 1968 that decorate their first two albums have Robbie Robertson, Levon Helm, Garth Hudson, Richard Manuel, and Rick Danko standing on a dusty dirt road in the Catskills. Dressed in dark three-piece suits, wearing old-time felt hats, and sporting thick beards, they look as though they had walked out of the 1860s rather than the 1960s. It's an obvious contrivance, a fiction. These were not the clothes they wore every day. But the photos are no more or less authentic than Henry Diltz's photos of the Eagles taken for their *Desperado* album cover: the group dressed up as . . . well, cowboy desperados and photographed at the Paramount Ranch Western film set.

But it was ever thus. As we have seen, a legend like Jimmie Rodgers inhabited a largely invented persona. Woody Guthrie's parents were far from being poor Okies; his father was, among other things, a local politician who made and lost a small fortune speculating on land prices in a boom-and-bust oil town. Bob Dylan is a character played by Robert Zimmerman, the son of a middle-class electrical retailer. Is it all just showbiz? All an illusion? All just another aspect of the same dog-and-pony show that Americana first rejected?

What all these artists have or had was a visceral connection to a music with roots. Many folk music academics derided Pete Seeger. In *Romancing the Folk* (2001), an analysis of the American folk music tradition, Benjamin Filene describes both the father of modern folk (that is, Woody Guthrie) and Bob Dylan as "folk stylists . . . figures who grew up outside the regional or ethnic traditions that produced roots music but who became public performers of and emissaries for that music."

Seeger was all about using music to help the working man and his family. He aspired to use song to create a sense of bonding through a shared musical history and community. Fans of Americana or contemporary folk may be attaching themselves to a simpler time, to a community, real or imagined, where there was always a member of the family who could play a guitar to amuse those sitting round the dinner table. These days a guitar can easily be at hand, but the unmistakable sound of acoustic Americana streamed via Spotify and played by four middle-class high-school boys from London will do perfectly well. It doesn't really matter how many of the twelve million people who bought Moby's trip-hop electronica album *Play* (1999) realized that its primary source material was Alan Lomax's *Sounds of the South* (1959), his collection of American field recordings. Surely what does matter, and should be celebrated, is that the plaintive voices of rural blues-gospel singer Bessie Jones

("Sometimes") and country-blues singer Vera Hall ("Trouble So Hard") are still being heard.

• • • • • •

Today the acoustic guitar is much more than just an instrument of Americana. In the hands of British singer-songwriter Ed Sheeran, who regularly sells 150 million albums annually, it has reached a much, much bigger audience than Jimmie Rodgers could ever have imagined. In mid-2018, Sheeran led the race for the best-selling album and singles artist of the year. At one point, he had sixteen songs in the British top 20, while his three albums were all in the top 5. The only act that could keep him from remaining at the top of the charts was Taylor Swift. These days Swift rarely plays guitar in her videos, but onstage, and in front of her largely young, female audience, she is still a singer-songwriter, still a "folk singer." That is, if we define folk music as the music that we remember, that we whistle or hum or turn to when we need cheering up or comforting.

A well-relic'd dreadnought.

New Old Guitars

On Thursday nights, the long, low-ceilinged function room of the Dagenham Roundhouse public house served as a community bingo hall. But on Friday and Saturday evenings from 1969 to 1975, the cream of British rock bands filled the room to capacity, turning it into the world's loudest sauna.

The pub had a well-deserved reputation for attracting a rough crowd from the massive Becontree housing estate; it was also home to the Village Blues Club. East London's self-proclaimed "Premier Rock Music Venue" was host to any of the dozens of hard-working rock bands flogging their way up, down, and across the breadth of the British Isles most nights through the '70s.

As a fourteen-year-old teenager in 1969, living with my parents in a council house on the Becontree Estate, opportunities to see live rock music without going "up to London" were nonexistent—until the Village Blues Club opened for business.

On Saturday, April 19, 1969, I told my parents I was going to a friend's house for the evening to listen to records. Changing into a pair of green velvet flared trousers behind the garden shed, I walked the mile to the Dagenham Roundhouse to see my first live gig, a "bluesrock power trio" called Taste featuring, according to the previous week's *Sounds* music paper, "the best guitarist you'll ever see." That guitarist, also lead singer and the band's main songwriter, was Rory Gallagher. From a small town in Southern Ireland, he would be lauded in the 2000s as "the greatest rock guitarist you've never heard of."

The Village Blues Club was a licensed premises, so I was too young to pay the one-shilling (5p/6 cents) membership or seven shillings and six-pence (37p/45 cents) entrance fee to enter by the front door. But a few coins in the hand of the same security guy who had refused me entry at the front door who now guarded the fire exit got me in. Waiting for the 1,500-capacity room to get hot enough for the fire door to be opened to let some heat out and fresh air in, I heard both the support act (Steamhammer) and the first couple of songs from Taste through the muffle of the tiny and clearly inadequate ventilation grill. Once I'd finally sneaked in it took me five minutes to worm my way to the front of the crowd and the low stage. The young, long-haired Gallagher wore a thick plaid-check shirt, faded denims, and white baseball boots, although, with dark lamb-chop sideburns, he looked like a cross between a lumberjack and a Victorian butcher. He had just unplugged his electric guitar and sat down with a shiny metal-bodied acoustic unlike any guitar I had seen before. Using a glass bottle-neck, he made the guitar sound like nothing I had heard before.

Impressed by what I much later learnt was a National resonator, I listened entranced while Gallagher played two more tunes to finish the acoustic solo set and, rejoined by the bass player and drummer, strapped back on his electric guitar. The next song he played was "What's Going On?," a Gallagher original with a ridiculously catchy riff and a fiery and frenetic solo. To top it all he made his guitar make amazingly sustained squealing noises. I was only a few feet from him and despite the pressure of a couple of hundred sweaty bodies pinning me to the apron of the stage tried to figure out what he was doing. It was years before I realized he was playing "pinch harmonics." The sound that Brian May, Slash, Edge, Eddie van Halen, Billie Gibbons and countless other electric guitarists borrowed from him.

Taste disbanded not long after I saw them, but I was fortunate enough to see Rory Gallagher play a few more times in the '70s, always at the Roundhouse.

Only years later did I realize how lucky I had been to live just a short walk from such an amazing rock venue. The young promoters seemed able to lure both rock bands like Led Zeppelin, Pink Floyd, and King Crimson and folk groups like Pentangle and folk-rock groups like Fairport Convention to the shabby function room, primarily on the reputation of always providing an appreciative and musically knowledgeable audience.

Gallagher was immensely popular with live audiences, always insisting that the house lights stayed up so he could see the crowd. He always included a number of acoustic songs in his shows and seemed to attract an audience looking for rock, folk, Celtic-soul, and acoustic blues. At the time I was trying to play finger style and was intrigued to see him use both a flat-pick and two fingers. Only later did I appreciate he was playing like bluegrass flat pickers, able to achieve great speed as well as the delicacy of straight fingerpicking. When I saw Fairport Convention play, I realized that Gallagher and Fairport's Richard Thompson had similar technique.

• • • • • •

The other thing I remember from that night back in 1970 was the state of disrepair of Gallagher's electric guitar, a Fender Stratocaster. Interviewed many times about the iconic look of his guitar, he once said, "It was in good condition . . . but it's got so battered now it's got a kind of tattoo quality about it."

Aside from the normal dents and nicks expected of a well-used touring musician's guitar, the most remarkable thing was that virtually all the original sunburst paint finish on Gallagher's 1961 Fender Stratocaster had worn away or peeled off.

Most other Fenders I saw in the years following that night were shiny. From the bright red Stratocaster owned by Hank Marvin of the Shadows (thought to be the first Fender that entered Britain after the embargo on American luxury goods following World War II) to Eric Clapton's famed "Brownie" that he used on "Layla," they may have had the occasional nick or cigarette scorch mark on the headstock, but they were always shiny.

Thinking back to that night in the hot, steamy function room, I remember being amazed by how the sweat poured off Rory. By the end of the gig, his long hair was soaked. Playing both rhythm and lead guitar, he was in constant motion, and each time he swung round to face the crowd, an arc of sweat sprayed over all of us in the first couple of rows. His manager and brother, Dónal, interviewed after Rory's death in 1995 (when he was just forty-seven), stated that Rory's unusual blood type made his sweat particularly acidic. After hundreds of nights being played in hot, sweaty clubs, the guitar's original sunburst lacquer finish had all but disappeared.

Gallagher talked about swapping out the sweat-soaked necks of the guitar every few days. Having lost its protective lacquer finish, the bare wood became so damp that the neck needed to be allowed to dry out. Despite this, Gallagher never had the guitar restored or refinished, believing "the less paint or varnish on a guitar, acoustic or electric, the better. The wood breathes more."

Little could Gallagher have imagined that by the second decade of the 2000s, guitarists were paying premium amounts for "new old guitars" that were distressed specifically to look like his 1961 Stratocaster. It's what the guitar world knows as "relic-ing": building a brand-new, shiny guitar but making it look like it has spent a lifetime on the road.

The technique has been in use since the late 1960s, when guitar repair shops first learned how to reset necks from old acoustic guitars. If a vintage Gibson or Martin was valuable enough to be worth repairing by fitting a new neck, top, or back, the owner would ask for the new wood to be distressed to make the replacement part look like the original parts of the guitar—to effectively hide the repair.

It wasn't a big step for someone to ask if the whole of a newer, nonvintage guitar could be aged a little. Sometimes for purely aesthetic motives, sometimes for less honest reasons. The art and antique world had been "ageing" furniture, ceramics, and paintings for centuries. According to luthier Wayne Henderson, the violin world was also doing it centuries before. "I heard a story that [Niccolò] Paganini played a Stradivarius violin and he brought it to [nineteenth-century French luthier Jean-Baptiste] Vuillaume to have repair work done. Vuillaume said it would take two weeks and Paganini reluctantly agreed. When he came back, Vuillaume had made an absolute copy of it. Paganini didn't know which was which—and he was a doggone expert."

What had originally been a do-it-yourself process of ageing a new guitar by beating the painted body with a motorcycle chain and sanding the paint finish at strategic points with different grades of glass-paper became much more professional. Big-name brands relic-ing from new hit the electric guitar business in 1995, when Jay Black and Vince Cunneto joined the Fender Custom Shop. They had specialized in ageing electric guitars in small numbers for professional players but noticed in the late '80s and '90s that more amateur players wanted guitars that looked like they had played a thousand grunge nights at the Showbox in Seattle. In particular, guitarists wanted Fender Stratocasters and

Telecasters from the early 1960s because they sounded better as well as having more vintage mojo. But their popularity and increased rarity also increased their price. What a few years earlier was just an old guitar was now something special. Acquiring a guitar that looked *and* sounded the part was becoming big business.

In 1997, Fender, having approached the estate of Rory Gallagher, produced a limited run of replica Gallagher 1961 Stratocasters. Peeling paint, mismatched tuning pegs, cracked and beaten edges, tarnished or even rusted metalwork were all carefully reproduced. "Warts and all" replicas, including mods to switchgear, wiring, and pickups that never originated in the Fender factory. They sold out immediately, helping Fender, and other makers, to realize there was enormous potential not only in the factory reissue market but in professionally aged instruments.

By 1999, the Fender Custom Shop was getting more ambitious, handcrafting even more perfectly flawed reissues via their Time Machine program. It introduced six levels of distress. From *New Old Stock*: "As if you went back in time (to 1954) and bought it" from a guitar store; *Closet Classic*: "With subtle indications of the ages" like "slight oxidation" of metalware. For more wear, they offered the *Journeyman Relic*: With "'friendly' down to wood nicks." For the brave they offered *Heavy Relic*: "Designed to evoke decades of the most punishing play and touring."

So perfectly convincing was each guitar that Fender started stamping the word RELIC into the back of the headstock lest some future owners be hoodwinked into believing they were buying an actual vintage Fender.

Relic-ing addressed a business problem heritage-brand guitar companies like Fender and Gibson had. Their vintage electrics were being bought for many multiples of what any of their current models could command. The frustration for a company like Gibson was that they had made only $25 when they first sold a Les Paul Custom through a dealer in 1957. They didn't make a cent when, sixty years later, that very same guitar sold through a vintage dealer for $400,000.

While relic-ing partially addressed the issue, up until the mid-2010s, it only applied to the electric guitar world. The logic was that the sound of an electric guitar is the sum of three fundamentals: The original solid body plus the pickups and the way the electrics are wired make up what is effectively the "signal chain." Accurately reproduce those three elements, and in theory you can recreate the sound of any electric guitar. Distressing the paint and lacquer, tarnishing the metalwork and matching peripherals like tuners, control knobs, and pick guards don't affect the sound; they're just aesthetics. But they complete the package, enabling modern electric players to buy a guitar that looks, feels, and sounds like a guitar from the '60s for a fraction of the price of a true vintage instrument.

But the frustration remained for makers in the acoustic world.

In the 1990s, Martin had unknowingly started addressing the problem of their old guitars massively outstripping the price tag of modern models when they issued two commemorative-edition models. The first, an edition of ninety-four Perry Bechtel models, celebrated the first fourteen-fret OM guitar. The second, sixty-six Gene Autry models produced in 1995, each sold for a cool $22,000. In 1995, they started developing a line of signature editions, replicas of earlier models favored by professional players. With the introduction of the Clapton 000-42EC in 1996, they seemed to have found both a silver bullet and a new price point for the business.

Martin continued producing signature editions, along with various commemorative editions over subsequent years, each carrying the signatures of players known to choose Martin instruments. None were ever as popular as the Clapton 000s, and after producing guitars with the signatures of Johnny Cash, Willie Nelson, Merle Haggard, and Crosby, Stills & Nash inlaid in the fretboard (although never Young), they continued at a steady rate. More recently they've found themselves issuing guitars related to more obscure musicians. But the business logic is sound. If an artist has a reasonably significant fan base, their signature guitar would appeal to the guitarists in that fan base. It is also a relatively low-risk enterprise. One or two prototypes are revealed each year at the annual NAMM trade show where dealer interest is gauged. Subsequent preorders govern how many are eventually produced of each model.

However, when Martin produces a signature guitar, the emphasis is on crafting one that looks like the precise model chosen and used by the professional, whether it's Eric Clapton's 000-42 *Unplugged* guitar or British skiffle star Lonnie Donegan's 1967 000-28. Each signature guitar is delivered into the customer's hands as shiny and perfect as it would have been when the original was made. The Martin name on the headstock is the guarantee of build quality, and for most people Martin still builds the finest guitars money can buy. However, while they may have looked authentic and sounded great, they didn't sound vintage.

And that was becoming increasingly important as a growing body of opinion decreed that vintage acoustics sounded significantly better than any new guitar, even a new Martin, ever could. I wasn't totally convinced until, in 2015, I found my "birth year" Martin, a 1955 0-18. It was loud and woody, with exquisite forward-sounding musical trebles. A little road weary, it was still a fabulous-sounding guitar. I had tried a few vintage Martins over the years, but by playing the 0-18 every day on my two-month road trip across America researching this book, I finally knew what all the fuss was about. I understood why getting the vintage sound was the holy grail for so many players and makers.

• • • • • •

On the wall in my writing room I have two guitar tops on display. One is a Sitka spruce top from a 1995 Santa Cruz 000. It is the guitar's original top, ruined by an eight-inch crack. After being dropped from a Los Angeles hotel luggage trolley somewhere between reception and my room, SCGC kindly replaced it and returned the original broken top as a reminder to never entrust a guitar to an airline clerk *or* a hotel porter. Alongside the Santa Cruz is a Bourgeois guitar top given to me by Dana Bourgeois after I attended a workshop he ran at the 2015 Fretboard Summit. He was teaching the rudiments of voicing a guitar top to a small group of nonluthiers and had brought along a dozen prebraced tops that we were allowed to voice by shaving the braces.

Leaving my desk, I pulled down the two tops and spent fifteen minutes comparing the tap-tones of each.

The SCGC top is now twenty-eight years old and sounds wonderfully mellow. Over five minutes I convinced myself that I could hear it changing, becoming ever livelier.

The Bourgeois top is twenty years younger. Yet it has the crisp, woody sound, with a strong low end you'd want alongside the musical treble snap of a vintage top. I'm even tempted to ask Dana to turn it into a whole guitar.

It sounds that way, that good, because in 2015 "something" arrived that would be a game changer for contemporary builders trying to achieve the impossible—to create, from new, guitars that sound vintage.

That something is torrefaction: Baking wood, specifically red spruce, at a high temperature in an oxygen-free environment oxidizes it and thereby changes the acoustic signal chain.

Curing it in an oven dries the moisture in the wood. For centuries, craftsmen working with fine timber have stored their wood to let it settle and dry, thus ensuring that the finished piece doesn't twist or crack as it naturally dries out.

Kiln-drying timber over several days rather than air-drying it over months or years oxidizes not just water but any number of naturally occurring volatiles—sugar, oils, pitch. The resulting timber is lighter and stiffer, and because the internal structure of the cells changes, it delivers what back in 2015 the luthier Dana Bourgeois called "aged tone."

Bourgeois was the first high-end luthier to try the new torrefied Adirondack top wood offered by a Canadian timber supplier. He was surprised to find that the oven-baked spruce not only looked older but sounded like old wood. Over the years, Bourgeois experimented with glues and finishes that worked with the new type of tonewood and began offering aged-tone vintage guitars.

But the guitar world is divided on torrefaction. Is artificially speeding up the process of ageing a shortcut too far? Bourgeois is a believer, as is Martin, who offers it on some models. Aged wood is a large component in tone, but if we subscribe to makers like Thompson, Borges, and John Slobod, the magical sound of an old guitar is due only in part to the wood.

But even guitars built with torrefied wood still largely look like new guitars, and there is still appeal in owning a pre-aged guitar that looks like it's lived a life without having to pay $100,000 for the privilege.

Dick Boak, who spent most of his working life at Martin guitars, has a compelling opinion. "Unfortunately, old guitars can be tricky. Hide glue that has dried up can lead to loose braces and warped tops; the pull of heavy strings over decades can leave the action unplayably high. So instead of dealing with a vintage guitar that comes with issues, some consumers have turned to buying factory-fresh instruments that are pre-distressed."

To partially solve the problem—and recognizing that we not only eat with our eyes but listen with our ears—Martin recently introduced "custom ink" to their $3,000 D-28 Street Legend guitar. This process involves effectively screen-printing a photograph of an old Martin vintage top onto a new spruce top.

But rather than superimposing a photo of an aged top, physically adding actual wear marks to pristine, beautifully crafted acoustic guitars involves much more than attacking the instrument with a rotary sander. The wear on most vintage acoustics is subtle, made over the years through a combination of pick wear, sweat erosion, and belt-buckle marks familiar to anyone who regularly plays standing up using a guitar strap—typically bluegrass players.

But it still seems odd, or perhaps plain wrong, to pay a luthier extra money to distress a perfectly made guitar.

One small company that specializes in meeting such challenges is Pre-War

Guitars. Ben Maschal and Wes Lambe started the North Carolina company in 2014 and now work with just a few skilled artisans to contour both the sound and the look of their "new old" prewar instruments. The company primarily looks to recreate the look and sound of Martin guitars made between 1934 and 1941. That's a narrow window, but one from which they believe the best-sounding guitars derive.

They apply the same philosophy as Slobod, Thompson, and Borges, but they go that extra, crazy step to physically distress the finely crafted guitars they produce. Moreover, they believe the distressing adds to the authenticity of the sound.

And, not unlike Fender, they offer different levels of distressing. Every guitar gets torrefied tops and bracing as well as receiving an ultra-thin coat of nitro cellulose lacquer that is artificially "checked" to relieve the stress level of the finish on the top.

From there, the levels move from "New Old Stock" through "Well loved, well played" to "The Road Warrior" and finally to "Awesome," the latter indicating the sort of guitar that vintage enthusiasts dream of finding in an old junk shop in the back of beyond staffed by an old lady who is about to retire.

When I saw bluegrass flat-picking prodigy Molly Tuttle play with Tommy Emmanuel, they both played Pre-Wars, hers a dreadnought. I have no idea if they bought them or were given them, but they sounded authentic.

As of June 2023, Pre-War's Double Aught in mahogany, with a red spruce torrefied top, cost a little over $5,000. That's about what you would pay for a 1960s Martin 00-18 in what Pre-War would call "Road Warrior" condition.

I guess you pays your money and you makes your choice.

In my own guitar travels, I've spoken to many players whose choice has been to move from high-end production brands like Guild, Gibson, and Martin to smaller, low-volume boutique makers like Bourgeois, Collins, Huss & Dalton, and Froggy Bottom. Santa Cruz has developed into a custom maker; Richard Hoover estimates that well over half of his builds are now custom buys. They are spec'd by and destined for the potential owner in collaboration with the Santa Cruz Guitar Company.

When I met with Hoover while first researching this book in late 2015, I asked him why he thought people acquired multiple guitars, especially in the bespoke or custom sector. After all, isn't a bespoke, custom-built instrument the pinnacle, the ultimate, and therefore the last guitar you'll ever need to purchase?

He reminded me, as a Santa Cruz owner, that

the thrill of acquiring the guitar probably overwhelms most other things, even, for some, the actual playing and ownership of the instrument. The guitar-buying experience is 99 percent of what we at Santa Cruz deliver. It's the service we, as primarily a custom shop, give to our customers. For that experience to be meaningful, we understand that there is "the before": discussing the possibilities, finalizing the detailed brief, understanding the choice and selecting tonewood, establishing expectations.

Then there is "the during": continuing and reinforcing the relationship, the customer's ability to call in and to speak to the team here, making that connection with the workshop and our craftsmen, talking through progress, looking at pictures of the developing instrument or physically coming here to look at the build in person. It's also about our recognizing that a customer's questions are not necessarily to get answers but to enable them to be part of the build process.

All of that "before" and "during" makes the final stage, "the arrival," just awesome, a beautiful thing. For many it inspires "that was so good, let's do it again!"

In none of the above is Hoover gainsaying either his continuing passion for guitar making or the quality of what the sixteen professional builders working at SCGC make. Neither is he talking down the importance and joy derived from playing the instrument and the continuing ownership experience. But, in conversations with many collectors and serial acquirers, it is apparent that the "before" and "during" can definitely be the most exciting part of the experience.

I'm lucky enough to own more than a few Santa Cruz guitars. My first was bought back in 1996, straight off the wall from a guitar store in Southern California. It played and sounded like a dream, and at the time I knew nothing about SCGC, just that this was a beautifully made instrument. I bought it blind; there was no "before" or "during," just, in Hoover's terms, the "arrival." My second was a custom-build in 1998 and offered the holy trinity of guitar acquisition. I had the chance to discuss what I wanted in a small-bodied guitar, to select woods, and to understand the possibilities available within what was their standard parlor guitar design. Looking back, the anticipation of the acquisition was incredibly satisfying. I had a variety of conversations as the ten-week build proceeded. And even though I wasn't present, I probably thought every day about how the build was progressing five thousand miles away. The arrival, a few weeks later, was the brilliant culmination of a five-month process.

It certainly inspired in me the response, "That was fun, we must do it again," because in 2000 that's exactly what I did.

Santa Cruz guitars with sought after tonewoods and high levels of decoration regularly sell for sums between $7,000 and $20,000. You would be forgiven for thinking that Hoover and his team must be living the good life. But as I travelled around the United States and Europe meeting guitar makers and owners of multiple guitars, I was encountering a completely new phenomenon—collectors who were seemingly just keen to support the craft of the guitar builder. Every one of them knew that even the very best builders often lived a hand-to-mouth existence.

These buyers weren't all wealthy, modern-day Medicis. Many were just regular players who felt some sense of responsibility to support the craft skills of artisanal guitar making.

One roundtable session at the Fretboard Summit in 2015 included five makers: flat-top builders Richard Hoover, Bill Collings, and Michael Gurian; and archtop builders Steve Grimes and Tom Ribbecke. They each spent time talking about their individual careers and all had one thing in common—what Ribbecke described as the years living with "the terror of having no money or having spent a year building a guitar that just won't sell."

Ribbecke had spent over thirty years making archtop guitars, and only in relatively recent times had he been able to sell every one of the twelve guitars he makes each year for what he thinks is a fair price.

Successful archtop makers today can be counted on the fingers of two hands, but their small market of buyers is prepared to pay eye-watering amounts for what many consider to be the zenith of the guitar maker's craft. Ribbecke now sells some of his Masterpiece models ("unique instruments differentiated by material and thematic detail and made without compromise") for more than $50,000 to clients who may buy a new guitar from him every few years.

He remembered that "for the first seven years we couldn't afford a bed; we slept on a mattress on the floor. When I started in 1972 there was no real market for archtops, but I was stupid enough to carry on. I had guitars that I'd spent hundreds of hours making and no buyers."

Today he reckons it takes him around two hundred hours to produce one of his $20,000 base-model guitars, which, after allowing for costs, still seemed to me a low hourly rate for an artisan craftsman of Ribbecke's caliber.

He looked pained when he told his audience that "I have a graph at home that shows how much I actually made during the first fifteen years of my career. It was like a flatline. Only when I average out all my years building guitars, and take into account the good years, only then do my average lifetime earnings equate to a living wage."

Some weeks later in London, I discussed this imbalance between skill, profile, and the maturity of the builder with Ben Montague and Michael Watts.

Ben runs the North American Guitar, a boutique "salon de guitar" he started in London. A European equivalent of Paul Heumiller's Dream Guitars, it represents a small number of single guitar makers from Europe, South Africa, and the United States and sells instruments to buyers across the globe. His business is now headquartered in Nashville and has acquired both Cotten Guitars and Carter Vintage Guitars. Along with George Gruhn, it is the leading guitar store in "Guitar Town" Tennessee.

But back to when they were a boutique operation in London.

Watts is a talented guitarist and an acclaimed "connoisseur of tone" in the guitar world. He can clearly and precisely articulate both how a guitar plays and describe its tone in ways equaled only by a world-class wine expert describing the bouquet of fine wine. Watts teaches workshops on the finer points of finger-style playing, esoteric subjects like "Finding Your Own Tone" and "Texture, Timbre and Touch." Guitar builders use him as an independent critic on experimental instruments. He also helps them explore what their guitars can do in the hands of a top player.

When we talked about how little money many guitar builders make in a lifetime, both Michael and Ben talked about Jason Kostal, a maker from Phoenix, Arizona. Kostal had employed a different philosophy from the start of his career and appeared to be almost prosperous compared to many makers.

The pair explained that Kostal had apprenticed under Ervin Somogyi, but they believed his prowess as a builder was more than just what he'd learned in his years under the master luthier.

> Jason had a first career in the US military, and like all the makers I've worked with, he brings not just great craft but amazing rigor to the way he works. When you visit his workshop, you notice that there is not a thing out of place. Every tool that he uses gets placed back precisely where it belongs. Every tool is sharpened to a critical edge every time he uses it. Like another maker we represent, Michael Greenfield, he spends a couple of hours at the end of each working day clearing and preparing the workshop so that he can extract the maximum out of the next working day. When he arrives next morning, all is calm, everything is ready and in its place. It sounds fanatical, but both builders find it difficult to operate if they don't have order. And

I think that is reflected in their guitars. In the case of Jason, it also reflects in his lifestyle—he works enormously hard every day he is in his shop but nowadays he has a rich work-life balance, rare in the world of luthiery.

Ben continued,

Because of the way he brought himself into the industry, Jason has been able to command top dollar for the limited number of guitars he makes each year from pretty early in his career. I know he regularly pulls eighteen-hour days, but he is so organized and has such a strong work ethic that he regularly takes a month off to travel, enjoy fine food, and recharge his batteries. When he returns to the workbench, he is hungry to get started again. His meticulously built guitars regularly arrive with our customers ahead of schedule.

Michael played a Jason Kostal modified dreadnought for me. It had a top of German spruce and a body made of a rarified quilted mahogany called simply (or perhaps rather pompously) "the Tree."

I gulped when I saw the price tag, but at that point I didn't know about the provenance of the tonewood.

The Tree was found in the Honduran rainforest in 1965. A huge, hundred-foot-tall mahogany of the genus *Swietenia macrophylla*, the Tree was initially destined for the fine furniture industry. It was felled before the CITES treaty restricted logging in that part of Central America.

Dragging the 350-year-old tree out of the forest proved a logistical challenge for the loggers, and a mishap resulted in the trunk falling deep into a ravine, thereby rendering it irrecoverable for commercial purposes. Ultimately, and no doubt after many tall tales and a lively bidding war, what was becoming a minor legend in the commercial timber world was purchased in situ by a dealer in fine timber. Loggers abseiled into the ravine, and the huge log was sawn crudely on site to allow more manageable pieces to be floated a hundred miles downriver to a steam-powered sawmill for proper dissection. Further inspection revealed that the timber extracted was so wildly and exquisitely figured that the dealer, no doubt with an eye to enhanced profit, dubbed his harvest "the Tree."

One of the first luthiers to obtain some of the finer tortoiseshell-figured timber from the Tree was Richard Hoover of the Santa Cruz Guitar Company. He pronounced the resulting two guitars sounded "more like rare Brazilian rosewood than mahogany"; whereas Brazilian rosewood is regarded as the very best, mahogany tonewood is normally regarded as being at the entry level for fine guitars. Sets of the Tree soon started trading at Brazilian rosewood prices, with the promise of a tone that has "all the woody dryness of mahogany but the top end brilliance and warm bass richness of rosewood." At this point, it's best to not entertain any thought that these differences would be difficult for most mortals to appreciate. Whatever the hyperbole, a holy grail of guitar tonewood had been uncovered, and the Tree had become a celebrity in its own right.

Unsurprisingly, some of the Tree found its way into the workshop of Ervin Somogyi and put into the hands of Jason Kostal, just finishing the third year of his apprenticeship with the mercurial master builder. Kostal was atypical of many of today's builders; he did not start with a background in woodworking or guitar repair but rather with a passion for playing since he was a young man.

After graduating from West Point and serving ten years in US Army Special Operations, Kostal completed his post-Army MBA, heading for a planned career in supply-chain logistics in the corporate world. While he was at graduate school, there had been an informal weekend apprenticeship with a local Atlanta guitar maker that planted in him a deep seed for guitar making. On leaving graduate school and following a year pursuing his corporate career, Kostal decided that it wasn't what he wanted out of life.

Instead of doing "what society wanted [him] to do" and continuing with a financially rewarding but unfulfilling existence, he made the decision to follow his heart. Against all the advice of his friends and parents, he left the world of reason and studied at the Roberto-Venn School of Luthiery, where, after graduation, his talent was recognized and he was asked to stay on as a postgraduate tutor.

Most graduates from Roberto-Venn immediately put their name on the shingle and start the long trek up the mountain of subsistence living that guitar building offers. For Kostal, ten hours teaching basic guitar building at the school each day was followed by nights perfecting building techniques alongside making guitars until two or three in the morning.

Although he now knew how to build a guitar, he sought out an apprenticeship with legendary West Coast builder Ervin Somogyi to "learn to build a world-class guitar." A largely unpaid apprenticeship with Somogyi lasts for three years, and even so a slot is difficult to get. Somogyi sets a final task for those who manage to get through the grueling first stages of the interview process: to build an "exquisite" but small box out of a roughhewn block of wood using only hand tools. "Perfection" is their only brief, and Somogyi gives very few clues as to what that means. It is a Zen-like test that apparently most fail.

As I played the modified dreadnought that Kostal built for Michael Watts, I bore in mind that this guitar was built while Kostal was technically still an apprentice under Somogyi. I wondered what quality of guitar he was building five years later. The Kostal guitar built using the Tree was a thing of visual and sonic beauty, although Watts was keen to stress that even though his guitar was made from a piece of wood known as much for its visual appeal as its aural qualities, "the specifications for my guitar were purely sonic rather than aesthetic." Watts reiterated that Kostal had built the instrument while still technically learning how to make a guitar "by taking as much time as necessary to do it perfectly."

• • • • • •

Many guitar commentators agreed that by 2015 we were living in "a new golden age of acoustic luthiery."

The venerable Martin was, according to George Gruhn, "once again making some of the best guitars of their almost two-hundred-year history." Chris Martin was still chairman and CEO, but would soon step down from the day-to-day. Gibson, while still experiencing a merry-go-round of ownership and management, was, after many years, making some consistently good guitars.

The small pantheon of low-volume boutique makers, such as Bourgeois, SCGC, Collings, and Froggy Bottom, were undoubtedly making some of the finest acoustic guitars we have ever seen. Makers like John Slobod and Dale Fairbanks were reimagining Martin and Gibson vintage creations to a level unimaginable even a decade earlier. There were also more talented single luthiers producing outstanding one-off instruments, providing you had $10–15,000 in your pocket.

Over the past thirty years virtually all the guitars I've acquired have been made in the United States by American builders who are, hopefully, earning a fair wage. But I realize I'm lucky to be able to afford to buy that level of quality.

I say "virtually all," because in the early 1990s, I looked at a small-bodied Englemann spruce and mahogany 00 guitar made in collaboration between the US-owned brand Recording King and Eric Schoenberg (the co-creator, with Dana Bourgeois, of the Schoenberg OM Soloist). All Recording King guitars are manufactured in the Far East, and this model sold for around $1,000 versus the $6,000 or more for an original US-made Schoenberg Soloist. After much consideration, I didn't buy that guitar, but in 2015 I did purchase a Recording King RP16-C made in China. What swung it was that this model had a torrefied Adirondack red spruce top with mahogany back and sides and cost $499. It sounded great, played great, looked great.

I never liked the idea of buying guitars made in the factories of the Far East, but Recording King guitars all seemed extremely well made, regardless of the price.

So perhaps it's surprising that one of the most interesting instruments I acquired during this period was a Gretsch G9500 Jim Dandy flat-top, purchased brand new in 2013 for just $200 (£175). I bought it untried by mail-order from a German online retailer. I was spending a couple of weeks at a friend's house in France, and I didn't want to take a "good guitar" on and off planes or run the risk of it being left in the sun or picked up by visiting children or pets.

The Jim Dandy was based on a range of guitars the original Friedrich Gretsch company marketed in the 1920s under the Rex brand. They were built in the Kay factory in Chicago and distributed across America via the Sears and Montgomery Ward catalogs. My new Asian-built, small-bodied Gretsch was delivered by the French postal service the day after I arrived in France. The label inside said it was made in Indonesia, and it was even in tune when I pulled it out of the plastic bag it had left the factory in.

It played well and had an acceptable sound; in fact, it sounded authentically woody, despite much of it being made out of what looked like birch plywood. The frets were well finished, the tuners were basic but accurate. It was easy to play.

What's not to like? I got a great little guitar. Although I did wonder what a guitar factory in Indonesia that turns out $200 guitars this good looked like or how it operated. I also started to consider who gets paid or makes what out of a $200 guitar.

Dealers usually expect to receive 50 percent of the sales price as profit. The importer probably wants around 20 percent, with 10 percent usually going to shipping and distribution. Which meant my Gretsch Jim Dandy left the factory in Indonesia probably costing the manufacturer no more than $60. Most manufacturers expect 50 percent margin, so I shuddered to think what the workers got paid for making a guitar. After a bit of digging, I discovered that the biggest guitar manufacturer in the world today, making about 30 percent of all guitars sold globally, is the South Korean company Cor-Tek, whose manufacturing plants were originally in Korea, then expanded into China, before another massive expansion into Indonesia, where no doubt wages were lower. It seems that Indonesia is likely to be Cor-Tek's main production base in the future and therefore the world's largest production center for guitars. They make some incredible guitars, especially the electrics they produce for brands like PRS, Fender, G&L and the maker's own brand, Cort.

If my little Gretsch or 00 Recording King had been my first beginner's guitar, I would have been delighted to start playing either rather than my original, heavy-weight Eko Ranger. Access to guitars with easy action and fine sound has to be good news for the industry and music lovers. As long as the makers are being paid a fair wage.

Taylor Swift playing a Taylor GS6 Grand Symphony and Ed Sheeran playing a Martin LX1 "Little Martin."

The Acoustic Guitar, Taylor's Version

Ask a grade school child to draw you a picture of a "country singer," and chances are you'll get a white man in a cowboy hat playing a big old acoustic guitar. The six-string flat-top guitar has been synonymous with country music from its earliest days—at least since the 1930s when Mother Maybelle and the Carter Family had sold seven hundred thousand records and ruled the radio airwaves, to today when modern stars like Luke Combs strut their version of the genre and achieve digital streams in the multimillions. Thanks largely to radio shows like *National Barn Dance* and its successor, the *Grand Ole Opry*, country was for a good while America's most popular music. Today it runs a close third to rock and pop, but it's still big and growing in popularity. In 2023, country music tunes were streamed 20 billion times, an increase of 23.7 percent on the previous year. It also has proved to have global reach. In the spring of 2024, pop diva Beyoncé released her country album, *Cowboy Carter*, which garnered 76 million streams globally on its first day alone.

But from much of my research in and around the history of country music in all its various manifestations over the last eleven decades, it seems that female artists and African American musicians in particular have often had a difficult relationship with country music and the country music establishment—the primarily white, conservative males who run the Opry, the CMA, the major country music publishers and record labels, and the country music charts and radio station playlists that both power and shape the country music business.

By contrast, the business of pop and rock music has always been driven largely by individual entrepreneurs whose primary aim is to monetize the creativity of the artists they represent. From legendary manager-negotiators like Albert Grossman to record company moguls Ahmet Ertegun, Berry Gordy, or David Geffen, they made millions managing and producing many of the fickle creative geniuses of the music industry. They were all largely independents, whereas country music, more than any other genre, is still an intensely close-knit, often incestuous industry in cahoots with itself. While country is now a global business, it is still largely headquartered in Nashville.

Nashville decided what country music sounded like and looked like.

In the first two decades of the *Grand Ole Opry*, from 1925 to 1945, of the eighty-seven solo performers regularly featured, only 13 percent were women. This set a precedent for the following decades: a study conducted by Jada Watson at the University of Ottawa found that female artists accounted for only 16 percent of the top songs played by country radio between 2000 and 2018.

In 1955, fourteen-year-old country and proto-rockabilly singer Wanda Jackson took the stage at the Ryman Auditorium for the first time wearing a dress that revealed her arms and bare shoulders. She was instructed to replace the outfit with a long-sleeve, floral, prairie-homestead dress in the style that the *Grand Ole Opry* management preferred to see female singers wear.

When the *Opry* started broadcasting in the 1920s, its opening signature music was a lively harmonica piece. The virtuoso playing was by DeFord Bailey, introduced as the "Harmonica Wizard" by the show's founder and regular MC, "Judge" George Hay. Although he was one of the founding performers and an audience favorite, Bailey was fired in 1941, long before most listeners knew he was a Black musician. It would not be until 1967 that singer-guitarist Charley Pride would become the next Black singer to appear on the Opry stage. Ray Charles released his groundbreaking LP *Modern Sounds in Country and Western Music* in 1962, but it received minimal airplay on country radio stations until Charles's cover of Don Gibson's "I Can't Stop Loving You" got to the top of the charts and stayed there for over a month.

In 1969, Linda Martell became the first Black female solo singer to appear on the *Opry*.

In 2014, singer and guitarist Darius Rucker, formerly lead singer and guitarist for Hootie and the Blowfish, would join DeFord Bailey and Charley Pride to become only the third African American inductee into the Grand Ole Opry Hall of Fame.

Despite the contributions of many Black musicians to the roots genres that evolved into country music—hillbilly, old-time, and early blues—Black players and their innovations have been excluded by the genre's many gatekeepers. In her book *Black Country Music* (2022), Francesca Royster writes in terms of the "controlled visibility" of Black artists in the world of mainstream country.

In 2019, a controversy arose that helped break through this gate, at least a little. The rapper Lil Nas X, then twenty-two, released his song "Old Town Road," which in his own words was "country rap," unmistakably including elements of both genres. Originally self-released in a two-minute version, it hit number 16 on the Billboard Country Top 100 before Billboard removed it from the country charts. It offered the excuse that it "did not have enough elements of today's country music." Billy Ray Cyrus then sang vocals on an extended cut, which mentioned horses, tractors, back porches, bull riding, backroads, "geetars," and enough horse tack to float a rodeo, but even then it was not reinstated to the country charts. It did however spend a record-breaking nineteen weeks at number one on the Billboard Hot 100 chart.

The song opens with an instrumental hook that sounds like a cross between a banjo and an acoustic guitar, immediately grounding the listener on the back porch of an old country shack. It is, in fact, a studio-manipulated sample of an obscure Nine Inch Nails guitar riff.

When Beyoncé made her own push against the country music gatekeepers in February 2024, it surprised no one that she was going to do it her way. Nor would she be told that it was inauthentic. The first single she released was "Texas Hold 'Em," which enlisted old-time banjo superstar Rhiannon Giddens to play the opening riff on a gut-string banjo, about as authentic to country's musical roots as it gets. Giddens's credentials include her work with the Carolina Chocolate Drops and with the group Our Native Daughters, whose album *Songs of Our Native Daughters* (2019) was released on Smithsonian Folkways.

Given what had happened with "Old Town Road," it's unsurprising that not many hours after the digital release of "Texas Hold 'Em," stories were flying around the internet that numerous country radio stations in the American South had banned the record. Everyone, including those applauding the ban and those against it, was outraged. Like many internet tempests, the story was inaccurate. In reality, one radio station out of Oklahoma had emailed a listener after they had asked if the station would play the song on their request show. The response was: "Hi, we do not play Beyoncé on KYKC as we are a country music station. Thank you." Maybe the station could be criticized for not being up-to-the-minute; after all, this was only Beyoncé's second country release, after "Daddy Lessons," a hit in 2016. That track featured the Chicks (who as the Dixie Chicks had been banned by a fair number of country radio stations themselves), so perhaps she was on somebody's watchlist as a provocateur.

Cowboy Carter is an authentic sounding and hugely successful example of country music's possibilities. It received eleven nominations at the 67th Annual Grammy Awards and won best country album and overall album of the year. It can only be a positive step for country music that an artist like Beyoncé is proud to play music celebrating her own Texas roots, following decades in which Black artists were unwelcome to participate in country music, despite having played such a pivotal role in its development. Regardless of the global success of both the single and the album, the CMA chose not to nominate either at the 2024 awards. Beyoncé herself declared "this a Beyoncé album not a country album." The exclusion was and is controversial.

Hopefully, one day, when another grade schooler is asked to draw a simple picture of a "country singer," we'll get a drawing of a Black artist in a Gucci cowboy hat playing their acoustic guitar while riding a white horse. This would be a great thing, not least because music styles that don't change tend to die.

• • • • • •

In completing this, the final chapter of this book, I was torn between looking back over nearly two hundred years of American guitar making or looking into the future and trying to predict where the American flat-top guitar will find itself as the new millennium rolls on. Will it face a precarious or prosperous time? Does acoustic-guitar-led music itself have a future? Will we be playing the same sort of flat-top guitars thirty or forty years from now?

As I assembled my thoughts, I came across two articles about Joni Mitchell in my newspaper. The first was a review of a CD: *Joni Mitchell at Newport*

(2023), a live recording of her surprise appearance at the Newport Folk Festival in 2022. It was a larger scale, public version of the "Joni Jams" that her friend Brandi Carlisle had been curating at Mitchell's Los Angeles home since 2020.

Carlisle recounted that Mitchell, still recovering from the brain aneurysm she suffered in 2015, announced to her over dinner that "there was something missing in her life that she eagerly wanted to bring back." She said that she could handle the fact that she didn't play music anymore, but she did regret that no music was being made in her house these days "with all these old instruments and these dulcimers and these great guitars." Mitchell suggested that Carlisle invite some of her own musician friends to come and jam. Friends like Hozier, Chaka Khan, and Marcus Mumford arrived. Mitchell's own friends heard about the nights, so Paul McCartney, Elton John, and Herbie Hancock dropped by too.

Mitchell had last played Newport Folk Festival in 1967 as a relative unknown. On the Newport stage that night in July 2022, Carlisle recreated a version of Mitchell's LA sitting room, setting the stage with couches and lamps and some of the people who had come to the house over the previous two years . . . Carlisle of course, but also Marcus Mumford, Celisse Henderson, and others. It's a joyous listen, Joni's now alto voice chiming with those of her friends/fans.

The second article was a review of a Joni Mitchell concert at the Gorge Amphitheatre in rural Washington State. In her first headline show in twenty-three years, she played alongside her "Joni Jam" friends to an adoring audience of 27,000.

I had last *seen* Mitchell when she was just about well enough to attend Joni 75, a tribute concert held in 2018, back when friends and old lovers sang their own versions of her remarkable back catalogue, many written on her guitar, often in her own unique tunings. As I watched that broadcast, I thought that was probably the last shout for a musician whose music I had lived with and loved all my adult life. I had even prepared myself for Mitchell's passing a few years back. I asked my family if they might go out for the day when she passes so that I could sit alone, play every one of my collection of original Joni vinyl, and wallow in the tears. But despite having to learn to talk, walk, and play guitar again, there appears to be a new energy in the maestro.

By coincidence, a few weeks after seeing the CD review and having now drafted multiple versions of this final chapter, I saw the front cover of a magazine with a picture of a teenage Paul Simon holding a guitar. It was taken in 1957, when Simon would have been sixteen, around the time he and Garfunkel released their first single, "Hey Schoolgirl," under the name Tom and Jerry. The headline was "My Generation's Time Is Up." Simon, no longer "the only living boy in New York," is now an octogenarian, living, in part due to a partial hearing loss, with the sound of silence on his Texas ranch. In the article, he reflects on the recent passing of fellow '60s Greenwich Village troubadour Gordon Lightfoot and British rock guitarist Jeff Beck. His conclusion: "My generation's time is up."

Simon had just released the album *Seven Psalms* (2023). It contains some interesting stuff, but we would be very fortunate if he were writing the equal of what he produced in the 1960s: "The Sound of Silence," "Homeward Bound," and "America"; in the 1970s: "Bridge over Troubled Water," "The Boxer," "50 Ways to Leave Your Lover," and "Still Crazy After All These Years"; or the sort of work that led his 1986 album *Graceland* to sell 16 million copies. Maybe he can't put his guitar away. Perhaps he has to keep writing to stay sane. Maybe he has more to say. Unlike Mitchell, who seems genuinely delighted to reimagine her old songs and to perform them, Simon dreads a return to live performance. He fears becoming "a Paul Simon cover band" and scolds himself to "get off the road and go home." I would want to hear him sing the old songs again, but only if *he* wants to.

My love of the guitar has always drawn me to singer-songwriters like Mitchell and Simon as well as to folk, bluegrass, country-blues, and Americana artists. That love of the acoustic guitar, and the music it best lends itself to, has led me to continue listening to the music from my youth, often music liked by a minority. Since the heyday of acoustic-based music in the late 1960s and early '70s, acoustic artists have not had the mass appeal of other styles. But I have always tried to keep in tune with the new material the acoustic guitar inspires.

Even the most successful and talented singer-songwriters and folk performers have enjoyed only modest record sales compared to pop and rock performers. Mainstream country and western artists, playing what was once the most popular genre of music on American radio, now tend to be confined to smaller concert halls when they tour, with only the most successful stars filling arenas. But in recent years, two singer-songwriters have changed that. America's Taylor Swift and England's Ed Sheeran have both recently enjoyed global stadium tours that put them in front of millions of their fans.

Starting in 2023, Swift's Eras tour covered five continents and exceeded 150 shows. Just the initial US leg of the tour, with fifty-three shows, ranked as the highest-grossing tour ever for a female artist. Multiple teams of riggers and sound engineers and an assorted army of support staff prebuilt, loaded in, and loaded out the three identical and lavishly expansive sets that these shows demanded. Each stadium show saw Swift dive into and swim under what appeared to be a glass-topped stage. Designing, building, and transporting all of this for the first fifty US dates of a tour that the *New Yorker* described as "megaspectacles, simultaneously intimate and colossal," cost an estimated $100 million. Each show lasted more than three and a half hours, during which time the thirty-five-year-old Swift performed over forty songs, covering the different eras of her ten-album studio career. Alongside the live shows and filmed over three nights at the beginning of the tour, *Taylor Swift: The Eras Tour* looks set to be the highest-grossing concert movie ever.

Swift was back in London in August 2024 playing to a capacity crowd of 90,000 at Wembley Stadium. This, her 131st show of the two-year tour, closed out her European leg, making Eras the biggest tour of all time (gross earnings exceed $2 billion). The highlight of every show is Swift's closing acoustic set. The shows featured Ed Sheeran and her songwriting partner Jack Antonoff playing a guitar-backed medley and her trademark surprise songs.

Swift turned semiprofessional at fourteen as a Nashville-based country singer-songwriter. Having come to the notice of Bob Taylor of Taylor Guitars (she still plays her personal diamanté-encrusted Taylor Grand Auditorium model onstage), Swift spent a few years appearing as an unknown at Taylor Guitar town hall meetings and factory get-togethers before progressing to entertaining Taylor Guitar dealers at NAMM shows in the early 2000s. In 2005, at sixteen, she signed with Big Machine Records. At twenty-four, she had become a multigenre, tent-pole global artist. Her act was no longer pure country but a country-flavored "singer-songwriter" amalgam, with heavy hints of rock, electronica, and pop. Not the sort of music Hank Williams would recognize as country, but I would bet he'd raise a shaky glass to her undoubted talent, tenacity, and hard-won success. She has achieved that rarest of feats—becoming a genuine crossover artist from niche country to mainstream pop.

Amid her journey, the *New York Times* had criticized her for becoming a "too-cool-for-country" pop star. But, as if in reply, she spent the pandemic lockdown (which began around April 2020) producing a pair of raw-edged, alt-country albums, *Folklore* and *Evermore*. The albums, both collaborations with indie-rock writer-producer Aaron Dessner, featured guest appearances by alt-country artists Bon Iver, the National, and Haim and embraced indie-folk, new-country, and a broad smattering of fingerpicked acoustic guitar. Some of the material brought her full circle, almost back to the fiddle-and-banjo backed yearning teen-romance angst sound of her 2006 debut single, "Tim McGraw." Like what she does or not, industry experts estimate that when the Eras tour is over in late 2024, her net earnings will have been in excess of $1 billion.

Ed Sheeran started his career around the same time as Swift, but in rural Suffolk as a folksy teenage street busker. At some point in autumn 2004, when he was thirteen, he saw Scottish female singer KT Tunstall perform "Black Horse and the Cherry Tree" with an acoustic guitar, a headless tambourine, and a $100 looper pedal on Jools Holland's weekly late-night music show on British TV.

Tunstall was herself a last-minute fill-in when the original act had dropped out twenty-four hours before the broadcast. The next day, one lone female guitarist with a Gibson Dove copy, using a basic Akai loop pedal, built up layers of percussion, guitar slap, and vocals to wow the studio audience and the half million watching on TV. She was "a whole one-woman band in a box." Tunstall was herself influenced by 1970s folk-trip guitarist John Martyn's use of an Echoplex analog delay/loop machine to build layers of music during live shows. Martyn's 1970s setup was crude by comparison to a modern loop pedal board—a Martin D-28 rigged with two pickups and a tangle of cables and pedals. But it also wowed his small coterie of fans and at some point caught the attention of Tunstall, then fifteen, for her to make her updated version the center of her debut TV appearance in 2004.

Sheeran, equally inspired by what was possible for a solo acoustic guitarist with a basic loop pedal, and in an attempt to find an audience, took his three-quarter-sized Martin travel guitar, now with a more advanced loop pedal and a battery-powered amp, from the street into coffee shops, folk clubs, soul and R&B clubs, and finally to hip-hop nights in rooms above pubs. When he reached London, he formed an unlikely friendship with Jamal Edwards, a young entrepreneur using his underground SBTV YouTube channel to break lots of young UK rappers, hip-hop, and grime artists by giving them a voice when traditional media ignored them. With Jamal's continued support, and now sleeping on his sofa, Sheeran started to get noticed. With Jamal's help, he built a young insider audience. By collaborating with edgy underground rappers, he became the young, geeky, ginger-haired kid still playing a mini-guitar but now with friends in low and high places. A record label and a manager soon found him. He carried on working six nights a week in increasingly bigger clubs and then halls while still making quick, on-the-fly videos for SBTV on YouTube. In 2011, he released "The A Team," the song that broke him to a mass audience.

By 2014, Sheeran and Swift were collaborators and firm friends. He first supported her on the US leg of the RED Tour. A European leg followed, including five nights in London at the 15,000-capacity O2 Arena, where she pulled him up onstage. Half the audience already knew him, and the words to all his songs. He was by now also a strong multigenre writer and performer, except that he had made a habit of regularly collaborating with well-regarded artists, whether pop, hip-hop, rock, drum 'n' bass, reggaetón, afrobeats, Latin-rap, and even controversial subgenres like grime and drill. In 2019, he set up a studio in a rented house in Nashville. As artists he admired, regardless of genre, came through Guitar Town, he would, in his own words, "Hit them up and they would come to the house. We'd make a song, and the record [*No.6 Collaborations Project* (2019)] was made over the course of three months, with lots of people I like."

Cuban American star Camila Cabello actually looked him up first, and they wrote and recorded "Bam Bam" (2022), an atypical break-up song. The subsequent video features Sheeran playing an acoustic. For all the Latino beats and slick production, the song was clearly carved out on Sheeran's guitar before transforming into a Latin-pop hit.

Since the late 2010s, Sheeran has dominated the UK music industry as the nation's most played artist. From a different route, he was at one point almost as big as Swift globally. However, except for the presence of an acoustic guitar, his tour persona and live show modus operandi couldn't be more different. His stadium tours are acoustic-guitar led, still him with his small travel guitar, currently the Sheeran signature model from Irish luthier George Lowden, hooked through a loop station. He usually appears onstage in a pair of jeans, trainers, and a lumberjack shirt, perhaps a nod to Rory Gallagher. No fancy costumes. No dancers. No fireworks or swimming pools. Only relatively recently has he added a couple of backing singers—I guess to give his voice a little help in his long solo sets. When in 2017 he headlined Glastonbury, one of the world's largest open-air music festivals, it was still with what was effectively his standard acoustic guitar and loop pedal setup. One man, one guitar, and a few pedals played for two hours in front of a live crowd of 90,000 and a digital streamed audience of over 30 million.

It just goes to show that even today a young kid with an acoustic guitar plus boundless talent and drive can make it.

Sheeran and Swift still have a lot in common. They have both been criticized for moving away from their singer-songwriter roots. They both can write a good hook and play a flat-top acoustic reasonably well. They are both at their core smart, hardworking, prolifically creative, genre-busting, fiercely independent, highly protective of their work, and, obviously, relentless tourers.

Despite annually outselling most other artists in album sales and digital streams, they know their fame is likely to be transitory and that they need to enjoy it and exploit it while they can. They also understand the economics of the music business. Back in the '60s, '70s, and '80s, artists like Paul Simon and Joni Mitchell toured primarily to promote their current album and generate record sales. They made little money from touring; it was all about visibility and promotion. They went on the road when they had new product to sell, usually every other year. Today, with revenue from physical sales disappearing and royalties from streams sparse, unless your buying audience is massive, the real money is in touring. Albums and digital single releases sustain the fan base between tours, keeping them interested and in lock-step with the artist's evolution. When the tour comes to town, or to the stadium or arena nearest to them, fans are prepared to unlock their piggy banks to pay hundreds of dollars to worship at the altar . . . and buy a T-shirt or two on the way home.

But you don't have to move away from your roots to find an audience.

In 2022, the thirty-year-old Grammy Award–winning bluegrass guitarist Billy Strings played his first proper gig outside of the United States. It was in the Islington Assembly Rooms, a 1930s art deco theatre in North London. As I waited in line for the doors to open and mingled with the expectant crowd, what surprised me was that it felt like at least half the capacity crowd of around nine hundred were American. London has a big resident American community, but it seemed most people I spoke with had flown over from America especially to see Strings. He played just two nights at the one venue, and most people had been to the previous evening's show. One fan from Billy's home state of Michigan told me Billy plays about a hundred gigs across America every year—and he had seen him over twenty times.

Taylor Swift has her Swifties: über fans who follow her around and effectively "collect" shows. These fans spend small fortunes seeing her as often as funds allow—I guess the reason she bothers to make every show unique. Billy Strings has his "Goats" (a play on billy goat), who appear to do the same. As I talked to a few Goats before Billy's second Islington show, it was apparent that many had seen the thirty-something many times.

When the house lights dimmed, all of us, including the Goats, went quiet.

Billy walked onstage with a brand-new Preston Thompson dreadnought strapped across his shoulders. It looked like one of the boutique Oregon maker's rare DBA-45s, its dark Brazilian and sunburst Adirondack top competing with a lot of abalone inlay. The audience cheered as they recognized the first few notes of "Turmoil & Tinfoil." They all knew the words, relating to String's troubled youth and the struggles with opioid addition he and his family endured. They all joined in with "Springtime is coming to the mountains," the opening words of Ralph Stanley's version of the old spiritual "A Robin Built a Nest on Daddy's Grave." The same happened with Jimmy Driftwood's "Tennessee Stud." They cheered the opening notes of "Little Maggie," standing spellbound at Strings's perfect high-speed cross-picking. But when the band segued into a medley that blended classic bluegrass songs with snatches of Pink Floyd and Hendrix before cutting back to Doc Watson, the crowd erupted. Strings played Watson's trademark sixteen-bar solos note for note, although if anything he was faster than even Watson's usual blistering speed. I don't think I've seen anyone play as fast, clean, and crisp in a live setting. When he returned to the familiar chord progression, the crowd proceeded to pogo, two-step, and generally jig around, as they did through most of the whole two-hour set.

The prancing and dancing surprised me a little. I had seen String's bluegrass contemporary Molly Tuttle play, this time to a more reverential bluegrass audience. I had expected a similarly older and sober audience here to see a master guitar player. But Strings's audience was there to see their hero and hear good music but most of all have a good time. With which I had no complaint. I was delighted to see bluegrass enjoyed in the present rather than worshipped as something from the past.

Not long before he died in 2016, old-time singer and banjo player Ralph Stanley had enjoyed newfound popularity following the 2000 release of the Coen Brothers film *O Brother, Where Art Thou?* with its bluegrass and old-time soundtrack. Stanley's classic a cappella version of "O Death" gave him his biggest audience ever. It lured him back on the road with the Clinch Mountain Boys, touring America's many bluegrass festivals. Around that time, he was interviewed about the newfound popularity of old-time mountain and bluegrass music. Did he think it was a transitory surge in interest? "It's like 'Old Joe Clark,' that old fiddle tune. It was here yesterday, it'll be here tomorrow. These [recent] big hits'll be gone tomorrow. Garth Brooks—you'll never know he existed in forty-eight years. I've been in the business for forty-eight years. I don't know why it is they make more in a month than bluegrass will in ten years. Don't have to last, I guess."

If the popularity of young flat-pickers like Billy Strings and Molly Tuttle and the tunes they choose to play today is anything to go by, it looks like Ralph

Stanley is right. His songs were "here yesterday" and will almost certainly be "here tomorrow."

There seems to be a fresh resurgence in the "yesterday sound" of string-band music beyond bluegrass. Guitar maker John Slobod is noticing an increase in demand not just for the bluegrassers' favorite dreadnoughts but also for smaller-bodied guitars being used by duos like the Milk Carton Kids and intimate string-band ensembles like Nickel Creek.

The members of Nickel Creek were just teenagers in 2000 when they brought out their eponymous debut album, merging bluegrass with other musical styles alongside their own compositions. The record sold in the millions, and the band won a similar number of fans, making bluegrass younger and cooler than it had been for decades.

But Chris Thile, the superstar mandolin player of the trio, put Nickel Creek on hiatus in 2006 to "pursue other projects." In interviews, he cited the pursuit by "the bluegrass police" as the driver for the breakup. Nearly twenty years later, Nickel Creek has finally returned with an even more distant exploration of bluegrass that may cause even more police interest.

In the interim, one of Thile's earliest "other projects" was to form the Punch Brothers, a five-piece string band made up of fiddle, banjo, guitar, mandolin, and upright bass. Their music was described as showing "bluegrass instrumentation and spontaneity in the strictures of modern classics" as well as "American country-classical chamber music."

The quintet toured extensively, and when they came to play Glasgow, Scotland, they had their own Judas moment (shades of Dylan at Newport). Someone in the audience yelled out, "Oh, play some bluegrass, fi' Christ's sake!"

It seems younger bluegrass audiences are happy to hear unlikely covers of songs they and the band grew up with. The Punch Brothers regularly included Radiohead's "Morning Bell" in their live set and a version of the Strokes' "Heart in a Cage" appeared on their second album. Not everyone liked it, seeing it as some kind of betrayal. Another Judas moment. But in the age of social media, it was more than a voice from the darkness of a concert hall. The fan forums reached boiling point over the material they were playing. Contributors to one thread went ballistic over the inclusion of a swear word in a song the band didn't even author.

And I can see how too free an attitude over what is or isn't bluegrass, folk, or country is likely to rile traditionalists. Sadly, when fans latch on to a musician, they often want more of what first attracted them. Neil Young has regularly made it clear that first and foremost he writes music to please himself, material that satisfies his own definition of good. The fans are welcome to come along, but on his terms.

Creative souls are restless. And they need the right tools to inspire their creativity. For musicians with a leaning toward old-time tunes, songs that were first popular in the 1920s and '30s, they naturally lean toward the banjo, mandolin, and acoustic guitar to reflect a time when these instruments were all you needed to make that kind of music.

And so it is today, and probably tomorrow, when players like Swift, Sheeran, Strings, or Tuttle set out to create music that will comfort or cheer us and even experiment and create new sounds, they do what countless musicians for the past 150 years have done. They will hopefully still grab that most accessible of instruments, the steel-string flat-top acoustic guitar.

• • • • • •

Pinned to the wall by my writing table is a passage from John Steinbeck's *The Grapes of Wrath*. A guitarist has been playing, mesmerizing a crowd of Okie migrants on their way to California. His music draws the group together, comforts them as darkness falls and sleep beckons. At dawn they will continue their long journey into the unknown.

> And after a while the man with the guitar stood up and yawned.
> Good night, folks, he said.
> And they murmured, Good night to you.
> And each wished he could pick a guitar, because it is a gracious thing.

Picking a 1934 National Trojan.

Gratitude and Acknowledgments

I started writing my first book about the guitar, *The Devil Is in It*, in the late summer of 2014, sitting in a harbor-side cafe on the small Greek island of Symi.

Using a small school exercise book and a cheap pencil bought from a local hardware store, I imagined that a brief book describing the process of commissioning the crafting of a hand-built guitar would be completed within a few months. Five years later, researching and writing the book seemed to have become a constant in my life, occupying all my spare time and interrupting every family meal and conversation.

The eventual scope and scale of *The Devil Is in It* and the original hand-bound edition of five hundred books meant that I had leaned very heavily on the patience of my family and a collection of friends and guitar enthusiasts and experts. Without the support of these individuals, completing the endeavor would not have been possible.

So, initially I must thank again:

Those who helped me with the original research, including George Gruhn of Gruhn Guitars, Nashville; Greg Johnson of the University of Mississippi Blues Archive; Joe Spann, an expert on the history of early Gibson guitars; Greig Hutton, a specialist researcher and scholar on the history of Martin guitars; and Jim Bollman, an authority on the history of the banjo in America.

I want to thank those who were generous with their time in speaking with me, often repeatedly and at great length (the most generous often being the busiest people!). These include the guitar maker Jason Kostal; Ben Montague and his team at the North American Guitar, London; the guitarist Michael Watts; Richard Hoover and his team at the Santa Cruz Guitar Company;

Andy Powers of Taylor Guitars; the late Bill Collings; Eric Schoenberg; Matt Umanov; the late Bill Luckett, civil rights attorney, co-owner of the Ground Zero Blues Club, and former mayor of Clarksdale, Mississippi; and the family of the late Stan Jay of Mandolin Brothers. I especially thank Dick Boak, formerly of Martin guitars, for his time and for allowing me access to Martin's extensive archive and photo library.

This new edition of the book is largely thanks to Robert Devens, my editor and the director of the University of Texas Press. I had not initially realized back in 2023 that Robert was not only passionate about guitars but had, back in 2020, acquired one of the first collector's editions of my original, independently published book. Having finally connected, we jointly conceived the idea of a revised, more accessible version of *The Devil Is in It* focused on what had been the backbone of the original book, the sizeable history section, expanded here to the present day. He has been a patient, insightful, and always encouraging collaborator and guide.

Having completed a much-revised manuscript, I am also grateful to Jason Mellard and the anonymous peer reviewer, who together further challenged me to dig even deeper into more research sources to make this new edition broader in both scope and detail.

These revisions and additions, which have taken the best part of a year, could not have been completed without the help of my son Jeremy, who has not only been my eyes and typing fingers; he's also been a researcher and has helped me to untangle my grammar and has also brought the crucial perspective of a younger generation to key parts of the story.

I also thank the extremely talented illustrator Drew Christie for his time and generosity in providing the illustrations for the original book plus two new creations for this edition. His original pen-and-ink portrait of C. F. Martin has been pinned above my desk since the start of this project.

Finally, I will always be in debt to those friends who got me started. Those who read early drafts of the original book; encouraged me to include certain topics and pleaded that I delete or abbreviate others; asked intelligent questions; spurred me to sharpen my thinking and often helped sort order out of chaos. In particular, I thank Andrew Cracknell, who not only sailed me to that small harbor in Symi but who inspired me to get out from behind my desk, venture across and around America, and seek out and talk in person to guitar players, makers, retailers, and enthusiasts. And lastly, to my daughter Olivia for her untiring support, and to my wife Lynda, who has both figuratively and literally held my hand for the last forty-five years.

A Note on the Sources

When I first started my research for this book, I turned to the guitar and music books that fill the bookshelves and much of the floor space of my writing room. I surprised myself to discover that over the years I've been playing acoustic guitar, I had acquired over 150 titles about guitars; the people who made them and played them; and the music they helped create.

However, the start point for my research was a book I bought in the early 1980s, after I began to develop a passion for the guitar in all its forms.

Tom and Mary Evans's *Guitars: From the Renaissance to Rock*, while now nearly fifty years old, remains one of the few books that treat the guitar, regardless of form, as a totality. The book's own extensive bibliography still provides an excellent resource for anyone wanting to read deeper into the style, construction, music, and social history of all types of guitars, from classical, flamenco, and acoustic flat-top to the electric instrument. The Evanses, working well before the internet was even imagined, supplemented their clearly extensive book-based research with numerous interviews with a wide range of notable makers, players, and music experts.

A decade after the Evans's book was published, two Nashville-based vintage guitar collectors and dealers began systematically commissioning archival-quality photographs of notable guitars. Across the following five years, they had obtained access to an unrivalled collection of vintage guitars and associated fretted instruments—including mandolins, ukuleles, and banjos. Their initial objective was to "collect and preserve" on film what were already rare instruments.

Their final collection of photographs could have filled several books, but in

1993, the best were selected and made into *Acoustic Guitars and Other Fretted Instruments: A Photographic History*. At first glance, it could be mistaken for what has become known as "guitar porn"—an almost random collection of fabulous guitar photographs assembled into a glossy coffee-table book. But George Gruhn and Walter Carter's book is in many ways a photographic companion to the Evanses' seminal book. Equally well written but shorter than that created by the Evanses, its original color photographs are meticulously and thoughtfully curated and allow readers to get as close as most of us are ever likely to get to the rarest and most significant guitars of the previous 150 years. It also tells not just the story of the evolution of the guitar but also of the many inventions and developments behind that evolution.

Together, the two books discussed above contain everything most casual guitar enthusiasts would need to know about the development of the modern guitar. However, if, as is likely, that enthusiast is also a guitarist, they are more than likely to play the most ubiquitous of guitars, the steel-string flat-top acoustic. Furthermore, the information gleaned from the two books would inevitably lead them to realize that the modern acoustic flat-top, while bearing a passing resemblance to the European classical guitar, is largely an American invention. They would also quickly realize that the German luthier C. F. Martin, and the company he founded in New York in 1833, would pioneer and ultimately dominate the development of the flat-top to the present day.

In 2003 Philip Gura published *C. F. Martin and His Guitars, 1796–1893*. While the Martin brand and company were well known, very little was known about its founder and the early days of the Martin company. Gura's access to the company's extensive (but then largely unexplored) archives gives unique insight into the company's founder, working practices, and how America's growing economy impacted the growth in popularity of the guitar. The book makes clear that after only twenty years in business, the small Martin company was a success, often unable to meet demand from its many direct, retail, and wholesale customers. Although the book's focus on the Martin company limits the attention Gura gives to other manufacturers, it was clear that Martin had much competition.

I was keen to understand what contribution these less-famous builders made to the evolution of the acoustic guitar and why few had survived beyond the early 1900s.

Chapter 4 of Gura's book, "Ashborn, Tilton and the Battle for New York," described some of Martin's competitors and their wares. But I had many more questions. The answers came with the publication of a collection of essays edited by Robert Shaw and Peter Szego. *Inventing the American Guitar* (2013) helps explain how Martin, along with other East Coast American makers, transformed what was originally a European invention into the American flattop that still dominates the guitar world today.

• • • • • •

The notes and the accompanying bibliography contain what I found to be the best books to further inform and deepen any guitar enthusiast's understanding.

In addition, if you're reading this book, you're probably already at least an occasional reader of both *Acoustic Guitar* magazine and perhaps *Fretboard Journal*. If you're not, I would recommend taking out subscriptions and buying any back numbers you come across.

I first started buying *Acoustic Guitar* in the early 1990s. Living in England meant it was a matter of grabbing one whenever I spotted a rare, imported copy. In early March 1995, I found one with a front cover featuring a photograph of a vintage Martin 000-45. It was promoting an article, *The Lost Martin*. I read that article many times across the following weeks and eventually raised the cash to buy my first Martin guitar, a 1983 Martin Custom Shop 00-42. A few years later, I held my breath and commissioned Martin to make me a version of the 000-45 that I had seen on the magazine cover in 1995.

The first copy of *Fretboard Journal* came out in the winter of 2005. On a shelf in my home office/writing room-*cum*-studio is a complete set of the quarterly magazines, each festooned with yellow sticky-notes bookmarking the many articles I have used as resources for this book.

What follows is a chapter-by-chapter reference to my primary sources followed by a complete bibliography.

INTRODUCTION

Highway 61: Samuel Willcoxon, "Highway 61: Good Roads, Great Migrations, and Delta Blues"; and Tammy Ingram, *Dixie Highway*.

Convict labor: Robert Burns, *I Am a Fugitive from a Georgia Chain Gang!*; and Mitchel Roth, *Prisons and Prison Systems*.

QUOTES

"He appeared through the trees": Shirley Collins interview on *Desert Island Discs*, BBC Radio 4, August 6, 2023.

CHAPTER 1: THE ORIGINS OF THE ACOUSTIC GUITAR

BEFORE 1833

Musical instrument competency: NAMM 2017 Survey, Associated Board of Royal Schools of Music (UK), 2014 Research Project.

Sousa: *A Sousa Reader*; and Patrick Warfield, *Making the March King.*

Elizabethan music: Katherine Butler, *Music in Elizabethan Court Politics.*

Broadside ballads: Lucie Skeaping, *Broadside Ballads.*

Guitar antecedents, including English guittar: Tom Evans and Mary Anne Evans, *Guitars: Music, History, Construction.* In addition, see Philip Gura, *C. F. Martin and His Guitars, 1796–1893*, for the physical development of the guitar and the role that guitar virtuosos of the period, from Paganini to Fernando Sor, played in helping contemporary makers perfect the instrument. These virtuosos, Sor in particular, played a major part in popularizing the Spanish instrument in England, while his various method books also made their way to America.

German emigration to America: Andrew Popp, "Christian Frederick Martin (1796–1873)," at Immigrant Entrepreneurship, https://www.immigrantentrepreneurship.org/.

"Guitaromanie": Robert Shaw and Peter Szego, *Inventing the American Guitar*; and Gura, *C. F. Martin and His Guitars.*

QUOTES

"Awash with pianos, violins, guitars" and all other quotes and paraphrases from Sousa are from John Philip Sousa, *Sousa Reader.*

"Well all the songs I heard in my life is folk songs": Spoken introduction to "This Train (Bound for Glory)," recorded October 25, 1956, at Northwestern University, Folkways 1908 Trouble in Mind.

"Any young woman unable to take her proper place": Butler, *Music in Elizabethan Court Politics.*

"The sweetness and brilliancy of sound peculiar to the Guittar": Geminiani, *Art of Playing the Guittar or Cittra.*

CHAPTER 2: THE BIRTH OF MARTIN GUITARS

1833–1860

European guild system: Christopher Friedrichs, *The Early Modern City, 1450–1750.* How guild strictures played a key role in bringing C. F. Martin to New York in 1833 is informed by the early chapters of Greig Hutton, *Hutton's Guide to Martin Guitars: 1833–1969*; Gura, *C. F. Martin and His Guitars*; and essays contained in Shaw and Szego, *Inventing the American Guitar.*

C. F. Martin's early years in Europe: Gura, *C. F. Martin and His Guitars*; Hutton, *Hutton's Guide to Martin Guitars*; Benjamin Hebbert's 2020 lecture to the Violin Society of America, "Violin Making in Northern Europe in the Time of the Amatis"; author's conversations with Dick Boak at Martin & Co., interviews and many telephone conversations with George Gruhn, and telephone conversations and emails with Greig Hutton, the archivist with unique access to the Martin company's extensive archives. Greig's recently published *Hutton's Guide to Martin Guitars* carries fresh and consolidated analysis of the Martin archive and contextualizes much of the early history of the Martin company, including C. F. Martin's struggles with the violin makers' guild in Germany. For more information and analysis, see Greig Hutton's website, www.theguitarphile.com.

Development of the guitar in America: Gura, *C. F. Martin and His Guitars*, and his article "Manufacturing Guitars for the American Parlor." Gura's work, together with essays contained in Shaw and Szego, *Inventing the American Guitar*, explain how Martin ran his business in America. These books put Martin into broader context, illustrating that despite his enormous influence, he was not the only maker.

New York music houses: Gura, *C. F. Martin and His Guitars*; Hutton, *Hutton's Guide to Martin Guitars*; and Shaw and Szego, *Inventing the American Guitar.*

Señora Delores Nevares de Goñi: Including de Goñi's creative relationship with Martin guitars and the introduction of X-bracing in Gura's *C. F. Martin and His Guitars*; Hutton, *Hutton's Guide to Martin Guitars*; and Shaw and Szego, *Inventing the American Guitar.*

QUOTES

"Nothing more than mechanics": James Westbook, "Johann Georg Stauffer and the Viennese Guitar," in Shaw and Szego, *Inventing the American Guitar*.

"New York guitar wars": Gura, *C. F. Martin and His Guitars.*

"With [Knoop] there is a sweet Spanish Lady": Longfellow, *Letters*, vol. 2, 1837–1843.

"Before leaving New York, I feel compelled to express my satisfaction": Shaw and Szego, *Inventing the American Guitar*, 134.

CHAPTER 3: POPULAR MUSIC IN THE CIVIL WAR AND BEYOND

1861–1899

Blackface minstrelsy: Eric Lott's magnum opus *Love and Theft*; Annmarie Bean, James Hatch, and Brooks McNamara, *Inside the Minstrel Mask*. (Both books contributed to the section in this chapter on Stephen Foster and the influence of blackface minstrelsy on popular culture.) Lott's *Love and Theft* helped clarify the many potential and conflicting origins of the first minstrel troupes and how minstrelsy developed from the 1840s onward as a racial political force. Michael Pickering's *Blackface Minstrelsy in Britain* helps us appreciate that blackface minstrelsy was not solely an American invention. Hans Nathan's *Dan Emmett and the Rise of Early Negro Minstrelsy* explains how blackface minstrelsy originally developed and explores its popularity in America.

Development of the banjo: George Gruhn and Walter Carter's *Acoustic Guitars and Other Fretted Instruments* provides a concise explanation of the development of the banjo in the early part of chapter 5, "String Banjos: Minstrel to Bluegrass."

DURING THE WAR

E. Lawrence Abel, *Singing the New Nation*; Christian McWhirter, *Battle Hymns*; and Anne Elise Thomas, *Music of the Civil War.*

AFTER THE WAR

The Thirteenth Amendment to the US Constitution: John C. Willis, *Forgotten Time.*

RECONSTRUCTION

Reconstruction: Eric Foner, *Reconstruction: America's Unfinished Revolution.*

Black codes and Jim Crow laws: Gunnar Myrdal, *An American Dilemma*, vol. 2, *The Negro Problem and Modern Democracy*; Stetson Kennedy, *A Jim Crow Guide to the USA* (a mock guidebook); C. Vann Woodward, *The Strange Career of Jim Crow* (originally published in 1955 and hailed by Martin Luther King Jr. as "the bible" of the civil rights movement); and Joel Williamson's classic work, *The Crucible of Race.*

American folk dancing: Phil Jamison's *Hoedowns, Reels, and Frolics* explains the influence of African American and Native American dancers on American folk dancing, outlining its ethnic diversity and dispelling the myth of isolation and whiteness in Southern backcountry dancing.

The Dibblee family: Interviews with Roy Regester of the Santa Barbara Historical Museum via various emails and telephone conversations across 2015–2016.

QUOTES

"I propose now closing up by requesting you play": Bernard, *Lincoln and the Music of the Civil War.*

"Every town and village had its ballroom": Jamison, *Hoedowns, Reels, and Frolics.*

"A new battle emerged": Debbie Levy, *Soldier Song.*

"The Dibblee House": Gertrude Franklin Atherton, *San Francisco Evening Post*, October 18, 1890.

"Save the guitar, save the guitar!": *Santa Barbara Daily News*, August 17, 1931.

"I started reading (old) newspaper articles about": Bob Dylan's semiautobiographical *Chronicles, Vol. 1.*

CHAPTER 4: MINSTRELSY AND THE BLUES

THE 1900s

Guitar tuition: Peter Danner, *The Guitar in America*; Elijah Wald, *How the Beatles Destroyed Rock 'n' Roll*; Robert Ferguson, "Henry Worrall (1825–1902): Anglo-American Guitarist"; and Bert Weedon obituary, *London Daily Telegraph*, April 21, 2012.

VHS: Shawn Michael Glinis, "VCRs: The End of TV as Ephemera."

John Renbourn: For the section on John Renbourn's research into American parlor music, see Jas Obrecht's *Talking Guitar.*

Stephen Foster: The section on Stephen Foster was initially informed by John Tasker

Howard's *Stephen Foster: America's Troubadour*, for many years the standard reference work on Foster; see also Ken Emerson, *Doo-Dah! Stephen Foster and the Rise of American Popular Culture*; and Joanne O'Connell's more recent *The Life and Songs of Stephen Foster.*

Banjo evolution: Philip Gura and his friend and associate, banjo aficionado and collector James Bollam, *America's Instrument*; Cecelia Conway, *African Banjo Echoes in Appalachia.*

W. C. Handy: W. C. Handy, *Father of the Blues*; Eileen Southern's 1971 history, *The Music of Black Americans*; David Robertson, *W. C. Handy: Life and Times*; and Alan Lomax, *The Land Where the Blues Began.*

British migrants in Appalachia: David Hackett Fischer, *Albion's Seed*; Barry Hankins, *The Second Great Awakening and the Transcendentalists*; and Paula M. Kane's thesis, "American Revival Songs, 1820–1850."

Appalachian dialect: Erik Thomas, "Rural White Southern Accents," in *Atlas of North American English* (online).

Orville Gibson and Gibson guitars: Gruhn and Carter, *Acoustic Guitars and Other Fretted Instruments*; Erlewine, Whitford, and Vinopal, *Gibson's Fabulous Flat-Top Guitars*; Walter Carter, *Gibson Guitars*; and Joe Spann, *Spann's Guide to Gibson, 1902–1941.*

Mandolin craze: Walter Carter, *The Mandolin in America*; and Spann, *Spann's Guide to Gibson.*

QUOTES

"His lyrics were conversational": Francis Davis, *History of the Blues.*

"What he loved to do was clown": Sleepy John Estes, quoted in Bill Wyman and Richard Haver, *Bill Wyman's Blues Odyssey.*

"If you can imagine a field hand": 1992 letter from British guitarist John Renbourn to Jas Obrecht, author of the anthology *Talking Guitar.*

"(Lyon & Healy) producing 100,000 instruments annually": Gruhn and Carter, *Acoustic Guitars and Other Fretted Instruments.*

CHAPTER 5: UKULELES AND HAWAIIAN GUITARS

THE 1910s

C. F. Martin in 1910s: Richard Johnston and Dick Boak, *Martin Guitars: A History*; Gruhn and Carter, *Acoustic Guitars and Other Fretted Instruments*; and Hutton, *Hutton's Guide to Martin Guitars.*

Mandolins: Carter, *The Mandolin in America*; and Paul Sparks, *The Classical Mandolin.*

Vahdah Olcott-Bickford: Jim Washburn and Richard Johnston, *Martin Guitars: An Illustrated Celebration*; and Hutton, *Hutton's Guide to Martin Guitars.*

Martin archives: Hutton, *Hutton's Guide to Martin Guitars.*

Lyon & Healy and Washburn: The story of companies like Lyon & Healy, makers of Washburn and Bay State instruments, has been based variously on sparsely written records, hearsay, guesswork, or the exaggerated claims of the companies' own catalog copy and advertising. Fortunately, Hubert Pleijsier's *Washburn Prewar Instrument Styles* finally brought careful and thorough research to the table. Pleijsier cleared the muddied waters created by earlier books published by a variety of recent owners of the Washburn brand.

Martin & Co.: Johnston and Boak, *Martin Guitars: A History*; Gruhn and Carter, *Acoustic Guitars and Other Fretted Instruments*; and Hutton, *Hutton's Guide to Martin Guitars.*

Statute of St. Anne: Mark Rose, "The Public Sphere and the Emergence of Copyright"; and Rose, *Authors and Owners.*

Larson brothers: Robert Hartman, *The Larsons' Creations.*

Ukulele: Jim Beloff, *The Ukulele: A Visual History*; and Jim Tranquada and John King, *The Ukulele: A History.*

Hawaii: Charles Garrett, *Struggling to Define a Nation*; Beloff, *The Ukulele: A Visual History*; and Tranquada and King, *The Ukulele: A History.*

Hawaiian steel guitar: John Troutman, *Kīkā Kila.*

QUOTES

"Bright, sweet sound": Lyon & Healey 1889 catalog; Gruhn and Carter, *Acoustic Guitars and Other Fretted Instruments.*

CHAPTER 6: THE BIRTH OF JAZZ AND COUNTRY MUSIC'S BIG BANG

THE 1920s

Context: Kathleen Drowne and Patrick Huber, *The 1920s*; Lawrence Broer and John Walther's collection of essays, *Dancing Fools and Weary Blues*; David Goldberg, *Discontented America.*

Birth of jazz: Alyn Shipton, *A New History of Jazz*; Nat Shapiro and Nat Hentoff, *Hear Me Talkin' to Ya.*

Early jazz recordings in Berlin and London, Rainer Lotz: Tom Wolfenden (producer), *Black Music in Europe.*

Black Swan Records/OKeh race records: Amanda Petrusich, *Do Not Sell at Any Price*; Tim Brooks, *Lost Sounds.*

First recorded guitar players, Sylvester Weaver, and Charlie Jackson: Shipton, *New History of Jazz*; and Southern, *The Music of Black Americans*, esp. chapter 10, "The Jazz Age."

Female blues guitarists: Valerie Turner, "Out of the Shadows"; and "Women of Early Blues Guitar," University of North Carolina Libraries Podcast, October 2022, https://www.youtube.com/watch?v=i8L61kB6xB0.

Lydia Mendoza: Yolanda Broyles-González, *Lydia Mendoza's Life in Music.*

Lydia Mendoza's guitars: Todd Cambio, "Lydia Mendoza and Her Acosta 12 String."

Radio age: Eric Barnouw, *History of Broadcasting in the United States*, vol. 1, *A Tower in Babel.*

Rural square dancing: Jamison, *Hoedowns, Reels, and Frolics*; and Peter La Chapelle, "Antisemitism and Henry Ford's Old-Time Music Revival," in *I'd Fight the World.*

Grand Ole Opry and border blasters: Chet Hagan, *Grand Ole Opry*; Joe Klein, *Woody Guthrie: A Life*; Gene Fowler and Bill Crawford, *Border Radio*; and Jon Langford, *Nashville Radio.*

Clarksdale, Son House, and Muddy Waters: Lomax, *Land Where the Blues Began*; and Davis, *History of the Blues.*

Bristol Sessions: Charles Wolfe and Ted Olson, *The Bristol Sessions*; and Benjamin Filene, *Romancing the Folk.*

Jimmie Rodgers: Barry Mazor, *Meeting Jimmie Rodgers*; and Nolan Porterfield, *Jimmie Rodgers: Life and Times.*

Carter Family and Ralph Peer: Bernard MacMahon and Allison McGourty, *American Epic*; and Philip Hirsch, *Voices from the Hollow.*

Lloyd Loar: Sparks, *The Classical Mandolin*; Gruhn and Carter, *Acoustic Guitars and Other Fretted Instruments*; Erlewine, Whitford, and Vinopal, *Gibson's Fabulous Flat-Top Guitars*; Carter, *Gibson Guitars: 100 Years*; Spann, *Spann's Guide to Gibson*; and Carter, *The Mandolin in America.*

QUOTES

"The rhythmic beat of our everyday lives": Edward Jablonski, *Irving Berlin.*

"Now get down to earth with us in a shindig of Grand Ole Opry!"; Hagan, *Grand Ole Opry.*

"You didn't need a radio aerial": Author's interview with WSM engineers, October 2015.

"I made more money in Clarksdale": Handy, *Father of the Blues.*

"Can You Sing or Play": MacMahon and McGourty, *American Epic.*

"He was a performer of force without precedent": Dylan, *Chronicles, Vol. 1.*

"They just had an old building that we recorded in": Maybelle Carter, 1961 interview by Ed Kahn and Archie Green, Archie Greene Papers, Southern Folklife Collection, Wilson Library, University of North Carolina at Chapel Hill.

"They wander in": Ralph Peer, 1958 interview by Lillian Borgenson, John Edwards Memorial Foundation Records, Southern Folklife Collection, Wilson Library, University of North Carolina at Chapel Hill.

CHAPTER 7: THE DEPRESSION AND THE EMERGENCE OF THE MODERN FLAT-TOP

THE 1930s

Context: Edmund Lindhop, *America in the 1930s*; and Frederick Allen, *Since Yesterday*, "September 3, 1929, to September 3, 1939."

Martin Dreadnought: Johnston and Boak, *Martin Guitars: A History*; Gruhn and Carter, *Acoustic Guitars and Other Fretted Instruments*; and Hutton, *Hutton's Guide to Martin Guitars.*

Gibson flat-tops: George Gruhn, author interview October 2015; Gruhn and Carter, *Acoustic Guitars and Other Fretted Instruments*; Erlewine, Whitford, and Vinopal,

Gibson's Fabulous Flat-Top Guitars; Carter, *Gibson Guitars: 100 Years*; and Spann, *Spann's Guide to Gibson.*

Robert Johnson: Elijah Wald, *Escaping the Delta*; Gayle Wardlow, *Chasin' That Devil Music*; Bruce Conforth and Wardlow, *Up Jumped the Devil*; Peter Guralnick, *Searching for Robert Johnson*; Mack McCormick, *Biography of a Phantom*; and Steve Cheseborough, *Blues Travelling.*

The Delta: Douglas Hurt, *African American Life in the Rural South*; W. J. Cash, *The Mind of the South*; James Cobb, *Most Southern Place on Earth* and *Redefining Southern Culture*; Willis, *Forgotten Time.*

Black female singers: Daphne Harrison, *Black Pearls*; and Paul Oliver, *Story of the Blues*, esp. chapter 6, "Rabbit Foot and Toby Time."

Dobro/National guitars: Bob Brozman *The History and Artistry of National Resonator Instruments*; and Gruhn and Carter, *Acoustic Guitars and Other Fretted Instruments.*

Early electric guitars: Richard Smith, *The History of Rickenbacker Guitars*; Gruhn and Carter, *Acoustic Guitars and Other Fretted Instruments*; Carter, *Gibson Guitars: 100 Years*; and Steve Waksman, *Instruments of Desire.*

Delta scouts and Henry. C. Speir: Wardlow, *Chasin' That Devil Music.*

Cinema and singing cowboys: Holly George-Warren, *Public Cowboy No. 1.*

Banjos and archtop guitars: Gruhn and Carter, *Acoustic Guitars and Other Fretted Instruments.*

Perry Bechtel/OM: Johnston and Boak, *Martin Guitars: A History*; Gruhn and Carter, *Acoustic Guitars and Other Fretted Instruments*; and Hutton, *Hutton's Guide to Martin Guitars.*

Epiphone: Gruhn and Carter, *Acoustic Guitars and Other Fretted Instruments.*

QUOTES

"Collectors of fine instruments care about who made it": Author interview with George Gruhn, October 2015.

"Played the old, cheap Stella guitars": Wardlow, *Chasin' That Devil Music.*

"And such a racket you never heard!": Son House interview with John Fahey et al.

"When he came back . . . me and Willie Brown": House interview with Fahey.

"Getting on all fours and howlin' like a mad dog": Honeyboy Edwards interviewed by Pete Welding, *Blues Unlimited* 54 (June 1958).

"Cotton obsessed, Negro obsessed": Robert Vance quoted in Cobb, *Most Southern Place on Earth.*

CHAPTER 8: THE MOST POPULAR FRETTED INSTRUMENT

THE 1940s

Context: Henry Finder, *The 40s.*

Country and western: Charles Wolfe, *A Good-Natured Riot*; Nicholas Dawidoff, *In the*

Country of Country; Diane Pecknold, *Hidden in the Mix*; and Francesca Royster, *Black Country Music.*

Honky tonk: Ronnie Pugh, *Ernest Tubb.*

Birth of bluegrass: Robert Cantwell, *When We Were Good*; Kip Lornell, *Capital Bluegrass* and *Exploring American Folk Music*; and Dawidoff, *In the Country of Country.*

"Authenticity" in country music: Richard Peterson, *Creating Country Music*; and Karl Hagstrom Miller, *Segregating Sound.*

Evolution of Martin Dreadnought: Hutton, *Hutton's Guide to Martin Guitars.*

Political folk music: Stephen Petrus and Ronald Cohen, *Folk City*, chapter 5, "Political Activism and the Folk Music Revival"; and Jack Whalen and Richard Flacks, *Beyond the Barricades.*

Woody Guthrie: Klein, *Woody Guthrie: A Life*; and Cantwell, *When We Were Good*, chapter 3, "Ballad for Americans."

Pete Seeger: Cantwell, *When We Were Good*, chapter 7, "He Shall Overcome"; Winkler, "*To Everything There Is a Season*"; Petrus and Cohen, *Folk City*; and Pete Seeger, *In His Own Words.*

The Almanac Singers and the Weavers: Petrus and Cohen, *Folk City*, chapter 1, "New York and the Origins of the Folk Music Revival"; and Cantwell, *When We Were Good*, chapter 3, "Ballad for Americans."

Gibson electrics: Carter, *Gibson Guitars: 100 Years.*

QUOTES

"*Here. Woody Guthrie, I want you to meet Pete Seeger*": Winkler, "*To Everything There Is a Season.*"

"*Bar owners are asking all the time for records that can cut through*": Pugh, *Ernest Tubb.*

"*I discovered there was good music in my country*": Seeger, *Pete Seeger in His Own Words.*

"*When we got Earl*": Dawidoff, *In the Country of Country.*

"*It sounded like the gates of heaven*": St. John, *Clapton's Guitar.*

"*Learn about ourselves, and . . . learn about each other*": Petrus and Cohen, *Folk City.*

CHAPTER 9: SKIFFLE AND A GUITAR CRAZE IN BRITAIN

THE 1950s

Context: Henry Finder, *The 50s*; and Peter Hennessey, *Having It So Good.*

British skiffle: Chas McDevitt, *Skiffle: Definitive Inside Story*; Billy Bragg, *Roots, Radicals and Rockers*; Karel Reisz and Tony Richardson, dirs., *Momma Don't Allow*, short documentary filmed in the North London Fisherman's Arms pub and featuring the Chris Barber Band with the Irish blues singer Ottilie Patterson; and Mark Lewisohn, *The Beatles: All These Years*, chapter 4, "Scufflers to Skifflers."

British guitars: Grimshaw Guitars UK website, grimshawguitars.co.uk; and Tony Bacon, *The Ultimate Guitar Book.*

Fender: Tony Bacon, *50 Years of Fender.*

Trad jazz, including Ken Colyer: Alyn Shipton's *New History of Jazz*, esp. "The New Orleans Revival and Mainstream Jazz"; Mike Pointon and Ray Smith, *Goin' Home.*

Lonnie Donegan: Patrick Humphries, *The Lonnie Donegan Story*, and *Lonnie Donegan and the Birth of British Rock & Roll.*

Lennon and McCartney: Mark Lewisohn, *The Beatles: All These Years.*

British blues: Harry Shapiro, *Alexis Korner*; Bob Brunning, *Blues: British Connection*; Roberta Schwartz, *How Britain Got the Blues.*

Modern jazz in America: Shipton, *New History of Jazz*, chapter "From Swing to Bop."

Josh White: Dorothy Siegel, *The Glory Road*; Elise Luray, "The Josh White Guitar," *History Detectives*, interview with Josh White Jr., 2009; Elijah Wald, *Josh White*; and Eric Bentley, *Thirty Years of Treason.*

Wanda Jackson: Billy Poore, *Rockabilly: Forty-Year Journey*; Leah Bransetters, "Women in Rock and Roll's First Wave"; and Andrew Hickey, "A History of Rock 'n' Roll in 500 Songs" (podcast), episode 43, July 27, 2019.

Hank Williams: Lillian Stone and Allen Rankin, *Life Story of Our Hank Williams*; Colin Escott and Kira Florita, *Hank Williams: Snapshots*; and Colin Escott, George Merritt, and William MacEwen, *Hank Williams: The Biography.*

QUOTES

"People were wandering London's Charing Cross Road": As of May 1, 2023; and Christian Hoyer, "A History of the Karl Hofner Company, 1887–2007."

"You couldn't buy anything": As of May 1, Hoyer, "History of the Karl Hofner Company."

"I found this Hofner violin bass": *FarOut* magazine, July 2023.

"The Skiffle group which takes over during the intervals at the London Jazz Club": Humphries, *Lonnie Donegan and the Birth of British Rock.*

"This was living": Pointon and Smith, *Goin' Home.*

"In Britain we were separated from our folk music tradition": Lonnie Donegan interview in *Melody Maker*, May 1970.

"Even his wife, Delphine, was resented": Pointon and Smith, *Goin' Home.*

"The sound of his guitar stirred me": Wald, *Josh White.*

"The guitar that Josh White plays is as eloquent": Wald, *Josh White.*

"Drunk or sober, it didn't matter": Escott, Merritt, and MacEwen, *Hank Williams: The Biography.*

"You gotta make a choice boy": Paul Hemphill, *Lovesick Blues.*

"You sorry son of a bitch": Hemphill, *Lovesick Blues.*

"Starts out like a sad, sappy country ballad": Poore, *Rockabilly: Forty-Year Journey.*

"Elvis didn't see it coming": Bruce Springsteen, *Born to Run.*

CHAPTER 10: BRITISH BLUES, AMERICAN GUITARS

THE 1960s IN BRITAIN

Overview: Peter Hennessy, *Winds of Change*; Dominic Sandbrook, *White Heat*; and Joe Boyd, *White Bicycles.*

Traditional folk: Dave Harker, *Fakesong: Manufacture of British "Folksong"*; and Georgina Boyes, *The Imagined Village.*

Folk clubs: J. P. Bean, *Singing from the Floor.*

Paul Simon in Britain: Robert Hilburn, *Paul Simon: The Life*; Spencer Leigh, *Simon & Garfunkel: Together Alone*; and Bean, *Singing from the Floor.*

Big Bill Broonzy: Bob Reisman, *I Feel So Good*; Max Jones, "Big Bill Broonzy: 1951 UK Tour Recalled," *Melody Maker*, August 23, 1958; and Studs Terkel radio interview, "Big Bill Broonzy," WFMT Chicago, 1958.

Rev. Gary Davis: Ian Zack, *Say No to the Devil.*

Bert Jansch: Colin Harper, *Dazzling Stranger.*

Beat and Merseybeat: Spencer Leigh, *Twist and Shout!*

The Beatles in Hamburg: Mark Lewisohn, *The Beatles: All These Years*, is the definitive history of the Beatles' early years; and Craig Brown, *One Two Three Four.*

QUOTES

"Music of delinquents" and *"rhythm crazed teenagers"*: *Daily Sketch*, 1956.

"For the rest of us it was bed by ten": Andrew Cracknell, "Under the Bomb," *Financial Times*, August 2005.

"For a start, the British didn't seem to own anything": Boyd, *White Bicycles.*

"It's strenuous work"; *"I have now taken down 250 tunes"*; and *"We tramped"*: Cecil Sharp's Appalachian diaries, 1916–1918, in Michael Yates, *Cecil Sharp in America.*

"A man who, with unbelievable dedication": Michael Yates, editor of the EFDSS *Folk Music Journal*, "Jumping to Conclusions," http://www.bluegrassmessengers.com/jumping-to-conclusions—michael-yates.aspx.

"A land without music": Oskar Schmitz, *Land Without Music.*

"Put a stop to everybody bringing a guitar and having to tune the entire front row": Peggy Seeger, in Bean, *Singing from the Floor.*

"At the time there were very few": Jimmie McGregor quoted in Bean, *Singing from the Floor.*

"He really knew his way around the fretboard": Author interview with club singer Gordon Wright at Brentwood Folk Club, 1975.

"The first time I saw Paul Simon": Bean, *Singing from the Floor.*

"I had the facility": Will Hodgkinson, *Guitar Man.*

"The music got so exciting": Ian A. Anderson quoted in Bean, *Singing from the Floor.*

"Encapsulated everything I wanted": Richards quoted in Stefan Grossman, "Linear Notes" from *The Guitar of Big Bill Broonzy*, Guitar Workshop DVD, 1980.

"The music alone would have been tremendously captivating": Clapton quoted in Grossman, "Linear Notes."

"What I saw and heard changed my life": Thomas Kitts, *Ray Davies.*

"Do they serve Whisky & Chips?" and *"Whatever Bill played"*: Author conversation with Martin Carthy, 2002.

"He was this huge man coming into the room": Val Wilmer quote from *Blues and Beyond with Cerys Matthews and Val Wilmer*, BBC4, June 25, 2022.

"Ringo's not even the best drummer in the Beatles": Wrongly attributed to Lennon and for a decade or two to British comedian Jasper Carrot. According to Beatles scholar Mark Lewisohn, a gag from a 1981 edition of the BBC Radio 4 comedy sketch show *Radio Active.*

"With an air that we associated more with an English drawing room": Finder, *The 60s*, part 5, "The Beatle Man."

"I think that America is ready for the Beatles": Epstein interview, *New Yorker*, December 28, 1963.

CHAPTER 11: GONE ELECTRIC

THE 1960s IN THE USA

Overview: Finder, ed., *The 60s: Story of a Decade.*

The Beatles in America and effect on US music scene: Mark Lewisohn, *The Complete Beatles Chronicle*; Stephen Stark, *Meet the Beatles.*

US guitar sales in the 1960s: Spann, *Spann's Guide to Gibson*; Carter, *Gibson Guitars: 100 Years*; and Andy Babiuk, *Beatles Gear.*

The polka craze: Richard March, "American Polka in the Media"; and Victor Greene, *A Passion for Polka.*

Imported European guitars, including Rickenbacker: Bacon, *Ultimate Guitar Book*; and Smith, *History of Rickenbacker Guitars.*

Second American folk music revival: Benjamin Filene, *Romancing the Folk*; Boyd, *White Bicycles.*

New York folk scene: Cantwell, *When We Were Good*; Petrus and Cohen, *Folk City*; Dave van Ronk, *Mayor of MacDougal Street.*

Mississippi John Hurt: Paul Oliver, *Story of the Blues.*

The Byrds: Johnny Rogan, *Byrds: Requiem for the Timeless.*

Newport Folk Festival: Boyd, *White Bicycles*; and Elijah Wald, *Dylan Goes Electric!*

Bob Dylan: Dylan, *Chronicles, Vol. 1*; Sean Wilentz, *Bob Dylan in America*; Greil Marcus, *Invisible Republic*; and Mark Polizzotti, *Dylan: Highway 61 Revisited.*

House Un-American Activities Committee: Bentley, *Thirty Years of Treason.*

The Band: Barney Hoskyns, *Across the Great Divide*; Robbie Robertson's autobiography, *Testimony*; and Greil Marcus, *Invisible Republic* and *Mystery Train.*

Fairport Convention: Boyd, *White Bicycles*; and Rob Young, *Electric Eden.*

Woodstock: Michael Lang, *Road to Woodstock*; and Barney Hoskyns, *Small Town Talk.*

QUOTES

"I was listening to the music and to me": Phil Everly interviewed in 1980 on BBC TV Arena, "The Everly Brothers: Songs of Innocence and Experience," November 2, 1984.

"When John and I first started to write songs": McCartney interviewed on the death of Phil Everly, *Los Angeles Times*, January 10, 2014.

"They all believed that their chances with members of the opposite sex": Ruy Castro, *Bossa Nova.*

"You can have anything in here": Author interview with Matt Umanov, New York, 2015.

"If you travelled from god knows where": Al Kooper interviewed by Richard Jinman for *The Independent*, July 25, 2015.

"Gigantic tambourine . . . as big as a wagon wheel": Dylan, *Chronicles, Vol. 1*; Wald, *Dylan Goes Electric!*

"Some of Bob's stuff is really hard to play!": Nanci Griffith, *Other Voices.*

"Fingering, like any common stool pigeon": Seeger, *In His Own Words.*

"People say music changes the world": Joan Baez interview, PBS, *Craft in America*, "Music," season 7, episode 1, November 20, 2015.

"Dylan may well become the country's most creative troubadour": Pete Seeger in Charles Nicholl, "That Wild Mercury Sound," *London Review of Books*, December 1, 2016.

"[It] was like receiving a letter from the other side of the world": Elvis Costello quoted in Hoskyns, *Across the Great Divide.*

"Cosmic in the sense of being cutting edge": See "What Is Cosmic American Music?," *No Depression*, March 21, 2018.

"Open space, low-volume, high-intensity": Clive James on Sandy Denny, "In a Lonely Moment," *Let It Rock* magazine, March 1974.

"Tin Pan Alley is gone": Liner notes from Dylan's *Biograph* LP, 1985.

"A wider definition of 'whiteness' emerged": David Roediger, "Critical Studies of Whiteness."

CHAPTER 12: THE SINGER-SONGWRITER AND THE D-28

THE 1970s

Context: Turner, *Crisis? What Crisis?*; Thomas Borstelmann, *The 1970s*; David Hepworth, *1971—Never a Dull Moment*; Boyd, *White Bicycles*; and Richard Morton Jack, *Galactic Ramble.*

The D-28: "Gearbox: Joni Mitchell," *Acoustic Guitar*, August 1996.

Woodstock: Lang, *Road to Woodstock.*

The Dick Cavett Show: Dick Cavett and Christopher Porterfield, *Cavett*; and DVD liner notes, *The Dick Cavett Show*, "Rock Icons," 2005.

Joni Mitchell: Malka Marom, *Joni Mitchell: In Her Own Words*; and David Yaffe, *Reckless Daughter.*

Laurel Canyon: Harvey Kubernik, *Canyon of Dreams*; and Lisa Robinson, "It Happened in Laurel Canyon."

Tony Rice's D-28: "58957: Tony Rice and His Holy Grail Martin D-28," *Fretboard Journal*, Spring 2007.

Nick Drake: Boyd, *White Bicycles*; Richard Morton Jack, *Nick Drake*; and Gabrielle Drake, *Nick Drake: Remembered for a While.*

Nick Drake, Volkswagen ad: "I knew this was different," T*he Guardian*, July 5, 2022; "From Obscurity to Hit in One TV Commercial," *Los Angeles Times*, April 11, 2001.

Bridget St. John: Mike Fiorito, "The Gentle Songs of Bridget St. John," interview with Bridget St. John in *Atwood* magazine, July 2, 2021.

Dandelion Records: Owen Adams, "Label of Love," *The Guardian*, October 7, 2009.

John Martyn: John Neil Munro, *Some People Are Crazy*; Graeme Thomson, *Small Hours*; and Boyd, *White Bicycles.*

QUOTES

"Annus Mirabilis of the long playing album": Hepworth, *1971—Never a Dull Moment.*

"[They] raised their voices together": Marom, *Joni Mitchell.*

"Carol Kaye . . . could do anything": Quincy Jones, *Autobiography.*

"It was the beginning of very big changes": Kubernik, *Canyon of Dreams.*

"What Joni Mitchell did was far and above": Robinson, "It Happened in Laurel Canyon."

"Eric is just staring at me playing guitar": Marom, *Joni Mitchell.*

"Once I got the open tunings": Marom, *Joni Mitchell.*

"When they cleared the wreckage": Jeffrey Pepper Rodgers interview with Joni Mitchell, *Acoustic Guitar*, August 1996.

"Really tender song[s] filled with despair": Jackson Browne between-song commentary, European tour, 2007.

"Stephen Stills . . . was the first guy": Jackson Browne between-song commentary, European tour, 2007.

"(CSNY) . . . helped fortify the market": George Gruhn, interview with author, October 2015.

"Before that the electric and acoustic markets were very much separate entities": George Gruhn, interview with author, October 2015.

"I saw that old D-28 and it didn't have a name on the headstock": "58957: Tony Rice and His Holy Grail Martin D-28," *Fretboard Journal*, Spring 2007.

"I remember sitting at home on the couch with my mother": Lol Tolhurst, *Cured: Tale of Two Imaginary Boys.*

"I cannot think of anybody else I've ever recorded" and *"I knew this was different"*: John Wood, Nick Drake's producer and recording engineer, *The Guardian*, July 5, 2022.

"At a local club I sang the usual blues numbers": Robin Frederick, in the family-produced memoir *Nick Drake: Remembered for a While.*

"Found myself a job, playing in a night club": Letter from Nick Drake to his parents, July 1967, in *Nick Drake: Remembered for a While.*

"John was a boozer and a stoner": Mike Chapman quoted in Munro, *Some People Are Crazy.*

"In awe": Gabrielle Drake in *Nick Drake: Remembered for a While.*

"Roughly speaking, it goes like this": Andy Childs, "Talking with John Martyn," *ZigZag* magazine, April/May 1974.

CHAPTER 13: BEYOND MARTIN AND GIBSON

THE 1980s

Context: Turner, *Rejoice! Rejoice!*; and Marlene Brill, *America in the 1990s.*

Tracy Chapman and the Nelson Mandela Wembley concert, 1988: Ayun Halliday, "How an Unscheduled, Last-Minute Performance," Open Culture/In Music website, February 9, 2024.

Martin guitar sales: Longworth, *C. F. Martin Guitars: A History* (the original single volume produced in 1988); Johnston and Boak, *Martin Guitars: A History* and *Martin Guitars: A Technical Reference.*

American Dream: Siobhan Braun interview with Sam Radding, *San Diego Reader*, July 1, 2015.

Taylor: Author interview with Andy Powers, the master guitar designer and a partner at Taylor, conducted September 2016; Bob Taylor, *Guitar Lessons*; and Siobhan Braun interview with Kurt Listug, *San Diego Reader*, July 1, 2015.

The Fender Company: Bacon, *50 Years of Fender*; and Forrest White (former general manager of the Fender company), *Fender: Inside Story.*

Roger Rossmeisl and Fender acoustic guitar design: Rossmeisl Guitar Legacy website, curated by Peter McCormack, 2004.

John D'Angelico and James D'Aquisto: Paul William Schmidt, *Acquired of the Angels.*

Renaissance of hand-built guitars: Kathryn Marie Dudley, *Guitar Makers*; author interviews with guitar makers Richard Hoover and Bill Collings at the Fretboard Summit in California; and author interviews at the Santa Cruz Guitar Company, Santa Cruz, California, October 2015.

Schoenburg and OM guitars: Much of the information regarding the playing of ragtime on Martin guitars and the rebirth of the OM guitar derives from two extensive interviews the author conducted with Eric Schoenberg in San Francisco in October 2015. Subsequent interviews with Dick Boak of Martin Guitars and Dana Bourgeois added detail to the Schoenberg interview and the OM story.

QUOTES

"The music scene was healthier": Turner, *Rejoice! Rejoice!*

"Mass-produced fluorescent 'superstrats' from Kramer": Author interview with George Gruhn, October 2015.

"Soulless, factory-made, mass-produced guitars": Dudley, *Guitar Makers.*

"When you open up a Gibson from the '80s": Author interview with Dave King, April 2015.

"Disgusted with what has happened": Stu Mossman, from 1960s Mossman Guitars catalog.

"The sensation of doing the final shaping of the neck": Author interview with Dave King, April 2015.

"Designed to be played standing up" and *"modified in outline"*: Ervin Somogyi, *The Responsive Guitar.*

"During the '60s and '70s, Martin had little knowledge": Author interview with George Gruhn, October 2015.

CHAPTER 14: UNPLUGGED

THE 1990s

The "business" of the music business: Simon Napier-Bell, *Ta-Ra-Ra-Boom-De-Ay* and *White Powder, Black Vinyl*; David Byrne, *How Music Works*; and Boyd, *White Bicycles.*

Lilith Fair, Jewel: Jessica Hopper, "Building a Mystery"; and Quentin Harrison, "Portrait of a Phenomenon: Lilith Fair."

Sales performance of Martin & Co.: Johnston and Boak, *Martin Guitars: A History* and *Martin Guitars: Technical Reference.*

MTV Unplugged: Roger Cormier, "19 Electric Facts About MTV Unplugged"; Elaine Louie, interview with MTV executives Robert Small and Jim Burns, *New York Times*, February 9, 1992; and Andy Greene, "MTV Unplugged: The 15 Best Episodes."

Vintage guitar collecting: Deke Dickerson, *The Strat in the Attic.*

Martin archtops: Johnston and Boak, *Martin Guitars: A History.*

Martin signature models: Dick Boak, *Martin Guitar Masterpieces.*

Nick Lucas and the Gibson Nick Lucas Special: Whitford, Vinopal, and Erlewine, *Gibson's Fabulous Flat-Top Guitars.*

James Olson: Dudley, *Guitar Makers*; author interview with Bob Page, owner of Buffalo Brothers, Encinitas, California, in 1995; Olson Guitar Shop interview produced by Thomas Strand, 2014.

Wayne Henderson: Allen St. John, *Clapton's Guitar.*

QUOTES

"He said what I would let you do is sit down": Johnny Cash, MTV News interview, 2005.

"He wasn't well enough to tour anymore": Rick Rubin interview on *Desert Island Discs*, BBC Radio 4, October 2022.

"My fondest memories are just": Rick Rubin interviewed by Paul Rees, *Q* magazine, October 2009.

"In 1984 a buyer could have acquired": Author interview with George Gruhn, October 2015.

"A business to run that feeds me" and *"I was the go-to guy"*: Author interview with Matt Umanov, September 2015.

"Most valuable Martin, possibly the most valuable guitar": Autry Museum of the American West, Los Angeles.

"I was a wood whacker": Interview with Jim Olson conducted by guitarist Will Ackerman, 2016.

"Until you've been making guitars for at least fifteen years": Author interview with British guitar maker Dave King, September 2014.

"For everything I do to be for a higher purpose" and subsequent quotes are from author interview with Paul Heumiller, Asheville, North Carolina, October 2015.

CHAPTER 15: AMERICANA AND AN ACOUSTIC REVIVAL

THE 2000s

Billy Bragg and Mermaid Avenue: Bragg, *Roots, Radicals and Rockers.*

Alt-country, American roots music, and Americana: Grant Alden and Peter Blackstock, *The Best of No Depression.*

Three chords and the truth: Dawidoff, *In the Country of Country.*

Merle Haggard: David Cantwell, *Merle Haggard: The Running Kind.*

Johnny Cash: Johnny Cash, *The Autobiography.*

Black banjo: Diane Pecknold, *Hidden in the Mix*, and specifically Erika Brady's essay, "Contested Origins: Arnold Shultz and the Music of West Virginia."

QUOTES

"Against everything that Maggie Thatcher stood for": Turner, *Rejoice! Rejoice!*

"Who do you think you are?": "Merle Haggard Receives Award and Gets Rowdy," Saving Country Music.com, March 6, 2009.

"There's only two kinds of music, the blues and Zip-a-Dee-Doo-Dah": Van Zandt quoted by Gillian Welch during performance, Hammersmith Apollo, London, November 2011.

"I have a Gibson LG-1 that I've had sitting in my office for a long time": Billy Bragg interviewed by Jamie Dickson, *Guitar World*, April 12, 2022.

CHAPTER 16: NEW OLD GUITARS

THE 2010s AND BEYOND: THE GUITAR

Rory Gallagher: Gary Blankenburg, "Rory Gallagher: 1945–1995"; and Lauren Alex O'Hagan, "Fashioning the 'People's Guitarist.'"

Martin signature guitars: Boak, *Martin Guitar Masterpieces.*

Ben Montague, Michael Watts, Jason Kostal, and "the Tree": Author interviews, November 2014.

QUOTES

"The less paint or varnish on a guitar" and other quotes about Gallager's guitars are from Rorygallagher.com, retrieved June 13, 2019.

"I heard a story that Paganini played a Stradivarius": Wayne Henderson quoted in Clifford Hall, "To Relic or Not to Relic," *Guitar World*, July 5, 2018.

"Unfortunately, old guitars can be tricky": Interview with Dick Boak, *Guitar World*, July 2018.

"Jason had a first career in the US military": Author interview with Ben Montague of North American Guitar [November–December 2015].

"We are not a factory and we aren't a single builder": Author interview with Richard Hoover, October 2015.

CHAPTER 17: THE ACOUSTIC GUITAR, TAYLOR'S VERSION

THE 2010s AND BEYOND: THE PLAYERS

Politicization of country music: Louise Callahan, "America's Sound," *Sunday Times*, June 2, 2024.

Black artists in mainstream country: Royster, *Black Country*.

Punch Brothers: *Fretboard Journal*, No. 10 (Summer 2008).

Paul Simon: Matt Everitt, "The First Time with . . . Paul Simon," BBC Radio 6 Broadcast, May 2016, https://www.bbc.co.uk/programmes/b07d727g; *Sunday Times* interview, May 20, 2023.

Women in contemporary country music: Marissa Moss, *Her Country*.

QUOTES

"Hit them up and they would come to the house": Sleeve notes for *No.6 Collaborations Project* (2019), Asylum Atlantic Records.

"It's like 'Old Joe Clark', that old fiddle tune": Ralph Stanley quoted in Dawidoff, *In the Country of Country*.

"Oh, play some bluegrass, fi' Christ's sake!" Pete Paphides interview with Chris Thile, *The (London) Times*, January 25, 2008.

"You should get off the road and go home": Dan Cairns interview with Paul Simon, *Sunday Times Magazine*, May 21, 2023.

Bibliography

Abel, E. Lawrence. *Singing the New Nation: How Music Shaped the Confederacy, 1861–1865*. Mechanicsburg, PA: Stackpole Books, 2000.

Alden, Grant, and Peter Blackstock, eds. *The Best of No Depression: Writing About American Music*. Austin: University of Texas Press, 2005.

Allen, Frederick Lewis. *Since Yesterday: The 1930s in America*. New York: Harper Perennial, 1986.

Babiuk, Andy. *Beatles Gear: All the Fab Four's Instruments from Stage to Studio*. London: Backbeat Books, 2016.

Bacon, Tony. *50 Years of Fender: Half a Century of the Greatest Electric Guitars*. London: Backbeat Books, 2000.

Bacon, Tony. *The Ultimate Guitar Book*. London: Dorling Kindersley, 1991.

Barker, Martin, and Julian Petley, eds. *Ill Effects: The Media Violence Debate*. Rev. ed. Abingdon-on-Thames, UK: Routledge, 2013.

Barnouw, Eric. *A History of Broadcasting in the United States*. Vol. 1, *A Tower in Babel: To 1933*. Oxford: Oxford University Press, 1966.

Barraclough, Nick. *Three Chords and the Truth*. London: BBC Radio 4 Broadcasts, 2005.

Bean, Annmarie, James V. Hatch, and Brooks McNamara, eds. *Inside the Minstrel Mask: Readings in Nineteenth-Century Blackface Minstrelsy*. Middletown, CT: Wesleyan University Press, 1996.

Bean, J. P. *Singing from the Floor: A History of British Folk Clubs*. London: Faber & Faber, 2014.

Bellson, Julius. *The Gibson Story*. Kalamazoo, MI: Julius Bellson, 1973.

Beloff, Jim. *The Ukulele: A Visual History*. San Francisco: Backbeat Books, 2003.

Bentley, Eric, ed. *Thirty Years of Treason: Excerpts from Hearings Before the House Committee on Un-American Activities, 1938–1968*. New York: Nation Books, 2001.

Bernard, Kenneth A. *Lincoln and the Music of the Civil War*. Caldwell, ID: Caxton Printers, 1966.

Blankenburg, Gary. "Rory Gallagher: 1945–1995." *20th-Century Guitar*, 1995. http://www.roryon.com/20th.html.

Boak, Dick. *Martin Guitar Masterpieces: A Showcase of Artists' Editions, Limited Editions, and Custom Guitars*. London: Palazzo Editions, 2003.

Borstelmann, Thomas. *The 1970s: A New Global History from Civil Rights to Economic Inequality*. Princeton, NJ: Princeton University Press, 2010.

Boyd, Joe. *White Bicycles: Making Music in the 1960s*. New York: Serpent's Tail, 2007.

Boyes, Georgina. *The Imagined Village: Culture, Ideology, and the English Folk Revival*. Manchester, UK: Manchester University Press, 1994.

Bragg, Billy. *Roots, Radicals and Rockers: How Skiffle Changed the World*. London: Faber & Faber, 2017.

Brand, Neil. *Sound of Song: The Recording Revolution*. London: BBC4 Documentary, January 2015.

Brandfon, Robert L. *Cotton Kingdom of the New South: A History of the Yazoo Mississippi Delta from Reconstruction to the Twentieth Century*. Cambridge, MA: Harvard University Press, 1967.

Bransetter, Leah. "Women in Rock and Roll's First Wave." Women in Rock Project. https://www.womeninrockproject.org/.

Brill, Marlene Targ. *America in the 1990s*. New York: Twenty-First-Century Books, 2009.

Broer, Lawrence R., and John D. Walther, eds. *Dancing Fools and Weary Blues: The Great Escape to the Twenties*. Bowling Green, OH: Bowling Green State University Popular Press, 1990.

Brooks, Tim. *Guitar: An American Life*. New York: Grove Press, 2005.

Brooks, Tim. *Lost Sounds: Blacks and the Birth of the Recording Industry, 1890–1919*. Appendix by Dick Spottiswood. Urbana: University of Illinois Press, 2004.

Brown, Craig. *One Two Three Four: The Beatles in Time*. London: Fourth Estate, 2020.

Broyles-González, Yolanda. *Lydia Mendoza's Life in Music*. Oxford: Oxford University Press, 2001.

Brozman, Bob. *The History and Artistry of National Resonator Instruments*. Anaheim, CA: Centerstream, 1993.

Brunning, Bob. *Blues: The British Connection*. London: Helter Skelter, 2002.

Burns, Robert E. *I Am a Fugitive from a Georgia Chain Gang!* Athens: University of Georgia Press, 1997.

Butler, Katherine. *Music in Elizabethan Court Politics*. Martlesham, UK: Boydell Press, 2015.

Byrne, David. *How Music Works*. London: Canongate, 2012.

Cambio, Tod. "Lydia Mendoza and her Acosta 12 String." Fraulini Guitar Co., June 2014. https://fraulini.com/2014/06/lydia-mendoza-and-her-acosta-12-string/.

Cantwell, David. *Merle Haggard: The Running Kind.* Austin: University of Texas Press, 2022.

Cantwell, Robert S. *When We Were Good: The Folk Revival.* Cambridge, MA: Harvard University Press, 1996.

Carter, Walter. *Gibson Guitars: 100 Years of an American Icon.* Los Angeles: General Publishing, 1994.

Carter, Walter. *The Mandolin in America: The Full Story from Orchestras to Bluegrass to the Modern Revival.* London: Backbeat Books, 2016.

Cash, Johnny, and Patrick Carr. *The Autobiography.* London: HarperCollins, 1999.

Cash, W. J. *The Mind of the South.* New York: Knopf, 1941.

Castro, Ruy. *Bossa Nova: The Story of the Brazilian Music That Seduced the World.* Chicago: A Capella Books, 1990.

Cavett, Dick, and Christopher Porterfield. *Cavett.* New York: Harcourt, 1974.

Charters, Samuel B. *The Country Blues.* New York: Holt Rinehart, 1959.

Cheseborough, Steve. *Blues Travelling: The Holy Sites of Delta Blues.* Jackson: University Press of Mississippi, 2009.

Cobb, James C. *The Most Southern Place on Earth: The Mississippi Delta and the Roots of Regional Identity.* New York: Oxford University Press, 1994.

Cobb, James C. *Redefining Southern Culture: Mind and Identity in the Modern South.* Athens: University of Georgia Press, 1999.

Conforth, Bruce, and Gayle Dean Wardlow. *Up Jumped the Devil: The Real Life of Robert Johnson.* London: Omnibus Press, 2019.

Conway, Cecelia. *African Banjo Echoes in Appalachia: A Study of Folk Traditions.* Knoxville: University of Tennessee Press, 1995.

Cormier, Roger. "19 Electric Facts About MTV Unplugged." *Mental Floss*, August 18, 2017.

Danner, Peter. *The Guitar in America.* Melville, NY: Mills Publishing, 1978.

Davis, Francis. *The History of the Blues: The Roots, the Music, the People from Charley Patton to Robert Cray.* Boston: Hyperion, 1995.

Dawidoff, Nicholas. *In the Country of Country: A Journey to the Roots of American Music.* London: Faber & Faber, 1997.

Denning, Michael. *The Cultural Front: The Laboring of American Culture in the Twentieth Century.* New York: Verso, 1997.

Dickerson, Deke. *The Strat in the Attic: Thrilling Stories of Guitar Archaeology.* Minneapolis: Voyageur Press, 2013.

Drake, Gabrielle, and Cally Callomon, eds. *Nick Drake: Remembered for a While.* London: John Murray, 2014.

Drowne, Kathleen, and Patrick Huber. *The 1920s.* Westport, CT: Greenwood Press, 2004.

Dudley, Kathryn Marie. *Guitar Makers: The Endurance of Artisanal Values in North America.* Chicago: University of Chicago Press, 2014.

Dylan, Bob. *Chronicles, Vol. 1*. New York: Simon & Schuster, 2004.

Emerson, Ken. *Doo-Dah! Stephen Foster and the Rise of American Popular Culture*. New York: Simon & Schuster, 1997.

Eriksson, Björn. "The Beatles and Their Rickenbacker Guitars." Björn Eriksson's Rickenbacker Page, 1999. https://rickbeat.com/.

Erlewine, Dan, Eldon Whitford, and David Vinopal. *Gibson's Fabulous Flat-Top Guitars: An Illustrated History and Guide*. San Francisco: Miller Freeman Books, 2006.

Escott, Colin, and Kira Florita. *Hank Williams: Snapshots from the Lost Highway*. Cambridge, MA: Da Capo, 2001.

Escott, Colin, George Merritt, and William MacEwen. *Hank Williams: The Biography*. San Francisco: Little, Brown, 1994.

Evans, Tom, and Mary Anne Evans. *Guitars: Music, History, Construction and Players from the Renaissance to Rock*. London: Paddington Press, 1977.

Ferguson, Robert. "Henry Worrall (1825–1902): Anglo-American Guitarist." *Soundboard Scholar* 2 (2016).

Filene, Benjamin. *Romancing the Folk: Public Memory and American Roots Music*. Chapel Hill: University of North Carolina Press, 2000.

Finder, Henry, ed. *The 40s: The Story of a Decade*. New York: Modern Library, 2015.

Finder, Henry, ed. *The 50s: The Story of a Decade*. New York: Modern Library, 2016.

Finder, Henry, ed. *The 60s: The Story of a Decade*. New York: Modern Library, 2017.

Fiorito, Michael. "The Gentle Songs of Bridget St. John." *Atwood* magazine, July 2, 2021.

Fischer, David Hackett. *Albion's Seed: Four British Folkways in America*. New York: Oxford University Press, 1989.

Foner, Eric. *Reconstruction: America's Unfinished Revolution*. Updated ed. New York: Harper Perennial Modern Classics, 2014.

Fornatale, Pete. *Back to the Garden: The Story of Woodstock and How It Changed a Generation*. New York: Touchstone, 2010.

Fowler, Gene, and Bill Crawford. *Border Radio: Quacks, Yodelers, Pitchmen, Psychics, and Other Amazing Broadcasters of the American Airwaves*. Rev. ed. Austin: University of Texas Press, 2002.

Fox, Jo. "From Documentary Film to Television Documentaries: John Grierson and *This Wonderful World*." *Journal of British Cinema and Television* 10, no. 3 (July 2013): 498–523. https://doi.org/10.3366/jbctv.2013.0152.

Friedrichs, Christopher R. *The Early Modern City, 1450–1750 (A History of Urban Society in Europe)*. London: Longman, 1995.

Garrett, Charles Hiroshi. *Struggling to Define a Nation: American Music and the Twentieth Century*. Berkeley: University of California Press, 2008.

Geminiani, Francesco. *The Art of Playing the Guittar or Cittra*. Edinburgh: n.p., 1760.

George-Warren, Holly. *Public Cowboy No. 1: The Life and Times of Gene Autry*. New York: Oxford University Press, 2007.

Gibson, Chris, and Andrew Warren. *The Guitar: Tracing the Grain Back to the Tree.* Chicago: University of Chicago Press, 2021.

Gioia, Joe. *The Guitar and the New World: A Fugitive History*. Albany, NY: SUNY Press, 2013.

Glinis, Shawn Michael. "VCRs: The End of TV as Ephemera." MA thesis, University of Wisconsin-Milwaukee, 2015. Theses and Dissertations, Paper 806. http://dc.uwm.edu/etd/806.

Goldberg, David J. *Discontented America: The United States in the 1920s*. Baltimore: Johns Hopkins University Press, 1999.

Greene, Andy. "MTV Unplugged: The 15 Best Episodes." *Rolling Stone*, September 2017.

Greene, Victor. *A Passion for Polka: Old-Time Ethnic Music in America*. Berkeley: University of California Press, 1992.

Griffith, Nanci, and Joe Jackson. *Nanci Griffith's Other Voices: A Personal History of Folk Music*. Maidstone, UK: Amber Waves, 1998.

Gruhn, George, and Walter Carter. *Acoustic Guitars and Other Fretted Instruments: A Photographic History*. San Francisco: GPI Books, 1993.

Gura, Philip F. *C. F. Martin and His Guitars, 1796–1873*. Chapel Hill: University of North Carolina Press, 2003.

Gura, Philip F. "Manufacturing Guitars for the American Parlor: James Ashborn's Wolcottville, Connecticut Factory, 1851–56." *American Antiquarian Society* (1994): 117–155.

Gura, Philip F., and James F. Bollam. *America's Instrument: The Banjo in the Nineteenth Century*. Chapel Hill: University of North Carolina Press, 1999.

Guralnick, Peter. *Searching for Robert Johnson: The Life and Legend of the "King of the Delta Blues Singers."* New York: Plume Books, 1988.

Hagan, Chet. *Grand Ole Opry: The Complete Story of a Great American Institution and Its Stars*. New York: Henry Holt, 1989.

Handy, W. C. *Father of the Blues: An Autobiography*. London: Hassell Street Press, 1941.

Hankins, Barry. *The Second Great Awakening and the Transcendentalists*. Westport, CT: Greenwood Press, 2004.

Harker, Dave. *Fakesong: The Manufacture of British "Folksong" 1700 to the Present Day.* Milton Keynes, UK: Open University Press, 1985.

Harper, Colin. *Dazzling Stranger: Bert Jansch and the British Folk and Blues Revival.* London: Bloomsbury, 2000.

Harrison, Daphne Duval. *Black Pearls: Blues Queens of the 1920s*. New Brunswick, NJ: Rutgers University Press, 1988.

Harrison, Quentin. "Portrait of a Phenomenon: Lilith Fair, 1997–1999." Albumism, July 5, 2022. https://albumism.com/.

Hartman, Robert Carl. *The Larsons' Creations: Guitars and Mandolins*. Centennial ed. Anaheim, CA: Centerstream, 2007.

Hebbert, Benjamin. "Violin Making in Northern Europe in the Time of the Amatis." *Violins & Violinists*, October 19, 2020. https://violinsandviolinists.com/.

Hemphill, Paul. *Lovesick Blues: The Life of Hank Williams*. New York: Penguin, 2005.

Hennessey, Peter. *Having It So Good: Britain in the Fifties*. London: Allen Lane Publishing, 2006.

Hennessy, Peter. *Winds of Change: Britain in the Early Sixties*. London: Allen Lane Publishing, 2019.

Hepworth, David. *1971—Never a Dull Moment: Rock's Golden Year*. London: Bantam Press, 2016.

Hilburn, Robert. *Paul Simon: The Life*. New York: Simon & Schuster, 2018.

Hirsch, Philip. *Voices from the Hollow: What Happened When the Blue Bloods Met the Blue Ridge*. Boston: Mariner, 2006.

Hodgkinson, Will. *Guitar Man: A Six-String Odyssey, or, You Love That Guitar More Than You Love Me*. London: Bloomsbury, 2006.

Holley, Chuck. *A Perfectly Good Guitar: Musicians on Their Favorite Instruments*. Austin: University of Texas Press, 2017.

Hopper, Jessica. "Building a Mystery: An Oral History of the Lilith Fair." *Vanity Fair*, September 30, 2019.

Horstman, Dorothy. *Sing Your Heart Out, Country Boy: Classic Country Songs and Their Inside Stories by the People Who Wrote Them*. New York: Dutton, 1975.

Hoskyns, Barney. *Across the Great Divide: The Band and America*. London: Pimlico Books, 2003.

Hoskyns, Barney. *Small Town Talk: Bob Dylan, the Band, Van Morrison, Janis Joplin, Jimi Hendrix and Friends in the Wild Years of Woodstock*. London: Faber & Faber, 2016.

Houghton, Mick. *Becoming Elektra: The True Story of Jak Holzman's Visionary Record Label*. London: Jawbone, 2010.

Howard, John Tasker. *Stephen Foster: America's Troubadour*. New York: Crowell, 1934.

Hoyer, Christian. "A History of the Karl Hofner Company, 1887–2007." Steve Russell's Vintage Hofner webpage. https://www.vintagehofner.co.uk/.

Humphries, Patrick. *Lonnie Donegan and the Birth of British Rock & Roll*. London: Robson Press, 2012.

Humphries, Patrick. *The Lonnie Donegan Story, 1931–2002: Puttin' On the Style*. London: Virgin Books, 2003.

Hurt, R. Douglas, ed. *African American Life in the Rural South, 1900–1950*. Columbia: University of Missouri Press, 2011.

Hutton, Greig. *Hutton's Guide to Martin Guitars: 1833–1969*. Anaheim, CA: Centerstream, 2022.

Indelicato, M. J. *Guitar Man: Six Strings of Separation*. Milwaukee, WI: Hal Leonard, 2015.

Ingram, Tammy. *Dixie Highway: Road Building and the Making of the Modern South, 1900–1930*. Chapel Hill: University of North Carolina Press, 2014.

Jablonski, Edward. *Irving Berlin: American Troubadour*. New York: Henry Holt, 1999.

Jack, Richard Morton. *Galactic Ramble: The 60s and 70s UK Music Scene*. London: Foxcote, 2009.

Jack, Richard Morton. *Nick Drake: The Life*. London: John Murray, 2023.

Jamison, Phil. *Hoedowns, Reels, and Frolics: Roots and Branches of Southern Appalachian Dance*. Champaign: University of Illinois Press, 2015.

Johnston, Richard, and Dick Boak. *Martin Guitars: A History*. Updated from the original work by Michael Longworth [1975]. San Francisco: Hal Leonard, 2008.

Johnston, Richard, and Dick Boak. *Martin Guitars: A Technical Reference*. San Francisco: Hal Leonard, 2008.

Jones, Quincy. *The Autobiography of Quincy Jones*. New York: Doubleday, 2001.

Kane, Paula M. "American Revival Songs, 1820–1850: The Christian Lyre and Spiritual Songs for Social Worship." Thesis, College of the Holy Cross, 1980. https://crossworks.holycross.edu/fenwick_scholar/19.

Kellerman, Jonathan. *With Strings Attached: The Art and Beauty of Vintage Guitars*. New York: Ballantine, 2008.

Kennedy, Stetson. *A Jim Crow Guide to the USA: The Laws, Customs, and Etiquette Governing the Conduct of Nonwhites and Other Minorities as Second-Class Citizens*. London: Lawrence and Wishart, 1959.

Kitts, Thomas M. *Ray Davies: Not Like Everybody Else*. London: Taylor & Francis, 2007.

Klein, Joe. *Woody Guthrie: A Life*. New York: Knopf, 1980.

Kubernik, Harvey. *Canyon of Dreams: The Magic and the Music of Laurel Canyon*. New York: Sterling, 2009.

La Chapelle, Peter. *I'd Fight the World: A Political History of Old-Time, Hillbilly, and Country Music*. Chicago: University of Chicago Press, 2019.

Lang, Michael. *The Road to Woodstock*. London: Ecco 2010.

Langford, Jon. *Nashville Radio: Art, Words, and Music*. Portland, OR: Verse Chorus Press, 2006.

Leigh, Spencer. *Simon & Garfunkel: Together Alone*. Carmarthen, Wales: McNidder and Grace, 2018.

Leigh, Spencer. *Twist and Shout! Merseybeat, the Cavern, the Star-Club and the Beatles*. London: Nirvana Books, 2004.

Levy, Debbie. *Soldier Song: A True Story of the Civil War*. New York: Hyperion, 2017.

Lewisohn, Mark. *The Beatles: All These Years*. Vol. 1, *Tune In*. London: Little Brown, 2013.

Lewisohn, Mark. *The Complete Beatles Chronicle: The Definitive Day-by-Day Guide to the Beatles' Entire Career*. Chicago: Chicago Review Press, 1996.

Lindhop, Edmund. *America in the 1930s*. Minneapolis, MN: Twenty-First Century Books, 2009.

Lomax, Alan. *The Land Where the Blues Began*. New York: New Press, 2002.

Longfellow, Henry Wadsworth. *Letters of Henry Wadsworth Longfellow*. Vol. 2, *1837–1843*. Edited by Andrew Hilen. Cambridge, MA: Harvard University Press, 1967.

Lornell, Kip. *Capital Bluegrass: Hillbilly Music Meets Washington, DC*. New York: Oxford University Press, 2020.

Lornell, Kip. *Exploring American Folk Music: Ethnic, Grassroots, and Regional Traditions in the United States*. Oxford: University Press of Mississippi, 2012.

Lott, Eric. *Love and Theft: Blackface Minstrelsy and the American Working Class*. New York: Oxford University Press, 1993.

Luray, Elyse. "The Josh White Guitar." *History Detectives: Special Investigations*, PBS, season 6, episode 11, 2009.

Lynskey, Dorian. *33 Revolutions per Minute: A History of Protest Songs, from Billie Holiday to Green Day*. London: Faber & Faber, 2010.

MacMahon, Bernard, and Allison McGourty. *American Epic: The First Time America Heard Itself*. New York: Atria Books, 2017.

March, Richard. "American Polka in the Media: Next to Nothing to 24/7." *Transatlantica: American Studies Journal* (2019). https://doi.org/10.4000/transatlantica.14042.

Marcus, Greil. *Invisible Republic: Bob Dylan's Basement Tapes*. New York: Henry Holt, 1998.

Marcus, Greil. *Mystery Train: Images of America in Rock 'n' Roll Music*. New York: Plume, 2015.

Marom, Malka. *Joni Mitchell: In Her Own Words*. Toronto: ECW Press, 2014.

Mazor, Barry. *Meeting Jimmie Rodgers: How America's Original Roots Music Hero Changed the Pop Sounds of a Century*. New York: Oxford University Press. 2009.

McCormack, Peter R. "The Rossmeisl Guitar Legacy." Rickenbacker forum, 2004. https://www.rickresource.com/rrp/theroger.html.

McCormick, Robert "Mack." *Biography of a Phantom: A Robert Johnson Blues Odyssey*. Edited by John Troutman. Washington, DC: Smithsonian Books, 2023.

McDevitt, Chas. *Skiffle: The Definitive Inside Story*. London: Robson Books, 1998.

McWhirter, Christian. *Battle Hymns: The Power and Popularity of Music in the Civil War*. Chapel Hill: University of North Carolina Press, 2012.

Miller, Karl Hagstrom. *Segregating Sound: Inventing Folk and Pop Music in the Age of Jim Crow*. Durham, NC: Duke University Press, 2010.

Molloy, Peter. *1945: The Savage Peace*. BBC2 Documentary, May 2015.

Morton-Jack, Richard. *Galactic Ramble: The 60s and 70s UK Music Scene*. London: Foxcote Books, 2009.

Moss, Marissa. *Her Country: How the Women of Country Music Became the Success They Were Never Supposed to Be*. New York: Henry Holt, 2022.

Munro, John Neil. *Some People Are Crazy: The John Martyn Story*. Edinburgh: Polygon, 2007.

Myrdal, Gunnar. *An American Dilemma*. Vol. 2, *The Negro Problem and Modern Democracy*. New York: Harper & Row, 1944.

Napier-Bell, Simon. *Black Vinyl, White Powder: The Real Story of the British Music Industry*. London: Ebury Press, 2007.

Napier-Bell, Simon. *Ta-Ra-Ra-Boom-De-Ay: The Dodgy Business of Popular Music*. London: Unbound, 2014.

Nathan, Hans. *Dan Emmett and the Rise of Early Negro Minstrelsy*. Norman: University of Oklahoma Press, 1962.

Obrecht, Jas. *Talking Guitar: Conversations with Musicians Who Shaped Twentieth-Century American Music*. Chapel Hill: University of North Carolina Press, 2017.

O'Connell, JoAnne. *The Life and Songs of Stephen Foster: A Revealing Portrait of the Forgotten Man Behind "Swanee River," "Beautiful Dreamer," and "My Old Kentucky Home."* Lanham, MD: Rowman & Littlefield, 2016.

O'Hagan, Lauren Alex. "Fashioning the 'People's Guitarist': The Mythologization of Rory Gallagher in the International Music Press." *Rock Music Studies* 9, no. 2 (2022): 174–198. https://doi.org/10.1080/19401159.2022.2048988.

Oliver, Paul. *The Story of the Blues: The Making of Black Music*. Boston: Northeastern University Press, 1969.

Pecknold, Diane, ed. *Hidden in the Mix: The African American Presence in Country Music*. Durham, NC: Duke University Press, 2013.

Peterson, Richard A. *Creating Country Music: Fabricating Authenticity*. Chicago: University of Chicago Press, 1997.

Petrus, Stephen, and Ronald D. Cohen. *Folk City: New York and the American Folk Music Revival*. New York: Oxford University Press, 2015.

Petrusich, Amanda. *Do Not Sell at Any Price: The Wild, Obsessive Hunt for the World's Rarest 78 RPM Records*. New York: Scribner, 2014.

Pickering, Michael. *Blackface Minstrelsy in Britain*. Abingdon-on-Thames, UK: Routledge, 2008.

Pleijsier, Hubert. *Washburn Prewar Instrument Styles: Guitars, Mandolins, Banjos and Ukuleles, 1883–1940*. Anaheim, CA: Centerstream, 2008.

Pointon, Mike, and Ray Smith. *Goin' Home: The Uncompromising Life and Music of Ken Colyer*. Ken Colyer Trust, 2010.

Polizzotti, Mark. *Bob Dylan: Highway 61 Revisited*. New York: Bloomsbury, 2006.

Poore, Billy. *Rockabilly: A Forty-Year Journey*. Milwaukee, WI: Hal Leonard Corp., 1998.

Popp, Andrew. "Christian Frederick Martin (1796–1873)." Immigrant Entrepreneurship: German-American Business Biographies, 1720 to the Present. Last modified November 2020. https://www.immigrantentrepreneurship.org/.

Porterfield, Nolan. *Jimmie Rodgers: The Life and Times of America's Blue Yodeler*. Oxford: University Press of Mississippi, 2007.

Pugh, Ronnie. *Ernest Tubb: The Texas Troubadour*. Durham, NC: Duke University Press, 1998.

Quantick, David. "The Blaggers Guide to the Guitar." *Blaggers Guide*. BBC Radio 2, 2014.

Reisman, Bob. *I Feel So Good: The Life and Times of Big Bill Broonzy*. Chicago: University of Chicago Press, 2011.

Reisz, Karel, and Tony Richardson, dirs. *Momma Don't Allow: The Wood Green Jazz Club*. Documentary. London: BFI Screenonline, 1956.

Robertson, David. *W. C. Handy: The Life and Times of the Man Who Made the Blues*. New York: Knopf, 2009.

Robertson, Robbie. *Testimony*. London: Windmill Books, 2017.

Robinson, Lisa. "It Happened in Laurel Canyon." *Vanity Fair*, February 6, 2015.

Roediger, David R. "Critical Studies of Whiteness, USA: Origins and Arguments." *Theoria: A Journal of Social and Political Theory* 98 (2001): 72–98.

Rogan, Johnny. *Byrds: Requiem for the Timeless*. Vol. 1. London: Rogan House, 2011.

Rose, Mark. *Authors and Owners: The Invention of Copyright*. Cambridge, MA: Harvard University Press, 1993.

Rose, Mark. "The Public Sphere and the Emergence of Copyright: Areopagitica, the Stationers' Company and the Statute of Anne Tulane." *Tulane Journal of Technology and Intellectual Property* 12 (Fall 2009).

Roth, Mitchel P. *Prisons and Prison Systems: A Global Encyclopedia*. Westport, CT: Greenwood Press, 2006.

Royster, Francesca T. *Black Country Music: Listening for Revolutions*. Austin: University of Texas Press, 2022.

Russ, Tom. *Four Guitars: (More or Less)*. New York: Xlibris, 2011.

Sandbrook, Dominic. *White Heat: A History of Britain in the Swinging Sixties*. London: Abacus, 2007.

Scarborough, Dorothy. *On the Trail of Negro Folk Songs*. New York: Folklore Associates, 1963.

Schmidt, Paul William. *Acquired of the Angels: The Lives and Works of Master Guitar Makers John D'Angelico and James L. D'Aquisto*. Lanham, MD: Scarecrow Press, 1988.

Schmitz, Oskar. *The Land Without Music*. London: Jarrolds, 1925.

Schwartz, Roberta Freund. *How Britain Got the Blues: The Transmission and Reception of American Blues Style in the United Kingdom*. Aldershot: Ashgate, 2007.

Seeger, Pete. *Pete Seeger: In His Own Words*. Selected and edited by Bob Rosenthal and Sam Rosenthal. Abingdon, UK: Routledge, 2012.

Shapiro, Harry. *Alexis Korner: The Biography*. London: Bloomsbury, 1996.

Shapiro, Nat, and Nat Hentoff. *Hear Me Talkin' to Ya: The Story of Jazz as Told by the Men Who Made It*. New York: Dover Books, 1966.

Shaw, Robert, and Peter Szego, eds. *Inventing the American Guitar: The Pre-Civil War Innovations of C. F. Martin and His Contemporaries*. Milwaukee, WI: Hal Leonard, 2013.

Sheehy, Michael. "Woodstock: How the Media Missed the Historic Angle of the Breaking Story." *Journalism History* 37, no. 4 (2012): 238–246. https://doi.org/10.1080/00947679.2012.12062864.

Shipton, Alyn. *A New History of Jazz*. London: Continuum, 2001.

Siegel, Dorothy Schainman. *The Glory Road: The Story of Josh White*. San Diego, CA: Harcourt, 1982.

Simmons, Michael John. *Boutique Acoustics: 180 years of Handbuilt American Guitars*. London: Backbeat Books, 2015.

Skeaping, Lucie, ed. *Broadside Ballads: Songs from the Streets, Taverns, Theatres and Countryside of 17th-Century England*. London: Faber & Faber, 2003.

Smith, Richard R. *The History of Rickenbacker Guitars*. Anaheim, CA: Centerstream, 1987.

Somogyi, Ervin. *The Responsive Guitar*. Oakland, CA: Luthiers Press, 2009.

Sousa, John Philip. *A Sousa Reader: Essays, Interviews, and Clippings*. Edited by Bryan Proksch. Chicago: GIA Publications, 2016.

Southern, Eileen. *The Music of Black Americans: A History*. New York: Norton, 1971.

Spann, Joe. *Spann's Guide to Gibson, 1902–1941*. Anaheim, CA: Hal Leonard, 2011.

Sparks, Paul. *The Classical Mandolin*. Oxford: Oxford University Press, 2005.

Springsteen, Bruce. *Born to Run*. New York: Simon & Schuster, 2016.

Stark, Steven D. *Meet the Beatles: A Cultural History of the Band That Shook Youth, Gender, and the World*. New York: HarperCollins/Dey Street Books, 2005.

St. John, Allen. *Clapton's Guitar: Watching Wayne Henderson Build the Perfect Instrument*. New York: Free Press, 2005.

Stone, Lillian, and Allen Rankin. *Life Story of Our Hank Williams: The Drifting Cowboy*. Atlanta: Philbert Publications, 1953.

Taylor, Bob. *Guitar Lessons: A Life's Journey Turning Passion into Business*. Hoboken, NJ: Wiley, 2011.

Thomas, Erik R. "Rural White Southern Accents." *Atlas of North American English*. 2006. https://www.academia.edu/15229307/Rural_Southern_White_Accents.

Thomas, John. *Kalamazoo Gals: A Story of Extraordinary Women and Gibson's "Banner" Guitars of WWII*. Staunton, VA: American History Press, 2013.

Thomson, Graeme. *Small Hours: The Long Night of John Martyn*. London: Omnibus Press, 2020.

Tolhurst, Lol. *Cured: The Tale of Two Imaginary Boys*. London: Quercus, 2016.

Tranquada, Jim, and John King. *The Ukulele: A History*. Honolulu: University of Hawaii Press, 2012.

Troutman, John W. *Kīkā Kila: How the Hawaiian Steel Guitar Changed the Sound of Modern Music*. Chapel Hill: University of North Carolina Press, 2020.

Turner, Alwyn W. *Crisis? What Crisis? Britain in the 1970s*. London: Aurum Press, 2007.

Turner, Alwyn W. *Rejoice! Rejoice! Britain in the 1980s*. London: Aurum Press, 2010.

Turner, Valerie. "Out of the Shadows: Undersung Women of Blues Guitar." *Acoustic Guitar* (March/April 2021).

Unterberger, Richie. *Eight Miles High: Folk-Rock's Flight from Haight-Ashbury to Woodstock*. San Francisco: Backbeat Books, 2003.

van Ronk, Dave, and Elijah Wald. *The Mayor of MacDougal Street: A Memoir*. Cambridge, MA: Da Capo, 2005.

Waksman, Steve. *Instruments of Desire: The Electric Guitar and the Shaping of Musical Experience*. Cambridge, MA: Harvard University Press, 2001.

Wald, Elijah. *Dylan Goes Electric! Newport, Seeger, Dylan, and the Night That Split the Sixties*. New York: HarperCollins/Dey Street Books, 2015.

Wald, Elijah. *Escaping the Delta: Robert Johnson and the Invention of the Blues*. New York: HarperCollins/Amistad, 2004.

Wald, Elijah. *How the Beatles Destroyed Rock 'n' Roll: An Alternative History of American Popular Music*. New York: Oxford University Press, 2009.

Wald, Elijah. *Josh White: Society Blues*. London: Routledge, 2002.

Wald, Elijah, and John Junkerman. *The Mississippi: River of Song*. PBS 4-Part TV documentary (1999).

Wald, Elijah, and John Junkerman. *River of Song: A Musical Journey Down the Mississippi*. New York: St. Martin's Press, 1998.

Wardlow, Gayle Dean. *Chasin' That Devil's Music: Searching for the Blues*. San Francisco: Backbeat Books, 1998.

Warfield, Patrick. *Making the March King: John Philip Sousa's Washington Years, 1854–1893*. Champaign: University of Illinois Press, 2013.

Washburn, Jim, and Richard Johnston. *Martin Guitars: An Illustrated Celebration of America's Premier Guitar Maker*. Emmaus, PA: Rodale Press, 1997.

Whalen, Jack, and Richard Flacks. *Beyond the Barricades: The Sixties Generation Grows Up*. Philadelphia: Temple University Press, 1989.

White, Forrest. *Fender: The Inside Story*. San Francisco: Backbeat Books, 1994.

White, Josh, and Ivor Mairants. *The Josh White Guitar Method*. London: Boosey & Hawkes, 1956.

Wilentz, Sean. *Bob Dylan in America*. New York: Doubleday, 2010.

Willcoxon, Samuel. "Highway 61: Good Roads, Great Migrations, and Delta Blues." University of Mississippi Honors Thesis, 2019. 1000. https://egrove.olemiss.edu/hon_thesis/1000.

Williamson, Joel. *The Crucible of Race: Black-White Relations in the American South Since Emancipation*. New York: Oxford University Press, 1984.

Willis, John, C. *Forgotten Time: The Yazoo-Mississippi Delta after the Civil War*. Charlottesville: University of Virginia Press, 2000.

Winkler, Allan M. *"To Everything There Is a Season": Pete Seeger and the Power of Song*. New York: Oxford University Press, 2009.

Wolfe, Charles K. *A Good-Natured Riot: The Birth of the Grand Ole Opry*. Nashville, TN: Vanderbilt University Press, 1999.

Wolfe, Charles K., and Ted Olson, eds. *The Bristol Sessions: Writings About the Big Bang of Country Music*. Jefferson, NC: McFarland, 2004.

Wolfenden, Tom, producer. *Black Music in Europe: A Hidden History*. Documentary. London: Loftus Media/BBC Radio 4 Broadcasts, 2018.

Woodward, C. Vann. *The Strange Career of Jim Crow*. Commemorative ed. New York: Oxford University Press, 2001.

Wyman, Bill, and Richard Havers. *Bill Wyman's Blues Odyssey: A Journey to Music's Heart and Soul*. New York: Dorling Kindersley, 2001.

Yaffe, David. *Reckless Daughter: A Portrait of Joni Mitchell*. Toronto: HarperCollins, 2017.

Yates, Mike. *Cecil Sharp in America: Collecting in the Appalachians*. Stroud, Glos., UK: Musical Traditions, [1999]. http://www.mustrad.org.uk/articles/sharp.htm.

Young, Rob. *Electric Eden: Unearthing Britain's Visionary Music*. London: Faber & Faber, 2010.

Zack, Ian. *Say No to the Devil: The Life and Musical Genius of Rev. Gary Davis*. Chicago: University of Chicago Press, 2015.

Index

Page numbers in *italics* refer to illustrations and photos.